# BLACK LIGHTNING
## POETRY-IN-PROGRESS

# BLACK LIGHTNING

## POETRY-IN-PROGRESS

Alexander, Amirthanayagam, Berssenbrugge,
Cabalquinto, Chin, Foster, Hagedorn,
Hahn, Hongo, Lee,  Liu, Mura, Sze, Yau

By Eileen Tabios

# Black Lightning

*By Arthur Sze*

A blind girl
stares at me,
then types out ten lines
in braille.

The air has a scent
of sandalwood and
arsenic; a night-blooming cereus
blooms on a dark path.

I look at the
short and long flow
of the lines:
and guess at garlic,
the sun, a silver desert rain,
and palms.

Or is it simply
about hands, a river of light,
the ear of a snail,
or rags?

And, stunned, I feel
the nerves of my hand flashing
in the dark, feel
the world as black
lightning.

BLACK LIGHTNING is for all poets and their "Others"
who would read and love their poems.

BLACK LIGHTNING: POETRY-IN-PROGRESS benefited from a 1997 Poetry Grant provided by the Witter Bynner Foundation as well as those organizations who support The Asian American Writers Workshop: National Endowment for the Arts, the New York State Council on the Arts, the Department of Cultural Affairs, New York Community Trust, Jerome Foundation, Greenwall Foundation, Witter Bynner Foundation for Poetry, Axe-Houghton Foundation, AT&T, Anheuser-Busch, Bell Atlantic, Two St. Mark's Corporation, Los Angeles Cultural Grant, and the generosity of AAWW individual members. Additional support for publishing this book was provided by OENOPHILES FOR POETRY (Dan and Mari Dawley, Robert and Meryl Messineo, Don and Shelley Meltzer, Michael Offen/Bear Stearns & Co. Monterey Fund, Fred McConkey, Alice Brody, Barbara Friedlander and Thomas Pollock); A. Stabile Memorial Fund; Michael G. Price; Mr. and Mrs. Fran and Vinnie Antonnacchio; Philip Wexler; Margaret and Michelle DeMeo; Virgilio and Edna Cabalquinto; Mr. and Mrs. Elmer Basbas; Luis and Gloria Cabalquinto; V.C. Igarta; Yolly and Rey Corpus; Irma Corpus; Teresita Tagura; and Celita Sulat.

Cover Photo: "TWL," 20" by 20" by Theresa Chong.
1997 Oil on Wood. (Photo by Tom Powel; Courtesy of Danese)

Art Directors: Crazy Art (Ji Young Lee, Jue Yee Kim)

Distributed by
**Temple University Press**
Philadelphia
*tel* 1-800-447-1656    *fax* 215-204-4719

# ACKNOWLEDGMENTS

*BLACK LIGHTNING: POETRY-IN-PROGRESS* would not have been possible without the contributions and encouragement of others: Thomas Pollock whose brilliant eye first taught me poetry; Curtis Chin and Bino Realuyo, in whose vision for the Asian American Writers Workshop (AAWW) I found a writer's re-birth; Eric Gamalinda, Barbara Tran and Andrea Louie, AAWW's publication directors; Julie Koo, Soo Mee Kwon, Karen Hwa, Hun Ohm, Purvi Shah and Ishle Park, former and current editors of *The Asian Pacific American Journal* (*The Journal*); Peter Ong, Ray Hsia, Parag Khandar, Nerio Brillantes, Erna Hernandez, Miwa Yokoyama, Derek Nguyen, Alice Fung, Jeannie L Wong and other volunteers who ensure AAWW and *The Journal* thrive; Arthur Sze, whose generosity helped birth the project; Resa Alboher, copy editor and much needed source of "positive energy"; my editorial assistants Cristina Natividad, Dayna Poon and Zahera Saed; AAWW's current Board of Directors (Edward Boland, Curtis Chin, David Eng, Gordon Kato, Albert Kim, Holly Kim, Sunaina Maira, Alan Marks, Peter von Ziegesar, Michael Yi) as well as former Board President Marie Lee; Sesshu Foster whose encouragement was heartening during the early days of this project; John Yau for his aid on Art, including the book's cover art; Nick Carbo, whose loving exhortations helped immensely whenever my energies flagged; Elena Alexander and Ruel Espejo of "MAD ALEX Presents" for their help on computer technologies (and more); and *BLACK LIGHTNING*'s poets: Meena Alexander, Indran Amirthanayagam, Mei-mei Berssenbrugge, Luis Cabalquinto, Marilyn Chin, Sesshu Foster, Jessica Hagedorn, Kimiko Hahn, Garrett Hongo, Li Young Lee, Timothy Liu, David Mura, Arthur Sze and John Yau.

Earlier versions of some of these works first appeared in *The Asian Pacific American Journal* (editors Eric Gamalinda, Karen Hwa, Julie Koo, Soo Mee Kwon); *The Clackamas Literary Review* (editors Jeff Knorr and Tim Schell); *phati'tude* (editors G. David, Regie Cabico, Tony Medina); and *Crab Orchard Review* (editors Richard Peterson, Jon Tribble and Carolyn Alessio).

# TABLE OF CONTENTS

# INTRODUCTION

*Illustrating The Polysemous Nature of Poetry*

*BLACK LIGHTNING* is a unique collection. There have been other anthologies of Asian American poetry, including *Breaking Silence* (Greenfield Review Press, 1983), *The Open Boat* (Anchor/Doubleday, 1993), and *Premonitions* (Kaya Production, 1995). But *BLACK LIGHTNING* features poetry-in-progress drafts of selected poems and interviews fourteen Asian-American poets concerning their craft and vision. Eileen Tabios initiated the series as an editor of *The Asian Pacific American Journal*, and it soon grew into a book-length project. Tabios gives acute and insightful readings of the poems and has a keen appreciation for the poetic process.

Critical discussion of Asian-American poetry lags behind artistic accomplishment. The discourse tends to center on race and identity, and it is just beginning to address theory and practice and the polysemous nature of the work. In considering the poets included in this collection, I would like to stress the depth, diversity, and range of concern. Each poet raises different issues.

Indran Amirthanayagam delves into *cante jondo* to balance political and social impulses. Meena Alexander's "gold horizon" traces the arc of her journey in a litany of place names. Mei-mei Berssenbrugge balances epistemological inquiry with the immediate presence of her family to create a continuum between the abstract and the concrete, the immaterial and the material. Luis Cabalquinto sifts out the diffuse to simplify and intensify. Marilyn Chin's deep knowledge of classical Chinese poetics and her feminist perspective are harnessed in a form of "controlled entropy" to create something new and striking. Sesshu Foster's sinuous prose-based poems are human landscapes reflecting his careful listening to people in East Los Angeles. Jessica Hagedorn finds in James Rosenquist's series of dolls a slightly menacing as well as seductive image of our time. Kimiko Hahn's image-based poems incorporate an ongoing dialogue with feminist critics and create distinctive parallaxes. Garrett Hongo's "On the Last Performance of Musume Dojoji at the Nippon Kan of the Astor Hotel, Seattle, Washington," shows how his live-wire lines build to an emotional crescendo through a process of luminous concretion. Li Young Lee initially compares the fateful form of a poem to iron filings drawn into a singular configuration by the mind's magnetism but later recognizes that a new poem requires a new mind. Timothy Liu's unfolding drafts of "Canker" are a revelation in how the prose poem can incorporate silences that are active points of resistance. David Mura's "The Colors of Desire" reveal how the dark knot of race, identity, sexuality, history and politics, become a single intertwined knot that will not unravel. John Yau's sharp juxtapositions, layerings, and use of *ut pictura poesis* exemplify his idea of a "fractured self" that embodies the mystery and multiplicity of existence . . . . These are some of the splendors in this book.

By illuminating the creative process of fourteen poets, *BLACK LIGHTNING* widens and deepens our understanding of what it means to be an Asian American writer today. At the same time, *BLACK LIGHTNING* makes an important contribution to contemporary *American* poetry and poetics.

— **Arthur Sze**

# ARTHUR SZE

Arthur Sze has published six books of poetry: *The Redshifting Web: Poems 1970-1997* (Copper Canyon Press, 1998); *Archipelago* (Copper Canyon, 1995); *River River* (Lost Roads, 1987); *Dazzled* (Floating Island, 1982); *Two Ravens* (1976: revised edition, Tooth of Time, 1984); and *The Willow Wind* (1972: revised edition, Tooth of Time, 1981). He is the recipient of a Guggenheim Fellowship (1997), a Before Columbus American Book Award (1996), a Lannan Literary Award in Poetry (1995), three Witter Bynner Foundation for Poetry fellowships (1983, 1994, 1997), two National Endowment for the Arts Creative Writing fellowships (1982, 1993), a George A. and Eliza Gardner Howard Foundation Fellowship, Brown University (1991), a New Mexico Arts Division Interdisciplinary Grant (1988), Santa Fe Council for the Arts grants (1979, 1980, 1982), and the Eisner Prize from the University of California at Berkeley (1971). He has taught in artist-in-schools and prison writing workshops in Alaska and New Mexico, and in writing programs at Brown University, Bard College, and Naropa Institute. He is currently a Professor of Creative Writing at the Institute of American Arts in Santa Fe.

In response to the question, "What advice would you give to a young poet?" Arthur Sze responds:

> Read the chapter "Reflections and Aphorisms" contained in *The Art of Rosanjin* by Sidney Cardozo and Masaaki Hirano (Kodansha, Tokyo, Japan, 1987).

# Arthur Sze: Mixing Memory and Desire

*A poet is, before anything else, a person who is passionately in love with language.*
— *W.H. Auden*

A 1990 visit to the Ryoanji temple in Kyoto; an uncle's tale about the death of two brothers in China; a stabbing; the sound of milk bottles clinking; a ceremony in the San Ildefonso pueblo in New Mexico — these are among the metaphorical islands in Arthur Sze's poem, "Archipelago." Although seemingly separate, these islands are derived from the same submarine land mass, the earth's core. Sze appreciates the connection, calling the metaphor of archipelago "the epistemology of the poem: the One and the Many."

However, Sze notes that an archipelago is not only a group of islands but also "an expanse of water with many scattered islands" — the silence and space of that water, which provides the poem "its resonance, the core of the poem: memory and desire, the flashbacks of memory and the yearnings of desire." From such resonance flows the images that Sze offers the reader, not unlike the poem's Pueblo dancers who throw "licorice, sunflower seeds, pot scrubbers, aprons, plastic bowls" to their audience. Sze says, "I throw images that incorporate a series of empty spaces where attentive readers will find a certain resonance."

In "Archipelago," Sze designed the sequence of the poem's nine sections to symbolize a solitary traveler's voyage through an archipelago — solitary as a reader's unaccompanied perusal of a poem — stopping at islands as well as navigating a boat through the "expanse of water." Some sections ("the chengdu effect," "april snow," "the center," "smoke," "the smash") seem to relate more to land and the others ("the silences," "the shards," "the throw, "the double throw") to water. By the order of the sections, the voyage can be marked as *land, water, land, land, land, water, land, water, water*. The order of the sections (particularly the way it ends) places emphasis on the "expanse of water" to affect the resonance Sze hoped readers would feel as they read his poem.

Sze originally wrote "Archipelago" in ten sections (featured below), but later deleted the section with a working title of "the elements of composition." For the poem's Final Draft, Sze also discarded the section titles as he had intended them only to facilitate his drafting process. He says he used the titles as "phrases that set up a certain kind of resonance" that he wished to explore — a "kind of marker" given his intent to write a lengthy poem. "I knew I wanted to write something long and, indeed, this became the longest poem I had ever written up to that point." ("The Redshifting Web" is his longest poem to date.)

The original ten sections were written over a ten-month period from September 1990 to May 1991. He wrote hundreds of drafts (of sections) of "Archipelago" before arriving at what he laughingly calls "the 201st draft" which we reproduce in part below. Due to his arduous drafting process, he also ended up using the floor as his entire desk. He said he set up piles of drafts and would move from one pile to another to continue the writing.

Featured below is the "201st" draft with some discussion of the poem's development. We did not attempt to "explain or explore the poem in its totality" because, as Sze notes, the reader's journey through the poem has to do with the reader's own nature of attentiveness.

—ɯ—

**ARCHIPELAGO — "201ST" DRAFT WITH REVISIONS AND DISCUSSION:**

*Editing Marks:   Underlined words = insertions; Strikethroughs = deletions; [New L] = new line break; and [Del L] = delete line break.*

1.       the elements of composition

        stopped at a light, he sees a woman,
        in a car with the license plate "zazen," smoking,
        and, in the other lane, in a red pulsar

        with the license plate "tina s.," tina.
        an owl is to full moon as mind is to appearance?
        it is obtuse to think that the more

        one is blind to the exterior world,
        the more one can become luminous,
        play ping-pong by candlelight in a greenhouse.

        he remembers seeing, after garbage collectors
        picked up trash, apples strewn in the driveway.
        stones are to path as islands are to sea?

        the elements of composition in a garden
        include stones, lanterns, pathways, basins,
        plantings, fences, but require in calculated

        landscape the casual movement of the viewer.
        so a day may appear to be a stretch of raked sand
        but has the infinite strength of water

Sze deleted this section because, as he succinctly explains, "It's really bad!"  Although he often recycles parts of discarded poems, Sze saw fit to reuse only one of this section's phrases: "playing ping -pong by candlelight in a greenhouse" which was used in section 9, "the throw." Nevertheless, the inspiration underlying this section — as hinted by "apples strewn in the drive-way,/ stones are to path as islands are to sea" — is fleshed out by the overall structure of the poem, emblematic of the soul existing past the demise of the body.

2.       the chengdu effect

        desire is to memory as an azalea is to a stone?
        during the cultural revolution, the youngest brother
        of the peng family was executed against a wall
        in chengdu for being a suspected guomindang agent.

years earlier, the eldest brother was executed
at that ~~very~~ wall for being a suspected communist.
this chengdu effect has no end, but if you interiorize,
~~you can feel how~~ a series of psychological tragedies
~~have~~ has the resonance of stone-and-gravel waterfalls.
a first frost sweetens the apples; i want them sweeter
but discover a second frost makes the cores mush;
so essential shapes are destroyed starting at the center.
a woman and man must have a series of betrayals
before they can begin to bicker at the dinner table.
i water hyacinth bulbs planted in shallow pots
in the cool, dark bathroom, and, though it feels
odd to do so when walnuts are rotting on the ground,
a thought of spring is inadvertent pleasure:
a policeman ~~stopped~~ pushed a dancer ~~on a dirt road, [Del L] pushed him~~ against
        ~~the hood of the~~ a car, ~~and~~ said, "sure,"
when he insisted he had marigolds, not marijuana.

Sze says an uncle told him the story about the two brothers in Chengdu. "It may have
happened," he says, "but I used it as a paradigm — the Chengdu story made me think of intention
and effect." The "intention and effect" illustrated by the story become universal with Sze's addi-
tion of the last three lines — which show that in places as different as Santa Fe and Chengdu,
individuals can be caught in similar(ly unfortunate) circumstances beyond their control.

3.        the silences

                rope ~~strung~~ at ankle level,
                a walkway sprinkled with water
                under red and orange maples along a white-plastered wall;

                moss covering the irregular ground
                under propped-up weeping cherrry trees;

                in a corral~~: the air is wine-colored~~
                ~~as~~ a woman is about to whisper and pat the roan's neck;

                an amber chasm inside a cello;

                in a business conversation,
                the silences are eel farms passed on a bullet train;

                a silence in the shape of a rake;

                a thin sheet of ice floating along a dock;
                the texture of icy-black basil leaves at sunrise;

a shaggy mane pushing up through ~~the~~ asphalt ~~of a parking lot~~;

a woman wearing a multicolored dress of a silk-screened naked women
about to peel a hard-boiled egg;

three stones leading into a pond.

This section is the first of similar sections listing what would seem to be unconnected images (the other sections being "the shards," "smoke," "the throw" and "the double throw").

4.      april snow

~~i~~ ~~you~~ i walk along the length of a stone-and-gravel garden
and feel without looking how the fifteen stones
appear and disappear. ~~i~~ ~~you~~ i had not expected the space
to be defined by a wall made of clay boiled in oil
nor to see above a series of green cryptomeria
pungent in spring. ~~i~~ ~~you~~ i stop and feel an april snow
begin to fall on the stones and raked gravel and see
how distance turns into abstraction desire and ordinary
things: from the air, corn and soybean fields ~~become~~ are
a series of horizontal and vertical stripes of pure color:
viridian, yellow ocher, raw sienna, sap green. ~~i~~ ~~you~~ i
remember in istanbul at the entrance to the blue mosque
two parallel and extended lines of shoes humming [Del L] at
[New L] the threshold of paradise.  up close, it's hard to know
if the rattle of milk bottles will become a topaz,
or a moment of throttled anger tripe that ~~you~~ is
~~chew and chew~~ chewed and chewed. in the distance, you feel drumming
and chanting and begin to see a line of pueblo women [Del L] dancing
[New L] with black-on-black jars on their heads~~,~~ ; they [Del L] lift
[New L] the jars high then start to throw them to the ground.

Sze's reference to "fifteen stones" was inspired by his 1990 visits to the Ryoanji Zen garden in Kyoto.  He recalls, "Three of the four sides of the Ryoanji garden are walled so that visitors can walk along only one side.  The fifteen stones in the garden are placed specifically so that a visitor can never see all of them at the same time.  Thus, you can only see fifteen stones through feeling — imagination."

He adds that he considers the "april snow" section to be about distance: "How you may be really close to something and still not see it, then you go away and when you return, it's transformed."  The poem's narrator feels rather than observes the snow.  The snow hides "desire and ordinary things" and offers the narrator an abstraction that stimulates associations with other thoughts including memories.

The lines, "up close, it's hard to know/ if the rattle of milk bottles will become a topaz," seem unexpected in their placement even though the concept is an expansion of Sze's ideas about distance. If the reader is surprised at encountering these lines, Sze thought that readers might stop to ponder the thoughts generated by them — in a stillness of time captured by the idea of a topaz.

The last four lines of the section depict a real-life incident that occured in the pueblo of San Ildefonso. Sze recalls, "There was a wedding at a church. The bride and groom had left. Then there were a bunch of guys drinking and one ended up stabbing another. The women of the pueblo felt so bad that they created black-on-black pots and invited the public to a ceremony where they raised the pots to the crowd and then threw them on the ground." The "throw" symbolizes creating a connection with the crowd, which Sze seizes as a metaphor for his poem.

In this section, Sze shifts from the first person to the third. He felt the shift appropriate as he delved more into the writing process. It is worth noting that when Sze later revised the order of the sections of the poem, he returned to the first person pronoun. After deciding to begin the poem with "april snow," he switched back to the first person because he felt a need to "personalize the poem."

5.        the center

men dressed in cottonwood leaves ~~are dancing~~ dance
in the curving motion of a green rattlesnake.
~~i feel~~ ~~you dream~~ i am walking along a sandstone trail
and stop in a field of shards~~,~~ : here is a teal zigzag
and there is a blood-red deer's breath arrow,
women dancers offer melons to the six directions
then throw them to the ground. ~~you~~ ~~i feel~~ a wave
~~rock~~ rocks through the crowd as the melons are smashed open.
~~you feel you~~ i know i have have walked along a path lit
by candles inside open-mesh cast-iron carp.
~~you~~ i stop at a water basin, and as ~~you~~ i bend to
ladle water, ~~you~~ see~~,~~ reflected, a sweet gum leaf~~,~~ .
as a cornmeal path becomes a path ~~again,~~ to the gods
[New L] then a cornmeal path again, ~~you~~ i see the line
of women dancing with black-on-black jars on their heads.
they raise the jars with macaw and lightning patterns
to the six directions then form a circle
and throw them down on the center-marking stones.
~~for a second the singing and drumming stops,~~
~~a sexual wave of singing rocks in the blood and mind.~~

The Pueblos recognize six directions: above, below, north, west, south and east. "In the pueblo, one can be in the center of a three-dimensional world," Sze explains. Structurally, this section is quite accomplished: in describing pueblo life, Sze points "below" with the narrator's "bend to ladle water" and "above" with the "cornmeal path becomes a path to the gods"; "above" and "below" are echoed later when the women raise the jars before throwing them down.

Sze deleted the last two lines because they "go on far too long and reveal too much; cutting it short makes it more effective."

"go kiss a horse's ass."

"he hanged himself from the flagpole."

"i just do what i'm told."

she wanted him to hold her and say nothing.

"depression is due to loss or guilt."

who heard shrieks?
in the morning,
a mutilated body was found behind the adobe church.

he saw that "A or B" was not a choice since A and B had been predetermined.

"i hated that painting painting so I burned it."

hair on the woodstove.

"i'm so glad."

after fallopian surgery, she checks her scar, combs her hair, puts on makeup.

the red phoenix tattoos on the arms of a locksmith.

"a man's character is his fate."

he had two cameras but was always pawning one to ~~get~~ <u>release</u> the other ~~back~~.

they slept a mediterranean sleep: sun, sand, water;
the bed had the soft motion of waves.

"no, no, no, no, no, no, no!"

~~he saw that a sunny weather forecast was no solution to grief.~~

<u>"water is the koan of water."</u>

~~ocean horizon.~~

Sze deleted "ocean horizon" from the Final Draft because he thought that the resulting last line, "water is the koan of water," was sufficient to tie together the different "shards" in this section.

7.    smoke

she puts jars in a pit, covers them with sawdust,
adds a layer of shards and ~~again~~ covers them,
builds a fire, and, when the burn is intense,
smothers it with sheep dung.  she will not know
for a few hours if the jars have turned completely
black and did not break cooling.  for now
no one sees or knows; i inhale smoke, ~~seeing~~ see
vendors along the ~~bosporus~~ docks selling grilled
corn smelling of charcoal, the air at dusk
plangent with cries from minarets up on the hill —
the cries resembling the whirring waves of starlings
that always precede the pulsing wing-beat Vs
of sandhill cranes.  oh, you can glow with ~~jealousy~~ anger,
but it leaves the soot of an oil burner
on the windows and walls. if anguish is an end
in itself, you walk into a landscape of
[New L] burned salt cedar [Del L] ~~burned~~ along ~~the banks of~~ a river.  i remember
seeing hungry passengers disembark at the docks ~~;~~ .
~~they seemed so possessed by hunger that biting~~
~~into a cobra's egg was the only way for them to see.~~

  Sze says that he considered the last two lines unnecessary.  The change also opens up
the ending of "the smoke," creating that resonant space Sze wishes to achieve.


8.    the smash

i look at fourteen stones submerged at varying depths
in a sea of gravel.  i do not know under which stone
is a signature but guess that a pin-sized hourglass space,
separating intention and effect, is a blind point
where anger may coalesce into a pearl.  i may sit here
until the stones have a riparian shine and are buoyant
in september starlight, yet never live to see
how grief turns into the effortless stretch of a fisherman
casting a fly onto a stream.  when i slept on ~~a~~ the float house
i became accustomed to the rise and fall of the tide,
so that when i walked on the rain forest island
i was queasy.  i wanted a still pellucid point
but realize the ~~tragic but~~ necessary and sufficient condition
is to feel the pin-sized space as a point of resistance,
as a smash that is a beginning wave of light.
the dancers reappear and enter the plaza in two lines.
shifting feet in rhythm to the shifting drumming,

they approach the crowd under the huge yellow cottonwood.

This section presents a sense of contemplation — a consideration, perhaps, of what has been addressed in earlier sections of the poem. Thus, Sze offers "fourteen stones" versus the "fifteen stones" mentioned in section 4. The inspiration is related to Ryoanji — specifically that one can see only fourteen (of the fifteen) stones from the exit.

"(T)he pin-sized hourglass shape" evokes the earlier reference to "topaz" in section 4 — a moment or space of time where there is a "possibility of transformation."


9.    the throw

mating above the cattails, red dragonflies —

sipping litchi tea, eating fried scallion pancakes —

bamboo slivers under the fingernails —

playing ping-pong by candelight in a greenhouse —

digging up and rotating soil in the flower beds —

pulling and pullling at her throat until it bleeds —

scraping the skin of the earth —

finding ~~shaggy manes~~ shaggymanes have deliquesced into black ink —

releasing endorphins in the brain —

~~*blak, black*~~ —

archipelago:
an expanse of water with many scattered islands —

a python coiling around sixteen white oblong eggs —

waking in the dark to pungent hyacinths —

blooming the pure white curve of blooming —

dancers are throwing
~~lollipops,~~ licorice, sunflower seeds, pot scrubbers, aprons, plastic bowls.

This section contains Sze's first mention of "archipelago." Although the reader could take these lines as a link of all of the poem's elements, Sze says he was keeping in mind the particular definition of "archipelago" as "expanse of water" because that definition achieves his desire for "the poem to resist closure — like in a Pueblo ceremony where they (end) by opening out the ceremony to the audience." In addition, the words "expanse of water" relate again to the resonance that Sze had sought to portray with his images.

Sze moved the words, "blak, black" to the next section, the "double throw." He also changed "lollipops" to "licorice" because he thought " 'lollipops' was too whimsical and its tone not quite right" for the poem.

Like the sections "the shards," "the throw" and "the double throw," this section also lists seemingly unconnected images as he carves up poetic space. His goal for this technique may be captured by an excerpt from one of his old poems that was printed in his 1982 book, *Dazzled* (Floating Island Publications), "Viewing Photographs of China." In this excerpt, one can see how the poet's philosophy came to manifest itself in a poem like "Archipelago" nearly two decades later — all for "a clear light, a clear emerging/ view of the world":

> . . . instead of insisting that
> the world have an essence, we
> juxtapose, as in a collage,
> facts, ideas, images:
>
> the arctic
> tern, the pearl farm, considerations
> of the two World Wars, Peruvian
> horses, executions, concentration
> camps; and find, as in a sapphire,
> a clear light, a clear emerging
> view of the world.

10.    the double throw

> plastic bowls, aprons, pot scrubbers, sunflower seeds, ~~lollipops~~ licorice —
>
> the shadow of a hummingbird —
>
> crab apple blossoms scattering in the street —
>
> a silence in the shape of a chanterelle —
>
> a turkey feather hanging from a branch of mountain ~~mahogany~~ ash —
>
> the forms of lightning —
>
> a yellow iris blooming near the house marker, 1932 —
>
> river stones marking the noon solstice —

black, *blak, blaec* —

following the thread
[New L] of recollection through ~~all the places~~ [Del L] ~~of~~ a lifetime ~~and vanishing~~
—

the passions becoming the <u>chiming</u> sounds of ~~struck~~ jade —

blue corn growing in a field of sand —

the *chug chug, ka ka* of a cactus wren —

a black-_and-_yellow butterfly closing and <u>then</u> opening its wings —

egrets wading in shallow water at low tide.

"There is only one (physical) throw," Sze says, referring to the section title. "The second does not exist except as my metaphorical throw of images to the reader. I call it 'chromatic effacement' — where I 'throw' a series of resonances at the reader. What I throw incorporates a series of empty spaces where there is nothing. If you're attentive, however, there is a resonance and erasure of time."

"Blak" and "blaec" are, respectively, the Middle English and Old English spellings of "black" which Sze discovered while looking up "black" in a dictionary. Sze recalls, "This 'black, blak and blaec' was interesting. So I thought to myself, I should ask somebody about this etymology." He ended up asking the opinion of Murray Gell-man who, in addition to being a Nobel Prize-winning physicist, is an "incredible linguist" whom Sze sometimes consults on poetry. "I asked him about the sounds of the words, pronouncing the Old and Middle English versions exactly like 'black'," Sze remembers. "When he confirmed that the words were homonyms, I knew I wanted to keep them for my poem." Thus, Sze used the words, symbolizing a return to the past — as in the next line's "thread of recollection" — from current to Middle to Old English.

—ᵚᵚ—

After finishing the "201st" draft, Sze reorganized the order of the sections. He began by retyping the poem to insert capital letters where appropriate — he writes all early drafts of his poem in lower case because he finds the use of capitals "disruptive to my associative process." He then uses the act of capitalizing words in the final stages of the writing process "to slow me down and think again about how the poem works, to consider what I'm writing."

The following table compares the order of the sections in the chronological order in which they were written in the 201st draft, versus the order of the sections in the final version of the poem:

| Working Title | 201st Draft Order | Final Draft Order |
|---|---|---|
| elements of composition | 1 | deleted |
| the chengdu effect | 2 | 3 |
| the silences | 3 | 2 |
| april snow | 4 | 1 |
| the center | 5 | 5 |
| the shards | 6 | 6 |
| smoke | 7 | 4 |
| the smash | 8 | 7 |
| the throw | 9 | 8 |
| the double throw | 10 | 9 |

Sze considered "april snow" a better beginning for the poem, less "abrupt" than "the chengdu effect." Sze sequenced the poem's sections to make the poem a "walk through . . . a meditation on existence" for the reader.

The poem now starts with "I walk along the length of a stone-and-gravel garden . . ." From this beginning, there is a smoother, more logical flow in reading through the rest of the poem. The last three lines of the new first section depict "Pueblo women dancing . . . they lift the jars high then start to throw them to the ground." The implied shards connect to the list of images — or the shards — presented by the second section, "the silences." This also is the "chromatic resonance" Sze wishes to achieve: the shards of the first section turning into pieces of empty space in the next section.

Both "april snow" and "the silences" also serve as an introduction to the third section, which describes "the chengdu effect," a specific story — a specific island — that was a key inspiration for the poem. In presenting the story of the incident in Chengdu, Sze recalls that he had wished to "ground the story in time" through an association with a Pueblo ceremony. These references begin with the last two lines of "the chengdu effect" and continue to flow through the next two sections, "smoke" and "the center."

The next section, "the shards," features more "empty spaces" designed to aid the reader's exploration of the "certain resonance" Sze wishes to offer with his poem and, thus, smoothly flows into the next section, "the smash." By recalling the effect of the Ryoanji garden, "the smash" calms the reader into a more meditative flow. By the time the reader reaches the lines in the middle of the section that define "archipelago," the reader is tempted to feel a sense of closure, interpreting the invocation of "archipelago" as a link of the disparate elements featured in the poem. Sze, however, crafts his poem "to resist closure like in a Pueblo ceremony where they (end) by open(ing) out the ceremony to the audience."

At about this stage of Sze's drafting process, he shared his poem with Mei-mei Berssenbrugge, another resident of New Mexico. Berssenbrugge's input is reflected in revisions that primarily involve technical aspects, e.g. rhythm, style and diction. The two poets often share final drafts of their poems to "clarify the structure." As a result of their discussions, Sze's changes included:

Section: "the silences"
First line: "rope strung at ankle level" was changed to "rope at ankle level."

Section: "the chengdu effect"
Thirteenth line: "a woman and man must <u>have</u> a series of betrayals" was changed to "a woman and man must <u>ache from</u> a series of betrayals."

Nineteenth to twenty-first lines: "a policeman stopped a dancer on a dirt road,/ pushed him against the hood of the car and said, "sure,"/ when he insisted he had marigolds, not marijuana" was changed to "a policement pushed a dancer against a car, said, "sure,"/ when he insisted he had marigolds, not marijuana."

Section: "smoke"
Eighth line: the line, "vendors along the bosporus docks selling grilled," dropped the word "bosporus."

Thirteenth line: " . . . oh you can glow with <u>jealousy</u>" was changed to " . . . oh, you can glow with <u>anger</u>."

Sixteenth and seventeenth lines: the lines "in itself, you walk into a landscape of salt cedar/ burned along the banks of a river. I remember" was changed to "in itself, you walk into a landscape of/ burned salt cedar along a river. I remember."

Section: "the center"
First line: "men dressed in cottonwood leaves <u>are dancing</u>" was changed to "men dressed in cottonwood leaves <u>dance</u>."

Section: "the shards"
Thirteenth line: "after fallopian surgery, she <u>checks</u> her scar, . . ." was changed to "after fallopian surgery, she <u>touches</u> her scar"

Sixteenth line: "he had two cameras but was always pawning one <u>to get the other back</u>" was changed to "he had two cameras but was always pawning one <u>to release the other</u>"

Three years later as Sze was putting together the book manuscript that he titled after "Archipelago," Sze incorporated two more changes to the version published in *The Paris Review* (Summer 1992). The changes were suggested by editors at Copper Canyon Press including Sam Hamill. "Mr. Hamill read the poetry manuscript as a whole and asked me to do a second read because he thought I used the phrases, 'I feel' and 'You feel' too often throughout the book." As a result, Sze deleted "I feel" from the seventh line of "the center." With this change, Sze professes no discomfort.

However, he says he is still wondering about the other change: the insertion of a comma after the word, "anger," in the sixteenth line of the "april snow" section: "or a moment of throttled anger, tripe that is."

"I'm unsure of whether I should have done that," Sze muses.

It seems ironical that — after the lengthy, complicated process required to finish his poem — Sze continued wondering if he should have conceded to that small puntuation mark. I noted to Sze that if he looked up the word, "comma" in the dictionary, he would see it defined partly as a "mark of separation" — perhaps not in keeping with the poem's epistemology. Symbolically,

Sze's slight unease would seem to possess a certain logic.

A few days after our interview, Sze called to say that as a result of discussing "the process of the poem, I have decided to remove that comma." Thus, *BLACK LIGHTNING*, is pleased to present the — for now — *final* draft of "Archipelago." It is the version published in his Copper Canyon book but without a certain comma. For, as Sze suggests, it is often in a "pin-sized hourglass space" where transformation may occur.

—∿—

## ARCHIPELAGO

**1**

I walk along the length of a stone-and-gravel garden
and feel without looking how the fifteen stones
appear and disappear. I had not expected the space
to be defined by a wall made of clay boiled in oil
nor to see above a series of green cryptomeria
pungent in spring. I stop and feel an April snow
begin to fall on the stones and raked gravel and see
how distance turns into abstraction desire and ordinary
things: from the air, corn and soybean fields are
a series of horizontal and vertical stripes of pure color:
viridian, yellow ocher, raw sienna, sap green. I
remember in Istanbul at the entrance to the Blue Mosque
two parallel and extended lines of shoes humming at
the threshold of paradise. Up close, it's hard to know
if the rattle of milk bottles will become a topaz,
or a moment of throttled anger tripe that is
chewed and chewed. In the distance, you feel drumming
and chanting and begin to see a line of Pueblo women dancing
with black-on-black jars on their heads; they lift
the jars high then start to throw them to the ground.


**2**

Rope at ankle level,
a walkway sprinkled with water
under red and orange maples along a white-plastered wall;

moss covering the irregular ground
under propped-up weeping cherrry trees;

in a corral
a woman is about to whisper and pat the roan's neck;

an amber chasm inside a cello;

in a business conversation,
the silences are eel farms passed on a bullet train;

a silence in the shape of a rake;

a thin sheet of ice floating along a dock;
the texture of icy-black basil leaves at sunrise;

a shaggymane pushing up through asphalt;

a woman wearing a multicolored dress of a silk-screened naked women
about to peel a hard-boiled egg;

three stones leading into a pond.


**3**

Desire is to memory as an azalea is to a stone?
During the Cultural Revolution, the youngest brother
of the Peng family was executed against a wall
in Chengdu for being a suspected Guomindang agent.
Years earlier, the eldest brother was executed
at that wall for being a suspected communist.
This Chengdu effect has no end, but if you interiorize,
a series of psychological tragedies
has the resonance of stone-and-gravel waterfalls.
A first frost sweetens the apples; I want them sweeter
but discover a second frost makes the cores mush;
so essential shapes are destroyed starting at the center.
A woman and man must have a series of betrayals
before they can begin to bicker at the dinner table.
I water hyacinth bulbs planted in shallow pots
in the cool, dark bathroom, and, though it feels
odd to do so when walnuts are rotting on the ground,
a thought of spring is inadvertent pleasure:
a policeman pushed a dancer against a car, said, "Sure,"
when he insisted he had marigolds, not marijuana.


**4**

She puts jars in a pit, covers them with sawdust,
adds a layer of shards and covers them,
builds a fire, and, when the burn is intense,
smothers it with sheep dung.  She will not know

for a few hours if the jars have turned completely
black and did not break cooling.  For now
no one sees or knows; I inhale smoke, see
vendors along the docks selling grilled
corn smelling of charcoal, the air at dusk
plangent with cries from minarets up on the hill —
the cries resembling the whirring waves of starlings
that always precede the pulsing wing-beat Vs
of sandhill cranes.  Oh, you can glow with anger,
but it leaves the soot of an oil burner
on the windows and walls. If anguish is an end
in itself, you walk into a landscape of
burned salt cedar along a river.  I remember
seeing hungry passengers disembark at the docks.


### 5

Men dressed in cottonwood leaves dance
in the curving motion of a green rattlesnake.
I am walking along a sandstone trail
and stop in a field of shards: here is a teal zigzag
and there is a blood-red deer's breath arrow,
Women dancers offer melons to the six directions
then throw them to the ground.  A wave
rocks through the crowd as the melons are smashed open.
I know I have have walked along a path lit
by candles inside open-mesh cast-iron carp.
I stop at a water basin, and as I bend to
ladle water, see reflected, a sweet gum leaf.
As a cornmeal path becomes a path to the gods
then a cornmeal path again, I see the line
of women dancing with black-on-black jars on their heads.
They raise the jars with macaw and lightning patterns
to the six directions then form a circle
and throw them down on the center-marking stones.


### 6

"Go kiss a horse's ass."

"He hanged himself from the flagpole."

"I just do what I'm told."

She wanted him to hold her and say nothing.

"Depression is due to loss or guilt."

Who heard shrieks?
In the morning,
a mutilated body was found behind the adobe church.

He saw that "A or B" was not a choice since A and B had been predetermined.

"I hated that painting painting so I burned it."

Hair on the woodstove.

"I'm so glad."

After fallopian surgery, she checks her scar, combs her hair, puts on makeup.

The red phoenix tattoos on the arms of a locksmith.

"A man's character is his fate."

He had two cameras but was always pawning one to release the other.

They slept a mediterranean sleep: sun, sand, water;
the bed had the soft motion of waves.

"No, no, no, no, no, no, no!"

"Water is the koan of water."


**7**

I look at fourteen stones submerged at varying depths
in a sea of gravel. I do not know under which stone
is a signature but guess that a pin-sized hourglass space,
separating intention and effect, is a blind point
where anger may coalesce into a pearl. I may sit here
until the stones have a riparian shine and are buoyant
in September starlight, yet never live to see
how grief turns into the effortless stretch of a fisherman
casting a fly onto a stream. When I slept on the float house
I became accustomed to the rise and fall of the tide,
so that when I walked on the rain forest island
I was queasy. I wanted a still pellucid point
but realize the necessary and sufficient condition
is to feel the pin-sized space as a point of resistance,
as a smash that is a beginning wave of light.

The dancers reappear and enter the plaza in two lines.
Shifting feet in rhythm to the shifting drumming,
they approach the crowd under the huge yellow cottonwood.


**8**

Mating above the cattails, red dragonflies —

sipping litchi tea, eating fried scallion pancakes —

bamboo slivers under the fingernails —

playing Ping-Pong by candlelight in a greenhouse —

digging up and rotating soil in the flower beds —

pulling and pullling at her throat until it bleeds —

scraping the skin of the earth —

finding shaggymanes have deliquesced into black ink —

releasing endorphins in the brain —

archipelago:
an expanse of water with many scattered islands —

a python coiling around sixteen white oblong eggs —

waking in the dark to pungent hyacinths —

blooming the pure white curve of blooming —

dancers are throwing
licorice, sunflower seeds, pot scrubbers, aprons, plastic bowls.


**9**

Plastic bowls, aprons, pot scrubbers, sunflower seeds, licorice —

the shadow of a hummingbird —

crab apple blossoms scattering in the street —

a silence in the shape of a chanterelle —

a turkey feather hanging from a branch of mountain ash —

the forms of lightning —

a yellow iris blooming near the house marker, 1932 —

river stones marking the noon solstice —

black, *blak, blaec* —

following the thread
of recollection through a lifetime —

the passions becoming the chiming sounds of jade —

blue corn growing in a field of sand —

the *chug chug, ka ka* of a cactus wren —

a black-and-yellow butterfly closing and then opening its wings —

egrets wading in shallow water at low tide.

# KIMIKO HAHN

Kimiko Hahn's poetry was first collected in book form in *We Stand Our Ground* (IKON, 1988), a collaboration with poets, Gale Jackson and Susan Sherman. That volume was followed by *Air Pocket* (Hanging Loose Press, 1989); *Earshot* (Hanging Loose Press, 1992) which won the 1995 Theodore Roethke Poetry Award and an Association of Asian American Studies Award in Literature; *The Unbearable Heart* (Kaya Productions, 1995) which won a 1996 American Book Award from the Before Columbus Foundation; and *Volatile* (Hanging Loose Press, 1998). She has appeared in numerous anthologies and publications including *Best American Poetry 1996* and has been awarded fellowships from the National Endowment for the Arts and the New York Foundation for the Arts. Hahn has taught poetry and literature at Barnard, Goddard, Sarah Lawrence and Yale, and currently is an associate professor in the English Department at Queens College/CUNY. She is working on a fifth poetry collection, *Mosquito and Ant*, which includes poems in *BLACK LIGHTNING*; and is revising a prose manuscript, *Afterbirth*.

In response to the question, "What advice would you give to a young poet?" Kimiko Hahn responds:

Take risks. Leave the map at home.

# Expressing Self and Desire, Even If One Must Writhe

*It occurs to you*
*only women and wounded soldiers*
*writhe.*
*— from "Her First Language" by Kimiko Hahn*

Kimiko Hahn was not exposed to much literary theory as a student. She recalls reading mostly primary texts as she majored in English and East Asian Studies at the University of Iowa and while studying for her Master's in Japanese Literature at Columbia University. Consequently, during her academic breaks from teaching creative writing and literature at Queens College/CUNY, she likes to read literary theorists. During the winter 1996 academic break, she focused on several essays by such feminists as Hélène Cixous, Luce Irigaray, Catherine Clément and Adrienne Rich, and birthed a group of poems that were "triggered" by fragments from those essays.

"I excerpted quotes from these writers to 'talk back' to them, hopefully engage with them deeply," she says. "I found their psychological bent interesting and, for the most part, I agreed with their ideas."

Among the poems generated from that period were "The Notice" and "Responding to Light." The former poem was triggered by the words, "obliging him to see," which is a phrase from Clément's essay, "The Guilty One." The latter poem was triggered by a series of phrases from Irigaray's essay, "Body against Body: In Relation to the Mother."

"I think these poems are more pointedly feminist than anything I've written before. I think of my work as rising from a feminist place although not always directly. These do, in part, because I was talking back to the French feminists," she says. "They write such incredibly lush stuff."

Hahn also remembers that the birth of the poems, as a writing technique, was first suggested to her in a workshop with Michael Burkhard who she studied with at age 18. "I recall him saying that if you're ever stuck, find a quote you like and respond to it," she explains. "I don't know if I consciously thought of this technique but it's one I've used with other poems, such as 'Cruising Barthes' and poems inspired by (tenth century Japanese novel) *The Tale of the Genji.*"

For Hahn, whose busy schedule includes raising two daughters, this device is also useful given her limited writing time. She does have a routine, however, and is as committed to it as she is to her teaching schedule. This obviously places pressure on those hours. She often leaves her apartment for local cafes to get away from the domestic energy — or lethargy — but notes that she doesn't have time to "sit and wait for the poem."

"When I write, I don't think. I really try to work off whatever is at hand — to respond, to generate raw material. After the initial draft, I then try to figure out where the poem is going," she says.

Upon reflecting on these first drafts, Hahn states, "The triggering lines are very specific. But I realized afterward that in some cases the poems are no longer about those quotes — as in 'The Notice.' Still, I would like to publish the poems with the lines because I think it's interesting (for a reader) to see (what an author) is reading at the time, what influenced the work."

Hahn says she usually takes some time before sending her poems to potential publishers, even after she reaches what she senses may be the final draft. To help her determine whether the poems are written to her satisfaction, she "tries them out" at poetry readings, noting that she particularly likes reading at the New York reading spaces of the Asian American Writers Workshop and the Poetry Project at St. Marks because she knows she can take a lot of "risks" at those venues. By "risks," Hahn refers to publicly exploring new material without being conscious of all the layers; with such exploration — such "risk" — she says that her poems may suggest new themes to her.

To date, neither poem has been published. Partly based on the positive feedback she's received from audiences, Hahn now feels both poems — written a year-and-a-half ago — are ready for publication.

—〰—

The following presents both poems from their beginning, hand-written drafts to their final drafts. A discussion about the poems' progression is featured along with the drafts. *(Editing Marks: [New P] denotes new stanza break; [Del P] denotes deletion of prior stanza break; [New L] denotes new line break; [Del L] denotes deletion of prior line break; underlined words denote added words; words with strike-through marks denote deleted words; and capitalized and/or italicized comments present Hahn's notes on the margins of her poems' drafts.)*

Also featured below are excerpts from Clément's and Irigaray's essays. Though Hahn notes that the poems ultimately transcended their triggering thoughts, it is, indeed, interesting to see the context of the poems' origins.

I.    **The Notice**

Hahn first wrote her poem under a different title, "Seeing," triggered by the phrase "obliging him to see" from Clément's essay, "The Guilty One." Hahn read the essay in *The Newly Born Woman* by Cixous and Clément (translated by Betsy Wing, University of Minnesota Press, 1986). A biography in the book describes Clément as "diplomat in charge of cultural exchanges at the French Ministry of External Relations. Formerly editor of cultural science for the Parisian newspaper *Le Matin*, she is the author of books on structuralism, psychoanalysis, and Marxism, and has written several novels."

In the Introduction to *The Newly Born Woman*, Sandra M. Gilbert (an English professor), says the "mutual focus (of Clément and Cixous) is on the sometimes oppressive, sometimes privileged madness fostered by marginalization, on the wilderness out of which silenced women must finally find ways to cry, shriek, scream, and dance in impassioned dances of desire." Indeed, what Gilbert calls "the heart" of the book is the story of a southern Italian ritual, the tarantella.

The tarantella is described in Clément's essay which, in Gilbert's words, "discusses the rebellious 'celebrations' with which repressed (female) subjects have responded to their subjugation by patriarchal hierarchies. Clément tells a tale of women in the Mezzogiorno who can be cured of imaginary spider bites only by doing a ceremonial dance. . . . At the end of the episode, she transcends 'the divine bite' and 'leave[s] risk behind . . . . to settle down again under a roof, in a house, in the family circle of kinship and marriage . . . the men's world.' But she has had her interlude of orgasmic freedom."

Clément's "The Guilty One" addresses specifically the images of the sorceress and the hysteric as exemplifying women's rebellion against oppression. The phrase that triggered Hahn's poem was within the context of a discussion about the "cunning" public nature of the way the hysteric and the sorceress rebel. Cunning, because the oppressor is forced to witness — thus, also suffer from — the act of rebellion. The following excerpt from Clément's essay sets the poem's triggering phrase, "obliging him to see," in context:

> The hysteric and the sorceress are more cunning: the attack is mimed on their own body, implicating the other in the celebration, <u>obliging him to see</u>, since he has the 'fantastic desire' to do so, but also obliging him to endure the attack's indefinite repetition. Fair's fair: spectacle in exchange for repetition of spectacle. . . .(T)he hysterical attack provides) a return to regular rhythm. The device—setting in complement, face to face, the ones who look and the ones who suffer, the women who suffer— requires it. The device requires that 'victims and torturers alike recall their earliest youth' . . .The child . . . watching someone fall cries.

The following is the draft Hahn first hand-wrote in response to the phrase, "obliging him to see."


**A.**    **Handwritten First Draft**

### Seeing

". . . obliging him to see . . ."
Clément P. 18

The only lights are the lights from the
neighbor's <u>back</u> ~~windows~~ facing your back windows:
their kitchen florescence into your bedroom.
There are no stars in the City,
even Brooklyn though if all the lights
were extinguished perhaps the ceiling
would lift, the reddish black night lift,
and <u>the</u> constellations we read about
come into their ambiguous focus.
You want him. You
want him to want you first
but in the angled light know
he will sleep soon so you must
tap his last moments of wakefulness
in the hopes the mother in the black brassiere
has not appeared, nor the sister in the white lace, —
because you want his want.
All of it.
And you want him to see
that under your XL t-shirt
is the apparel of the black widow

sans blade unless the ~~labia minor~~ <u>clit</u>
is just that.  Unless his own cock.


Your students wince at that word, clit.
They do not like the sound.
But *you* love the consonants.


*Look at this.*


You want to rise to stand in the center
of the hard mattress and pull the shirt over your head.
You want to be *a spectacle.*
You want to be the one who can revisit ~~memory~~ painful <u>memory</u>
You want to be the one who can travel from his to your own.
You want to straddle him ~~acrobatically~~ flexing your inner thighs


Hahn says she can't recall what she was thinking as she wrote this draft but she often begins with a place, here the bedroom, and sees what happens there.  "I probably had a feeling there would be some kind of 'performance' given the triggering line," she suggested.  "So I began in the 'master bedroom.'"

As she was reading the essay, Hahn says she was "trying to understand what one wants for one's self.  My mother — and other people's mothers — never really asked themselves what they want.  Girls — maybe boys, too, but certainly girls — are not taught to ask themselves, 'What do I really want?'  In my generation when a girl said she wanted something, she was seen as demanding: sassy or bitchy, an attitude that could even be punished.  If one doesn't ask oneself or if one doesn't let others know what she wants — she may not acquire what she needs to be whole.  But to be whole is dangerous: that is why women are so often 'in pieces.'  Perhaps that is why the word 'want' appears so often in this draft.  Also I like the simplicity of it — how it differs from 'desire' or 'need'."

In Gilbert's Introduction, there is a passage containing the word "tarantella" that may have triggered the words, "black widow" in the poem; it also seems to correlate Hahn's motivation with that of the life of a poet:

(T)he country of writing ought to be a no where into which we can fly in a tarantella of rage and desire, a place beyond 'vileness and compromise' where the part of ourselves that longs to be free, to be an 'it' uncontaminated by angel or witch (or by sorceress or hysteric) can write itself, can dream, can invent new worlds.


**B.**  **A Combination of the First Two Typewritten Drafts, with Editing Marks Showing Changes From Handwritten Version:**


**Seeing**
"... ~~obliging~~ <u>Obliging</u> him to see ..."
Clément ~~P.~~ ( 18 )

The only lights are the lights from the

neighbor's back window facing your back ~~windows~~ <u>window</u>:

their kitchen florescence into your bedroom.

There are no stars in the City ~~;~~ .

~~even~~ <u>Even</u> Brooklyn though if all the lights

were extinguished perhaps the <u>reddish black</u> ceiling

would lift~~, the reddish black night lift~~,

and the constellations we read about

come into their ~~ambiguous~~ <u>ambivalent</u> focus.

You want him. You

want him to want you first

but in the angled light know

he will sleep soon so you must

tap his last moments of wakefulness

in the hopes the mother in the black brassiere

has not appeared, nor the sister in the white lace, —

because you want his want.

All of it.

And you want him to see

that under your XL t-shirt

is the apparel of the black widow

sans blade unless the clit               INSTRUMENT?

is just that. ~~Unless his own cock.~~


Your students wince at that word, clit.

They do not like the sound~~.~~

<u>but you do.</u> ~~But you~~ <u>You</u> love the consonants ~~:~~ <u>,</u> like

[Del P] ~~Look~~ <u>look</u> at this.


You want ~~to rise~~ to stand in the center

of the hard mattress and pull the shirt over your head.

You want to be <i>a spectacle.</i>

You want to be the one who can revisit painful memory

~~[ New P]~~

~~[~~[Del P] You want to be the one who can travel

[New L] from his to your own. ~~[~~

<u>You want to be the one feeling all the time</u>

<u>as if breathing through skin.</u>

You want to straddle him flexing your inner thighs.


                                    NEEDS MISTREATMENT

                                    LOOKS FOR IT


It is apt to note the reference to "black widow," given <i>The Newly Born Woman</i>'s refer-
ences to the tarantella. Hahn says the reference was probably made consciously as it resulted
partly from a discussion with a friend about the themes discussed in Clément's essay. "A black

widow, as a powerful female figure," she notes, "possesses a concealed weapon (hence the reference to 'blade' in the second-to-last line of the first stanza). She has a means to get what she wants and does not shrink from that desire."

My reading had associated *tarantella*, spider with *black widow*; from black widow, there seemed some association with "mother in the black brassiere." Interestingly, the mother and black undergarments have appeared before in Hahn's poetry, as in her 1989 book *AIR POCKET* (Hanging Loose Press) which includes a poem, "IMAGINATION," that features the lines, "It enters/ his dream/ like a mother/ in a black slip." Further, in *EARSHOT* (Hanging Loose Press, 1992), the poem "Infra-Red" contains this closure: "Maybe she will always be the one/ in a bra and half-slip/ kissing the boy *morning*." What are all these boys' mothers doing? "I guess I am in a hot competition," Hahn suggests.

The last stanza also reflects the influence of Clément's essay, especially in the lines:

> You want ~~to rise~~ to stand in the center
> of the hard mattress and pull the shirt over your head.
> You want to be *a spectacle*.
> You want to be the one who can revisit painful memory
> [ New P]
> [Del P] You want to be the one who can travel
> [New L] from his to your own. ⊔

The following are excerpts from Clément's essay that could relate to the last stanza (underlining of words is mine for emphasis).:

> These women, to escape the misfortune of their economic and familial exploitation, chose to suffer spectacularly <u>before an audience of men</u>: it is an attack of <u>spectacle</u>, a crisis of suffering. And the attack is also a festival, a celebration of their guilt used as a weapon, a story of seduction. All that, <u>within the family</u>."

> "Why do people bitten by the tarantula find such prodigious relief in song and different melodies?" . . .Once again it is a question of <u>expelling the foreign body</u>, the venom, through a violent and irksome action. A forced dance, a tragic happiness, but even more — the <u>repetition of a distant past</u>.

> The three central figures, madman, wildman, and child, who always simultaneously signify origin, exclusion and the future norm are mixed up in the inversion, in the obvious conjunction between a regression to origin and the underside of social life. Woman partakes of all three and she beats all: madwoman, wildwoman, childwoman. The madmen's festival, the savages' wild celebrations, the children's parties: <u>woman is the figure at the center</u> to which the others refer, for she is, at the same time, both loss and cause, the ruin and the reason. She, once again, is the guilty one.

In the margin of her first typewritten draft, Hahn had questioned, in the first stanza, the choice of the word "ambiguous" and whether the phrase "Unless his own cock" was necessary. She later deleted the phrase, as well as amended the word "ambiguous" to "ambivalent" as the word contained "greater personification" than "ambiguous."

In the first typewritten draft, her notes in the margin also reflect her thought that the last stanza seems to need "MORE MISTREATMENT." This resulted, in the second typewritten draft, of her addition of the lines, "<u>You</u> want to be the one feeling all the time/ as if breathing through skin." Oftentimes in later drafts she finds the need to intensify the emotional content: "get ruthless, get vicious,. . . really explore the material without hesitation." This stage may mean cutting back to give focus but can also mean adding sharp edges.

Hahn also addresses why she used the second person, "you," instead of the more common first person. "I think I wanted the poem to contain a sense of the speaker speaking to herself, but also, the speaker including the reader, I think. I can't recall why I unconsciously chose the second person in the first draft, but in choosing to keep it, I'll stay with this possible explanation."

**C.    Third Typewritten Draft, with Editing Marks**
**Showing Changes From Previous Typewritten Version:**

### ~~Seeing~~ <u>The Notice</u>

". . . Obliging him to see . . ."
Clément (18)

The only lights are the lights from the
neighbor's ~~back window facing your back window:~~ [Del L] ~~their~~ kitchen
florescence <u>facing</u>
[New L] ~~into your~~ <u>our back</u> bedroom <u>window</u>.
There are no stars in the City ~~:~~ <u>--</u>
[ ~~Even~~ <u>even</u> Brooklyn ] though if all the lights
were extinguished perhaps the reddish<u>-</u>black ceiling
would lift
and the constellations we read about
come into their ambivalent focus.
You want him. You
want him to want you first
but in the angled light know
he will sleep soon so you ~~much~~ <u>must</u>
tap his last moments of wakefulness
in the hopes the mother in the black brassiere
has not appeared, nor the sister in the white lace, --
because you want his want.
All of it.
~~And you want him to see so~~
~~that under your XL t-shirt~~
~~is the apparel of the black widow~~
~~sans blade unless the clit~~
~~is just that.~~

~~Your students wince at that word, clit.~~
~~They do not like the sound~~
~~but you do. You love the consonants , like~~
~~*look at this*.~~

[Del P] You want to stand in the center
of the hard mattress and ~~pull the shirt over your head~~ open the iridescent
    kimono.
~~You want to be *a spectacle*.~~
~~You want to be the one who can revisit painful memory~~
~~[Del P] You want to be the one who can travel~~
~~from his to your own.~~
~~You want to be the one feeling all the time~~
~~as if breathing through skin.~~
~~You want to straddle him flexing your inner thighs.~~
You want him to see
the blade of your sex, open.

In exploring what "one wants for one's self (in order to exist)," Hahn again mentions turning her reflection to girls in her generation being considered "demanding" when they express their desires. "But to demand something is not bad or wrong," Hahn says. Consequently, in her third typewritten draft, she changed the title to "The Notice" as a wordplay on the concepts of "Notice Me" and, concurrently, "I AM GIVING NOTICE."

During this stage, Hahn also deleted the stanza related to "students winc(ing) at that word, clit." Though the integration of "students" reflects her teaching career, in response to whether the reference perhaps caused her to think about the poem's (potential) audience, she replies, "I don't often think of 'audience' when I write — I write talking to myself in a sense — even in these 'talking back' pieces. The poem is in part 'about' audience, however, or at least dialoging with Clément in this case." In any event, Hahn says she subsequently deleted the references to shorten the poem. "I was trying to narrow the poem down to a single scene, and that moment seemed to veer off. I like to veer off but not in this short a poem," she explains.

She says she cut much of the end to "focus on the spectacle rather than talk about it." Also, she didn't want to detour to "his" needs as suggested in the lines, "travel/ from his [pain] to your own." And again the straddling is implied in the spectacle so she did not feel it necessary to "spell it out."

Hahn also cut much of the last stanza because the lines felt too 'interpretive': that is, that she was explaining the poem. In addition, she didn't want the poem to stop being a poem although she "likes to flirt with the poem-as-essay." Thus, rather than relying on this list of "wants," she tried, again, "to narrow the image down to one 'spectacular' one (in the sense of 'spectacle'): one that challenges."

**D.** **Draft with Editing Marks Showing Changes**
**Between Third Typewritten Version and Final Draft:**

**The Notice**

"~~. . . Obliging him to see . . .~~"
~~Clement (18)~~

The only lights are the lights from the
neighbor's kitchen florescence facing
our back bedroom window.
There are no stars in the City —
[~~even Brooklyn~~] though if all the lights [Del L] were extinguished
[New L]  perhaps the reddish-black ceiling
would lift
and the constellations we read about
come into their ambivalent focus.
You want him. You
want him to want you first
but in the angled light know
he will sleep soon so you must
tap his last moments of wakefulness
in the hopes the mother in the black brassiere
has not appeared, nor the sister in the white lace, —
because you want his want.
All of it.
You want to stand in the center
of the hard mattress and open the iridescent kimono.
You want him to see
the blade of your sex , open :
for fun.

Triggering Line: " . . . Obliging him to see." Catherine Clément (18)

Hahn acknowledges that "there are a lot of sexual references in my poems especially since my second book (*EARSHOT*). I've been kidded about the intensity — but I've also kidded back that when there's a lot of sex in a work, it's not about sex; and when sex is not there in the work, the work is about sex. This isn't entirely true for my poems or anyone else's — but some-what true. For example, a poem's concerns with sexuality and the body may circle subverting patriarchy and racism. And there are also issues of identification — not limited to the feminist view — for example, how does one view one's self; where does one find importance in one's life? If one feels empowered as a female, a very sexual female, then can't it potentially empower those around her? Perhaps this poem circles these concerns — though of course I wasn't conscious of these ideas as I was writing."

Then Hahn laughs and says, "Ultimately, no one should ever listen to what writers say about their own work."

Hahn's display of humor is mirrored in the last line she added to the poem: "for fun." Given that fun is typically associated with laughter, it may be worth noting that Clément described how, after the end of the "sabbat" or witches' celebration, in which the sorceress participated, the sorceress is "alone," but "that is when she takes off —laughing."

> She laughs, and it's frightening — like Medusa's laugh — petrifying and shattering con-
> straint. . . .All laughter is allied with the monstrous. . . . Laughter breaks up, breaks out,
> splashes over. . . . It is the moment at which the woman crosses a dangerous line, the
> cultural demarcation beyond which she will find herself excluded.  To break up, to touch
> the masculine integrity of the body image, is to return to a stage that is scarcely constitut-
> ed in human development; it is to return to the disordered Imaginary of before the mirror
> stage, of before the rigid and defensive constitution of subjective armor. . . .An entire fan-
> tastic world, made of bits and pieces, opens up beyond the limit, as soon as the line is
> crossed.  For the witch (the hysteric), breaking apart can be paradise, but for another, it is
> hell. . . . And for the hysteric, caught in the contradiction between cultural suffering and a
> tacit paradise that is secret, hidden in a little implicit smile through even the most intense
> pain. Thus the ambiguity of the witch and her daughter, the hysteric, is gradually
> explained.  From her archaic point of view, it is pleasure in breaking apart; but from the
> other's point of view, it is suffering, because to break apart is to aggress. . . . So Freud's
> strange remark, 'Victims and torturers alike recall their earliest youth in the same way,'
> can be explained.  Between the two parts of the couple — inquisitor-witch, psychiatrist-
> hysteric — circulate suffering and pleasure, paradise and hell.

Hahn recalls about the line, "for fun," that she "kept taking it on and off" the poem dur-ing her drafting process.  She retained the line because, she says, "I liked the figure of the black widow but I didn't want the poem to close with a kind of ultimate isolation for the female. Rather, I wanted to have an inviting figure.  My intent was provocation."  Part of the provocation surfaces in the previous line that begins with "the blade of your sex."  Hahn says that was inspired by the black widow's "concealed weapon."

She adds that she also likes "for fun" because it is "ambiguous.  It can be for fun as in, 'let's play' or it can be 'it's fun for me but I don't know if it's fun for you'."

Fun, indeed, is important to Hahn who notes, "How many poems are there where the woman is having fun?  I feel passionate about poems where women are in control, but I also want them to have fun.  It's not just about seizing power but also having fun."

Hahn, herself, begins to have fun as she continues discussing this concept: "Whenever I hear 'fun' I think of Jessica Hagedorn who often uses the phrase about projects that she may get involved in, 'Well, I hope it's fun.'  We both take our work seriously and work hard, but we also want it to be fun."

In fact, Hahn says she often counsels her students, "If it's not fun, why bother?"  As she describes how some of her students complain that rough drafts are tough work, Hahn groans and says she sometimes chides them, "Give me a break — go home then and watch MTV!"

**E.** **Final Draft:**

### The Notice

The only lights are the lights from the
neighbor's kitchen florescence facing
our back bedroom window.
There are no stars in the City
though if all the lights were extinguished
perhaps the reddish-black ceiling
would lift
and the constellations we read about
come into their ambivalent focus.
You want him. You
want him to want you first
but in the angled light know
he will sleep soon so you must
tap his last moments of wakefulness
in the hopes the mother in the black brassiere
has not appeared, nor the sister in the white lace,
because you want his want.
All of it.
You want to stand in the center
of the hard mattress and open the iridescent kimono.
You want him to see
the blade of your sex open
for fun.


*Triggering Line: "... Obliging him to see." Catherine Clément*

—ᚿᚿ—


## II.    RESPONDING TO LIGHT

Among the poems Hahn wrote in her dialogues with feminist writers, she says her favorite is "RESPONDING TO LIGHT," a poem in which she intended to explore the elements of a parent-daughter relationship. The poem was triggered by several phrases from Irigaray's essay, "Body against Body: In Relation to the Mother" which Hahn read in *Sexes and Geneaologies* (translated by Gillian C. Gill, Columbia University Press, 1993. The original was published in 1987 by *Les Éditions de Minuit*). In this case, Hahn decided to hold on to these "triggering lines" in the poem itself.

Irigaray is a leading French feminist and psychoanalyst. She holds doctorates in both linguistics and philosophy. Her books in English include *Speculum of the Other Woman, This Sex*

*Which Is Not One* and *Marine Lover of Friedrich Nietzsche*. Gill is the English translator for three of Irigaray's books. A biographer and writer, Gill is also the author of *Agatha Christie: The Woman and Her Mysteries*.

In *Sexes and Geneaologies*, Irigaray addresses what she calls "the ethics governing the relationship between sexes." In so doing, she notes that "Claims that men, races, sexes are equal in point of fact signal a disdain or a denial for real phenomena and give rise to an imperialism that is even more pernicious than those that retain traces of difference. . . . social recognition have to be negotiated on the basis of identity — not equality. Without women, there is no society. Women have to proclaim this message loud and clear and demand a justice that fits their identity instead of some temporary rights. . . . To achieve this goal, women must learn how they relate both to gender and kinship. Sexual difference represents one of the great hopes for the future. It is not to be found in reproduction (whether natural or artificial) but in the access the two sexes have to culture. . . . Our culture has in some ways become too simple, in other ways too complex. We need to regain places where measure is possible, and I believe this can be done if we look at the cultural becoming of the sexes, as defined in relation to their genealogies."

By "genealogies," Irigaray means how genders have developed over time — and that "no social and cultural relationship between the sexes is possible without that double consideration." Irigaray posits that:

> . . . our History has collapsed male and female genealogies into one or two family trian-
> gles, all sired by the male. The oedipus complex as elaborated by Freud is one example
> of such triangles. But Freud's model can be traced back at least as far as ancient Greece.
> In order to fuse two genealogical trees, it is always necessary to have recourse to a tran-
> scendent and unique God-Father. Sometimes his name is Zeus, sometimes Jupiter. He is
> also God the Father of Judeo-Christian tradition. Respect for God is possible as long as
> no one realizes that he is a mask concealing the fact that men have taken sole possession
> of the divine, of identity, and of kinship. Once we give this whole issue the attention
> and serious consideration it deserves, however, it becomes obvious that God is being
> used by men to oppress women and that, therefore, God must be questioned and not
> simply neutered in the current pseudoliberal way. Religion as a social phenomenon can-
> not be ignored.

In the essay that triggered Hahn's poem, Irigaray explores the nature of woman as moth-
er, asking, "What is woman, apart from her social and material function in reproducing children, nursing, renewing the work force?" Irigaray notes that "the maternal function underlies the social order" in a, for women, limiting fashion:

> The maternal function...is always restricted to the dimension of need. Once individual
> and collective needs have been met there is often nothing left of maternal female potency
> to satisfy desire, particularly in its religious dimension. Her desire, the desire she has, this
> is what the law of the father, of all fathers, moves to prohibit: the fathers of families,
> fathers in religion, father teachers, father doctors, father lovers, etc. Whether moral or
> immoral, all these fathers intervene to censure, repress, the mother's desire. For them it's
> a matter of good sense, good health or even of virtue and holiness!

The result, says Irigaray, is but another form of silencing women, and another cause for the "madness" of women — similar to some of the themes touched on by Clément . Ultimately, Irigaray says in her essay that was first delivered at a conference on mental health with the theme, "Women and Madness," that our "urgent task" is to recover the self of the woman that is obviated by the social role of acting as mother:

> Our urgent task is to refuse to submit to a desubjectivized social role, the role of mother, which is dictated by an order subject to the division of labor — he produces, she reproduces — that walls us up in the ghetto of a single function.  When did society ever ask fathers to choose between being men or citizens?  We don't have to give up being women to be mothers....

## A.     Handwritten First Draft

The handwritten first draft features six sections.  After each section will be a brief discussion of the elements of Irigaray's essay that informed, as well as some of Hahn's thoughts as she developed, the poem.

### THE PINK DOGWOOD
I.

"Every desire has a relation to madness"
Irigaray (10)

In the house with windows that looked out
~~over~~ into the branches of a forest, into
the sunset of dinners where no one is allowed to speak
over the 5 o'clock news and no one
can see the television screen but the father
or if dark enough the mother can see its reflection
in ~~those~~ that same window of branches—
here, the daughters will make them larger than desired
than desire itself.  The father's money buys the red meat
the mother's hands stew it.
The silent daughters are silenced
then call a girlfriend, or boy, or begin math problems.
One finesses the answers in order to finish
without ~~any~~ excess boredom, the evening's requirement
to douse desire.  She will not omit what ~~she~~ feels
like power and insecurity both.

*

In the house with the rooms
where fingers and feet are always cold
no one is allowed to go barefoot—
*hadashi* — the word for it.

Cover up the naked soles.
Wrap up the tender ~~calloused~~ skin <u>calloused</u> islands
and never put things in your mouth
like a baby puts things in *his mouth*:
toes, fist, nipple, plastic horse, spoon handle, keys.
See if this makes sense. See if
following directions leads to sanity
or to a ~~the~~ covenant that one can feel virginal always
or ~~live~~ inhabit a betrayal
[New L] like a forest
across the street.

*

In the house with ~~the~~ one ~~bedrooms~~ <u>bedroom</u>
the daughters share that bedroom
and the parents sleep in the dining room.
The table cleared, the leaves folded, the hottray pushed aside.
They sleep in the smell of ~~coffee~~ <u>caffeine</u>
knowing the daughter's door is closed
and the windows are to branches.                    LEAD? LEVEL?

*

In the house with ~~paintings~~ <u>the father's</u> still lives
of ~~large~~ <u>massive</u> sea shells and slippery sea life, of dead chickens, of
~~the~~ sieves of onions and scallions,
the daughters imagine they are windows.
Mistake them for windows without blinds.
There are no people.
The younger one especially likes one with ochre.
When they leave for school on the road by the trees
they wonder about the gnarled branches
they grow downward ~~away from light~~ beneath the soil
away from clouds and towards the water table.

*

For the older one's apartment, since she will never afford a house,
there are curtains in the front ~~kitchen~~ parlor and in the back bedroom.
Her own daughter shares a room in the center,
a large room with two doors and one airshaft.
It is painted yellow to recall the ~~sun~~ <u>morning</u>
when one decides to stay in the dreams that allow desire
instead of dressing for the worlds, ~~that~~ the words,
taught to limit the girlchild
so she learns to limit the boychild.
Today they share small ~~candied~~ foiled hearts:
the taste of chocolate stimulating and simulating what cannot

be ~~uttered to~~ said.  The mother, that older daughter, me,
wishes to allow them everything but hurt
which then equals her own limitations.
But I am pleased to talk about it
by the white dogwood in the courtyard
or the pink dogwood in the tiny backyard.


Hahn begins the poem with the image of "the sunset of dinners where no one is allowed to speak."  It is a haunting beginning, particularly when Part I's epigraph is set in the context of Irigaray's essay first commenting on the limited attendance by male physicians at the conference where she was presenting her paper: "The absence of male doctors is, in and of itself, one explanation of madness in women: their words are not heard."  Of the world Hahn creates, she notes, "There is a mother, daughters and a father: the females outnumber the lone male and yet serve him.  Yet, are silenced.  In this first draft I was pleased with the gray world I created — it felt accurate; so in working on these drafts I wanted to retain the air of madness with the repressive images.  I wanted to make them Grimm-like."  (She explains "Grimm-like" further below.)

Irigaray points out, "Women and their words are not given the keys to the city when it comes to developing the diagnoses and therapeutic decisions that concern them.  Serious scientific discourse and practice remain the privilege of men who have control of politics in general as well as of our most private sphere as women. . . . Everywhere and in everything men define the function and the social role of women, right down to the sexual identity that women are to have — or not to have."  Irigaray's thoughts may have informed Hahn's lines, "The father's money buys the red meat/ the mother's hands stew it./ The silent daughters are silenced/. . . the evening's requirement/ to douse desire" — she certainly is returning to the question of what the daughters might want — even if such desire is "doused."

Section I's epigraph is set within the context of Irigaray's discussion of the privileging of men's status — including the privileging of their madness, versus the madness of women:


. . . one particularly "honest" male friend admitted to me not long ago: "You know, you're right.  I always thought that all women were mad."  And he added, "Obviously that was one way of avoiding the issue of my own madness."

This is in fact how the question needs to be posed.  Each sex has a relation to madness. Every desire has a relation to madness.  But it would seem that one desire has been taken as wisdom, moderation, truth, leaving to the other sex the weight of a madness that cannot be acknowledged or accommodated.


Consequently, the second stanza's description of a house with cold rooms containing rules of behavior may be a metaphor for how patriarchal society expects mothers to behave in a certain way: "In the house with the rooms/ where fingers and feet are always cold/ no one is allowed to go barefoot—/ . . .Cover up the naked soles./ Wrap up the tender skin calloused islands/ and never put things in your mouth/ like a baby puts things in *his mouth:*/ toes, fist, nipple, plastic horse, spoon handle, keys./ See if this makes sense. See if/ following directions leads to sanity/ or to a covenant that one can feel virginal always."  Of rules, Hahn says, "They not only provide limits, they isolate and define the daughter's self.  The rules are Byzantine — religious and intricate.  And repressive.  I think a woman's relation to desire/madness is in part how she deals with an institutionalized repression."

The second stanza also seems to be informed by Irigaray's reference to the *Oresteia* where Orestes kills his mother, Clytemnestra, and subsequently is driven mad, as is his sister Electra.  Irigaray notes that Electra will remain mad but that the god Apollo, "lover of men rather than women, . . . helps Orestes shake off his madness."  Because Orestes had killed his mother to eliminate the powers of the earth mother —or *puissances* — Irigaray notes that "the murder of the mother is rewarded by letting the son go scot free, by burying the madness of women — and burying women in madness — and by introducing the image of the virgin goddess, born of the Father, obedient to his laws at the expense of the mother."  Her translator Gill notes that Irigaray, in her work, associates *La puissance* with the power associated with women: "ancient female authority and tradition as well as for the possible new, feminist world order."

"If I remember correctly, what I was trying to do in this section is respond to how adult madness is shaped by limitations in childhood," Hahn says.  "And, that is especially true of daughters in a patriarchy — to express one's self physically is somehow wrong unless it is in the context of, for instance, a dance recital which is exceedingly prescribed to begin with.  I wanted to create a world of small rooms and limited access to the rest of the world.  A confinement — the way one confines a hysteric."

Each of these stanzas open with "In this house" — about which Hahn explains, "As far as writing goes, it was my key into the poem and the material.  I often begin with a nature image or a location and in this case I described 'this house' in numerous ways, a kind of list that I later edit. Repetition can be useful in generating raw material — and can be cut back when it reaches a threshold.  Or one can choose the stuff that is closest to the emotional truth of the poem.  When I studied with Louise Gluck — as an undergrad — I recall she would tell us to *choose* in order to pare the poem back."

Her thoughts can be seen in the lines in the last stanza of this section, "When one decides to stay in the dreams that allow desire/ instead of dressing for the worlds, ~~that~~ the words."  As Hahn sees it, the "place for desire" is not often in the material world, not safely, because there is risk and punishment for physicality and even for being.

"I think that's why I like the wordplay, world/word — because I see the word sometimes as a world where one can risk desire.  Wordplay is an important element in my writing and, obviously, very associative writing (dare I say 'intuitive'? yes!) which means it is close to the unconscious.  It is close to the spirit and needs to be trusted.  Japanese literature uses a great deal of wordplay and although that is not where I acquired this fondness, studying Japanese certainly enabled me to appreciate the depth this kind of play can permit."

Later in the same stanza, Hahn writes, "The mother, that older daughter, me,/ wishes to allow them everything but hurt/ which then equals her own limitations."  The lines reflect Hahn's attempt to "try to address the person I am now: an older daughter who needs to, in a sense, mother herself — who needs to give permission to the child in her own childhood."  Permission plays an important role for her in art; even to write this, Hahn says, she unconsciously wrote in the third person which she discovered gave a kind of license and also added to the narrative/Grimm tone.  She permitted herself these images not out of some therapeutic need but out of a desire to explore, even to risk exploration — health perhaps a by-product.

II.

" . . . our society and our culture operate on the basis of an original matricide."

Irigaray (11)

Somewhere in the rooms or the small house
filled with small lamps
that spot places to sit and read or eat
the mother agreed to be disappeared
like a peasant not a revolutionary
in order for the father to assume control
over the oldest daughter's plump body
that was ~~already~~ too early sprouting hair
and too early though any time was too early,
~~sprouting~~ budding nipples — the *German blood*
      His blood not hers
She already knew since third grade that she would bleed
and had shivered uncontrollably
as if there was no such thing as warmth —
her mother had told her one night.
If I had told her I would have held her in my arms
and not let her go.  I would not leave,
let the father let me leave, let myself escape,
when the girl finally did bleed
in huge baggy cotton underpants
that she stuffed with toilet paper
then ~~and~~ hid.  Then hid.  ~~And of~~ No way.
~~I would do something el~~

            *

~~And~~

In the corners of the house
with more corner than walls
there are so many small spaces
one does not need to have their own room.
No, that's not true.
The oldest daughter, me, kept rearranging the furniture
in the shared room
to make her own room.  To shut out
the disappeared mother, the father, the sister who can barely speak
she is so much younger.  Her speech
comes out in a myriad noises
that grate in their ~~myriad needs~~ prism of needs.
Someday they will write letters ~~to~~
and ~~even later~~ decades later, e-mail notes
about their mother killed instantly on the passenger side
~~of the~~ when teenagers ran a red-light.

And then she was gone in such a way

that there was no imagination for return

except for the granddaughters who never questioned

the existence of heaven they see in cartoons

and hear in the prayers of strangers.

*


Who will be the mother, the idealized breast

when one has spent a lifetime in that constellation of mythologies

presumably renewed by the mother in their infancies before desire

because *there are no words*.  Who will be the mother.

Not sister, not girlfriend, not boyfriend.

Not daughters.

Must the mother mother her self?

Must she be the breast and mouth?

~~And what is more~~

The presexual breast and presexual mouth.

~~The~~ When devour does not equal desire

The window curtains were gauzy

because the street and neighbors were far from viewing inside

the interior of the house that resembled a house without blood.

Veins without color.  Shafts without warmth.

Desire discovered, known, to be perfect

in a world where ~~no~~ there's a belief in the perfectionist

but not in all ~~perfection~~ perfect.  This

is not the same as sucking cock or clit

Not the same as fucking in one position or another.

~~But in~~ It is not the same ~~in~~.


The epigraph in Section II comes within the context of Irigaray's notion that "not only in everyday events but in the whole social scene: our society and our culture operate on the basis of an original matricide."  By this, Irigaray refers to Greek mythology — to Clytemnestra's murder in the *Oresteia*:

For years and years (Agamemnon) has been away from home, off with other men to recapture the fair Helen.  This is perhaps the prototype of war among men.  In order to secure his military and amorous expedition, Agamemnon sacrificed Iphigenia, the adolescent daughter he had with Clytemnestra.  When he returns home, it is with another girl by his side, Cassandra, his slave and, no doubt, the latest in his string of mistresses.

Clytemnestra, for her part, has taken a lover.  But she believed her husband was dead, since she had been without news of him for many years.  When Agamemnon returns in triumph with his mistress she kills him.  She kills him out of jealousy, out of fear perhaps, and because she has been dissatisfied and frustrated for so long.  She also kills him because he has sacrificed their daughter in the cause of male conflicts, though this motive is often forgotten by the authors of tragedy.

But the new order decrees that she be killed in her turn by her son, who is inspired to do so by the oracle of Apollo, beloved son of Zeus: the God-Father. Orestes kills his mother because the empire of the God-Father, who has seized and taken for his own the ancient powers (*puissances*) of the earth-mother demands it.

As reflected in the beginning of this section, Hahn says that at the time of writing the poem, the idea of a "disappeared mother" was important. "At the time I was thinking about how, in my own family, my mother was almost invisible to me. For me, my father was the dominant presence. My mother, though, collaborated in her disappearance — I think it was a social agreement that she participated in. I didn't consciously decide to work in these images, though obviously the triggering lines were selected for their emotional charge — but the idea of a 'disappeared mother' was in my work way before my mother died. In 'The Room' there are the lines: 'When we grow older and she dies/ where is the breast then?' In 'Comp. Lit.' where I take on Genji/Murasaki I wrote towards the end: 'He looked behind every screen/ for one who resembled his mother, *for his mother*,' yet did not understand that the mother/ would always be dead. . . .' And again in 'The Izu Dancer': 'But I know even young girls break into a sweat/ in passion or terror,/ a terror, as if mother left the house one morning/ to buy milk and never returned. . . .Would we run around the house looking for mother?' Which is only to say that the Irigaray idea of 'original matricide' was very powerful and one that I felt I not only agreed with but had begun writing about in various pieces."

When asked how she felt her own mother disappeared, Hahn replies, "When I remember my mother in my own childhood, I think of her as someone always in another room. It's like the Blue Beard story — where one wife is unaware but probably unconsciously knows that the husband has a roomful of dismembered wives."

In the classic French fairy tale penned by Charles Perrault, the character Blue Beard is featured as courting a lady for his next wife — not an easy task as his blue beard was not considered attractive and he had been married several times before with no one knowing whatever happened to his ex-wives. After they had been married for some time, his new wife stumbles into a closet where lay the bodies of the ex-wives whom Blue Beard had murdered. The current wife would have been killed, too, had she not been rescued by her brothers.

After retelling the story, Hahn laughs at the oedipal triangle she had just suggested by identifying with the latest wife: the husband dead and the wife turned into the father, mother and daughter.

Hahn recalls that her parents seemed to agree that her father would be her primary child-rearer while her mother would take primary responsibility for her sister. She recalls her father being the one to drive her to flute lessons (whereas Hahn today is the one who drops off her two daughters, Miyako and Reiko, to their dance lessons) and lecture her on dating topics. Also, Hahn grew up in Westchester and she sometimes relied on her father driving her into Manhattan to see friends in Japanese school — that is, boyfriends. In her memory, therefore, Hahn characterizes her relationship with her father as having an "odd dependency"; needing him to take her to her boyfriend. (Later she took trains.) This concept may be seen from an excerpt from the middle draft of her poem with the working title of "Luce's Pulse." That draft features the lines, "Everytime she *sees* someone/ she betrays the father's prohibition/ never to leave *and* supports the parents/ goal for the child to become adult,/ even if it means the girl becomes a woman."

Consequently, says Hahn, she does not consider "as peculiar this idea that a mother's needs are not taken seriously and that she can even be disappeared in a kind of mythical matricide. How a daughter views that and unconsciously imagines that happening to herself is, I think, really frightening. I also, somehow, participated in her disappearance. So (poetically) I fight against this loss and by extension, against my own erasure."

Her fight against the mother's disappearance may be seen in such lines as "the mother agreed to be disappeared/ in order for the father to assume control/ . . . over the oldest daughter's plump body." Later, the stanza continues with "I would not leave,/ let the father let me leave, let myself escape,/ when the girl finally did bleed/ in huge baggy cotton underpants/ that she stuffed with toilet paper/ then hid. Then hid. No way." She comments, "Unless the mother is able and/or willing to speak to the daughter about her body, a budding woman's body, then the disappearance is in a way perpetuated. Our 'private parts' remain almost nonexistence. As you can see, however, some of these ideas ultimately get in the way of the poem — this first draft is too, what one friend called, 'cerebral.' I needed to cut back to the most fertile imagery."

"But when we don't feel the mother is present, then where is the mother?" Hahn continues. "We need someone to raise us. If we didn't know from experience that we (children) need to be raised by a mother, we learn it from reading fairy tales. In Hansel and Gretel, an important fairy tale for me, Gretel becomes her own mother. Will mother mother herself? I think this is partly why I chose to deepen the Grimm-tone — for the feeling of disassociation that fairy tales have, that all the events take place 'once long ago,' so that frightening experiences can be named and not paralyze us, in fact, just the contrary. Furthermore, there are many heroines in those stories. Again, in hindsight, it was important for me to stay with the third person point of view because it could undercut, in a disassociative manner, the autobiographical experience of my childhood and replace it in part with a more mythic-sounding one — the kind Irigaray describes. I want to participate in that transmission. Even desperately."

Continuing, Hahn notes in the last stanza: "Who will be the mother, the idealized breast/ when one has spent a lifetime in that constellation of mythologies/ presumably renewed by the mother in their infancies before desire/ because *there are no words*. Who will be the mother./ Not sister, not girlfriend, not boyfriend./ Not daughters./ Must the mother mother her self?/ Must she be the breast and mouth?" These lines also evoke Irigaray's notion of the murder of the mother in order to continue patriarchal domination. Irigaray notes:

> The genital drive is theoretically that drive by which the phallic penis captures the mother's power to give birth, nourish, inhabit, center. Doesn't the phallic erection occur at the place where the umbilical cord once was? The phallus becomes the organizer of the world through the man-father at the very place where the umbilical cord, that primal link to the mother, once gave birth to man and woman. All that had taken place within an original womb, the first nourishing earth, first waters, first sheaths, first membranes in which the whole child was held, as well as the whole mother, through the mediation of her blood. According to a relationship that is obviously not symmetrical, mother and child are linked in a way that precedes all dissociations, all tearing of their bodies into pieces.

> This primary experience is very unpopular with psychoanalysts: in fact they refuse to see it. They allude to a fetal situation or fetal regression and find nothing to say about it. A vague sort of taboo is in force. There would be a danger of fusion, death, lethal sleep, if the father did not intervene to sever this uncomfortably close link to the original matrix. Does the father replace the womb with the matrix of his language? But the exclusivity of

his law refuses all representation to that first body, that first home, that first love. These are sacrificed and provide matter for an empire of language that so privileges the male sex as to confuse it with the human race.

The order of this empire decrees that when a proper name (*nom*) is given to a child, it substitutes for the most irreducible mark of birth, the navel (*nombril*). The family name, and even the first or given name, always stand at one remove from that most elemental identity tag: the scar where the umbilical cord was cut. The family name, and even the first name, slip over the body like clothes, like identity tags — outside the body.

Hahn asks, "What is the patriarchy based on then? The silencing of half the world? Of one's grandmother, mother, wife and daughters? Disappearing and matricide?" . . . . "Are we that powerful? Are we that threatening? I guess so."

"A number of French feminists believe there is a 'woman's writing' — and while I am not sure what that means, what it might look like, I find the idea very compelling. Again, I look East to the Japanese Heian period where women were writing in the vernacular (men wrote in Chinese) and created a whole literature with a kind of female aesthetic. This is very inspiring. I am not consciously trying to create a women's language, but I think I participate in that possibility. It's a powerful possibility and one, I feel, that is based on desire."

In this context what does lack of desire mean? Hahn ends Part II of the poem with the lines, ". . . a house without blood./ Veins without color. Shafts without warmth./ Desire discovered, known, to be perfect/ in a world where there's a belief in the perfectionist/ but not in all perfect. This/ is not the same as sucking cock or clit/ Not the same as fucking in one position or another./ It is not the same." Or, as Irigaray calls women without desire: "perfect models of femininity, always veiled and clothed from head to toe, very respectable, can be recognized by this sign: they are extraordinarily attractive — which doesn't mean they attract — but they really aren't interested in making love."

Of the content in this section, Hahn comments, "Much of this material is all over the place — doesn't make sense really — and some is familiar territory from other works, which doesn't make it less worthwhile. What I needed to do in the next draft was figure out where this piece was headed, (especially in relation to the quotes, since I'd decided I wanted to keep them) and *choose* the areas that felt on course (to) begin to make sense out of the raw material."

For the Final Draft, Hahn also took out the line from the first stanza, "like a peasant not a revolutionary." She says she felt that the line "steered the poem into an enormous theme that I didn't want this poem to follow." The enormity of this theme may be gleaned from the following excerpt from *WE STAND OUR GROUND* (Ikon, 1988), Hahn's book of discussions and poems with poets Gale Jackson and Susan Sherman:

In the poem, "Revolutions," I open with the little-known fact that the 'golden age of literature' was dominated by women in Japan. This influence of theirs happened for social reasons because the men were writing in Chinese (the same as people wrote in Latin instead of in the vernacular) whereas the women were writing in the vernacular in Japanese. So the women's writing was an explosion; it was a release of material and feelings — so much so men would write in the female persona. The 'female sensibility' was that dominant. To me this is a very important piece of history and part of myself. It inspires and informs much of my own art.

Parallel to this was my political "awakening," beginning with a feminist orientation. . . . My own sexuality became a territory for me: my body is mine, my responsibility. This 'territory' also gave me an increasing awareness that women's bodies historically have not always belonged to them; for instance, fathers using their daughters as marital pawns or husbands using wives to produce sons.

. . . all my work is deeply commited to women's relationships (with one another, with men, with society) This is especially true of the poems . . . . "Seizure," (where) I view revolution not as a 'midwife' but as birth itself. 'Revolutions' is more or less about a female culture or aesthetic. . . .(Women's) work and concerns are very different from men's and it has something to do with biology (the powerful, mysterious and vulnerable uterus) and a lot to do with history. I'm not knocking male writers, rather expressing my particular need for other women's voices.

Even as Hahn did not want to weigh down the poem with the themes related to the lines, "the mother agreed to be disappeared/ like a peasant not a revolutionary," the sensibility as featured above is still relevant, e.g. the "disappearance" of women's desires, and certainly the need for social change.

III

". . . the threatening womb. Threatening because it is silent, perhaps?"

Irigaray (16)

He wants to bake. He wants to broil.
To roast. But the oven
is hot. Unless
he can force her to open it
or at least to go away
and leave him to make something for himself
though his own mother has instructed him
that boys ~~do not~~ stay out of the kitchen
of if she allowed him to cook
only with her.
He will ~~push~~ send her out.
He will figure out how to burn it soon.
*(Note: After the above section was written, Hahn immediately crossed out the first stanza.)*

She does not carry a purse.
Her nails are unlovely. Her lips, plain.
She must be an academic or dyke or both.

Hahn says in response to a question of why she deleted the first stanza, "I don't remember. I don't remember writing it and don't remember taking it out. Which is how I like to write. I try to trust the intuitive process asking myself, does it sound right? And trust the craft lessons

I've garnered."

The first stanza, though it ended up being deleted, captures the context of Section III's epigraph which was set in the context of Irigaray's discussion of society's denial of *puissance*, the power of the earth-mother.

The problem is that when the father refuses to allow the mother her power of giving birth and seeks to be the sole creator, then according to our culture he superimposes upon our ancient world of flesh and blood a universe of language and symbols that has no roots in the flesh and drills a hole through the female womb and through the place of female identity. A stake, an axis is thus driven into the earth in order to mark out the boundaries of the sacred space in many patriarchal traditions. It defines a meeting place for men that is based upon an immolation. Women will in the end be allowed to enter that space, provided that they do so as nonparticipants.

The fertility of the earth is sacrificed in order to establish the cultural domain of the father's language (which is called, incorrectly, the mother tongue). But this is never spoken of. Just as the scar of the navel is forgotten, so, correspondingly, a hole appears in the texture of the language.

Some men and women would prefer to identify maternal power, the phallic mother, as an ensnaring net. But such attribution occurs only as a defensive mesh that the man-father or his sons casts over the chasms of a silent and threatening womb. <u>Threatening because it is silent, perhaps</u>?

The second stanza relates clearly to Irigaray's point of women as "perfect models of femininity." That when, in Irigaray's words, these women refuse to be "always veiled and clothed from head to toe, very respectable, can be recognized by this sign: they are extraordinarily attractive," then they are mocked by patriarchal society. Or, in the poem's words, "She does not carry a purse./ Her nails are unlovely. Her lips, plain./ She must be an academic or dyke or both."

Hahn says she used the references to "academic or dyke or both" because she wanted to "present figures that are not considered lovely. I was playing with stereotypes, and chose women who, in stereotype, are strong and don't take any shit: women who talk back. In fact, they're strong *because* they talk back."

IV.
"corps-a-corps"
          Irigaray (9)

~~When~~ They were more daughters than sisters.

They traded their clothes.
They dried the dishes.
They practiced the flute.

The French title of Irigaray's essay is "*Le corps-a-corps avec la mere.*" Gill, as translator, says that the phrase "has no simple translation in English. The expression *corps-a-corps*, which recurs throughout the text (of the essay), usually denotes armed combat between two warriors — hand-to-hand fighting. However, it is the word *corps* (body) that is crucial to Irigaray, who is looking to some new relationship between mother and child that accepts the body of both parties and moves toward a new imaginary and a new symbolic." Patriarchal society, notes Irigaray, forbids any *corps-a-corps* with the mother. And Irigaray stresses:

> If we are not to be accomplices in the murder (the silencing) of the mother we also need to assert that there is a genealogy of women. Each of us has a female family tree: we have a mother, a maternal grandmother and great-grandmothers, we have daughters. Because we have been exiled into the house of our husbands, it is easy to forget the special quality of the female genealogy; we might even come to deny it. Let us try to situate ourselves within that female genealogy so that we can win and hold on to our identity.

The reference to "genealogy of women" may be seen in Hahn's line, "They were more daughters than sisters."

Of the structure of this little section, Hahn comments, "It is a list — and I was taught that all 'items' on a list must be equally extraordinary. That is the challenge. The other question may be: is it too long or long enough? Also I don't have any lists of this sort yet, so the staccatto nature of a list gives the whole a kind of break from the suggestion of 'narrative'. In a piece of this length it is important to have some variation apart from the quotes themselves."

V.

"we barely . . . have access to fiction!"

Irigaray (10)

The stories, even when they were told by father
even when never told but *seen,*
were mother's stories. We wanted all the stories,
the one about the shark beyond the coral reef,
the dance classes, the *poi* in kindergarten,
were her stories that we listened to
in our own heads in the house
with rooms ~~that~~ filled with the shadows
of ~~the~~ branches and gauze curtains.
And she never thought they were *important.*
She knew, though we knew she didn't know
how they would become not only our stories
but the granddaughter's ~~stories~~ tales to tell classmates
in the schoolyards filled with noise.

Section V's epigraph is taken from a section shortly after Irigaray called the limited attendance of male physicians — when men comprise the majority of practicioners — at the conference on the mental health of women as an example of men not listening to women:

Everywhere, in everything, men's speech, men's values, dreams and desires are law. Everywhere and in everything men define the function and the social role of women, right down to the sexual identity that women are to have — or not to have. Men know, men have access to the truth, not us. <u>We barely, at times, have access to fiction</u>!

"I think this section is about transmission. My mother's stories were transmitted to me and she, in fact, told me stories. But if, in my own mythology, she disappeared, then someone else needed to be the transmitter. This is essential because, according to the theorist Trinh T. Minh-ha (*Woman Native Other*), storytelling is the woman's role," Hahn says, adding as an example, "Not coincidentally, as in the medical world, the world of publishing is male-dominated. So, sure, some stories are about women — either because they've broken into the canon or because the father is telling grandmother and mother stories. In any case, the ones heard are selected by a patriarchal publishing culture."

Hahn notes that this section provided the final stanza of the Final Draft. "I wanted to end the poem with the idea of transmission and the figure of a daughter doing something active, like leaving. I didn't want (the section — featured as section VI below at this drafting stage — with the epigraph, "sentences that translate the bond between our body, her body, the body of our daughter"), which is a sensual moment, to be the end. I wanted to end with an active — and quest-type — section."


VI.


" . . . sentences that translate the bond between our body, her body, the body of our daughter." (18-19)


If she touches her body in the gray bathroom
the gray light lighting the small window—
squeezes [Del L] her nipple or flicks her vulva—
if she tastes her taste
she is tasting her mother and daughters'
proverbially mythical waves on the Pacific shoreline.
There where the marine life crawls back
from the tidal pool
or gives up the desire to breathe underwater ever again.
If she touches herself she can
find that pulse that penetrates like an echo.
All this without sound in the gray light off the green tiles.


As Hahn begins to end the poem, she also relates to the concluding sections of Irigaray's essay. Part VI's epigraph is taken from the following section:

We need to be careful in one . . . respect: not again to kill the mother who was immolated at the birth of our culture. Our task is to give life back to that mother, to the mother who lives within us and among us. We must refuse to allow her desire to be swallowed up in the law of the father. We must give her the right to pleasure, to sexual experience, to passion, give her back the right to speak, or even to shriek and rage aloud.

We also need to find, rediscover, invent the words, the sentences that speak of the most ancient and most current relationship we know — the relationship to the mother's body, to our body — sentences that translate the bond between our body, her body, the body of our daughter. We need to discover a language that is not a substitute for the experience of *corps-a-corps* as the paternal language seeks to be, but which accompanies that bodily experience, clothing it in words that do not erase the body but speak the body.

In Part VI, Hahn's poetic way of finding "words that do not erase the body but speak the body" offers the image of a woman touching herself and, in doing so, relating back to her female genealogy. Or, in Irigaray's words:

What this amounts to is that we need . . . to discover our sexual identity, the specialness of our desires, of our autoeroticism, our narcissism, our heterosexuality, our homosexuality. In this context it is important to remind ourselves that, since the first body we as women had to relate to was a woman's body and our first loves is love of the mother, women always have an ancient and primary relationship to what is called homosexuality. . . .

When analytic theory claims that the little girl must give up her love for and of the mother, abandon the desire for and of her mother if she is to enter into desire for the father, woman is thereby subjected to a normative heterosexuality, common in our societies but nonetheless completely pathogenic and pathological. Neither the little girl nor the woman needs to give up the love for her mother. To do so is to sever women from the roots of their identity and their subjectivity.

Again, Hahn begins with a location. But why the bathroom as opposed to a bed? "I have a lot of baths in my poems — especially in the long piece, 'The Hemisphere,' where a young girl discovers her mother in the bath and in a sense discovers her own body. And her mother is lovely as a mother, as a woman and as that forecast. The bathroom, unlike the shared bedroom, contains privacy — except for my mother when I walked in on her!" she says. "I guess I kept it as a location in later drafts because it leads to the tidal pools as a symbol of fertility."

When asked how she came to the title "The Pink Dogwood," Hahn notes, "The pink dogwood (perhaps the *exciting* dogwood as opposed to the cloistered one) is in the backyard and so it is something that no one would otherwise see." Her recovery of something otherwise ignored is seen in the ending lines of this draft: "But I am pleased to talk about it/ by the white dogwood in the courtyard/ or the pink dogwood in the tiny backyard." And, she, indeed, is *pleased to talk about it.*

B.    **First Draft Titled "LUCE'S PULSE" With Editing Marks Indicating Changes From Handwritten Draft Titled "THE PINK DOGWOOD"**

Hahn began this stage of drafting by retitling the poem, "Luce's Pulse," because she wanted the poem to be a dialogue with Luce Irigaray whom she admired.  But, Hahn notes, the reference also contains a wordplay: "it's both taking her pulse (the pulse symbolizing hot, healthy blood — energy) as well as being impulsive."


## ~~THE PINK DOGWOOD~~ Luce's Pulse

I.

> "Every desire has a relation to madness"
>
> Irigaray (10)


In the house with windows that ~~looked~~ <u>look</u> out
into the branches of a forest, into
the <u>dinner of</u> sunset<u>s</u> ~~of dinners~~ where no one is allowed to speak
over the 5 o'clock news and no one
can see the television ~~screen~~ but the father
or if dark enough the mother can see its reflection
in that same window of branches—
here, the daughters ~~will make them larger than desired~~ <u>chew the meal</u>
<u>that will make them larger than desired,</u>
than desire itself.
[New L] The father's ~~money buys~~ <u>paycheck purchases</u> the ~~red~~ meat
the mother's ~~hands stew it~~ <u>hand</u> stews.
The silent daughters are silenced <u>,</u>
~~then~~ <u>later</u> call<u>s</u> <u>to</u> a girlfriend ~~,~~ or boy ~~,~~ or ~~begin~~ <u>sharpening pencils for</u> math
                                        problems.
One finesses the answers in order to finish
without excess boredom,
[New L] the evening's requirement [Del L] to douse desire.
[New L] She will not ~~omit~~ <u>displace</u> what feels          DISPLACE/EVICT
like power and insecurity both.


        *


In the house with the rooms
where fingers and feet are always cold          REDUNDANT?
no one is allowed to go barefoot — <u>:</u>
~~badashi — the word for it.~~
~~C~~<u>c</u>over up the naked soles ~~:~~ <u>!</u>          BETRAYAL?
~~W~~<u>w</u>rap up the tender skin <u>with</u> calloused ~~islands~~ <u>punctuation</u>
and never put things in your mouth
like a baby puts things in *his mouth*:
~~toes, fist,~~ nipple, <u>toe, fist,</u> plastic ~~horse~~ <u>horsey,</u> ~~spoon-handle,~~ keys.
See if this makes sense. See if
following directions leads to sanity
or to a covenant ~~that~~ one can feel virginal always          WHERE
or inhabit ~~a~~ betrayal

50

like a forest [Del L] across the street.

\*

In the house with one bedroom
the daughters share , ~~that bedroom~~
~~and~~ the parents sleep in the dining room.
The table cleared, the leaves folded, the hottray pushed aside.
They sleep in the ~~smell~~ fragrance of caffeine
knowing the daughter's door is closed
and the windows ~~are to branches~~ level to the leaves.

\*

In the house with the father's still lives
of massive sea shells and slippery ~~sea~~ marine life,
[New L] of dead chickens, of sieves of [Del L] ── ~~on onions and~~ scallions,
the daughters imagine ~~they~~ the canvases are windows ~~:~~
~~Mistake them for windows~~ without blinds.
There are no people to compromise definitions.                TO COMPROMISE?
The younger one especially likes ~~one with~~ those with ochre.
When they leave for school on the road by the trees
~~they~~ ~~wonder~~ the younger asks about the gnarled branches
they grow ~~downwards beneath the soil~~
away from ~~clouds~~ air and towards the water table.

\*

~~For~~ Now ~~days~~ in the older one's apartment, ~~since she will never~~
~~[New L] afford a house,~~ [Del L] there are ~~curtains~~ windows
[New L] in the front parlor and in the back bedroom.
Her own daughters ~~shares~~ a room in the center,
a large room with two doors and one ~~airshaft~~ air shaft.
It is painted yellow to recall the morning
~~W~~when one ~~decides~~ desires to stay in the dreams that allow desire
instead of dressing for the worlds, the words,
taught to limit the girlchild
so she learns to limit the boychild.
Today they share small foiled hearts:
the taste of chocolate stimulating and simulating
[New L] what cannot [Del L] be said.  The mother, that older daughter, me,
wishes to allow them everything but hurt
which then equals her own limitations.
But I am pleased to talk about ~~it~~ this
by the white dogwood in the front courtyard
or the pink dogwood in the tiny ~~backyard~~ back yard.

*Note: Hahn's notes indicate that she is considering deleting all of the above stanza except the following lines: "Today they share small foiled hearts:/ the taste of chocolate stimulating and simulating/ [New L] what cannot [Del L] be said."*

During this drafting process, Hahn says she "wanted to zero in on the moments of revealing imagery, which is part of what revision is." For instance, she deleted the lines, "the evening's requirement " and "to douse desire" in the second stanza because they are "interpretative lines — I'm doing the work of the reader. The writer needs to trust the reader."

"As I mentioned, a friend called an early version 'cerebral'," Hahn adds, "and so, in this draft, I wanted to make the images and scenes work harder." Ultimately, this resulted in Hahn, too, deleting the second and third stanzas altogether from the Final Draft. In addition, her early notes in the margin questions the lines, "Today they share small foiled hearts:/ the taste of chocolate stimulating and simulating/ [New L] what cannot [Del L] be said"; ultimately these are two of the few lines she actually kept from these stanzas. "Cerebral is fine as long as it does not tell the reader WHAT to think — there needs to be some play. These lines present the sisters sharing, literally and figuratively."

II.

" . . . our society and our culture operate on the basis of an original matricide."

Irigaray (11)

Somewhere ~~in the rooms or~~ the small house <u>with no hallways</u>
~~(filled with small lamps [Del L] that spot places to sit and read or eat~~
the mother agreed to be disappeared <u>,</u>
~~in order for the father to assume control~~ <u>this before</u>
[Del P] ~~over~~ the oldest daughter's plump body <u>;</u>
~~that was~~ too<u>-</u>early sprout~~ing~~<u>ed</u> hair
and too early <u>,</u> though any time was too early <u>;</u>
~~budding~~ <u>budded</u> nipples <u>(</u>—— the *German blood,* ~~not the mother's).~~ [Del L] ~~His blood~~

 ~~not hers~~ [Del L] ~~She~~ <u>This daughter</u>
[New L] already knew since third grade ~~[New L]~~ [Del L] that she would bleed
and <u>in the telling</u> had shivered uncontrollably
as if there was no such thing as ——— ~~COAL/RADIATOR/FURNACE.~~ <u>radiators.</u>
~~When her mother had told her one night.~~
If I had told her <u>that early night</u>
[New L] I would have held her ~~in my arms~~
and not let her go. I would not leave,
let the father let me leave,                    ?????
[New L] let myself escape <u>from hormonal harpoons</u>
~~w~~<u>W</u>hen the girl finally did bleed
in ~~huge~~ <u>her</u> baggy cotton underpants
~~that she stuffed them each with toilet paper for two days~~
~~and then and hid them. Then hid~~ <u>Hid</u> ~~them for two days. No way.~~
<u>then hid it between wall and mattress.</u>

In the corners of the house
with more corner~~s~~ than walls
there are so many small spaces
one does not need to have ~~their~~ <u>her</u> own room.
No, that's not true.
The oldest daughter, me, kept rearranging the furniture
in the shared room
to ~~make~~ <u>create</u> her own ~~room~~. ~~To~~ <u>Then she</u> shut out
the disappeared mother, the father, the sister
[New L] who can barely speak
she is so much younger. (Her speech
~~comes~~ <u>flies</u> out in ~~a myriad~~ noises
that ~~grate in their~~ <u>reflect a</u> prism of needs.)
Someday ~~they~~ <u>the two</u> will write letters
and decades later, e-mail notes [Del L] about their mother <u>,</u>
[New L] killed ~~instantly~~ on the passenger side <u>of father's car</u>
when teenagers ran a red-light.
~~And t~~<u>Then</u> she ~~was gone~~ <u>had left</u> in such a way
that there was no imagination for return
except for the granddaughters who never questioned
the existence of <u>the</u> heaven they see in cartoons
and hear in the prayers of strangers.

*Note: Hahn's notes here indicate she was wondering whether she should delete the second stanza:*

*

Who will be ~~the mother,~~ the idealized breast          TENT OF MYTHS
when one has spent a lifetime in that
[New L] constellation of mythologies
~~presumably~~ renewed by the mother in their infancies
[New L] <u>presumably</u> before desire
because *there are no words*. Who will be the mother ~~:~~
<u>when the father was never the mother.</u>
~~Not~~ <u>When the</u> sister, ~~not~~ girlfriend ~~, not~~ <u>or</u> boyfriend.
~~Not~~ <u>or the</u> daughters <u>were not</u>.
Must the mother mother ~~her self~~ <u>herself</u>?
Must she be the breast and mouth?
The presexual breast and ~~presexual~~ <u>asexual</u> mouth.
When devour does not equal desire<u>.</u>
The ~~window~~ curtains were gauzy
because the street and neighbors were far
[New L] from viewing inside

the interior of the house that resembled
[New L] a ~~house~~ <u>heart</u> without blood.
Veins without color.  ~~(Shafts without warmth.)~~
~~Desire~~ <u>When desire is</u> discovered, ~~known, to be perfect~~ <u>who will be the model</u>
in a world where there's a belief in the perfectionist
but not in ~~be all~~ perfect.  This
is not the same as sucking cock or clit.
Not the same as fucking in one position or another.
It is not the same.


Hahn came to drop the second stanza as she felt that it "seemed to drag out what I'd already established.  The poem needed to move quicker."

She also deleted more "interpretative" lines: e.g. (i) in the first stanza of section II when she deleted the words, "and then and <u>hid them</u>.  Then hid <u>Hid them for two days</u>.  No way."; (ii) the ending where she deleted the lines, ""This/ is not the same . . . It is not the same."; and (iii) line three, "in order for the father to assume control," about which she comments, "This is obvious."  Hahn continues, "There is already a kind of density to the poem itself, so I needed to take care to cut any 'fat or gristle,' which is why I cut a lot in the first few lines.  It was too cluttered, the excess distracted from the poem itself."


III.
". . . the threatening womb.  Threatening because it is silent, perhaps?"
                    Irigaray (16)


~~She does not carry a purse.~~
~~Her nails are unlovely.  Her lips, plain.~~
~~She must be an academic or dyke or both.~~


<u>The womb wishes to speak, to say something like</u>
<u>*Come here so easy*</u>
<u>or *go away, come here/wanting*</u>
<u>And this one doesn't even have incisors.</u>


At this point, Hahn says she decided to focus on the womb.  "I've been fortunate to be able to talk with a handful of women friends about either the essays themselves or the ideas in them.  One playfully asked me, 'What do you think your uterus would say if it could speak?'  I feel that if that part of a woman's body could speak, it would be a threatening ability."

Hahn adds, "Oddly enough *what* the uterus says is what a child will say around one of her/his separation phases.  Independence is alluring and frightening, though not necessarily equivalent to isolation.  I don't know why I wrote those lines for the uterus — but I've kept them for the notion I just gave."  Part of "talking back" for Hahn is being able to approximate a dialogue with these feminists, but the material also becomes part of what she really talks about — "usually on the phone because having children can be isolating," she notes.  Hahn says that the myth of the vagina having teeth — *VAGINA DENTATA* in Latin — partly sparked the last line with its reference to incisors. "I guess this womb is not threatening for its potential teeth — but for its wish to speak. I guess that's why I saved these images."

As far as tone is concerned, she "wanted to have this bit of somewhat hysterical (yes, I know — uterus/hysteria) speech here to give relief to the narrative tone. This was not intentional as I was writing, rather, intentional in the revision." The minute monolog also breaks the largely third-person narrative. And, Hahn adds, "personifying a womb is wacky — and that is also a break from the Grimm-tone. Furthermore, I love the idea of women's body parts speaking."

IV.
"corps-a-corps"
       Irigaray (10)

They were more daughters than sisters.
[Del P] They traded their clothes.
They ~~dried the dishes~~ added and subtracted.
They practiced the flute.

~~V.~~ VI.
       "we barely . . . have access to fiction!"
          Irigaray (10)

The stories, even when ~~they were~~ told by father
even when never told but *seen,*
were mother's ~~stories~~. We wanted all the stories,
the one about the shark beyond the coral reef,
~~the dance classes,~~ the *poi* in kindergarten, the ~~laundry her mother hung —~~ red
               seaweed
[New L] warmed ~~on~~ onto the beach and collected for dinner
were her stories that we listened to
in our own heads in the house
with rooms filled with the shadows of limbs.
~~of branches and gauze curtains.~~
And she never thought they were *important.*
She knew ~~,~~ though we knew she didn't know
how they would become not only our stories       THE NOISE OF DESIRE
but the granddaughters' tales to tell classmates
in the schoolyard~~s~~ filled with ~~noise~~ wanting.

~~VI.~~ V. *Note: At this stage, Hahn reversed the order of sections V and VI, except for the last stanza which she made the last stanza of the new Section VI that ends the poem.*

" . . . sentences that translate the bond between our body, her body, the body of
our daughter." (  )

> If she touches her body in the gray bathroom
> the gray light lighting the small window—
> squeezes [Del L] her nipple or flicks her vulva—
> if she tastes her taste
> she is tasting her mother and daughters'
> ~~proverbially~~ mythical waves on the Pacific shoreline.
> There where the marine life crawls back
> from the tidal pool
> or gives up the desire to breathe underwater ever again.
> If she touches herself she can
> find that pulse that penetrates like an echo.
> All this without sound in the gray light off the green tiles.
> <u>All this is a body that is a vessel for itself</u>
> <u>and for mind and spirit.  One that resists and insists</u>
> <u>as the real waves on any shoreline.  Even lakes.</u>

> Everytime she *sees* someone
> she betrays the father's prohibition
> never to leave *and* supports the parents
> goal for the child to become adult,
> even if it means the girl becomes a woman.
> [Del P] Every time she *sees* someone
> she moves away from the rooms
> that imitate the ventricles that are finally only tissues.
> Everytime she speaks it is a leave-taking
> of abandonment
> ~~and~~ towards the figure even if figurative
> she thought was dead or dying
> in a sealed off room she knew existed.

Hahn reversed the order of the last two sections because, as discussed previously, she
wanted to end the poem with references to the concepts of "transmission" and of the daughter on
a "quest."

Her notes also indicate that she was questioning whether the last stanza should be part of
what she considers the "story section" (the section with the epigraph, "we barely . . . have access
to fiction!"") or the "body section" (the section with the epigraph, "sentences that translate the
bond between our body, her body, the body of our daughter").  In the Final Draft, this stanza's
references became part of the "story section" that ends the poem, partly because its references also
alluded to "the sealed room in the Blue Beard story.  But it could be any sealed off room in any
story, any folk tale," Hahn says.

The sealed room, too, may be part of what Hahn wishes the daughter-speaker of her
poem to leave as she begins her quest.

**C. Draft Showing Changes from Draft Titled "LUCE'S PULSE" To Draft Titled "RESPONDING TO LIGHT"**

At this point, Hahn decided to change the title again by alluding to Luce with the word, "light," and with the idea of *responding* to her rather than symbolically taking her pulse. In looking over the sections, she says she "found a lot of shadows, dark rooms, sealed rooms, gray rooms, etc. and decided that in such an environment, one would respond/grow towards what little light there might be. In this case the light itself becomes the words of the feminist."

~~Luce's Pulse~~ **Responding To Light**

I.

"Every desire has a relation to madness"
Irigaray (10)

In the house with windows that look out
into the branches of a forest, into
the dinner of sunsets ~~,~~
[New L] ~~where~~ no one is ~~allowed~~ permitted to speak
over the ~~5~~ five o'clock news and no one
can see the television but the father ~~.~~
~~or if dark enough the mother can see its reflection~~
~~in that same window of branches —~~
~~H~~here, the daughters chew the meal
that will make them larger than desired,
than desire itself. Here
~~t~~The father's paycheck purchases the meat
the mother~~'s~~ stews.
The silent daughters are silenced ~~;~~ .
~~later calls to a girlfriend , or boy , or sharpening pencils for math problems.~~
~~One finesses the answers in order to finish~~
~~without excess boredom,~~
~~the evening's requirement to douse desire. —~~
~~She will not displace what feels~~
~~like power and insecurity both.~~

*

~~In the house with the rooms~~
~~where fingers and feet are always cold~~
~~no one is allowed to go barefoot.~~
~~cover up the naked soles!~~
~~Wrap up the tender skin with calloused punctuation~~
~~and never put things in your mouth~~
~~like a baby puts things in *his mouth*:~~
~~nipple, toe, fist, plastic horsey, keys.~~

[Del P] See if this makes sense. See if
following directions leads to sanity
or to a covenant where one ~~can~~ feels virginal always
or ~~inhabit~~ to inhabiting betrayal
like ~~a forest~~ the undergrowth across the street.

*

~~In the house with one bedroom~~
~~the daughters share,~~
~~the parents sleep in the dining room.~~
~~The table cleared, the leaves folded, the hottray pushed aside.~~
~~They sleep in the fragrance of caffeine~~
~~knowing the daughter's door is closed~~
~~and the windows level to the leaves.~~

*

In the house with the father's still lives
of massive sea shells and slippery marine life,
~~of dead chickens, of sieves of scallions,~~
the daughters imagine the canvases are windows
without blinds. [Del L] There are no people ~~.~~
to compromise definitions.
~~The younger one especially likes those with ochre.~~
When ~~they~~ the two leave for school on the road by the ~~trees~~ elms
the younger one asks about the gnarled branches
~~they~~ that grow [Del L] away from air and toward the water table.

*

~~Now in the older one's apartment,~~
~~there are windows~~
~~in the front parlor and in the back bedroom.~~
~~Her own daughters share a room in the center,~~
~~a large room with two doors and one air shaft.~~
~~It is painted yellow to recall the morning~~
~~when one desires to stay in the dreams that allow desire~~
~~instead of dressing for the worlds, the words,~~
~~taught to limit the girlchild~~
~~so she learns to limit the boychild.~~
~~Today they~~ And once a year the girls share small foiled hearts:
the taste of chocolate stimulating and simulating
what cannot be said ~~. The mother, that older daughter, me,~~
~~wishes to allow them everything but hurt~~
~~which then equals her own limitations.~~

~~But I am pleased to talk about this~~
~~by the white dogwood in the front courtyard~~
~~or the pink dogwood in the tiny back yard~~.
<u>though there are noises.</u>

This section was deleted almost in its entirety as Hahn revised towards the Final Draft. In part, Hahn says she made her changes to narrow the focus on the young sisters in the past. The other deleted parts relate partly to the "danger that one will repeat the limitations from one's childhood in one's (subsequent way of) child-rearing. But it was too much to ask the poem to also deal with this question. I took out certain lines because I wanted to hold on to the focus of the speaker's childhood." She says she kept the house as a portrait of the family but tightened by cutting redundant or superfluous elements. At this point, too, she knew what the other sections contained and could delete here what might come up later, like the window image. She also needed to stop the "exposition": "taught to limit the girlchild . . . ."

II.
" . . . our society and our culture operate on the basis of an original matricide."
Irigaray (11)

Somewhere <u>in</u> the small house with no hallways
the mother agreed to be disappeared ~~;~~
~~this~~ <u>just</u> before [Del L] the oldest daughter's plump body ~~;~~
too-early sprouted hair
and too early, though any time was too early,
budded nipples. This daughter
already knew since third grade that she would bleed
and in the telling had shivered uncontrollably
as if there was no such thing as radiators.
If I had told her that early ~~night~~ <u>evening</u>
I would have held her
and not let her go. I would <u>have</u> not ~~leave~~ <u>left</u>,
let the father let me leave,
let myself escape from hormonal harpoons <u>.</u>
When the girl finally did bleed
in her baggy cotton underpants
<u>she stuffed them with toilet paper</u>
then <u>later</u> hid ~~it~~ <u>them</u> between wall and mattress.

<u>SOAR</u>
<u>SORE</u>
<u>SOEUR</u>
<u>SOUR</u>
<u>SUR</u>
<u>SURE</u>

*

~~In the corners of the house~~
~~with more corners than walls~~
~~there are so many small spaces~~
~~one does not need to have her own room.~~
~~No, that's not true.~~
~~The oldest daughter, me, kept rearranging the furniture~~
~~in the shared room~~
~~to create her own. Then she shut out~~
~~the disappeared mother, the father, the sister~~
~~who can barely speak~~
~~she is so much younger. (Her speech~~
~~flies out in noises~~
~~that reflect a prism of needs.)~~
~~Someday the two will write letters~~
~~and decades later, e-mail notes about their mother,~~
~~killed on the passenger side of father's car~~
~~when teenagers ran a red light.~~
~~Then she had left in such a way~~
~~that there was no imagination for return~~
~~except for the granddaughters who never questioned~~
~~the existence of the heaven they see in cartoons~~
~~and hear in the prayers of strangers.~~

*

Who will be the idealized breast
when one has spent a lifetime in that
constellation of mythologies
renewed by the mother in their infancies ,
presumably before desire
because ~~there are no words~~ there are no words.  Who will be the mother
when the father was never the mother.
When the sister, girlfriend or boyfriend.
~~O~~or the daughter~~s~~ ~~were~~ was not.
Must the mother mother herself?
Must she be the breast and mouth?
The *presexual* breast and *asexual* mouth.
When devour does not equal desire~~.~~ ?
The curtains were gauzy
because the street and neighbors were far
from viewing inside
the interior of the house that resembled
a heart without blood.  [Del L] Veins without color.
~~When desire is discovered, who~~ Who will ~~be the model~~ instruct

in a world where ~~there's a belief in the perfectionist~~ <u>one is asked to obey</u>
<u>in her own erasure?</u>
~~but not in perfect. This~~
~~is not the same as sucking cock or clit.~~
~~Not the same as fucking in one position or another.~~
~~It is not the same.~~

As regards the "SOAR...SURE" additions, "SUR" is French for ocean and "SOEUR" for sister. Hahn says, "I felt the density of the poem required some relief, although can't remember where these words came from. It's just luck that there's some French in there because I certainly wasn't reading the essays in French. I was probably just scribbling and felt it fit. I like that section because it accomplishes a lot without any kind of explanation."

By what it accomplished, Hahn mentions (i) aural juxtaposition; (ii) how the list brings up the "spine of the poem" by creating words that "crystallize the poem's" thematic concerns; and (iii) how the list breaks up the narrative. As regards the latter, she adds, "Quotes may also break up the narrative but it's pleasing to have an interlude, a different type of moment that's verbal but not narrative. Perhaps it's also a way of owning words — giving them added meaning through justaposition. I have produced this kind of 'interruption' in other pieces — in particular 'Wisteria' (in *The Unbearable Heart*). After all it's important to be playful with language."

At this point, Hahn also deleted the entire second stanza because she considered it "redundant and boring." With a smile, she adds, "And it was *not fun*."

III
". . . the threatening womb. Threatening because it is silent, perhaps?"
Irigaray (16)

The womb wishes to speak ~~;~~ . ~~to~~ <u>To</u> say something like
*Come here ~~so easy~~ go away*
or *go away, come here ~~wanting~~*
And this one doesn't even have incisors.

IV.
"corps-a-corps"
Irigaray (10)

~~They were more daughters than sisters.~~
~~They traded their clothes.~~
<u>They peeled carrots.</u>
They added and subtracted.
<u>They traded blouses.</u>
<u>They were more daughters than sisters.</u>
They ~~practiced the flute~~ <u>trimmed each other's hair and pierced their faces.</u>

As regards her changes in this section, Hahn notes, "As I've said before, after you write a list, you have to go over it and take out boring items and either add or leave 'more charged' ones. I hope I've done that here. This, like the section before it, is a modest section but it impresses. I like the idea of a womb speaking because it seems both outrageous and parallel to the feminist notion of a woman's language that ushers from the body. The little list in the next section presents the sisters as isolated from one another in a sense but, still, side-by-side. To be physically close leaves potential for intimacy and change."

V.

" . . . sentences that translate the bond between our body, her body, the body of our daughter." ( )

If she touches her body in the gray bahroom
the gray light lighting the small window — ,
squeezes her nipple or flicks her vulva —
if she tastes her taste
she is tasting her mother and ~~daughters'~~ daughter's
mythical waves on the Pacific shoreline.
There ~~where~~ the marine life crawls back
from the tidal pool
or gives up the desire to breathe underwater ever again.
If she touches herself she can
find that pulse that penetrates like an echo.
All this without sound in the gray light off the green tiles.
All this ~~is~~ for a body that is a vessel for ~~itself~~ the self.
~~and for mind and spirit.~~ One that resists and insists
~~as~~ like the real waves on any shoreline. Even lakes.

VI.

"we barely . . . have access to fiction!"
Irigaray (10)

The stories, even when told by father
even when never told but *seen,*
were mother's. We wanted all the stories ~~;~~ :
the one about the shark beyond the coral reef,
the *poi* in kindergarten, the red seaweed_
~~warmed~~ washed onto the beach and collected for dinner —
these were her stories ~~that~~ we listened to
in our own heads in the house
with rooms filled with the shadows of limbs.
And she never thought they were *important.*
She knew though we knew she didn't know
how they would become not only our stories

but the granddaughters' tales to tell classmates
in the schoolyards filled with ~~wanting~~ balls and ropes.

~~Everytime she *sees* someone~~
~~she betrays the father's prohibition~~
~~never to leave *and* supports the parents~~
~~goal for the child to become adult,~~
~~even if it means the girl becomes a woman.~~
The stories never reach their true closure
because the endings are those preferred
by the fathers, husbands and brothers.
They, the men and the endings, are against the senses.
So ~~E~~every time ~~she~~ the daughter *sees* someone
she moves away from the rooms
that imitate the ventricles that are finally only tissue~~s~~.
Every time she speaks it is a leave-taking
of abandonment
towards ~~the~~ her smaller figure even if figurative ;
the one she thought was dead or dying
in a sealed off room she knew existed all along.

"It's a little thing," Hahn says of the last words in the first stanza that have altered 'from 'noise' to 'wanting' to 'balls and ropes' — "because ultimately I needed an image to work the abstract without being as specific as 'wanting.'"

She added the lines — "The stories never reach their true closure/ because the endings are those preferred/ by the fathers, husbands and brothers./ They, the men and the endings, are against the senses." — as a result of another discussion with her friend with whom she had explored the black widow concept. ""We were discussing the story of Daphne and whether its ending is true," she recalls.

From Greek mythology, Daphne was a Greek mountain-nymph pursued by Apollo. In response to her prayer for help, she was changed by Mother Earth into a bay or laurel tree. To console himself, Apollo made himself a laurel crown which since has become a symbol of victory, e.g. it was worn by Virgil as described by Dante as well as Julius Caesar; also, the memory lingers in the word "baccalaureate." Petrarch also took great pride in the laurel crown he received in the Capitol in Rome for his poetry.

"But why should Daphne be punished? Why should she be the one to be turned into a laurel tree?" asks Hahn, whose memory of the myth includes the details that Daphne was also a hunter; daughter of a god and a mortal woman who is "disappeared" from the stories about Daphne; and someone who didn't want to get married. "She didn't want to marry because if you marry a god, you get exiled; whereas if you marry a mortal man you get to be a wife," she notes.

"So if the ending is not satisfactory, what's to keep us from not writing a new one? The endings of stories that we have often benefits the patriarchy," she continues, scoffing that the laurel crown ending up being used for the brows of victorious men. "As this friend pointed out, what's to keep us tied to these endings? Why shouldn't we keep re-writing these stories?" With no small amount of satisfaction, Hahn shares, "In my story, Daphne finds her mother again who helps her not to be a tree!"

"In adding this new section that begins with 'The stories', I repeat the opening of the first section. I know I wanted this repetition though I am not sure I realized that this paralleled the phrase in Section I: 'In the house.' " She continues, "The repetition offers emphasis, focus and cohesion. Because of the earlier repetition there is a spiraling motion from the opening to the closure. Also, the word, 'stories,' refers directly to 'fiction' — and, of course, transmission."

Referring to the draft, Hahn says, "In this section there is a recognition of women's stories as well as the potential to leave the patriarchal 'house.' What I've added may be a bit, again, 'cerebral' but I have loaded the section with charged images: from red seaweed to the red heart. I hope the images absorb an expository moment like the one about the senses or abandonment. It feels right. And it feels right to spiral back to the house/rooms image."

**D.       Final Draft**

**Responding To Light**
I.

> "Every desire has a relation to madness"

In the house with windows that look out
into the branches of a forest, into
the dinner of sunsets,
no one is permitted to speak
over the five o'clock news and no one
can see the television but the father.
Here, the daughters chew the meal
that will make them larger than desired,
than desire itself. Here
the father's paycheck purchases the meat
the mother stews.
The silent daughters are silenced.
See if this makes sense. See if
following directions leads to sanity
or to a covenant where one feels virginal always
or to inhabiting betrayal
like the undergrowth across the street.

In the house with the father's still lives
of massive sea shells and slippery marine life,
the daughters imagine the canvases are windows
without blinds. There are no people.
to compromise definitions.
When the two leave for school on the road by the elms
the younger one asks about the gnarled branches
that grow away from air and toward the water table.

And once a year the girls share small foiled hearts:

the taste of chocolate stimulating and simulating
what cannot be said
though there are noises.


II.
" . . . our society and our culture operate on the basis of an original matricide."

Somewhere in the small house with no hallways
the mother agreed to be disappeared,
just before the oldest daughter's plump body,
too-early sprouted hair
and too early, though any time was too early,
budded nipples.  This daughter
already knew since third grade that she would bleed
and in the telling had shivered uncontrollably
as if there was no such thing as radiators.
If I had told her that early evening
I would have held her
and not let her go.  I would have not left,
let the father let me leave,
let myself escape from hormonal harpoons.
When the girl finally did bleed
in her baggy cotton underpants
she stuffed them with toilet paper
then later hid them between wall and mattress.

SOAR
SORE
SOEUR
SOUR
SUR
SURE

Who will be the idealized breast
when one has spent a lifetime in that
constellation of mythologies
renewed by the mother in their infancies,
presumably before desire
because there are no words.  Who will be the mother
when the father was never the mother.
When the sister, girlfriend or boyfriend.
Or the daughter was not.
Must the mother mother herself?
Must she be the breast and mouth?
The *presexual* breast and *asexual* mouth.

When devour does not equal desire?
The curtains were gauzy
because the street and neighbors were far
from viewing inside
the interior of the house that resembled
a heart without blood.  Veins without color.
Who will instruct
in a world where one is asked to obey
in her own erasure?

III.
". . . the threatening womb.  Threatening because it is silent, perhaps?"


The womb wishes to speak.  To say something like
*Come here go away*
or *go away, come here*
And this one doesn't even have incisors.


IV.
"corps-a-corps"

They peeled carrots.
They added and subtracted.
They traded blouses.
They were more daughters than sisters.
They trimmed each other's hair and pierced their faces.


V.
" . . . sentences that translate the bond between our body, her body, the body of
our daughter."

If she touches her body in the gray bathroom
the gray light lighting the small window,
squeezes her nipple or flicks her vulva —
if she tastes her taste
she is tasting her mother and daughter's
mythical waves on the Pacific shoreline.
There the marine life crawls back
from the tidal pool
or gives up the desire to breathe underwater ever again.
If she touches herself she can
find that pulse that penetrates like an echo.
All this without sound in the gray light off the green tiles.

All this for a body that is a vessel for the self.
One that resists and insists
like the real waves on any shoreline.  Even lakes.


VI.

   "we barely . . . have access to fiction!"

The stories, even when told by father
even when never told but *seen*,
were mother's.  We wanted all the stories:
the one about the shark beyond the coral reef,
the *poi* in kindergarten, the red seaweed
washed onto the beach and collected for dinner —
these were her stories we listened to
in our own heads in the house
with rooms filled with the shadows of limbs.
And she never thought they were *important*.
She knew though we knew she didn't know
how they would become not only our stories
but the granddaughters' tales to tell classmates
in the schoolyards filled with balls and ropes.

The stories never reach their true closure
because the endings are those preferred
by the fathers, husbands and brothers.
They, the men and the endings, are against the senses.
So every time the daughter *sees* someone
she moves away from the rooms
that imitate the ventricles that are finally only tissue.
Every time she speaks it is a leave-taking
of abandonment
towards her smaller figure even if figurative;
the one she thought was dead or dying
in a sealed off room she knew existed all along.


*(All the quotes beginning each section are taken from Luce Irigaray's essay, "Body against Body: In Relation to the Mother" (— from* Sexes *and Geneaologies by Luce Irigaray, translated by Gillian C. Gill, Columbia University Press, 1993.  The original was published in 1987 by* Les Editions de Minuit.*)*

—◈—

After speaking at length about this poem, Hahn was anxious that she had "just explained" the contents. She says she is more interested in discussing process; but then, in thinking aloud, she suggested that describing what she was reading and discussing with friends is important — "showing influences is important to the process itself." So she says she hopes that "rather than interpret the poem for the reader here, I lend a dimension."

Just as Hahn was the oldest of two daughters, she is now the mother of two girls. "I take a mythological view about this. I feel we're part of a story. My two daughters are chapter two. I can't imagine any other family formation," she says.

And, yes, Miyako and Reiko also enjoy writing, just like their mother. "They like to write stories. Hopefully, they'll write novels and not compete with mom," Hahn adds jokingly.

Or, perhaps, Hahn was serious with her statement, even though she was just having fun.

# TIMOTHY LIU

Timothy Liu's poems have appeared in such journals as *Grand Street, Harvard Review, Kenyon Review, The Nation, Paris Review, Poetry, Salmagundi, Shenandoah, Witness* and *Yellow Silk*. He has published three books of poetry: *Vox Angelica* (Alice James Books, 1992), *Burnt Offerings* (Copper Canyon Press, 1995) and *Say Goodnight* (Copper Canyon Press, 1998). *Vox Angelica* won the Norma Faber First Book Award. He is currently working on a new poetry manuscript with a working title of *HARD EVIDENCE*. He has taught at Cornell College in Mount Vernon, Iowa, Hampshire College in Amherst, Massachusetts; and University of California at Berkeley.

In response to the question, "What advice would you give to a young poet?" Timothy Liu responds:

> Read all the poets (living and dead) you can so that you can then get in on the great conversation that poetry is, a conversation that exists both in time and in eternity. And during times when you're not reading or writing, fill your life with as much beauty as you can afford: great food, great art, great music, great sex. To apprehend what is great is to fill oneself with awe and gratitude as armor against the vile and the ugly and the small which is also life, a life that seeks to negotiate the abyss between what is imagined and what is real.

# TOWARDS REDEMPTION

*If your mother tells you love is decent,*
*don't believe her, until she tells the truth.*
*Understand me when I say I didn't*
*do it for sex. I did it for pity.*
*For the hundreds of men that I have loved*
*in airports, busstops, truckstops, interstate*
*reststops, shopping malls, locker rooms*
*and janitorial closets, wherever there's enough*
*room for two men to stand up face to face.*
*Don't ask me what it's like to go on*
*living, at first a high priest breaking bread*
*for hundreds of open mouths, finally*
*feeding myself in some airport snack bar,*
*smell of a stranger's sex on my fingers.*
*— from "SFO/HIV/JFK" by Timothy Liu*

Timothy Liu wrote "SFO/HIV/JFK" after a homosexual encounter in an airport restroom while traveling between San Francisco and New York. Drafting the poem in a snack bar, he melded together references to three topics which frequently surface in his poems: homosexuality, religion and his mother. Yet "SFO/HIV/JFK" also exemplifies Liu's poems transcending their real-life inspiration through poetic craft, enhancing resonance.

"I have always privileged the lyric over the narrative because I find narrative poetry to be long-winded and tedious when it's not well-written," Liu said. "Some of the things that have helped me write towards the lyric are a kind of image-based poetry, with the images grounded in both the real and the surreal. I like the mix of real and surreal so that if you get the right image in the poem, you can create or recreate a certain type of emotional space — so that the image, whether real or rooted in the mind, can still create that emotion."

Liu's first book, *Vox Angelica* (alicejamesbooks, 1992), reflects a turbulent period of his life when he was renouncing Mormonism, coming out of the closet, and just starting to seek therapeutical help for dealing with the effects of his mother's child abuse. Winner of the Norma Faber First Book Award, *Vox Angelica* contains poems written in 1988-1991 while Liu was an undergraduate at Brigham Young University as well as while he attended the University of Houston for his Master's in Arts.

"I was encouraged by various teachers to write about my background. So there's a strong confessional element in terms of my first two books," he said; in 1995, Liu's second book, *Burnt Offerings*, was published by Copper Canyon Press. "People can write about whatever they want to, but, for me, I do think we're getting a bit saturated; the scales are starting to become real heavy on confessional exploring of ethnicity, abuse and all that."

Consequently, Liu said he has focused on refining his craft during the past two to three years.

"I've been paying attention to language and syntax — a language that will not shield one from emotional experience but rather make it more available. I tend not to like experimental or avant garde writing that is merely pyrotechnic. I want soul in it! Right now I'm reading a lot of poetry (in whose styles) I'll never write but which teach me about language. So when I read a book by Arthur Sze, Mei-mei Berssenbrugge or Aaron Shurin, I'm not trying to borrow their forms but they interest me into asking what kind of questions they are exploring about language. And I think that helps me build my poetry into a new direction."

"It's a shift of an aesthetic balance," he continued. "In the beginning, I was interested in mainstream writing, from the kind of poets that win Pulitzers and National Book Awards, as well as a lot of South American and Eastern European poets. I think I'm also interested now in reading the poets that aren't so recognized, not in the mainstream, but are doing interesting things."

During his adolescent years, Liu said most of his work revolved around "rock lyrics." At age 18, he read *Ariel* by Sylvia Plath ("Awesome!" he recalled). He started reading poetry seriously at age 21 and, since then, has adhered to reading an average of five poetry books a week. To further develop his poetry, Liu also began recently to read poems in public while they are still works-in-progress; previously, he said he would only read finished works.

—⚔—

In an interview after Liu read his latest works — including poems-in-progress — at the Asian American Writers Workshop ("AAWW," New York City, 1996), I asked Liu to dredge his memories and discuss the background and inspirations for the poems in *Vox Angelica*. After the interview, we discussed in detail three poems, the title poem "VOX ANGELICA," "CANKER" and "THE ROAD TO SEDER." Liu chose the three poems as a fair representation of his poetry and poetics during the years reflected in his two books.

*Tabios:* The drafts you showed me of your poems include editing marks and suggestions by Richard Howard (poetry editor for *The Paris Review* who also wrote an introductory essay to *Vox Angelica*). How did your relationship with him occur?

*Liu:* Richard was my first teacher at the University of Houston. It was a time when I was leaving the Mormon church and coming out as a homosexual. He was very helpful to me as a mentor, being quite understanding of the difficulties I was going through in my personal life. He's generous with his time with students; I'm a pretty prolific poet and I showed him everything I wrote.

*Tabios:* Richard Howard referred to a "Devouring Mother" syndrome in his introduction to *Vox Angelica?* Is there a real-life basis to this term?

*Liu:* My mother's been a paranoid schizophrenic for about 20 years and was abusive when I was growing up. She has been a consuming figure who's taken up a lot of my energy. I think Richard liked that term, "Devouring Mother," because it's so appropos with Freud and the family romance — a drama I was exploring.

*Tabios:* In "CANKER," there's a scene where the infant is fearful of being touched by the mother. The excerpt is:

> Your aunt wrote me while you had stayed with them, still a baby. You'd scream if your mother came into the room where you were being bathed. Her sister told her not to touch you but she did.

*Liu:* That's a story that my father told when when I was 18 years old. That was the first time he told me about the child abuse, although I'd had my suspicions. The incident is described in

"CANKER," the scene where my father is driving me to school.

*Tabios*: How did you interact with your mother as you were growing up?

*Liu*: When I was ten years old, she was diagnosed with schizophrenia; it was also about the time my parents were getting a divorce, after a therapist seduced my mother. When the therapist abandoned my mother, she went into the (mental) hospital. So I lived primarily with my father. She was in and out of different mental hospitals. Her paranoid schizophrenia would act up certain times during the year, but she didn't live year-round in institutions. We used to visit her once a week, whether at a mental institution or her apartment.

*Tabios*: Is she still alive?

*Liu*: Yes. She lives in an apartment by herself. She gets by. She's a resourceful schizophrenic. She knows how far she can go before jeopardizing her freedom.

*Tabios*: Did you feel guilt towards your mother in terms of how she turned out?

*Liu*: I think children expect their parents to be healthy. And when the parents are not able to come up with good parenting, I think most children do feel guilt. It's a natural thing to do.

*Tabios*: A new poem you read (at AAWW) contained a line, "Mother, are you listening?" Is this the wound (in "CANKER") that won't heal?

*Liu (nodding assent)*: In an earlier draft of that new poem, "PROLEGOMENON," I got rid of all the lines surrounding the question, lines lamenting the fact that because my mother is sick, she can never understand my poetry. So, in a way, it was a rhetorical question because the answer is *No*, she's not listening — and she's never been listening. Not to the poetry or to anything I say to her.

Or, if it's not a rhetorical question, perhaps it's an imperative command: *Mother, Listen.*

I think a lot of poets feel this way: of not being able to share their creative lives with their immediate family. At least in the Olympics you can have them watch you win a medal.

*Tabios*: Religion, homosexuality, the relationship with your mother — these create what Richard Howard calls the "battleground" for your poetry?

*Liu*: Yes, for the first two books. But I'm also aware of what's not available yet in my poetry. I'm conscious that I think a lot about being Asian American in my life and I wonder why it's not available to me as poetry, although some of my unpublished poems have dealt with ethnicity. But, in some ways, we don't really choose our subjects. We just write about what's bothering us.

*Tabios*: I don't want to simplify the issue of your homosexuality. But in "CANKER," there was a scene linking your homosexuality with the "first time (you) remember being held" which was by your father. The excerpt is:

*. . .That night there was a canker in the back of my throat. I couldn't eat for days. My father opened cans of a protein drink he'd brought home from the hospital./ Drink, this. Now sleep. Good./ That was the first time I remember being held. I told my father at the end of our trip. I told him about the men who came into my life. The pain that made me feel alive.*

*Liu:* In this culture it's a stigma to be gay, so many people would wonder why one would be gay. In that poem I did wonder why it was that the intimacy and safety I could feel was with my father and not my mother. I also wonder why that was the first thing I felt in my sexual intimacy with men: finally to be safe, that I'm finally *home*.

I think everything forms our sexuality, so why not? I had an abusive mother when I was very young and I was terrified by her. Why wouldn't that have an influence? So that's why that comes up in the poem. The only retraction that I would give is this: many men who have been abused by their mothers are very heterosexual. I look at my gay friends and a lot do have domineering mothers and distant fathers but I have to remind myself that a lot of my straight friends have a similar background.

*Tabios:* I read the entire book, *Vox Angelica*, again recently and certain lines rose to the surface. I'd like to share these excerpts with you and have you respond as you wish. These lines caught my attention partly because I thought they were beautifully-written, but I suspect your responses to these lines will be relevant to the three poems we'll be exploring in more detail: "VOX ANGEL-ICA," "CANKER" and "THE ROAD TO SEDER."

*Liu:* Okay.

*Tabios:* From the poem "VOX ANGELICA" — *The words I speak I cannot revise./ All art is an afterthought,/ an attempt to interpret a dream/ that by its nature is perfected,*

*Liu:* I find the first part — *the words I speak I cannot revise* — contains a built-in irony because the whole poem has gone through so many revisions! Yet it's not ironic because the poem was first created by my speaking into a tape recorder; so, one of the things I was conscious of is that I wasn't going to be able to go back and erase what I'd said. (Note that) I didn't say, "the words I WRITE," but I "the words I SPEAK."

I was also trying to address the fact that all art is imperfect because art needs to be revised — it's not whole the way a dream is. I think what we try to do as poets is to work and work on a poem until it seems like a perfect dream. Whereas a dream — we get it once, we don't revise it and it's already whole. There's nothing to be done to it except to try to figure out what it means. So, in some ways, (the process of writing poetry) is backward.

One of my teachers at Houston was the poet Adam Zagajewski; he thought that dreams didn't make very good material for poems, but that a good poem is like a dream for everyone. That's such a beautiful thing: your dream is not going to be a good poem but a good poem is going to be a good dream for everyone.

*Tabios:*  From "ARIEL SINGING" — *It is not happiness . . . It is a world without song/ I flew right into. . . .Teach me/ how to sing in a grove of olive trees,/ to fall as a sparrow.  It is all I want."*

*Liu:*  I was very unhappy when I wrote that poem.  Many of the poems in *Vox Angelica* are poems I wrote before getting therapy.  During that time, I was also trying to publish in *The Quarterly*, edited by Gordon Lish.  And some of my friends had started publishing there when I was a senior.  So I had been sending my works to Gordon Lish for about a year — every three weeks I'd send him poems.

*Tabios:*  Every three weeks?

*Liu:*  Yes, there was a lot of correspondence.  He encouraged me a lot but he never accepted a poem.  So I was really depressed when I wrote "ARIEL SINGING" — I thought, *I have nothing: My relationship with the Church is gone.  I don't have a good love life.  If I can't write a good poem, then I'm really sunk — I have nothing!*  I wrote, "Teach me how to sing in a grove of olive trees" because it was at that point in my life when I was asking God to help me be a poet, since I couldn't be a Mormon in good standing.  But I was also addressing Gordon Lish.

I refer to the olive tree as a sacred place, not merely as a Christian reference but as an earthly thing.  I think "falling" is the image of descent.  *Falling* — I was trying to come down.  Mormonism is a kind of heavenly thing, and I thought poetry would be the thing that would somehow get me down to earth.

*Tabios:*  A three-line poem, "THE KORE" — *What was sacred was in my journey/ the whole way back, leaving her/ in pieces the way I had found her.*

*Liu:*  The Kore is a 5th century B.C. statue of a virgin.  This poem was written for the poet Linda Gregg.  I met her in 1990 when I went to Aspen for a writer's conference.  But it ended up becoming a poem about my mother.  Sometimes, the great comfort is that you're not going to heal or put things back together, but to leave things the way they are and just look at them in the way they are.  There's another poem, "SHE SINGS IN ALL HER SEASONS," that immediately precedes "THE KORE" in the book; its opening line is 'To see her for what she is" — and that's the same kind of idea as in "THE KORE."

*Tabios:*  From "APHRODITE AS I KNOW HER" — *It is not ruin but the tenderness/ I love.  Not what time destroys/ but what remains: the empty/ hands broken off at the wrists.*

*Liu:*  There's an echo of this poem to "ARIEL SINGING" which begins with the words, "It is not happiness" — it's the same kind of grammar.

I think dealing with therapy is not about changing the past but about re-seeing the past.  A lot of these lines you're quoting have to do with healing, which is not about changing the past but coming to terms with the past.

*Tabios:*  What I find unexpected in your responses to the lines I'm quoting is that they disagree with what I recall to be the thesis in Richard Howard's introduction to *Vox Angelica*.  From the introduction, he writes:

> *In Liu's text the ascent, the ecstatic apprehension of the divine . . . can be affected only by a demonic insistence upon abjection, on the descent. . . . He shrives himself and his poems show the marks of the lash — they are the lash . . . ."*

I find your answers would seem to disagree with Richard Howard's thoughts about your poetry.

*Liu:* Perhaps Richard saw me as a kind of self-flagellating monk — the marks and the lash — someone suffering for his sins. I think for me, yes, there's a lot about going into the wound and falling. But there's also *HOPE* — I don't know if *hope* is the right word, but I certainly look at poetry as some sort of a redemptive act. And that's the way I look at therapy — I don't think I would have gone into therapy if I hadn't believed that, afterwards, I would have a better life after working with it. And I feel that way about poetry, as well.

*Tabios:* From "CARCASS," *Feel my black wings/ buckle like beautiful knees/ going down on dead meat.*

*Liu:* The idea was of transforming the angel from a heavenly angel to a dark angel. Before Adam and Eve were created, there was a war in Heaven and a third of the angels fell with Lucifer. And those are the angels that I identify with more, not the ones floating around in the sky but the ones that fell. That's what black wings mean to me. The initial draft of that was written at about the same time as "THE ROAD TO SEDER" where we have what I call the "negative angel."

"Dead meat" — I was playing with two colloquial phrases: going down on someone as in oral sex and "dead meat" as a corpse. I thought of the words strangely as kind of metaphor for some sort of infected penis or some meat of death — I liked it.

*Tabios:* From "SEPARATION," *After the first loss, there is no other,/ the rest is repetition . . . .How rooms are emptied/by a single act. All through school I had a dream/ of roll being called and I not being there./ Everything rises up again, not like the stars/ climbing into heaven, but to that place I keep/ returning to late at night, a light, a desk,/ a chair, no different from what my parents have/ owned, knowing how this would be the poem I would write for the rest of my life.*

*Liu:* I laugh at that poem now because that first line was stolen from Dylan Thomas who had a poem titled "A REFUSAL TO MOURN THE DEATH, BY FIRE, OF A CHILD IN LONDON." Its final line is, "After the first loss, there is no other". I didn't realize that I had stolen that line until years after writing it and I was horrified.

To me, the idea of "SEPARATION" is that the first loss is the primary experience and everything else is an echo. It's like the poem I read last night, titled "ECHOES," which talks about abuse and its effect being like rings in water (spreading after the water is penetrated by something) — effects just reverberate through life. And the first loss is when you leave the mother's body.

*Tabios:* Then you and your mother "leaving" each other due to her illness which caused the abuse?

*Liu:* Right, then leaving home, going to college, moving on . . .

After the interview, I looked up Thomas' poem, "A REFUSAL TO MOURN THE DEATH, BY FIRE, OF A CHILD IN LONDON" — and was not surprised by Liu's unconscious reference to it in his poem, "SEPARATIONS." The last two stanzas in Thomas' poem are as follows:

> *The majesty and burning of the child's death.*
> *I shall not murder*
> *The mankind of her going with a grave truth*
> *Nor blaspheme down the stations of the breath*
> *With any further*
> *Elegy of innocence and youth.*
>
> *Deep with the first dead lies London's daughter,*
> *Robed in the long friends,*
> *The grains beyond age, the dark veins of her mother,*
> *Secret by the unmourning water*
> *Of the riding Thames.*
> *After the first death, there is no other.*

Featured below are Liu's drafts of three poems listed in the chronological order of their creation. The drafts are featured with Liu's comments on the poems' underlying inspirations, his thoughts as he wrote the poem and explanations for some of the changes he made in drafting the poems.

(_Editing Marks_: *strikethroughs = deletions; underlined words = insertions/additions; [Del L] - deleted line breaks; [New L] = new line breaks; [Del P] = deleted stanza breaks; [New P] = new stanza breaks; bracketed, italicized words denote handwritten notes about the text.*)

## I.      CANKER

Liu began "Canker" in April or May of 1989 when he was still attending Brigham Young University. "I was also working for IBM, developing a computer program that taught kids how to read for meaning. I wasn't a very good worker and wrote a lot of poems on the job. I wrote some sketchy notes for this poem and during the summer typed out what ended up being an eleven-line poem (the first typed draft featured below under "B")," Liu recalled. "I thought it was a pretty strong poem and showed it to Stewart James."

James, a friend, classmate and fellow poet, suggested — as Howard subsequently did — that Liu expand the poem. Liu recalled them saying that that he "open up the poem and tell them what's really on my mind: what is the wound that will never heal?"

Thus, "Canker," is significant in Liu's poetic development as it is, not only the first "major poem" written by Liu to address the effects of his mother's abuse but also, the first prose-poem he wrote. Indeed, Liu found himself forced to use the prose-poem format because he found the subject so overwhelming that he wanted to focus on the material instead of on poetic structure.

"It was a very difficult poem to write," Liu recalled. "After Stewart and Richard suggested I expand the poem, I locked myself in my apartment for two to three days to work on it. As I expanded the poem, I felt that I had to ignore the 'art' of the poem — like line breaks and all that stuff — in order to get at the material about my mother."

After writing "CANKER," Liu said he no longer had to use "the strategy of the prose poem format to bring forth the material related to his mother" — though this may be, in part, because he began therapy after writing "CANKER." ("VOX ANGELICA" also touches on Liu's mother but is written in the more traditional stanza form.)

Liu credited James for his help as he wrote the poem. After the first day of working to expand the poem, Liu said that he "became very upset and I called him and read the first page of what I had written. He felt that it was a real break through and so gave me the courage to complete the first handwritten draft of that poem" in its long version. To date, "CANKER" is Liu's only published poem utilizing the prose poem format.

A)      1st Holograph of CANKER, April/May 1989

**CANKER**

The wound in my mouth
would not heal for days
longer than I'd expected
which was really nothing
compared to the ~~wound~~ pain
that my mother ~~'s mouth~~ inflicted

———————

with her mouth upon my body
for life. Her bites were not the kind

Liu considered the above holograph "too abstract," leading to his first typed version below.

B)      First Typed Draft of CANKER, September, 1989

**CANKER**

The wound would not heal for days longer than I had
expected. It was nothing compared to my mother
who ran her mouth all over my body.
What people will do to be remembered.

The nurses cutting roses from cards I've sent
put stamps in a tub of scalding water
where kisses have come undone.

Tonight my face will bloom beside her bed,

working thorns into her lips, the words

of love I never knew how to say:  Mother,

nothing ~~completely~~ heals completely as long as I stay alive.

 

"The poem has many references to the mouth, including the second stanza 'where kisses have come undone'," Liu said.  "I was referring to when you lick a stamp and then unseal it in order to put it in a stamp collection.  But though you can unseal a stamp, you can't undo what she did."

In response to this version, Liu remembered James saying, "You're sitting on a volcano. Whatever it is, let us (the poem's audience) in on it."

Liu's "opening up" of the poem resulted in the following draft as a prose poem:

 

C)        Second Holograph in a Prose Poem Format, Fall 1989

**CANKER**

> *Nicodemus answered and said unto him, how can these things be?*
>
> John 3:9

The wound would not heal for days longer than I had expected.  It was nothing compared to my mother who ran her mouth all over my body.

What people will do to be remembered.

The nurses cutting roses from the letters I send — put them in a tub of scalding water where kisses have come undone

The stamps are all that she can save, collecting them in a book like all the photographs from a childhood I never had

I too have managed to piece together the pages she tore away ~~from me but~~ that she could not destroy

Like a box of letters that burn away, the ashes ~~could be~~ were not extinguished *entirely*. Poked and stirred throughout the years, a ~~new~~ blaze started in my eyes that cannot forget

The day my father and I were driving after the school break was over, that two-lane highway on fire ~~the~~ that autumn ~~before when~~ I ~~had~~ left for school, everything falls.

Yet they continued to live in the same town where I was born.

It seems to me now that their divorce was never final only *a precarious extension,* an image between two cliffs *over a river of fire~~that~~ I had walked on*

Of course we had a great distance to go.  I wanted as many miles from what was left of home as I could get without cutting off my supports

the ropes that suspended my life in that awful space between

We shared the burden of taking the wheel.  Yet I couldn't get over the fact my father never had a steady foot, only a start-stop rhythm that burned more fuel than I thought we'd have had before reaching

the next services.  But we would make it.  It was belief that kept us at each other's throats.

I remember blood on the dining room floor after I broke a wooden chair

over his back.  There wasn't much, just a few drops running down his cheek, like when you cry a little, almost in relief.

But it was more than that.  The chair could not be restored to its proper place at the table.  It wasn't damaged beyond repair — could still support its own weight — but it was put away in the attic.

And I thought, if only mother knew, but she had fallen apart by then, garbage strewn across the hallway just outside her apartment door

The day the city workers went and locked her up for the first time that year.  But we went over twice a week to water her plants.

What else could we do but ~~try to~~ keep what she had from dying?

I thought of her in the backseat that day in junior high when I was called from class.  She said to me,

*if you love me let me die,*

her head in my lap, floating in a pool of chemicals while ~~her friend who pulled me out from school~~ ~~the cleaning woman who couldn't get in to clean~~ her friend ~~because she couldn't get in to clean~~ drove us to the hospital

*let me die*

That's all I heard as he broke into her bedroom, the pills she didn't swallow scattered upon the floor like a broken necklace I couldn't put back together

That night there was a canker in the back of my throat.  It grew so painful,

I couldn't eat for days.  I watched them pump her stomach.  ~~She was saved~~ They scared her.  What could I do but cry myself to sleep, thanking God ~~my mother~~ she had been saved

But saved for what?

My father opened cans of a liquid protein drink he had brought home ~~from the hospital months earlier~~ from the hospital

*Drink, this will make you whole.*

It was the first time that I remember being held, later men would come into my life that I couldn't live without.  It was the pain that made me feel alive.

My father wept.

It was as if he knew my life would come to this.

So often I'd press my tongue into a sore to see how much I could endure if not ~~to~~ understand the pain.  I saw my father now pushing his tongue ~~the~~ <u>on</u> fire that ~~my mother could~~ <u>years had</u> not smothered.

*Her sister wrote while you ~~were staying~~ <u>had stayed</u> with them, ~~an~~ <u>an</u> infant.  You'd scream if your mother came into the room where ~~your aunt was bathing you~~ you were being bathed.  Her sister told her not to touch you, but she carried you away.*

I wanted ~~this~~ my father to stop.  Why ~~couldn't he~~ ~~didn't~~ <u>couldn't anyone</u> stop her?

*There are no photographs of you when you were young. She wouldn't have them in ~~the~~ <u>the</u> house reminding her of the space you filled that she could not destroy*

The ropes snapped.  My father caught me as if I were ~~a great bird~~ <u>an angel</u> he had wounded out of the sky.  I knew I couldn't be going back

the way that I had come:  a man can never enter a second time into his mother's womb and be born again.  She entered me

by way of a kiss.

I returned at Easter — flew upon the wings of a plane half-empty into the ~~first grey light~~ of day.
I couldn't bring her flowers, though I thought of how'd they'd look upon her grave

I wanted her in the earth, her ashes contained

not knowing the words she'd say to me would burn like a great pyre upon ~~her~~ my bed

*Your father lies. You must please God, not hurt your mother.  ~~We always loved you.~~*

*You were so difficult, always crying, crying. I could not shut you up. You did not want my milk, ————-only ~~your father~~ your father How could I live with myself?*

Tonight my roses will bloom beside her bed, working their thorns into her lips. The words of love I never knew how to say: Mother, nothing heals completely as long as I stay alive

We cried together, ~~for the last time~~ muting out the fire. I left her in that room, closed the door behind me.          *[Move above 2 lines before the previous stanza]*

The following were notes by Liu to himself on bottom of page as he was searching for ways to rephrase some of the words in the first draft:

*That night before I left for school*
*I prayed, she is in your hands*
*As the only son, I cannot take responsibility.*
*[But saved for what and textbook excerpt]*

About his notes, Liu recalled, "I was thinking of the possibility of expanding the poem with a section that would begin with the line, 'That night before I left for school.' At the time I had just left for UCLA and was telling God, 'I've taken care of her for 10 years and I'm leaving town. She's in your hands; I'm out of here.' "

D)          First Typed Draft of CANKER, November 1989

Liu showed this version to Richard Howard; all the editorial marks on this draft reflect Howard's thoughts. In addition, Howard occasionally bracketed words and phrases to question whether they were necessary. As evident below, Howard's proposed changes strengthen the poem's structure, e.g. diction, rhythm and tightening phrases. By the top margin of the page, Howard also had suggested that Liu delete the reference to John 3:9.

**CANKER**

*Nicodemus answered and said unto him, how can these things be?*
John 3:9

The wound would not heal for days [longer than I had expected.] [It was nothing compared to] my mother ~~who~~ ran her mouth all over my body.

What people will do to be remembered.

The nurses cutting roses from the cards I ~~send~~ sent have put them  in a tub of scalding water ~~whose~~  , the kisses have come undone.

~~The~~ stamps are all ~~that~~ she can save, putting them in a book like all the photographs from a childhood I never had.

I ~~too~~ have managed to piece together the pages she tore away from me [that she could not destroy]. ~~Like~~ Though the box of letters ~~that~~ burned ~~away~~, the ashes were not entirely extinguished— ~~poked and~~ stirred through the years, a blaze started in my eyes ~~that cannot forget~~.

the day ~~my father and I were driving after Christmas break was~~ after Christmas break my father was driving me back to school, the ~~over that~~ two-lane highway on fire, ~~the autumn I had left for~~

~~school,~~ everything falling.

Yet they ~~continued to live~~ went on living in the same town where I was born.

~~It seems to me now that~~ To me their divorce was never final, only a precarious extension, a bridge ~~between two cliffs~~ ~~that~~ I had learned to walk ~~on~~ between two cliffs.

Of course we had a great distance to go. ~~I wanted~~ as many miles from what was left of home as I could get [without cutting off my support,]

without cutting the ropes that suspended my life ~~in~~ over that awful space between.

We shared this burden, taking our turns at the wheel. ~~Yet I couldn't get over the fact that~~ my father never had a steady foot, only a start-stop rhythm that ~~burned~~ would burn more gas than I thought ~~we'd~~ we had ~~making it we had~~ before

~~to~~ the next ~~services~~ station. But we would make it. It was belief that kept us at each other's throats.

I remember blood on the dining room floor when I broke a wooden chair over his back. ~~There wasn't~~ Not much, just a few drops running down his cheek, like ~~when you cry a little,~~ a few tears wept ~~almost~~ in relief.

The chair could not be restored to its proper place at the table. It wasn't damaged beyond repair— ~~could still support its own weight~~ —but it was put away in the attic.

And I thought, if only mother knew, but she had fallen apart by then, garbage strewn across the hallway ~~just~~ outside her apartment door the day the county workers came and locked her up for the first time that year.

     *[On Liu's manuscript, Howard circled "fallen apart" signifying,*
     *Liu said, that the phrase is "lousy diction" which Liu should clarify.]*

We'd go ~~over~~ there twice a week to water her plants.

What else could we do but ~~try to~~ keep what she had from dying?

I still can hear her ~~in the backseat~~ that day in junior high when I was called out of class. She said to me in the backseat

*if you love me let me die*

her head bobbing in my lap, floating in ~~a~~ its pool of chemicals. ~~Her~~ The friend who couldn't get in to clean ~~that morning~~ drove us to the emergency room that morning.

*Let me die.*

That's all I heard ~~as~~ when I broke into her bedroom, the pills ~~she hadn't swallowed~~ scattered on the floor like a broken necklace ~~I couldn't put back together.~~

That night there was a canker in the back of my throat. ~~It grew so painful~~ *[Del P]* I couldn't eat for days. I watched them pump her stomach. They saved her. ~~What could I do but cry myself to sleep that night, thanking God~~ my mother had been saved ~~?~~ .

But saved for what?

My father opened cans of a protein drink he'd brought home from the hospital.

*Drink, this will make you whole.*

It was the first time I remember being held. I told my father ~~this~~ at the end of our trip. I told him of the men ~~I couldn't live without~~ who came into my life. ~~It was~~ the pain ~~that~~ made me feel alive. I could not live without them.

My father wept. *[Del P]* ~~It was as~~ As if he knew my life would come to this.

I pressed my tongue into that sore, ~~wanting to see~~ how much could I ~~could~~ endure if I could not understand the pain. I watched my father push his tongue into a fire that years could not put out:

    *[On Liu's manuscript, Howard underlined "tongue into a fire" signifying,*
    *Liu said, that the phrase "didn't make sense to him on a literal level."*

~~*Her sister*~~ *Your aunt wrote me while you had stayed with them,* ~~*an infant*~~ *still a baby* ~~*still*~~. *You'd scream if your mother came into the room where you were being bathed. Her sister told her not to touch you but she* ~~*carried you away*~~ *did.*

I wanted this to stop. Why couldn't he stop her?

*There are no photographs of you* ~~*when you were young*~~ *then . She wouldn't have them in the house reminding her* ~~*of the space you filled that she could not destroy*~~.

The ropes snapped. We swerved to the side of the road. My father caught me as though I were an angel he had wounded out of the sky. I knew I wouldn't be going back the way that I had come:

*a man can never enter a second time into his mother's womb and be born again.*

She entered me by way of a kiss.
> *[On Liu's manuscript, Howard questioned this phrase. Liu said that*
> *Howard "didn't understand if I was being literal or not."]*

At Easter break, I flew on a ~~plane~~ half-empty <u>plane</u> into the ~~red-eye~~ eye of night  I could-
n't ~~bring myself to~~ bring her flowers, though I thought of how they'd look ~~upon~~ on her
grave.

I wanted her in the earth, her ashes contained.

Not floating down a river of fire.  Not knowing the words ~~she'd~~ <u>she said</u> ~~say~~ to me that
night would burn like a great pyre:

*Your father lies. Please God, ~~not~~ <u>don't</u> hurt your mother. You were so difficult, crying and*
*crying. I could not shut you up. You did not want my milk. Only your father. How could*
*I live with myself?*

We cried as if for the last time.  I put out the light.  I left her in that room.  I closed the
door behind me.

Tonight my roses will bloom beside her bed, working their thorns into her lips, the words
~~of love~~ I never knew how to say:  *Mother,*

*nothing heals completely as long as I stay alive.*


E)      Liu's Version In Response to Howard's Suggestions and Comments

**CANKER**

The wound would not heal for days.  <u>But that was nothing compared to</u> my mother <u>who</u>
ran her mouth all over my body.

What people will do to be remembered.

The nurses cutting roses from the cards I sent have put them in a tub of scalding water,
the kisses have come undone.

Stamps are all she can save, ~~putting~~ arranging them in a book like <u>the</u> ~~all the~~ photographs
~~from a childhood I never had~~ <u>she could never take</u>.

I have managed to piece together the pages she tore away from me.  Though the box of

letters burned, the ashes were not entirely extinguished — ,
~~stirred through the years, a blaze started in my eyes.~~

The day after Christmas break my father was driving me back to school, the two-lane highway on fire, everything falling.

~~Yet they went on living in the same town where I was born.~~

To me their divorce was never final, only a precarious extension, a bridge I had learned to walk between two cliffs.

Of course we had a great distance to go [Del P] ~~as many miles from what was left of home as I could get~~

~~without cutting the ropes that suspended my life over that awful space between.~~

~~We shared this burden,~~ [Del P] taking our turns at the wheel. My father never had a steady foot, only a start-stop rhythm that ~~would burn~~ burned more gas than I thought we ~~had~~ would have before reaching

the next station. But we would make it. It was belief that kept us at each other's throats.

I remember blood on the dining room floor and a few drops down his cheek when I broke a ~~wooden~~ chair over his back. [Del P] ~~Not much, just a few drops running down his cheek, like a few tears wept in relief.~~

~~The chair could not be restored to its proper place at the table.~~ [Del P] It wasn't damaged beyond repair, but it was put away in the attic.

And I thought, if only Mother knew, ~~but she had fallen apart by then, garbage strewn across the hallway outside her apartment door the day~~ ~~the~~ The county ~~workers came and~~ had already locked her up for the first time that year : her neighbors had complained about sacks of garbage she threw from her balcony into the swimming pool below.

~~We'd go there twice a week to water her plants.~~

~~What else could we do but keep what she had from dying?~~

I still can hear her voice that day in junior high when I was called out of class. She said to me in the backseat,

~~if you love~~ Love me , let me die ,

her head bobbing in my lap, floating in its pool of chemicals. The ~~friend~~ woman who couldn't get in to clean drove us to the emergency room ~~that morning~~.

*Let me die.*

That's all I heard when I broke into her bedroom, the pills scattered on the floor like a broken necklace.

She lived. That night there was a canker in the back of my throat. I couldn't eat for days. [Del P] ~~I watched them pump her stomach. They saved her. my mother had been saved.~~

~~But saved for what?~~

[Del P] My father opened cans of a protein drink he'd brought home from the hospital.

*Drink ~~, this will make you whole~~ this. Now sleep. Good.*

~~It~~ That was the first time I remember being held. I told my father at the end of our trip. I told him ~~of~~ about the men who came into my life. The pain that made me feel alive. ~~I could not live without them.~~

My father wept as we swerved to the side of the road. [Del P] ~~As if he knew my life would come to this.~~

~~I pressed my tongue into that sore, how much could I endure if I could not understand the pain. I watched my father push his tongue into a fire that years could not put out.~~ [Del P] Then he began to speak, stoking a bed of ashes that years could not put out:

*Your aunt wrote me while you had stayed with them, still a baby. You'd scream if your mother came into the room where you were being bathed. Her sister told her not to touch you but she did.*

I wanted this to stop. Why couldn't he stop her?

*There are no photographs of you then. She wouldn't have them in the house reminding her.*

~~The ropes snapped. We swerved to the side of the road. My father caught me as though I were an angel he had wounded out of the sky. I knew I wouldn't be going back the way that I had~~
~~come.~~

~~a man can never enter a second time into his mother's womb and be born again.~~

~~She~~ My mother entered me ~~by way of~~ with a kiss.

At Easter break, I flew on a half-empty plane into the eye of night I ~~couldn't~~ didn't bring her flowers, though I thought of how ~~they'd~~ they would look on ~~her~~ a grave.

I wanted her in the earth, her ~~ashes~~ <u>body</u> contained.

Not floating down a river of fire.  Not knowing the words she said to me that night would burn ~~like a great pyre~~:

*Your father lies.  Please God, don't hurt your mother.  You were <u>always</u> so difficult, crying* ~~and~~ *, crying.  I ~~could not~~ <u>couldn't</u> shut you up.  You ~~did not~~ <u>didn't</u> want my milk.  Only your father.  How could I live with myself?*

~~We cried as if for the last time.~~  <u>After we cried,</u> I put out the light.  I left her in that room. I closed the door behind me.

Tonight my roses ~~will~~ bloom beside her bed, working their thorns into her lips, the words I never knew how to say: [New P] *Mother,*

*[Del P] nothing heals completely as long as I stay alive.*


Liu explained some of his drafting changes as follows (the number of the paragraphs refers to the version above, not the final draft version of the poem):

1)  Re. Epigraph:

"Nicodemus asked how a man can be born twice, referring to baptism and the Christian concept of being Born Again.  He was asking, how can a man enter the womb a second time," said Liu.  For a moment, Liu focused on the physical image of the metaphor and joked, "Well, first of all — who would want to?"

John 3:1-9 from *The Holy Bible, King James Version* (Meridian, 1974) says:

*1        There was a man of the Pharisees, named Nicodemus, a ruler of the Jews;*

*2        The same came to Jesus by night, and said unto him, Rabbi, we know that thou art a teacher come from God: for no man can do these miracles that thou doest, except God be with him.*

*3        Jesus answered and said unto him, Verily, verily, I say unto thee, Except a man be born again, he cannot see the kingdom of God.*

*4        Nicodemus saith unto him, How can a man be born when he is old? can he enter the second time into his mother's womb, and be born?*

*5        Jesus answered, Verily, verily, I say unto thee, Except a man be born of water and of the Spirit, he cannot enter into the kingdom of God,*

*6        That which is born of the flesh is flesh; and that which is born of the Spirit is spirit.*

*7        Marvel not that I said unto thee, Ye must be born again.*

*8        The wind bloweth where it listeth, and thou hearest the sound thereof, but canst not tell whence it cometh, and whither it goeth; so is every one that is born of the Spirit.*

*9        Nicodemus answered and said unto him, How can these things be?*

Liu said he deleted the epigraph because he considers epigraphs "notes to myself. Epigraphs can be a lazy thing to do in poetry."  Liu later transferred the reference to the 36th and

37th paragraphs which read partly as, "I knew I couldn't be going back/ the way that I had come: a man can never enter a second time into his mother's womb and be born again."

2) Re. 7th Paragraph: "Yet they continued to live in the same town where I was born"

"It's a historical fact that both of my parents live in San Jose, and it was always important for me to get out of town. But I deleted it because it's not important for the poem; it was just a note to myself," said Liu.

3) Re. 8th - 10th Paragraphs: "To me their divorce . . . that awful space between."

Liu compressed this section because he found it "too wordy." Also, he considered the deleted lines to be repetitive — that the idea of a bridge over "an awful space between" noted in the tenth paragraph had been addressed previously by the eighth paragraph's mention of "a bridge I had learned to walk between two cliffs."

4) Re. 12th Paragraph: changing "services" to "station"

Liu said he preferred the word "station" as it would refer to both a gas station and "stations of the cross. I wanted the words to have that duality."

5) Re. 15th Paragraph: "But it was more than that"

Liu said he deleted this line because it was borrowed from a poem by Wallace Stevens, "THE IDEA OF ORDER AT KEY WEST." As regards borrowing lines from other sources, Liu says, "T.S. Eliot said something to the effect that good poets borrow, great poets steal. I've always taken that to be a challenge and so I steal plenty — just discreetly."

The following is an excerpt from Steven's "THE IDEA OF ORDER AT KEY WEST" that ends with Liu's deleted line:

> For she was the maker of the song she sang.
> The ever-hooded, tragic-gestured sea
> Was merely a place by which she walked to sing.
> Whose spirit is this? we said, because we knew
> It was the spirit that we sought and knew
> That we should ask this often as she sang.
>
> If it was only the dark voice of the sea
> That rose, or even colored by many waves;
> If it was only the outer voice of sky
> And cloud, of the sunken coral water-walled,
> However clear, it would have been deep air,
> The heaving speech of air, a summer sound
> Repeated in a summer without end
> And sound alone. But it was more than that,

6)  Re. 16th Paragraph: "garbage strewn across hallway just outside her apartment door"

Liu said this image was based on the real-life event which caused his mother to become institutionalized.


7)  Re. 17th Paragraph: "went over twice a week to water her plants"

"This was a lie.  My mother never had plants," Liu said.  "I cut it because sometimes it's stronger to tell the truth."


8) Re. 19th Paragraph: "that day in junior high when I was called from class"

"My mother tried to kill herself when I was in tenth grade.  After we returned from the hospital, I had a canker.  In real life, I was in high school.  I made the incident based on junior high to make the protagonist younger, so that the episode would be more horrible; otherwise, I could have seemed more competent than I was," said Liu.


9) Re. 25th to 28th Paragraphs:  "That night there was a canker in the back of my throat. I couldn't eat for days. My father opened cans of a protein drink he'd brought home from the hospital. *Drink this.  Now sleep.  Good*"

"My father really gave me this drink in real life, a drink called 'Ensure'," Liu recalled, then joked as he pretended to hold up an invisible drink, "I should do a commercial:  *Drink Ensure!*"


10) Re. 35th Paragraph:  "There are no photographs of you when you were young"

"This is a true image. My mother disliked me so much that she had no photos of me around the house.  My older brother had all these photos and the only photo of a younger me is when I was three months old.  I used to think it was because I was the second born and all the novelty had worn off (in taking photos of the brothers as young children).  But Dad told me later that my mother hated me so much, and it was Dad who took that one photo of me.  I was an unwanted child, unexpected.  When I was born and after I was cleaned up, my mother didn't even want to hold me," Liu said.

Liu also considers the word, "you," to have a double reference: "It refers to the protagonist but also to my mother who didn't like to be photographed."


11) "Re. 40th paragraph: "I wanted her in the earth, her ashes contained"

"I wanted her dead, cremated like the letters burned," said Liu, referring to the sixth paragraph.  Liu, however, says in the sixth paragraph that after the letters are burned, the ashes were not "extinguished entirely."


12) Re. 42nd and 43rd paragraphs

While reviewing the 42nd paragraph, Liu said he realized something for the first time: that he had "silenced" his mother in "VOX ANGELICA" whereas he had allowed her a voice in "CANKER."

"In a dysfunctional family, parents have voices and the kids are silenced. So when I gave voices to my parents — as I did in "CANKER" — this was a gesture of love," said Liu. In the final draft of "CANKER," the 42nd paragraph depicts the mother saying, "Your father lies. Please God, don't hurt your mother. You were always so difficult, crying, crying. I couldn't shut you up. You didn't want my milk. Only your father. How could I live with myself?" (In contrast, Liu had deleted lines in "VOX ANGELICA" that discussed his mother's viewpoint — see below.)

The poem ends with the protagonist saying, "Mother, nothing heals completely as long as I stay alive." It was noted that in the earlier version (featured above), the protagonist characterizes this ending sentence as "words of love." Though he later deleted the description, Liu didn't dispute the initial characterization, saying, "Love is both painful and beautiful."


F)      Final Draft


**CANKER**


The wound would not heal for days. But that was nothing compared to my mother who ran her mouth all over my body.

What people will do to be remembered.

The nurses cutting roses from the cards I sent have put them in a tub of scalding water, the kisses have come undone.

Stamps are all she can save, arranging them in a book like the photographs she could never take.

I have managed to piece together the pages she tore away from me. Though the box of letters burned, the ashes were not entirely extinguished.

The day after Christmas break my father was driving me back to school, the two-lane highway on fire, everything falling.

To me their divorce was never final, only a precarious extension, a bridge I had learned to walk between two cliffs.

Of course we had a great distance to go, taking our turns at the wheel. My father never had a steady foot, only a start-stop rhythm that burned more gas than I thought we would have before reaching

the next station. But we would make it. It was belief that kept us at each other's throats.

I remember blood on the dining room floor and a few drops down his cheek when I broke a chair over his back. It wasn't damaged beyond repair, but it was put away in the attic.

And I thought, if only Mother knew. The county had already locked her up for the first time that year: her neighbors had complained about sacks of garbage she threw from her balcony into the swimming pool below.

I still can hear her voice that day in junior high when I was called out of class. She said to me in the backseat,

*Love me, let me die,*

her head bobbing in my lap, floating in its pool of chemicals. The woman who couldn't get in to clean drove us to the emergency room.

*Let me die.*

That's all I heard when I broke into her bedroom, the pills scattered on the floor like a broken necklace.

She lived. That night there was a canker in the back of my throat. I couldn't eat for days. My father opened cans of a protein drink he'd brought home from the hospital.

*Drink, this. Now sleep. Good.*

That was the first time I remember being held. I told my father at the end of our trip. I told him about the men who came into my life. The pain that made me feel alive.

My father wept as we swerved to the side of the road. Then he began to speak, stoking a bed of ashes that years could not put out:

*Your aunt wrote me while you had stayed with them, still a baby. You'd scream if your mother came into the room where you were being bathed. Her sister told her not to touch you but she did.*

I wanted this to stop. Why couldn't he stop her?

*There are no photographs of you then. She wouldn't have them in the house reminding her.*

My mother entered me with a kiss.

At Easter break, I flew on a half-empty plane into the eye of night I didn't bring her flowers, though I thought of how they would look on a grave.

I wanted her in the earth, her body contained.

Not floating down a river of fire. Not knowing the words she said to me that night would burn:

*Your father lies. Please God, don't hurt your mother. You were always so difficult, crying, crying. I couldn't shut you up. You didn't want my milk. Only your father. How could I live with myself?*

After we cried, I put out the light. I left her in that room. I closed the door behind me.

Tonight my roses bloom beside her bed, working their thorns into her lips, the words I never knew how to say:

*Mother, nothing heals completely as long as I stay alive.*

—∞—

## II.    VOX ANGELICA

Liu wrote "VOX ANGELICA" in the spring of 1990, at about the time he began therapy — a move that was triggered by problems he was experiencing in a personal relationship. However, Liu said, "My relationship was the catalyst but within a few weeks, the therapy became about my mother. And so that's how this poem got started."

Liu also was grappling with issues related to Mormonism and coming out of the closet. After a year, Liu stopped going to the therapist because he suspected that she was trying to prevent him from accepting his homosexuality as a healthy life style. When the therapist confirmed Liu's suspicions, he terminated therapy. "Still, I still found very useful all the work we did together surrounding my mother," he said. "The transference in the therapy was pretty strong, so 'VOX ANGELICA' is about my therapist. As I revised the poem, I realized that I was writing about my mother, too. The subject became a kind of composite figure."

Liu said he "stole" the title, "VOX ANGELICA," from the name of an art work by Max Ernst which was featured on the cover of his book. Subsequently, one of Liu's friends, the poet Daniel Hall, suggested that Liu call his book by the same name, rather than "UNDER PRESSURE," the title for the manuscript which was also his graduate thesis.

During this period where he was much "under pressure," Liu recalled he had a lot of dreams, some of which he would describe into tape recordings. "VOX ANGELICA" was birthed while Liu was in a car listening to tape recordings of his dreams. He was then inspired to create the poem by dictating it into the tape recorder as he continued to drive around Houston.

The following is a transcript of the tape Liu made of the poem. After each section, Liu's thoughts are presented.

A)  First Transcript of "Vox Angelica" From Audio Tape, 1990

1
In the tumulus hour, I sing
to a breeze that runs through the rafters,
a woman skinning a snake. She turns
but not enough for me to see her face.
In the sink, the peelings have begun to pile up
in a mound the color of dirt.

She hears the oil hissing on its own
and thinks of throwing something in —
ginger, garlic, chopped rings of green onion —
but doesn't, lets the oil brown
until the smoke rises
and fills the dark corners of the kitchen.
The birds tonight are louder than ever
flying under a river she has made
with a paring knife that falls so easily to her side.

Liu said he frequently remembers images of his mother cooking.  Other than the cooking
scene, he called everything else a symbol.  "The woman skinning a snake" is Freudian to me
because my mother was a castrating figure, a bitch," he recalled.  "I also liked the image of a 'fly-
ing fish' — like a dolphin.  This was important because it symbolized bringing together two
worlds, the spiritual and the material, the spiritual and the heavenly."


2
She turned to find me
but I was not there,
not in the half-light of dawn
nor in the multitude of stars.
They say death has a nobility of its own
but all she could hear was weeping —
it was not entirely a human sound
but a sound as if made by a machine
that played again and again in her mind
like a tape she could not erase.
On her way to the funeral, she remembered the dress
she had bought for another occasion
still zipped in a bag that smelled of cedar chips.
She could not keep her eyes on the road
with that hearse beside her, leaves
changing to a color she could no longer describe.
She tried to explain the sadness
of the roof on her house as warm as any mouth,
petrified wood from a holy forest.
How they had stood there, he chopping, she
watching pieces fly, recording
every scrap that fell from his lips.

"I later cut out the idea that this woman comes looking for me; somehow I felt that if she
weren't looking for me, then she would have a larger presence in the poem.  The gaze is only
one way — like in my poem, "PROLEGOMENON" that I read last night when I ask 'Mother, are
you listening?' and she isn't or can't," Liu said.
　　"The dress — that's my mother's wedding dress.  She used to keep her dress in a clothing

bag and fill it with moth balls. I thought cedar chips would be a nicer image. But what I was thinking of was that, somehow, her marriage was also a death for her. She had a master's degree in library science. And her whole life, she had tons of regret that she never had a real life because she got married. I think a lot of the guilt I felt came from that," he continued.

Liu smiled as he considered the ending of the stanza: "These are such bad lines but they are interesting to me," he said. "I was playing with the image of the roof of a mouth so that the sadness is also her house, which is also in her mouth — and the sadness is in her voice, but that she can't talk. Then you return to that chopping wood image because that petrified wood is her memories and she can't come to terms with her past. That's why so much of this poem is about my mother and grief."

Liu, however, subsequently deleted the lines referring to her mother's voice. During our interview when he read the early drafts of "VOX ANGELICA" and "CANKER," Liu realized something new — that while he had given his mother a voice (as an act of love) in "CANKER," he had silenced his mother in "VOX ANGELICA." Liu explained, "My anger came out in therapy and it was time for me to speak, not her!"

Liu was also surprised by the section's third from the last line, "How they had stood there, he chopping, . . ."

"The reference is a 'he' — wow! So the father then also participates in a kind of castrating action in cutting down all these trees," he said, surprised as he had forgotten about the original use of the male figure. "So, in some way, these trees — as phallic as these trees are — are actually (representing) a feminine versus masculine kind of force."


3

I must admit I have never attended a funeral
nor have I seen death
in any other form but a man stretched out
in someone else's vision.
How then can I tell you of this woman
who does not even see me,
as if some god
who had held her up by her strings for so long
finally let her go?
Is there atonement in what I have created?
Is the man she mourns lying
in a plot of ground that belongs to me?
I do not know his name
or what it would mean
if I whispered it into her ear.
Perhaps she would not hear me at all.


"There are some lines here that I adore, that if I were revising this poem again I would put back in," Liu said. "I love: 'How then can I tell you of this woman/ who does not even see me,/ as if some god/ who had held her up by her strings for so long/ finally let her go?' I'm sure I cut these lines because I couldn't make them work; I was thinking, could I really get away with this marionette image? A marionette is made of wood so there's some (relationship with) the trees."

Ultimately, Liu said he found the subject matter too difficult for him to manage to retain the lines. "What I couldn't deal with in this poem is that there's a woman searching for me and also that she couldn't see me. It was too hard for me to deal with," he recalled.

Liu added that he deleted the last line because he found it "too much of an echo of Eliot's LOVE SONG OF J. ALFRED PRUFROCK.' Eliot doesn't say these words but he asks this kind of question and that's why I got rid of it," he said.


4
The hour of the Bible is dead.
Neither dirt nor flowers
can keep the body warm enough.
She continues to keep her hands on the wheel
as if steadying herself
the way that silence holds each word in place,
a stranger standing beside the road
neither smiling nor waving.
She cuts the engine, but he is gone.
A car without plates, a voice
in the woods gone wild in her mind,
two lovers lying down
as earth is sprinkled over their eyes,
their mouths filling with dirt.
This is heaven, she thinks, to speak in a tongue that no one,
not even God, can understand.

"If I were to bring back that marionette image, I'd retain these words I've always liked, 'a voice in the woods gone wild in her mind.' I think I lost something by getting rid of those words," Liu said. "A lot of this poem I cut because the ideas are good but the language is not efficient — clumsy. Though I love what I was saying, for example, 'This is heaven, she thinks, to speak in a tongue that no one,/ not even God can understand.' "


5
There are always more birds singing
on the other side of the window,
night a black cat sitting on my chest,
claws extended toward my face,
the scar on my shoulder
a witness to the place
where the world had once been opened,
muscle and blood. Last night,
a man in a blue suit winked at me
between the marble urinals,
his suit turning gold,

stiletto at my throat.

My castrati scream reached two worlds

on both sides of the glass.

Everything happened twice

in the cat's eyes,

the slow engine of happiness

seducing me back to sleep.

"I remember going through the poem and deleting the words, 'Last night, a man in a blue suit winked at me/ between the marble urinals,/ his suit turning gold,/ stiletto at my throat.' I felt this scene didn't belong. I wanted the mother to be the central figure," Liu said. "I also deleted 'My castrati scream reached two worlds' because I wanted to deal with it in a more subtle way."

6

The words I speak I cannot revise.

All art is an afterthought.

An attempt to interpret a dream

that by nature is perfected,

the bed unmade, and me almost late

to my next appointment where more of me

must get cut out. The horror

of getting beyond the skin,

the small white abberation that I dreamed

would not grow back, not enlarge

to fill my entire conscious body.

Bly said the mystics read

by the light of their own bodies.

What a world of darkness that must have been

to read by the flaming hearts

turning into heaps of ash on the altar,

how everything in the end is made

equal by the wind.

"I deleted Bly because he didn't belong; the poem doesn't rely on contemporary time — it should be more timeless," Liu said. With a laugh he added, "Plus, I'm competitive; I didn't want to give credit to Bly." In the final draft of the poem, Liu changed this line to "I think of how the mystics read."

Liu dedicated "VOX ANGELICA" to James who had introduced Liu to Bly. "He showed me two of Bly's books, *A LITTLE BOOK ON THE HUMAN SHADOW* and *LEAPING POETRY: AN IDEA WITH POEMS AND TRANSLATIONS,*" Liu says. "Both books deal with the Jungian idea of shadows which was very influential on me. Jung defines the shadow as 'every part of ourselves that we consciously disown.' To retrieve this shadow is to free up vital energies that we use to repress the shadow."

7

The water beads

on my feverish face.

It dissipates

in the room, flying

upward to God

as I cling

to the shoulders of death,

my feet touching

neither heaven

nor earth.

For the poem's Final Draft, Liu deleted section #7 but moved its thoughts to the second section into which the seventh section "grafts nicely." Liu made the change because he wanted to end with the sixth section. The sixth section's last lines resonate beyond the end of of its words, "What a world of darkness that must have been/ to read by the flaming hearts/ turning into heaps of ash on the altar,/ how everything in the end is made/ equal by the wind."

B) Changes Made To Reflect The Draft Published in the Book, *Vox Angelica*

**VOX ANGELICA**

~~1~~

~~In the tumulus hour,~~ I sing [Del L] to a breeze that runs through the rafters ~~;~~ .

~~a~~ A woman ~~skinning~~ skins a snake. She turns

but not enough for me to see her face.

In the sink, the peelings have begun to pile up

in a mound the color of dirt.

She hears the oil hissing on its own

and thinks of throwing something in —

ginger, garlic, chopped rings of green onion —

but doesn't, lets the oil brown

until the smoke rises

and fills the dark corners of the kitchen.

The birds tonight are louder than ever

~~flying under~~ perched beside a river ~~she has made~~ of flying fish.

~~with a paring knife that falls so easily to her side.~~

~~2~~ *

~~She turned to find me~~

~~but I was not there,~~

~~not in the half light of dawn~~

~~nor in the multitude of stars.~~

The sweat on her feverish face

dissipates, flying upward
to God as she clings to the shoulders
of death, her feet touching
neither heaven nor earth.
They say death has a nobility of its own
but all she could hear was weeping —
~~it was~~ not entirely a human sound
but a sound as if made by a machine
that played again and again ~~in her mind~~
like a tape she could not erase.
~~On her way to the funeral, she remembered the dress~~
~~she had bought for another occasion~~
~~still zipped in a bag that smelled of cedar chips.~~
~~She could not keep her eyes on the road~~
~~with that hearse beside her, leaves~~
~~changing to a color she could no longer describe.~~
She tried to explain the sadness ,
the leaves changing to a color
she could no longer describe.
~~of the roof on her house as warm as any mouth,~~
~~petrified wood from a holy forest.~~
~~How they had stood there, he chopping, she~~
~~watching pieces fly, recording~~
~~every scrap that fell from his lips.~~


~~3~~ *
~~I must admit I have never attended a funeral~~
~~nor have I seen death~~
~~in any other form but a man stretched out~~
~~in someone else's vision.~~
~~How then can I tell you of~~ How can I love ~~this woman~~
~~who does not even see me,~~
~~as if some god~~ who held her
~~who had held up by her strings for so long~~
~~finally let her go?~~
~~Is there atonement in what I have created?~~
~~Is the man she mourns lying~~
~~in a plot of ground [New L] that belongs to me?~~
~~I do not know his name~~
~~or what it would mean~~
~~if I whispered it into her ear.~~
~~Perhaps she would not hear me at all.~~


4 *
The hour of the Bible is dead.
Neither dirt nor flowers

98

can keep ~~the~~ <u>her</u> body warm enough.

<u>Driving from the service,</u>

~~She continues to keep~~ ~~she keeps her~~ <u>I keep my</u> hands on the wheel

as if steadying ~~herself~~ <u>myself</u>

the way ~~that~~ silence holds each word in place ~~;~~ <u>.</u>

~~a~~ <u>A</u> stranger ~~standing~~ ~~stands~~ ~~beside the road~~

~~neither smiling nor waving.~~

~~She cuts the engine , but~~ <u>and</u> ~~he is gone.~~

~~A car without plates, a voice~~

~~in the woods gone wild in her mind,~~

~~two lovers she thinks of lying down~~ ~~next to him~~

<u>I imagine lying down next to her</u>

as earth is sprinkled over ~~their~~ <u>our</u> eyes,

~~their~~ <u>our</u> mouths fillling with dirt.

~~This is heaven, she thinks, to speak in a tongue that no one,~~

~~not even God, can understand.~~


~~5~~ <u>*</u>

~~There are always more~~ <u>The</u> ~~birds~~ angels are ~~always~~ singing

~~on the other~~ ~~cold~~ ~~side of the window,~~

<u>in the shadows of the house,</u>

night a black cat sitting on my chest,

claws extended toward my face,

the scar on my ~~shoulder~~ <u>body</u> [Del L]

[New L]a witness [New L] [Del L] to ~~the~~ <u>that</u> place ~~on my body~~

~~where the world had once been opened,~~

~~muscle and blood. Last night,~~

~~a man in a blue suit winked at me~~

~~between the marble urinals,~~

~~his suit turning gold,~~

~~stiletto at my throat.~~

~~My castrati scream reached two worlds~~

<u>where the world</u>

[New L] had once been opened, [Del L]muscle

[New L] and blood. How a vision

pinned me down ~~to the bed~~ [Del L] until my scream

[New L] reached two worlds

on both sides of the glass.

Everything happened twice

in the cat's eyes,

the slow engine of happiness

seducing me back to sleep.


~~6~~ <u>*</u>

The words I speak I cannot revise.

All art is an afterthought ~~:~~ <u>.</u>

~~An~~ <u>an</u> attempt to interpret a dream
that by <u>its</u> nature is perfected,
the bed unmade, and me almost late
to my next appointment where more of me
must get cut out.  The horror
of getting beyond the skin,
the small white abberation that I dreamed
would not grow back, not enlarge
to fill my entire conscious body.
~~Bly~~ <u>I think of how</u> ~~said~~ the mystics read
by the light of their own bodies.
What a world of darkness that must have been
to read by the flaming hearts
~~turning~~ <u>that turn</u> into heaps of ash on the altar,
how everything in the end is made
equal by the wind.


~~7~~ <u>*</u>
~~The water beads sweat~~
~~on my feverish face .~~
~~It dissipates~~
~~in the room, flying~~
~~upward to God~~
~~as I cling~~
~~to the shoulders of death,~~
~~my feet touching~~
~~neither heaven~~
~~nor earth.~~


*(N.B. The last stanza was deleted as Liu moved  its thoughts to the second stanza of the*
*Final Draft.)*


<u>C)  The Draft As Published in *Vox Angelica*</u>


**VOX ANGELICA**

I sing to a breeze that runs through the rafters.
A woman skins a snake.  She turns
but not enough for me to see her face.
In the sink, the peelings have begun to pile up
in a mound the color of dirt.
She hears the oil hissing on its own
and thinks of throwing something in —
ginger, garlic, chopped rings of green onion —

but doesn't, lets the oil brown
until the smoke rises
and fills the dark corners of the kitchen.
The birds tonight are louder than ever
perched beside a river of flying fish.

*

The sweat on her feverish face
dissipates, flying upward
to God as she clings to the shoulders
of death, her feet touching
neither heaven nor earth.
They say death has a nobility of its own
but all she could hear was weeping —
not entirely a human sound
but a sound as if made by a machine
that played again and again
like a tape she could not erase.
She tried to explain the sadness,
the leaves changing to a color
she could no longer describe.

*

The hour of the Bible is dead.
Neither dirt nor flowers
can keep her body warm enough.
Driving from the service,
I keep my hands on the wheel
as if steadying myself
the way silence holds each word in place.
I imagine lying down next to her
as earth is sprinkled over our eyes,
our mouths filling with dirt.

*

The angels are singing
in the shadows of the house,
night a black cat sitting on my chest,
claws extended toward my face,
the scar on my body
a witness to that place where the world
had once been opened, muscle
and blood.  How a vision
pinned me down until my scream
reached two worlds
on both sides of the glass.

Everything happened twice
in the cat's eyes,
the slow engine of happiness
seducing me back to sleep.


    *

The words I speak I cannot revise.
All art is an afterthought,
an attempt to interpret a dream
that by its nature is perfected,
the bed unmade, and me almost late
to my next appointment where more of me
must get cut out.  The horror
of getting beyond the skin,
the small white abberation that I dreamed
would not grow back, not enlarge
to fill my entire conscious body.
I think of how the mystics read
by the light of their own bodies.
What a world of darkness that must have been
to read by the flaming hearts
that turn into heaps of ash on the altar,
how everything in the end is made
equal by the wind.


Since *Vox Angelica* was published in 1992, Liu said that at poetry readings he often reads "VOX ANGELICA" differently from the version published in the book.  He either omits the fourth section entirely or replaces the word, "scream," with "dream" in the fourth section so that the revised lines would be ". . . How a vision/ pinned me down until my dream/ reached two worlds/ on both sides of the glass."  After reading the poem out loud a number of times, Liu said he felt, " 'Scream' is so melodramatic!  Our reading voices often make good editors."

—⁓—

**III.      THE ROAD TO SEDER**

Liu chose "THE ROAD TO SEDER" to illustrate his process in writing a short poem, but his process is not necessarily different from writing a long poem.  His primary focus remains the same: lyricism.  When asked whether he has a view on long versus short poems, Liu replied, "Charles Simic says every American poet's secret ambition is to write an epic poem.  But how? For me, in lyrical sections, the way I read (Emily) Dickinson's *COLLECTED POEMS* as a kind of epic."

Liu wrote "THE ROAD TO SEDER" at the same time that he wrote the other poems for the book, *Vox Angelica,* but held back on its publication to continue developing it; the poem appears in *Burnt Offerings.*  Liu began writing the poem while he was taking a Bible literature class at Brigham Young University.

"The Mormons feel that Judaism is the closest religion to Mormonism because, in some ways, the God Jehovah that the Jews are awaiting is the same Christ the Mormons are looking for to come again. So, for this Bible literature class, one of the events we had at the end of the year was the Seder feast — the Passover feast. Part of the story of Seder is to leave one chair vacant so that Elijah, the prophet, can come back and join the feast," Liu said. "For me, that became this idea of, what if Seder was not a feast but a location — a destination to get to. In my mind, when I was writing the poem, I kept thinking, what if you're waiting for God to come take that chair. And what if that chair is always empty?"

Liu's questions reflected what he was experiencing at the time, including ultimately giving up on Mormonism. "If there is no God, then religion is only a pair of crutches. There's also the image of a wheelchair of fire, apocalyptic but handicapped. Rather than there being some God enthroned, there is no God which is the handicap and, hence, the chariot broken down.

A)  First Holograph

**~~ELIJAH~~ ON THE ~~WAY~~ <u>ROAD</u> TO SEDER ~~CARRIED AWAY~~**

You showed me how my legs could carry me
a little further, to the sign of water.
It was then I noticed your legs were broken,
that if I moved, it would be away from you.
We cried, *Lord have mercy on the souls that thirst!*
An angel appeared in a black robe. We ~~could see~~ <u>saw</u>
the hump on his back where the wings were tucked,
~~the white~~ <u>not the white</u> parachute ~~now~~ falling where the wings were tucked,
as though we were being carried away in a cloud
the throne of God was a wheelchair of fire.
There was no God, only a pair of crutches left
behind, as though our presence had inspired him
~~or~~ frightened him. A long way off, the sun
continued to turn in its vast confusion
unable to penetrate the cloud layer where millions
of seeds were floating above the highest mountains,
~~like~~ <u>whose</u> abandoned ~~God~~ <u>ark</u> __ driftwood for the *furnace/oven/fire*.

Liu recalled that the "You" in the first line originally referred to someone with whom he was having romantic problems. "But I also wanted the 'Beloved' to be God — the ultimate Beloved. The poem pleads, *Lord have mercy on the souls that thirst!*" I wanted the reference to God to show that there was a much larger issue here than just a dumb love affair — that there was a larger hunger."

In the seventh and eighth lines, Liu said he was trying to conjure up the concept of the "negative angel" by recalling "deformed or un-beautiful things" like the hunchback of Notre Dame or the Greek god of fire, Hephaestus. Hephaestus was said to be born to the gods Zeus and Hera. One account says Hephaestus was thrown by Zeus from heaven to earth because Hera bore him without Zeus' consent. Hephaestus was lamed from the fall. Another account says that

Hera threw him down from heaven because he was already lame. Hephaestus also was a master craftsman and, at one point, built a throne for Hera. But when Hera sat on the throne, the throne bound her and she was unable to leave. Hephaestus refused to return to Olympus until Dionysus (god of wine) made him drunk and then took him back to heaven where he was forced to free Hera. Unlike Apollo who rides his chariot through the skies, Hephaestus makes his art by staying close to the earth.

Liu noted that the image of the "white parachute" was probably also inspired by his sky-diving experiences from a year before he wrote the poem, an event which ended up with Liu limping away from a field with a sprained ankle.

"*To be carried away in a cloud* alludes to the Mount of Transfiguration in the New Testament. On the mountain, Christ, Moses and Elijah give the promised keys of the priesthood to Peter, James and John," Liu said. "So I was thinking that if there is no God, then only the para-chute can save us — the parachute as a real thing, not visions."

B) Changes Made Between First Holograph and Final Draft

**~~ON~~ THE ROAD TO SEDER**

~~You showed me~~ how my legs ~~could~~ would have to carry me [Del L]
~~a little~~ further ~~,~~ [New L] to the sign of water. [Del L]
~~It was then I noticed your legs were broken,~~
~~that if I moved, it would be away from you.~~
~~We cried, Lord have mercy on the souls that thirst!~~
[Del L] An angel appeared [New L] in a black robe. There were no wings. ~~We saw~~
~~the hump on his back where the wings were tucked,~~
only a parachute closing all around us
as though we were being carried way in a cloud
[New P] the throne of God was a wheelchair of fire.
There was no God, only a pair of crutches ~~left~~
~~behind, as though our presence had inspired him~~
~~frightened him~~. thrown down. A long way off, the sun
continued to turn in its vast confusion
~~unable to penetrate the cloud layer where millions~~
~~of seeds were floating above the highest mountains,~~
~~whose abandoned ark __ (?) driftwood for the furnace/ oven/ fire.~~
a spiral of souls floating past the mountain.

The endings differ significantly between the first holograph and the final draft. Liu recalled that he held back from including the poem in *Vox Angelica* because he didn't think the original ending — "whose abandoned ark __ driftwood for the *furnace/oven/fire*" — worked. He later changed the ending after a visit to the Smith Art Museum (Smith College in Northampton).

"I was looking at engravings by William Blake with Linda Gregg. There was this one image of a wonderful vortex of spirits in a kind of plume floating upward. That image came to me later in this poem as the right image. I found that image beautiful and I liked the sound of the language: 'a spiral of souls floating past the mountain'."

He continued, "Also, I'm not well-read with mysticism, but I know that the spiral is a very fundamental image of the beginning of the galaxy. It felt right. Are these souls afloat and adrift in the universe, floating past the mountain? Does that mean that we're floating past the mountain and making it to somewhere heavenly? I think it's a poem that somehow affirms godliness even as it denies it. The affirmation comes when the poem says 'the sun/ continued to turn' — that the universe continues to turn. And, 'sun" is also 'SON' so that it doesn't matter how confused we are, godliness is always going to be here."

C) Final Draft:

## THE ROAD TO SEDER

How my legs would have to carry me further
to the sign of water. An angel appeared
in a black robe. There were no wings,
only a parachute closing all around us
as though we were being carried away in a cloud.

The throne of God was a wheelchair of fire.
There was no God, only a pair of crutches
thrown down. A long way off, the sun
continued to turn in its vast confusion,
a spiral of souls floating past the mountain.

—⁂—

Some of Liu's papers — including journals, drafts of poems, correspondence and early poetry collections (published and unpublished) — have been acquired by The New York Public Library's Berg Collection. Among those papers is Liu's April 1991 thesis for his M.A. degree which contains "CANKER," "VOX ANGELICA" and "THE ROAD TO SEDER." In the thesis' preface, Liu wrote:

Language is a kind of seduction. Like a vision of angels, it catches us by surprise. Then we are left to wrestle with it until it gives us what we want. We are the willing virgins transformed into harlots time after time. The maidenhead heals, only to be rent again, like a veil that shrouds the Holy of Holies. So we are officiating priests *and* the fitting sacrifices under the eyes of God. We look up and the sky becomes a mirror clouded over with His breath. Language is the face that gradually appears to us. We talk to it. It talks back. In making what is private public, we learn the art of revealing our secrets to the world.

As a freshman at UCLA, I read Sylvia Plath's *Ariel* and grew increasingly exhilirated and disturbed. What possessed her to commit those words to paper, to leave *that* testament? Later, my pantheon would enlarge to make room for others: Milton, Blake, Hopkins,

Yeats, Whitman, Dickinson, Frost, Stevens and Crane. How could I ever write with those voices in the world? Yet I refused to become paralyzed. Instead, horizons expanded. I accepted the quest, searching for answers to questions that continue to haunt me: What kinds of pressure were they under? What was it that really *bothered* them?

The poems in *Under Pressure* (title of Liu's thesis of poems) explore what bothers me. Not public issues, but private wounds that will not heal "as long as I stay alive." Scars are ugly enough. Why uncover them, examine them, reopen them? My father would frown whenever I dwelled too much on "the past." As if my life were not entitled to a history, unless it was a happy one. Or one that would not cast a dishonorable shadow on our family. I hardly existed at all, except to please others. When I couldn't please my parents any more, I turned to the Mormons, was even adopted into the House of Ephraim. However, neither time nor baptism would wash away the abuse I suffered at my mother's hands, or from my own emerging sexuality.

By my early twenties, I had learned how to repress a great deal. Although I had served a faithful mission in Hong Kong from 1984 to 1986, I returned to a double life of attending temples and paying tithes to the bishop on the one hand, while fornicating in "tea rooms" on the BYU campus on the other. Not knowing who I was or what I wanted made it difficult to get at my poetry. I reached a point where I could no longer deny my existence for the sake of some other person or group. To do so meant not really living at all. When I first read Plath, she not only spoke to me of her pain but of my own suffering. But more than that, she told me a *secret* about my own condition that I was not even aware of. Because it was *her* poem, she was able to trick me and get past my defenses.

Language that gets past the defences is a key for writers *and* therapists. To unlock the doors that lead to the dusty rooms of the psyche. I do not mean to equate poetry with therapy. They both require hard work and a willingness to come to an increased self-knowledge, but confession alone is not art. Yet it can change our lives. There are many times when I just can't get to my poetry. So much of our lives are hidden, lived in denial. Yet like a landmine, what is hidden remains under pressure. Rage. Shame. Guilt. The grief of a lifetime. Of lifetimes. Who dares to clean out the active volcanos — *qui ramona soigneusment ses volcans en activité?* This is the business of poetry, a dangerous trade.

So the questions remained: how could I write with those other voices already in the world, under that pressure, that "anxiety of influence"? It is true many poets continue to direct workshops, but they seldom *deliver*. I needed deliverance. To wrestle an angel for a blessing. Charles Simic was such a mentor. When I met him last summer, it was necessary not simply to sit at his feet but to learn the secrets of the trade. What he gave me not only informs my own work but testifies to what *can be taught*. Here is an excerpt from the notes I took my first day in workshop:

> A tendency in American poetry is to be long-winded. Assumes the reader is not too bright. Everyone's secret ambition is to write the long poem. Poetry isn't one thing or the other. It's always in between. You start writing about your

grandma and a dog appears. Then you have to choose. If you write about the dog, the world of the grandmother will enter. Poems come into being by fooling around with the language and images that are on the page. The realization that could take years is "that's what the poem is about!" it's kind of like a chess problem. There's a mistake here. It's just fucked up. The phone rings and you leave it. Then one day, you see the move through what Nabokov calls "a splendid insincerity." Another thing. The paucity of figurative language. The advantage of a terrific figure of speech is that it's the most beautiful thing in the world. The problem of overwriting and the lack of figurative language is connected. Experience is usually not interesting — it doesn't translate immediately into poetry. Poets will tell you the abuse that each has received for excessive metaphors, wildness, outrageousness. This is the risk. If you're making similes, it's safe to say, "my fingers are like breakfast sausages." You must take risks to have the great homiletic moment. To chicken out is to pay for it.

I join Simic in demanding a language that is strong enough to trick the psyche out of what it wants. The poem *is* smarter than the poet, if only the poet can trust words that invite the surreal and the real, the violent and the ordinary. Such language may be from this world or another. Mystery enters poetry as an uninvited guest enters a house. It is an arrival that comes to us when we sit long enough at the edge of a forest.

What am I after in my poetry? To find my way home through "lies and lullabies." My mother never sang to me. Nothing will ever change that. I don't want pity. I want to know my own grief. Wound speaks to wound. It is the "never ending work of grief" that has opened me up to others. It takes a lifetime to know the difference between craft and necessity, between knowledge and salvation. It has something to do with taking a long walk without knowing where we are going, with being seduced by language.

*Seduced by language?* Perhaps, but notwithstanding the "desecrated battleground" that underlies Liu's poetry, notwithstanding craft's "long walk without knowing where we are going," Liu concludes each battle with poems in whose craft a healing occured. Liu's poetry reveals that Liu mastered language as much as he was seduced by it. He did find his way to changing his manuscript's title from "UNDER PRESSURE" to "VOX ANGELICA." *Vox Angelica* — Latin for an angelic voice. Such is the nature of Liu's poetic redemption — whether Liu is the fallen angel remaining earth-bound, or attempting an ascent, Liu sings.

# LI YOUNG LEE

A 1995 Lannan Poetry Awardee, Li Young Lee has published two poetry books, *The City In Which I Love You* (BOA Editions, 1990), which won the 1990 Lamont Poetry Selection of the Academy of American Poets); and *Rose* (BOA Editions, 1986), which won New York University's Delmore Schwartz Memorial Poetry Award.  He also wrote a memoir, *The Winged Seed* (Simon & Schuster, 1995), which won an American Book Award from the Before Columbus Foundation.  A recipient of numerous grants and fellowships from the Guggenheim, National Endowment of Arts, Mrs. Giles Whiting Foundation, Illinois Arts Council and The Commonwealth of Pennsylvania, his poetry has been included in the *American Poetry Review* as well as *The Pushcart Prize VIII and IX and XI.*

In response to the question, "What advice would you give to a young poet?" Li Young Lee responds,

> The writing of poetry is a sacred endeavor and to never forget that.  So that even if the world doesn't find it marketable or translatable into coarse values, keep in mind that the writing of poetry creates soulful values, subtle values.  And remember, never lose heart; realize how important your work is.  It occurs to me that everything valuable is invisible, like love.  The creation of art is invisible and subtle.

# Li Young Lee's *Universe-Mind* — A Search For The Soul

*If someone were to ask me: why do we pray, why do we fast, why do we all perform our devotions and good*
*works, why are we baptized, why did God, the All-Highest, take on our flesh? — then I would reply: in order*
*that God may be born in the soul and the soul be born in God.*
*— from "Selected German Sermons" by Meister Eckhart (1)*

*One day, when this terrifying vision's vanished,*
*let me sing ecstatic praise to angels saying yes!*
*Let my heart's clear-struck keys ring and not one*
*fail because of a doubting, slack, or breaking string.*
*Let my streaming face make me more radiant,*
*my tiny tears bloom.  And then how dear*
*you'll be to me, you nights of anguish.*
*— from "Duino Elegies: The Tenth Elegy" by Rainer Maria Rilke (2)*

In 1994, the Art Institute of Chicago released a collection of writers responding to works in the museum's permanent collection.  Titled *Transforming Vision* (A Bulfinch Press Book, Little, Brown and Company, 1994), the collection was edited by Edward Hirsch and included Li Young Lee's poem, "The Father's House."  Lee's poem was inspired by an installation of sixteen paintings titled "Corban Ephphatha I" (1991-1992) by his brother, Li-Lin Lee.  However, the poem was published before Lee finished it.

Indeed, four years later, Lee is still working on "The Father's House."  Still, this isn't unusual for Lee.  He has said(3) that it required seven years to write his 1995 memoir, *The Winged Seed*, and that he could have kept on writing it but he had to meet Simon and Schuster's publishing deadlines.  Similarly, when Lee told Hirsch that "The Father's House" was not yet finished, Lee says Hirsch replied, "Listen, I know how you work.  Just send me the poem you have and you just keep on working on it."

Consequently, Lee concludes, "It's inconvenient: publishing."

Rather, Lee is focused on a never-ending search for the answer to a question that he concedes may be unanswerable: *What is the "fateful form" of a poem?*

"The fateful form — I used to think there must be an inevitable form, like (Ezra) Pound's idea of a magnet driving all the filings to it.  When I sit down to write a poem, it's as if I end up in some metaphysical space. There's some sort of magnetic field I'm entering and the feeling there should be in a form that I couldn't have written it any other way.  It had to be said that way.  But everytime I sit down, it comes out differently and I'm beginning to wonder if there is such a thing as this inevitable form."

In his essay, "The Wisdom of Poetry," Pound wrote, "The Art of Poetry consists in combining these 'essential to thought', these dynamic particles, *si licet*, this radium, with that melody of words which shall most draw the emotions of the hearer toward accord with their import, and with that 'form' which shall most delight the intellect."(4)

For Lee, however, the prosodial manifestations change significantly with each sitting, with no indication as to whether he is getting closer to the poem's "fateful form."  As he does for many poems, Lee says he ruminated for some time about "The Father's House" before beginning to write the poem.  He wrote three separate drafts of this poem, handing over the third draft to Hirsch for *Transforming Vision.*  He says he recalls reading the published poem in the book and thinking that perhaps one of the other versions was better.  But that quickly became irrelevant as he continued to work on the poem.

"This is how I am with my art. I'm like a cow chewing its cud. Finally, I'd sit down and write some passages and then I'd forget about them. But of course I don't really forget. My unconscious is thinking of them and then they might choose to assert themselves and surface and I'd yield myself to them once more. So much of writing the poem is allowing things to happen and my ability to read my own interior," he says.

Indeed, upon being reminded that "The Father's House" shared certain passages with his memoir, *The Winged Seed*, Lee notes, "If passages appear in *The Winged Seed*, I wasn't conscious of that at the time. Echoes (of "The Father's House") appear in it because I'm dealing all the time with 'the inevitable form' — but I don't know anymore if that exists. I don't even know if the passages fit more in the poem or the memoir."

The following presents some examples of lines from "The Father's House" and "echoes" of them in passages from *The Winged Seed* as Lee went through his search for the "fateful form":

I.

From the poem:

But when she lies down
at night, in the room of our arrival, she'll know

I called her, though she won't answer, who is on her way
to sleep, until morning, which even now,

is overwhelming, the woman combing her hair
opposite the direction of my departure.

From the memoir:

If it is a morning glory seed, you hold both the flower and where the flower closes at evening, where another country begins, and double doors open toward us, the seam of their parting widening to vanquish utter margins unto the first day: Noon, a woman is dressing for our journey together, combing her hair opposite the direction of our arrival. Her name appears in ledgers of ships whose masts have long passed out of view, dispelling any rumor of a horizon or setting sun.

II.

From the poem:

And only now and then do I lean at a jamb
to see if I can see what I thought I heard.

I heard her ask, My love, why can't you sleep?

From the memoir:

How many nights have I lain here like some drowned cabin of a ship through whose portals fish big and small swim in and out in the dominion of the octopus and clam, and allowed myself to remain an unguarded room, open to thoughts coming and going, passing head to toe, no single thought as shapely as the course of a various thinking, no one idea as grave as this dark traffic, in whose current I drift, wondering, Did I close the windows downstairs? What time is it? Is the basement flooding? Did I put the garden shears away? Did I leave them in the rain to rust? Did I finish writing that letter to my father, or did I let the pencil fall from my hand? My love, why can't you sleep?

III.

From the poem:

I sweep all three floors of our father's house,
and I don't count the broom strokes; I row

up and down for nothing but love: his for me, and my own
for the threshold, . . .

           Meanwhile, I hear the voices
of women telling a story in the round,

so I sit down on a rain-eaten stoop, by the saltgrasses,
and go on folding the laundry I was folding,

the everyday clothes of our everyday life,

From the memoir:

I remember! It was Chicago. The blanket belonged to your twin sister, Denise. Our niece was there. I called her my little olive. And our sons. They were there, and while I lay there, staring up into a closet of stars, waiting for the streaks, traces of a far broom sweeping, you twin mothers and our children began to sing and tell by turns a story in the round, a story about a needle rowing all night, rowing over and under miles of garment. And when it arrived at the sea, it went on rowing and, arriving at the moon, found it to be no stone of boundary. It was a right-handed needle you sang about, singing thistle, linen, and gorse, sewing the fine and the coarse, sewing a garment for the seed. But what is a needle worth? A needle is only worth its one eye a seed may pass through, a seed that had no place to rest, a seed which, born flying, flew. Awake, my love, don't sleep. It's your birthday.

" 'The Father's House' has become, for me, a writing exercise," Lee says. "I keep coming back to it. Writing the poem is an unearthing thing. *Unearthing*. But everytime I sit down, . . ."

Lee's voice trails off, and I am struck by a sense that it is both easy and hard for Lee to discuss poetry. Yet this contradiction of ease and difficulty seems appropriate, given Lee's views: "Poetry is yogic. The word, 'yoga,' is a 'yoke,' a 'link,' or a 'connection.' The word 'religious' is linked to 'religion' and is a 'link' or 'connection.' So poetry is yogic: it's a connection to a universe-mind that is manifold, eternal yet temporal, double by nature, light and dark at the same time, spirit and matter, wave and particle — contradictions that are true and stay together. It is harmony in what appears to be chaos, a negotiation between harmony and chaos, a negotiation between order and disorder. Poetry is contradictions co-existing in harmony."

Consequently, Lee says, "I probably have ambitions about Art that I know may not be realistic. I keep posing questions."

It is the questioning process related to Lee's long search for the poem's "inevitable form." But when I offer that there may be no answers to his search, given how he views poetry as "contradictions co-existing in harmony," he agrees, "That's right. There are no answers. What comes back in response to my questions are poems. That's the 'problem' — the angst — of my poetry."

Thus, "The Father's House" has become a model for "unearthing" regardless of whether it ever will be finished. By "unearthing," Lee also means the "rebirth" required of a poet whenever the poet writes a new poem. "A new mind is what's required to make a new poem," Lee says. "A new poem requires new rooms for thought and feeling to circulate."

In "The Father's House," Lee envisions each stanza or couplet as a room for generating feeling and thought. And because of Lee's views on poetry — a connection to the "universe-mind" with all its contradictions — the poem's couplets move across time and references with some of the incidents seemingly unrelated, such as the "father walk(ing) through his church at night and (set)ing all the clocks for spring," the inexplicable appearance of a woman, two brothers reading to each other and the poem's "I" sweeping the floors, folding laundry and listening to women tell stories.

"In the poem, the rooms don't have boundaries but play with the fudging of boundaries — that's what I find hopeful about it," Lee says.

In a related manner, the words "seed" and "night" resonate for Lee and find their way into "The Father's House," as they do in his other works. When asked why he finds the two words so meaningful, he says, "I don't know. But I'll venture something: it seems to me that seed and night are the same word. One is so tiny and packed and the other is immense and without boundary. But because they're opposite, they're the same. I feel they're the same because the infinite can be so small — like (William) Blake's seeing the universe in a grain of sand."

Lee's theme is repeated in Rainer Maria Rilke's "Duino Elegies" which he so admires, as in this excerpt:

And the night, oh the night when the wind
full of outer space gnaws at our faces; that wished for,
gentle, deceptive one waiting painfully for the lonely
heart — she'd stay on for anyone. Is she easier on lovers?
But they use each other to hide their fate.
You still don't understand? Throw the emptiness in
your arms out into that space we breathe; maybe birds
will feel the air thinning as they fly deeper into themselves.
**— from "Duino Elegies: The First Elegy"**

In addition, when looking at "Corban Ephphatha I," his brother's works that inspired "The Father's House," one sees a landscape that may be interpreted as manifesting the "universe-mind" — incorporating individual images (some fragmented, some whole), many of which have become symbolic, such as a chalice, a cross, a spiral evoking a cellular molecule, leaves, a bird, a sky, a mountain, all sorts of circles and, surely, seeds and night. The word, "Corban" means a sacrifice or offering to God among the ancient Hebrews, and Lee says that he is under the impression that the phrase, "Corban Ephphatha" is a phrase that Jesus Christ uttered whenever he healed people, that in healing the person Christ was offering "a gift of god to be opened."

Lee explains, "I think my brother and I would agree that Christ is a Supreme Artist — he is a poet, a visionary, a wild man who possessed the universe-mind and spoke from something deep within him. And we also would agree that Art is also a balm, a high form of healing."

Lee's brother, Li-Lin, says in an artist statement, ""The mind is like a powerful shark which moves at great speed through darkness voraciously consuming every experience since the time of its birth and storing it in a vast ancient warehouse. The mind stores everything automatically making no distinction between the actual and the imaginary. Everything is put through as in a funnel and catalogued; often in the form of abbreviated complete images with shape and color. What emerges at the other end of the funnel is a miraculous and new personal reality. A reality that changes its shape from moment to moment."

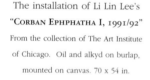

The installation of Li Lin Lee's
"CORBAN EPHPHATHA I, 1991/92"
From the collection of The Art Institute
of Chicago. Oil and alkyd on burlap,
mounted on canvas. 70 x 54 in.

*Changes its shape from moment to moment.* It evokes what Lee has concluded about the "inevitable" or "fateful" form -- or lack thereof -- of the poem.

"My brother and I talk a lot. He is never more himself than through his work. I am never more myself than through my poems. So when I see his paintings, I feel he's talking to me," Lee says. "When I look at his work, I see a plethora of images. He reminds me of someone who looks up at the night sky and sees thousands of constellations and not just one. I'd like to see that in my poetry -- that the heart is a star, the body is a star, the neck is a star, and each time you draw lines between them different constellations are formed.

"My brother's work is a grid of many paintings. It shows a large mind that he's trying to make a picture of. It's not a picture of a tree or of people but of a large mind. The longer he paints, the wider and more details are featured in his works. With my poetry, I also think of it as a picture of my mind, and I want that connection to a universe-mind."

Again, Lee refers to his concept of the "universe-mind, that which connects us to who we really are. If we remember who we are, the world would be better. If everyone walked around practicing divinity, we'd all be the better for it. How to remember divinity? Look at art, read a poem. Because art is the practice of the sacred, not the cultural event that I sometimes fear it's become."

Lee says he reads and revels in the sermons of 13th-century theologian Meister Eckhart, noting that he feels Eckhart's words are often applicable to poetry. The empathy is logical as Eckhart poses a complicated mindset related to Lee's notion of the "universe-mind." Scholar Oliver Davies has said about the 13th century thinker, "There is in Eckhart's system a complexity first of all of depth in that he explores many of the great technical themes of medieval theology, such as theory of analogy, metaphysics of the image, constitution of the human soul, epistemology (theory of knowledge) and ontology (theory of being). But there is in Eckhart's work no less a complexity of surface which results from his brilliant use of imagery and virtuosic ability to manipulate the forms and structures of language in order to communicate a metaphysical vision."

In addition, Davies has said that Eckhart's "primary perspective" is his "concept of unicity or oneness":

> A theology or philosophy of oneness has as its starting-point the belief that the ultimate principle of the universe is distinguished from all else by virtue of the fact that it is entirely one and undivided. All except this One is multiple, contingent and fractured. But, generally, the One is also understood to be in dynamic relation with the rest of the universe, which originates from it and which thus also 'looks back' to its source. The One is therefore everywhere present, since all exists only by reference to it, but it is also everywhere absent, since — for us — all objects of experience are multiple. The One alone is primal and permanent being (if indeed the term 'being' is attributable to it), while the being of all that is multiple shall inevitably decay. Redemption, . . . involves the ascent of the human mind away from the spheres of multiplicity and contingency back to a primal oneness which is grasped through an ecstasy of the mind. . . . Eckhart affirms that he does indeed find the notion of the One the most adequate way of speaking of God. . . . Oneness alone comes close to capturing something of God's essence in language, without clothing him in concepts which seem to owe more to our nature than to his.

About Lee's call for the practice of *divinity*, there is affirmation in what Eckhart has said about "divine virtues:"

> The effect of (God's) grace is to make the soul buoyant and responsive to all the works of God, for grace flows forth from the divine spring; it is a likeness of God that has the savour of God and makes the soul like God. Now when this grace and this savour enters the will, we call it love, and when this grace and savour enters our intelligence, we call it the light of faith. When the same grace and savour enters the irascible part, which is the dynamic power in us, then we call it hope. <u>That is why they are called the divine virtues, since they have divine effects in the soul, just as we can tell by the power of the sun that it quickens the earth, since it enlivens all things and sustains their being</u>.

That the two brothers share this sensibility is reflected, not only in the expansive landscape of
"Corban Ephatha I" but also, through another excerpt from Li-Lin Lee's artist's statement: "The
mind can also be a door to a place where we can see our self and discover our true origin. It is a
place where God is. That thingness at the core of all things. Painting is one of the most accessi-
ble and pure paths toward self realization for the painter and the viewer."

    *Self realization*, not just for the painter but also for the *viewer*. Similarly, Lee says the
poet's role is to "write silence. (With such silence), the poet is imparting the reader's true identity.
Poetry enacts out true identity."

    Once more, one sees empathy in Eckhart's sermons with Lee's attempts to "write silence"
— a view that may be captured by the poem's own title, "The Father's House." In one of his Latin
sermons, Eckhart wrote:

> My house is a house of prayer. Put the words in the following order: the house of prayer
> is my house. 'House' means freedom from passions. First note how far passion ranks
> below the soul according to its nature, . . . and thus how shameful it is to be in its power.
> Secondly, note the stillness of the soul. The reason for this is that the Word in which and
> through which and through whose descent into the soul the Father acts, is 'without
> sound', according to Augustine,' 'while everything preserved a deep silence', that is all
> that possesses being, life and knowledge. Therefore no hammer could be heard when
> the temple was being built.

The following presents the draft of "The Father's House" published in *Transforming Vision*:

## THE FATHER'S HOUSE

Here, as in childhood, Brother, no one knows us.
And someone has died, and someone is not yet

born, while our father walks through his church at night
and sets all the clocks for spring.  His sleeplessness

weighs heavy on my forehead, his death almost
nothing.  In the only letter he wrote to us

he says, *No one can tell how long it takes a seed*
*to declare what death and lightning told it*

*while it slept.  But stand at a window long enough,*
*late enough, and you may some night hear*

*a secret you'll tomorrow, parallel to the morning,*
*tell on a wide, white bed, to a woman*

*like a sown ledge of wheat.  Or you may never*
*tell it, who lean across the night and miles of the sea,*

*to arrive at a seed, in whose lamplit house*
*resides a thorn, or a wee man, carving*

*a name on a stone, at a fluctuating table of water,*
*the name of the one who has died, the name of the one*

*not born unknown.*  Someone has died.  Someone
is not yet born.  And during this black interval,

I sweep all three floors of our father's house,
and I don't count the broom strokes; I row

up and down for nothing but love: his for me, and my own
for the threshold, as well as for the woman's name

I hear while I sweep, as though she swept
beside me, a woman who, if she owns a face at all,

it is its own changing; and if I know her name
I know to say it so softly she need not

stop her work to hear me.  But when she lies down
at night, in the room of our arrival, she'll know

I called her, though she won't answer, who is on her way
to sleep, until morning, which even now,

is overwhelming, the woman combing her hair
opposite the direction of my departure.

And only now and then do I lean at a jamb
to see if I can see what I thought I heard.

I heard her ask, *My love, why can't you sleep?*
and answer, *Someone has died, and someone*

*is not yet born.* Meanwhile, I hear the voices
of women telling a story in the round,

so I sit down on the rain-eaten stoop, by the saltgrasses,
and go on folding the laundry I was folding,

the everyday clothes of our everyday life, the death
clothes wearing us clean to the bone, to the very

ilium crest, where my right hand, this hand, half
crab, part bird, has often come to rest on her,

whose name I know. And because I sat down,
I hear their folding sound, and know

the tide is rising early, and I can't hope
to trap their story told in the round. But the woman

whose name I know says, *Sleep*, so I lie down
on the clothes, the folded and unfolded, the life

and the death. Ages go by. When I wake, the story
has changed the firmament into domain, domain

into a house. And the sun speaks the day,
unnaming, showing the story, dissipating the boundaries

of the telling, to include the one who has died
and the one not yet born. Someone has died

and someone is not yet born. How still
this morning grows about the voice of one

child reading to another, how much a house

is house at all due to one room where an elder

child reads to his brother, and that younger
knows by heart the brother-voice.  How darker

other rooms stand, how slow morning comes, collected
in a name, told at one sill and listened for

at the threshold of dew.  What book is this we read
together, Brother, and at which window

of our father's house?  In which upper room?
We read it twice:  Once in two voices, to each

other; once in unison, to children,
animals, and the sun, our star, that vast office

of love, the one we sit in once, and read
together twice, the third time bosomed in

the future.  So birds may lend their church, sown
in air, realized in the body uttering

windows, growing rafters, couching seeds.

The poem's first two couplets relates closely to Lee's views on *ars poetica*.  The first couplet includes the phrase, "someone has died, and someone is not yet born."  The line, which Lee says was "a musical phrase that I kept hearing," is repeated (with minor modifications) four times throughout the poem.  Lee says he repeated the line for "grounding" since he was writing a long poem.  Equally important, he notes that the phrase evokes what he says about writing poetry: "Writing the poem entails a rebirth."

In the next couplet, there's a reference to "our father walks through his church at night/ and sets all the clocks for spring" — about which Eckhart says in another sermon:

I sometimes speak of two springs.  Even if it seems strange, we must nevertheless speak from our own understanding.  One spring, from which grace flows, is where the Father gives birth to his only-begotten Son; that same spring gives rise to grace and grace flows forth from it.  The second spring is where creatures flow out from God, and this is as far removed from that other spring, where grace emerges, as heaven is from earth.  Grace does not perform works.  Where fire is in its own nature, it cannot harm anything or set it on fire.  It is fire's heat which ignites things here on earth.  And even heat, where it exists in the nature of fire, cannot burn or harm anything.  Indeed, where heat exists in the nature of fire, it is as remote from the proper nature of fire as heaven is from earth.  Grace does not perform any works; it is too subtle for that and is as far from performing works as heaven is from earth.  An indwelling, an inhering and a union with God, that is what grace is and there 'God is with', for the words 'God is with you' immediately follow.

And that is where the birth occurs.

Rilke, too, has written about spring in a way with which Lee finds empathy:

And, oh, Spring would understand — the music
of your annunciation would echo everywhere.
First that tiny swell of questioning surrounded by
the purely affirmative day's magnifying stillness.
Then the calling-intervals, the rising steps up
to the future's dreamed-of temple; then the trill,
the fountain whose rising jet's already lured into
falling by the promise of play . . . And ahead of it, summer
**— *from "Duino Elegies: The Seventh Elegy"***

—ɯ—

How then does Lee poetically craft silence? To achieve the "numinous glow" of the "sacred"? To achieve the connection with the "universe-mind"?

On the surface, Lee's wish manifests itself through the poem's images from his everyday life. "Sometimes I'm thinking about where my actions reside in the context of harmony," he says. "And I'm sweeping, washing dishes, folding laundry, reading out loud to my sons. I'm not trekking on the silk road or doing some heroic things."

However, the poem is more than that narration of detail. Specifically, Lee considers his goal one of eliciting from the reader, "WOW!" Lee feels that his generation and the reader's response of "WOW!" is the connection with the "universe-mind."

"It's been said that narrative is background, that narrative and syntax are closely aligned and the story is the sentence. But in ancient Chinese poetry, there is no syntax. The Chinese poems proceeded as *perceived moments of eternity*. As in the haiku where there's a gap before the voltage (of the response). In the Italian Renaissance sonnet, one would call it 'volta'. In Chinese poetry, we call it 'raising the head'. It's that part of the poem when you see what it is you were thinking. As in this haiku:

*Such a moon:*
*The thief stops in the night*
*to sing*

Lee has long forgotten who wrote the above haiku, but it's a haiku that he holds permanently within his memory. Lee says the "volta" is not in the haiku's individual lines so much as the "pregnant silence" between them. It is this "writing silence" that he attempts, in which silence the reader can "raise the head" and respond: "WOW!" Or, as Eckhart said:

It is an amazing fact that something should flow out and yet remain within. That the word flows out and yet remains within is astonishing, that all creatures flow out and yet remain within is also astonishing. What God has given and has promised to give is astonishing, incredible and beyond belief. But this is as it should be . . . . God is in all things.

Among those poets to whose words Lee, himself, responds with the "WOW!" he lists ancient T'ang Dynasty poets such as Li Bai and Tu Fu; haiku poets such as Basho, Buson and Issa; and other poets such as Saigyo, Walt Whitman, Emily Dickinson ("a stark of puritanism but she's beautiful"), Laura Riding Jackson and Rainer Maria Rilke.

"Where's the WOW? That response is who we are and connects us to who we really are — the universe-mind. I read a lot of poems with a lot of descriptions but there's no WOW. (Those poems are) like acquariums with water and lots of little things, but no fish," Lee says.

That "WOW!" also manifests the interaction that Art should provoke with its audience, according to Lee, if the Art successfully reached what is "divine" in the audience. Indeed, it is similar to how Davies has described Eckhart's conception of "the divine image in the human person" as a *"potentiality. . . .* it is a transcendental potentiality within the soul through which the soul can enjoy a cognitive unity with God."

"All Art is a mirror," Lee stresses. "For example, I read Rilke's Duino Elegies and feel hope. In Rilke's elegies, just the way he wrote the sentence, Rilke's understanding of what it can carry — his sentences carry eternity, time, feeling, space and the information he provides he almost doesn't care about."

About this, too, Eckhart has something to say:

And here is another meaning of 'In the fullness of time': if someone possessed the skill and the power to draw time and all that has happened in time during these six thousand years or will happen before the end of time, into the Now of the present, then that would be the 'fullness of time'. This is the Now of eternity in which the soul knows all things new and fresh and present in God with the same delight which I have in those things that are present to me now.

Lee's admiration may be explained by this excerpt from Rilke's Third Elegy; it evokes a simmering response in the belly:

Look, we don't love like flowers
with only one season behind us: when we love,
a sap older than memory rises in our arms. O girl,
it's like this: inside us we haven't loved just some one
in the future, but a fermenting tribe; not just one
child, but fathers, cradled inside us like ruins
of mountains, the dry riverbed
of former mothers, yes, and all that
soundless landscape under its clouded
or clear destiny — girl, all this came before you.
### — from "Duino Elegies: The Third Elegy"

It's the same emotional response evoked by some of Lee's poems, such as this excerpt from his poem, "Always A Rose." Both offer lines who reach out to the reader but with a sense of containment, of (rhythmically) offering a potential for an emotion then retreating, offering then retreating again, until the reader is compelled to respond — thus be the one to complete or create the emotion whose potential the poem creates:

Listen now to something human.

I know moments measured

by a kiss, or a tear, or a pass of the hand along a loved one's face.

I know lips that love me,

that return my kisses

by leaving on my cheek their salt.

And there is one I love, who hid her heart behind a stone.

Let there be a rose for her, who was poor,

who lived through ten bad years, and then ten more,

who took a lifetime to drain her bitter cup.

And there is one I love, smallest among us —

let there be a rose for him —

who was driven from foreign schoolyards

by fists and yelling, who trembled in anger in each re-telling,

who played alone all the days,

though the afternoon trees were full of children.

### —*from "Always A Rose"*


"A new poem requires a new mind.  The avant garde don't realize it because they keep reshaping the old mind.  But I don't think their result is a poem because there's no new mind," says Lee.  "A new poem requires new rooms for thought and feeling to circulate.  It's like Dickinson trying to fashion a new room through a new mind.  Or Whitman knocking walls down so that his room is like a quadrant of a sea and other poems are all ocean."

Lee particularly appreciates such Whitman poems as "A Song of Occupation and "Song of the Broad Axe."  In the latter poem, Whitman has written, "Where speculations on the soul are encouraged . . ./There the great city stands," a comment on expansiveness that is echoed in this excerpt presenting, indeed, *an ocean for a room*:

The sum of all known value and respect I add up in
        you whoever you are;
The President is up there in the White House for you . . . .
        it is not you who are here for him,
The Secretaries act in their bureaus for you . . . . not you
        here for them,
The Congress convenes every December for you,
Laws, courts, the forming of states, the charters of cities,
        the going and coming of commerce and mails are
        all for you.

All doctrines, all politics and civilization exurge from you,
All sculpture and monuments and anything inscribed
        anywhere are tallied in you,
The gist of histories and statistics as far back as the
        records reach is in you in this hour — and myths and
        tales the same;
If you were not breathing and walking here where

would they all be?

The most renowned poems would be ashes . . . . orations

and plays would be vacuums.


All architecture is what you do to it when you look upon it;

Did you think it was in the white or gray stone? or the

lines of the arches and cornices?


All music is what awakens from you when you are

reminded by the instruments,

It is not the violins and the cornets . . . . it is not the oboe

nor the beating drums—nor the notes of the baritone

singer signing his sweet romanza . . . . not those of

the men's chorus, nor those of the women's chorus,

It is nearer and farther than they.

*—from "A Song For Occupations" by Walt Whitman*


True to Lee's feeling that Eckhart's sermons often apply to poetry, Eckhart has this to say about expansiveness:

What the masters tell us about the dimensions of the heavens beggars belief, and yet the least power in my soul is broader than the heavens, not to mention the intellect, in which there is breadth without breadth. In the head of the soul, in the intellect, I am as close to a point located a thousand miles beyond the sea as I am to the place where I am presently standing. In this expanse and wealth of God the soul attains knowing, nothing escapes her and she seeks nothing more.

To achieve the connection with the "universal-mind," Lee says he waits for the poem to surface and his role then is to accommodate the poem. For now, "The Father's House" seems to be resting or simmering. And Lee is content to wait, for as Eckhart has said:

'Speak the word, proclaim it, bring it forth and propagate it.' Proclaim it. That which is spoken into us from without is coarse, but this word . . . pronounced within(:) . . . 'Proclaim it' — that means become aware of what is in you.

And, while the poem remains deep within him, Lee says simply about the current state of the manuscript, "I have a rock on it."

—⁓—

The following presents a draft of "The Father's House" that shows some of the changes between the published version and the current version; as well as the current version of the poem that is resting beneath a rock. Following the current version will be a discussion about some of Lee's uncertainties about the poem's latest draft. *(Editing Marks: [New P] denotes new stanza break; [Del P] denotes deletion of prior stanza break; [New L] denotes new line break; [Del L] denotes deletion of prior line break; underlined words denote added words; and words with strike-through marks denote deleted words.)*

I.      <u>Changes From Published Draft To Arrive At The Current Working Draft Of The Poem</u>

**THE FATHER'S HOUSE**

Here, as in childhood, Brother, no one knows us.
And someone has died, and someone is not yet [Del P] born ~;~ .

[New P] ~while our~ <u>Our</u> father walks through his church at night
and sets all the clocks for spring.  His sleeplessness

weighs heavy on my forehead, his death almost
nothing.  In the ~only~ letter he <u>never</u> wrote to us

he says, *No one can tell how long it takes a seed*
*to declare what death and lightning told it*

*while it slept.  <u>And there are stars no one's heard from</u>*
*<u>yet, they have so far to fall toward the face foretold</u>*

*<u>prior to our names.</u> But stand at a window*
[New L] *long enough,* [Del L] *late enough, and you may* ~some night hear~

*<u>come to know: there's no</u> ~dark out there~ <u>night not first</u>*
*<u>and already in you.</u>  ~a~ A secret you'll tomorrow,*

[New P] *parallel to the morning,* [Del L] *tell on a wide, white bed,*
[New L] *to a woman* [Del P] *like a sown ledge of wheat.*

[New P]  *Or you may never* [Del L] *tell it, who lean across the* ~night~ *<u>dark</u>*
[New L] *and miles of* ~the~ <u>*an ageless*</u> *sea,* [Del P] *to arrive at a* ~seed~,

[New P] *in whose lamplit* ~house resides a thorn, or a wee man~ *<u>hand</u>*
~*resides a thorn, or a wee man, carving*~ <u>*unifying*</u> [Del P] *a name* ~on a stone, at a fluctuat-~
~*ing table of water,*~

[New P] *the name of the one who has died, the name of the one*
[Del P] *not born unknown.* Someone has died.  Someone

is not yet born.  And during this black interval,
[Del P] I sweep all three floors of our father's house,

[New P] and I don't count the broom strokes; I row
[Del P] up and down for nothing but love: his for me, and my own

[New P] for the threshold, as well as for the woman's ~~name~~ <u>voice</u>
[Del P] I hear while I sweep, as though she swept

[New P] beside me ~~;~~ <u>.</u> <u>She is</u> a woman who, if she owns a face
[New L] at all, [Del P] ~~it~~ is its own changing; and if I know her name

[New P] I know to say it so softly she need not
[Del P] stop her work to hear me.  But when she lies down

[New P] at night, in the room of our arrival, she'll know
[Del P] I called her ~~, though~~ <u>But</u> she won't answer, who is on her way

[New P] to sleep, until morning, which even now, [Del P] is overwhelming,
[New L] the woman combing her hair [Del L] opposite

[New P] the direction of my departure.
[Del P] And only now and then do I lean at a jamb

[New P] to see if I can see what I thought I heard.
[Del P] I heard her ask, *My love, why can't you sleep?*

[New P] and <u>I</u> answer, *Someone has died, and someone*
[Del P] *is not yet born.*  Meanwhile, I hear the voices [Del L] of <u>the</u> women

[New P] telling a story in the round ~~;~~ <u>.</u> [Del P] ~~so~~ <u>So</u> I sit down
[New L] on the rain-eaten stoop, by the saltgrasses,

[New P] and go on folding the laundry I was folding,
[Del P] the everyday clothes of our everyday life, the death [Del L] clothes

[New P] wearing us clean to the bone, to the very
[Del P] ~~ilium~~ <u>iliac</u> crest, where my right hand, this hand,

[New P] half [Del L] crab, part bird, has often come to rest on her,
[Del P] whose name I know.  And because I sat down,

[New P] I hear ~~their~~ <u>the women's</u> folding sound, and know
[Del P] the tide is rising early, and I can't hope [Del L] to trap

[New P] their story told in the round.  But the ~~woman she~~ <u>the woman</u> [Del P] ~~whose
name I know~~ says, *Sleep,*
[New L] so I lie down [Del L] on the clothes, the folded and unfolded,

[New P] the life [Del P] and the death.  Ages go by.  When I wake,
[New L] the story [Del L] has changed the firmament into domain,

[New P] domain [Del P] into a house.  And the sun speaks the day,
unnaming, showing the story, dissipating the boundaries

of the telling ; to include the one who has died
and the one not yet born.  Someone has died

and someone is not yet born.
[New L] How still [Del L] this morning grows about the voice

[New P] of one [Del P] child reading to another,
[New L] how much a house [Del L] is house at all due

[New P] to one room where an elder [Del P] child reads
[New L] to his brother, and that younger [Del L] knows by heart

[New P] the brother-voice.  How ~~darker~~ dark [Del P] other rooms stand,
[New L] how slow morning comes, collected [Del L] in a name, told

[New P] at one sill and listened for [Del P] at the threshold of dew.
[New L] What book is this we read [Del L] ~~together~~, Brother,

[New P] and at which window [Del P] of our father's house?
[New L] In which upper room? [Del L] We read it twice:

[New P] Once in two voices, to each [Del P] other ; , and
[New L] once in unison, to children, [Del L] animals, and the sun,

[New P] our star, that vast office [Del P] of love ~~,the~~ . The ~~one~~ sun we sit in
[New L] once, and read [Del L] together twice, the third time

[New P] bosomed in [Del P] the future.  So birds may lend their church,
[New L] sown [Del L] in air, realized in the body uttering

windows, growing rafters, couching seeds.


II.        Current Working Draft


**THE FATHER'S HOUSE**


Here, as in childhood, Brother,/ no one knows us./
And someone has died,/ and someone is not yet born./

Our father walks through his church/ at night
and sets all the clocks/ for spring.  His sleeplessness/

weighs heavy on my forehead, his death/ almost
nothing./   In the letter he never wrote/ to us

he says,/ *No one can tell how long/ it takes a seed*
*to declare/ what death and lightning told it/*

*while it slept.  And there are stars/ no one's heard from*
*yet,/ they have so far to fall/ toward ~~a~~ <u>the</u> face foretold/*

*prior to our names. ~~/~~ But stand at a window/*
*long enough, late enough, and/ you may ~~some night~~*

*come to know:/ there's no ~~dark out there~~ <u>night</u> not first/*
*and already in you./  A secret you'll tomorrow,*

*parallel/ to the morning, tell/ on a wide, white bed,*
*to a woman/ like a sown ledge of wheat./*

*Or you may never tell it, who lean across the ~~night~~ <u>dark</u>*
*and miles of ~~the~~ <u>an ageless</u> sea, to arrive at a ~~seed~~.*

*in whose lamplit ~~house resides a thorn, or a wee man~~ <u>hand</u>*
*~~carving~~ <u>unifying</u> a name ~~on a stone, at a fluctuating table of water,~~*

*the name of the one who has died, the name of the one*
*not born unknown.*  Someone has died.  Someone

is not yet born.  And during this black interval,
I sweep all three floors of our father's house,

and I don't count the broom strokes; I row
up and down for nothing but love: his for me, and my own

for the threshold.  As well as for the woman's voice
I hear while I sweep, as though she swept

beside me.  She is a woman who, if she owns a face
at all, is its own changing; and if I know her name

I know to say it so softly she need not
stop her work to hear me.  Though when she lies down

at night, in the room of our arrival, she'll know
I called her; but she won't answer, who is on her way

to sleep, until morning, which, even now, is overwhelming,

the woman combing her hair opposite

the direction of my departure.
And only now and then do I lean at a jamb

to see if I can see what I thought I heard.
I heard her ask, *My love, why can't you sleep?*

and I answer, *Someone has died, and someone
is not yet born.* Meanwhile, <u>I hear</u> the voices of <u>the</u> women

~~tell~~ <u>telling</u> a story in the round. So I sit down
on the ~~rough~~ <u>rain-eaten</u> stoop, by the saltgrasses,

and go on folding the laundry I was folding,
the everyday clothes of our everyday life, the death clothes

wearing us clean to the bone, to the very
iliac crest, where my right hand, this hand,

half paw, part bird, has often come to rest on her,
whose name I know. And because I sat down,

I hear the women's folding sound, and know
the tide is rising early, and I can't hope to trap

their story told in the round. But ~~she~~ <u>the woman</u> says *Sleep,*
so I lie down on the clothes, the folded and unfolded,

the life and the death. Ages go by. When I wake,
the story has changed the firmament into domain,

domain into a house, and the sun speaks the day,
unnaming, showing the story, dissipating the boundaries

of the telling to include the one who has died
and the one not yet born. Someone has died

and someone is not yet born.
How still this morning grows about the voice

of one child reading to another,
how much a house is house at all due

to one room where an elder child reads
to his brother, and that younger knows by heart

the brother-voice. How dark other rooms stand,
how slow morning comes, collected in a name, told

at one sill and listened for at the threshold of dew.
What book is this we read together, Brother,

and at which window of our father's house?
In which upper room? We read it twice:

once in two voices, to each other, and
once in unison, to children, animals, and the sun,

our star, that vast office of love. The sun we sit in
once, and read together twice, the third time

bosomed in the future. So birds may lend their church
sown in air, realized in the body uttering

windows, growing rafters, couching seeds.


Discussion On Current Working Draft:

      Though the poem contains autobiographical references, the narrative is not as important as evoking the feeling in the "metaphysical space" which Lee enters to write a poem — to achieve what Rilke accomplished in having his words weighted with "eternity, time, feeling, space." To this day, for example, Lee says he doesn't know who the woman is who surfaced in the poem. "I didn't plot the poem, though other references certainly are from my life," he recalls.

      In any event, Lee says he is not yet comfortable with the current draft because the poem's "body of feeling is not yet clear."

      For Lee, a poem is like a person in that both have several bodies: a physical body, a mental body that is more subtle than the physical body and a spiritual body that is even subtler. "And the poem is also a sonic or aural body — the poem is what you hear, but also the air and the feelings it generates," he notes.

      "I respond to poems with my whole body. The work that I really love affects my entire body. I can feel it in my stomach, my neck, my knees, the soles of my feet," says Lee. "When I'm reading a work, I pay attention to how my body responds. Like, whether it's all head, all about mentality."

      For instance, Lee says the body of T.S. Eliot's 'Four Quartets" is imbalanced. "Great as they are, with a physical body that is big, impressive, long sustained. And the intellectual body is also strong — very accomplished. But the spirit body seems dwarfed so that the poem seems to me to be imbalanced. The emotional body seems retarded."

      With "The Father's House," Lee feels that "there's a body there but it's hidden. I haven't found it yet."

      When asked to provide an example of his misgivings over the poem's current draft, he noted the latter part of the poem that begins to describe two brothers. "That section feels disconnected from the rest of the poem, perhaps because of the way the rhythm changes. But if I make it two parts, I might lose that disconnection and there might be something in that disconnection that shouldn't be lost," he says.

The poem has 39 couplets before the last one-line stanza, with the poem's number of couplets almost equally divided between each (variation of the) phrase, "Someone has died, someone is not yet born." If the poem was divided in four different sections, with each beginning with Lee's "grounding phrase, one indeed would see that there is a different rhythm to the last section that begins with the couplet depicting the two brothers. The later couplets are more compact and also rely less on consonance — contributing to a different type of resonance than in earlier sections of the poem (though the third part uses consonance as sparingly as the fourth section, somehow its lines maintain more of the emotional weight that seems to be lacking in the more straightforward fourth section). In the fourth section's more straightforward style, there seems less space for evoking the type of underlying feelings of passion that Lee so admires in Rilke's Duino elegies.

The first section also seems to bear the most feeling of all the four sections. In part, this may reflect the fact that Lee has worked mostly on this beginning section (based on the changes made from the published version). The addition of the middle phrases (underlined below) is particularly effective in expanding space, as evident by comparing the two sections before and after the added phrases:

Before additional phrases:

> Here, as in childhood, Brother, no one knows us.
> And someone has died, and someone is not yet born.
>
> Our father walks through his church at night
> and sets all the clocks for spring. His sleeplessness
>
> weighs heavy on my forehead, his death almost
> nothing. In the letter he never wrote to us
>
> he says, *No one can tell how long it takes a seed*
> *to declare what death and lightning told it*
>
> *while it slept. But stand at a window*
> *long enough, late enough, and you may*
>
> *come to know: there's no night not first*
> *and already in you. A secret you'll tomorrow,*
>
> *parallel to the morning, tell on a wide, white bed,*
> *to a woman like a sown ledge of wheat.*

After additional phrases:

> Here, as in childhood, Brother, no one knows us.

And someone has died, and someone is not yet born.

Our father walks through his church at night
and sets all the clocks for spring.  His sleeplessness

weighs heavy on my forehead, his death almost
nothing.  In the letter he never wrote to us

he says, *No one can tell how long it takes a seed*
*to declare what death and lightning told it*

*while it slept.  And there are stars no one's heard from*
*yet, they have so far to fall/ toward the face foretold*

*prior to our names.  But stand at a window*
*long enough, late enough, and you may*

*come to know: there's no night not first*
*and already in you.  A secret you'll tomorrow,*

*parallel to the morning, tell on a wide, white bed,*
*to a woman like a sown ledge of wheat.*

The current draft also depicts some line-breaks in the poem's first eight couplets. "Because the poem is not there yet, I started out with reconsidering the line breaks.  But I dropped it because I thought that was a superficial approach; it was a cosmetic problem.  Also, the poem came out as couplets the first time and I thought I'd trust that form," Lee says.  "I like couplets because of their audacity.  A couplet is a stanza and could be equal to any other and much longer stanza.  Since a couplet is about one line, the two-line stanza really should be freighted with, let's call it, 'the honey of poetry' for its form to dare itself."

—w—

For the moment, Lee's unconscious is reviewing "The Father's House."  When the poem will surface again for Lee to revisit the text may take place a day from now, a year from now, or much later.  Lee simply waits.  But what is likely is that what surfaces will be but another rainment in the wardrobe of, in Lee's lexicon, the seed.  For what is a *seed?*  It can be the most immense kingdom of all — "a new mind" — because a tiny seed suffices to contain thought.

As a reader, I see in "The Father's House" a garment whose shape is not yet known but whose feel I already know to be a caress, an embrace, an enfolding that, in turn, will open both my heart and mind.  This garment, as Lee described in The *Winged Seed*, is

. . . night itself, a waist of silk and immediate port, a myriad corner continuing; in your wrist and foot such arrival, and you are so near; lid and dark lash, you are such ankle; I can hardly say what elbow there is in the course of your river; nor what dark birds fly opposite our sleeping together, what winter oncoming.  Therefore I keep my hand moving over you, all the while knowing my hand may not move from glory to glory without it first moving shore to shore, your rib to hipbone, where, paused, my hand thinks with its wrist, the blood keeping count, as when the chariot, carrying two riders, flies down the stairs, the career of the vehicle gone to what's singing, loose in the driver's elbows, while the archer, braided, is let entirely to riding a swiveled bearing and axle tree, and the age beginning with the Yellow Emperor continues through me, whose history is in my face, my undoubled lid and alien eye, whose future is a question forming between my thighs, while you keep, or spend, which is a further range of keeping, the answer to our sufficiency, bed for seed.

I see in "The Father's House" an invitation to taste of the "honey of poetry" — to pursue divinity.  And if there are worldly things that must distract from this path of connecting with the "universe-mind," one must persevere, even if, as Lee wrote in *The Winged Seed*, one ends up acting like a thief at night sneaking into a house where "the thief who had been blind could see."  As Lee says, *Poetry enacts the true identity of the reader* and I — as the reader — see myself responding — reaching forth — to the poem, thus bringing something into the house rather than taking away from it.  I see myself sneaking in the silk I personally will have embroidered with soft, glistening thread to couch the waiting seed.

Footnotes:

(1) All excerpts from Meister Eckhart's sermons and Oliver Davies' statements about him are from Eckhart's *Selected Writings* (Edited and Translated by Oliver Davies, Penguin Classics, 1994)

(2) All excepts from Rainer Maria Rilke's "Duino Elegies" are translated by A. Poulin, Jr. (Houghton Mifflin Company Boston, 1977)

(3) from the Lannan Literary Video on Li Young Lee's poetry

(4) from Ezra Pound's *Selected Prose 1909-1965* (ed. William Cookson, New Directions, 1973)

# MEI-MEI BERSSENBRUGGE

Mei-mei Berssenbrugge has received numerous awards for her writing, including two National Endowment of the Arts Grants for literature, two Before Columbus American Book Awards and the PEN/West Award in Poetry. She serves as Contributing Editor to *Conjunctions* (Bard College) and is represented in many anthologies and journals. Her collections include *Summits Move With the Tide* (Greenfield Review Press, 1974), *Fish Souls* (Greenwood Press, 1974), *Random Possession* (I. Reed Books, 1979), *Packrat Sieve* (Contact II, 1983), *The Heat Bird* (Burning Deck, 1983), *Hiddenness* with Richard Tuttle *(The Whitney Museum Library Fellows, 1987),* *Empathy (Station Hill Press, 1989), Sphericity* (Kelsey St. Press, 1993), *Endocrinology* with Kiki Smith (U.L.A.E. and Kelsey St. Press, 1997) and *The Four-Year-Old Girl* (Kelsey St. Press, 1998). Her theatre work includes a play, *One, Two Cups*, directed by Frank Chin and produced by Basement Workshop and The Asian Exclusion Act; dance theater works with Morita Dance Company produced by Basement Workshop; and the play, *Kindness* with artist Richard Tuttle and composer Tan Dun. She has worked as an Artist-in-Residence with Basement Workshop and Arts Alaska, as well as served on the faculty of Brown University and the Institute of American Indian Arts. She received her MFA from Columbia University.

In response to the question, "What advice would you give to a young poet?" Mei-mei Berssenbrugge responds:

Advice: finding or creating a peer group; wide experience; wide reading.

# Mei-mei Berssenbrugge Bleeds
## A Poem That ~~Transforms~~ Transcends Heartbreak:
## "The Four Year Old Girl"

*Each night the sun slides out below the low clouds*
*and lights a section of the rainbow*
*which is actually solid in air around her*
*in her chair, or as a hummingbird moves in the garden*
*making it shimmer by friction. That's why there*
*are no mistakes*
*— from "Pack Rat Sieve" by Mei-mei Berssenbrugge*

Mei-mei Berssenbrugge has been ill for the past six years, ever since she was exposed to a pesticide, the effects of which she still feels. She also remains aware that her mother was a chronic sufferer of asthma from which she ultimately died. Both diseases are immune dysfunctions — a coincidence that facilitated the transmutation of reality into metaphor and inspiration for her poem, "The Four Year Old Girl."

"I think a lot about fate and if and how fate can be changed. I've had so much experience with illness that I came to see it as a crisis of being. And I began thinking of how not to pass on illness to my (then) four-year-old daughter, Martha," Berssenbrugge recalls. "My poem is the result of being desperately sick and trying to figure out a way spiritually to overcome illness."

As she pondered how to overcome this "crisis of being," the question developed to "thinking about what is psychologically determined by early experiences, and what can be changed. I decided to write about genetics and how to change one's own genetics. This became a poem about how a girl makes her identity if her genetics is disorganized as well as the mother's role in her daughter's fate," Berssenbrugge says.

To research her poem, Berssenbrugge reviewed a number of sources ranging from genetics and philosophy texts to art discourses. For "The Four Year Old Girl," she notes the importance of *Genetics In Medicine* by M. Thompson, Roderick McInnes and Huntington Willis; *Seminar of Jacques Lacan, Book II* (ed. Jacques-Alain Miller); and *Four Fundamental Concepts of Psychoanalysis* (ed. Jacques-Alain Miller). Other sources reflect her practice of reading books on Western philosophy and Buddhism in tandem whenever she is about to birth a new poem, such as *Buddha Nature* by Thrangu Rinpoche and *Theory of Religion* by Georges Bataille. (A comprehensive list of her sources is featured below.)

"I read in a trance. It's an unconscious level of reading and I make notes on what floats up to the surface," she says.

Berssenbrugge's process of reading and annotating her research material took nearly three months, after which she typed out the passages which caught her attention and printed them out on slips of paper. She then laid out the slips of paper, along with other visual notes — such as xeroxes of illustrations from the genetic books to family photos — on the 10' x 4' surface of a large table. As she perused the notes on the table, sometimes moving them around to form some sort of order, she typed what became the "First Draft" of the poem. Subsequently, to create a record that she calls "the first form of the poem" ("First Form"), she taped on paper the notes used in the First Draft as well as additional notes that she wished to reconsider for potential use.

(The First Draft and First Form are featured below.)

Berssenbrugge used only about one-tenth of her gathered notes in the First Draft. The following is a sampling of unused notes which address Berssenbrugge's underlying concerns about creating identity when coping with "disordered genetics:"

> Children growing up in homes with inadequate love, induce in themselves a deficiency of growth hormones for the pituitary and as a result they remain small and undeveloped in their physiques . . . . When these children are placed in loving surroundings, their condition can spontaneously reverse, and they quickly catch up with their peers in size. . . . . Bliss is when the world expands beyond its accustomed limits . . . . You cannot feel that you are intelligent, but you can feel bliss.
>
> — from *Quantum Healing* by Deepak Chopra, M.D.

> In nature there are no perfect circles or straight lines or equal spaces. . . . Because the Greeks sought guidance of their conscious mind their work is very inspiring to us because they were inspired, we are inspired by their work. . . . Today we realize that perfection is out of reach for us because we ourselves are a part of nature but it is still our greatest interest . . . . The individual by himself must move forward by inspiration in order to live . . . . We may wake up in the morning feeling happy for no reason. Abstract or nonobjective feelings are a very important part of our lives.
>
> — from *Writings* of Agnes Martin

Berssenbrugge's visual notes included snapshots photographed deliberately for her poem, e.g. a photo displaying scars on her elbow (a manifestation of her illness) in partial preparation for what became the first sentence of Part 5 of her poem's Final Draft as she imagined the "The Four Year Old Girl"'s disease: "On her fourth birthday, a rash on the elbow indicated enzyme deficiency." However, Berssenbrugge says she also includes family photos in her visual space while writing, without necessarily anticipating that they will become incorporated into the poem.

"My process is so cerebral that I try to get things in front of me that hold an emotional element — that's where the family pictures come in," she says. One of the family photos is of her daughter lying on a patterned bedspread. This photo made it into the Final Draft of the poem as the fifth sentence of Part 6: "Parallel woven lines of the blanket extend to water."

Berssenbrugge's process can be illustrated by comparing the following notes from her First Draft with what evolved into passages in the Final Draft. From Part 3 of the poem, she noted in her First Draft:

> an image of energy starting from a given point of the real (think of them as being like light, since that is what most clearly evokes an image in our mind — are reflected at some point on a surface, come to strike the corresponding same point in space. The surface of a lake might just as well be replaced by the area striata of the occipital lobe, for the area striata with its fibrillary layers is exactly like a mirror. In the same way as you don't need the entire surface of a mirror — for you to be aware of the content of a field or a room, in the same way as you obtain the same result by using a field or a room, in the same way as you obtain the same result by using a tiny little bit, so any small portion of the area striata can be put to the same use, and behaves like a mirror *OTHER*

All sorts of things in the world behave like mirrors. All that's needed is that the conditions be such that to one point of a reality there ____ correspond an effect at another point, a bi-univocal _____points in real space.

. . .

you never look at me from the place from which I see you

The above notes resulted in the following passages from the Final Draft; these passages are quite accomplished in discussing the nature and significance of perception:

The image, the effects of energy starting from a real point, is reflected at some point on a surface, a lake or area of the occipital lobe.

You don't need the whole surface to be aware of a figure, just for some points of real space to correspond to effect at other points.

There's an image and a struggle to recognize reception of it.

Nevertheless, Berssenbrugge's intellectualness did not prevent her sense of humor from poking its way into her process. As regards the title of her poem, she says, that, as she had anticipated, "A lot of friends thought it was about Martha because she was four years old at the time. But that was just an act of mischief on my part and it's not really about Martha."

Berssenbrugge originally had a working title of "The Lost Ring" for the poem, referring to a gift from her mother that Berssenbrugge thought she had lost. Subsequently, while developing the poem she concluded that the working title did not fit the developing poem. Berssenbrugge considers the final title appropriate. "Certainly, a lot for formative things are happening at age four," she notes.

Interestingly, some of Berssenbrugge's early drafts indicate that she was already conscious of the length of the final form of the poem while still in the early stages of composition. "I have a preconception about the number of lines in my poems. It's mystical but accurate. I may not know what the poem is going to be about — the poem will end up being simply what the poem will be. But I often know the number of lines the poem will contain. It's a question of scale. If I know a poem's length, then I know how to weight single lines," she says. By "weight single lines," Berssenbrugge refers to how much content will be encompassed by single lines, which she says could be different among poems of different lengths.

In addition, although the notes in the collage feature the type of technical or scientific language that permeate tomes about genetics, some of the jargon survived Berssenbrugge's revisions to make their way into the poem's Final Draft. For example, a caption to a photo of a radiograph of a premature (26 weeks gestation) infant includes the sentences, "The skull is relatively large and unmineralized, and was soft to palpation. The thoracic cavity is small, the long bodies of the arms and legs are short and deformed, and the vertebral bodies are flattened. All the bones are undermineralized." Part 4 of the poem opens with:

Her skull is large and soft to touch.

The thoracic cavity small, limbs short, deformed and vertebrae flattened.

All the bones are undermineralized.

The poem contains many examples of scientific language being co-opted into poetry. In part, this reflects her note-taking process wherein she says, "I look for linguistic structure as much as material meaning." Her co-optation of the technical language of the genetics textbook also reflects her long-time interest in feminizing technical jargon which started when she wrote *Random Possessions* (I. Reed Books, 1979), the book for which she won her first of two American Book Awards from the Before Columbus Foundation.

Since 1979, however, Berssenbrugge believes that a broader access to scientific language has become "established. Now, what I think I'm doing is trying to create a continuum between the abstract and the concrete, a continuum between the material and immaterial — to make a world like that. The time of my poems is not a narrative time; I write the beginning of the poem to occur (concurrently) as the end of the poem so that the whole thing rises up at the same time," she says.

"The Four Year Old Girl" exemplifies Berssenbrugge's mastery of poeticizing scientific language. It is a poem dotted with words like *biochemical, molecule, chromatin, mitosis, rhodopsin* and *substrate*. But it is a light poem, transcending the individual denseness of such words. The poem is as weightless as rhapsody, notwithstanding its body of six parts with each sentence fraught with implications. Her poem transforms technical jargon to resonate beyond the terms of their original, "masculine" usage. Here are a few examples from the poems' Final Draft and what the passages could be hinting within the context of the poem:

Part 1, Sentence 3 states, "Genetic disease is extreme genetic change, against a background of normal variability." This sentence raises questions as to whether "disease" truly exists because it is defined as relative — a matter of psychology as much as biology — as well as offers implications about separations, e.g. that "disease" is the nature of extreme separations between a parent/mother and child.

Part 1, Sentence 6 states, "The problem is not to turn the subject, the effect of the genes, into an entity." This sentence could hint that, notwithstanding "genetic disease," the subject ("the effect of genes") should not be considered an individual without membership in a family, without ancestors, i.e. without a mother.

Part 2, Sentence 4 states, "A fragile site recombines misaligned genes of the repeated sequence." Within the poem's canvas, "recombines" is a brilliant choice in words. Recombination is defined by *Webster's* as a "new combination of genes in progeny that did not occur in parents" — a definition that resonates with implications about a parent-child relationship, or the intangible sieve that edits heredity and/or parental influence.

Part 3, Sentence 2 states, "Rhodopsin from the unaffected gene can convert photons into retinal impulse, so she sees normally for years." This statement could be a metapor for a child who received poor parenting, and that the effects of poor parenting are not immediately apparent.

Part 3, Sentence 13 states, "Obedience to one's child is anxious, heartfelt, but not continuous, like a white mote in her eye." The sentence refers to one of Berssenbrugge's visual notes, a photo of a girl affected by retinoblastoma disease. In the photo, there is a white reflection of light which directly touched on the tumor surface in the girl's eye. This sentence could be raising the question of constraints on a mother from performing as a perfect parent.

Part 4, Sentence 11 states, "The phenotype, whose main task is to transform everything into secondary, kinetic energy, pleasure, innocent, won't define every subject." Notwithstanding the definition of phenotype as "the observable expression of the genotype as structural and biochemical traits," this sentence seems to imply that genetics is not the ultimate definition of a person (such as "The Four Year Old Girl") and that there are other realities besides biology or chemistry such as emotion, psychology and fate.

Part 4, Sentences 8, 9 and 14 state, "One creates a mouse model of human disease by disrupting a normal mouse gene in vitro, then injecting cells containing the mutated gene into host embryos./ DNA integrated into the mouse genome is expressed and transmitted to progeny./ By transferring functional copies of the gene to her, he might correct reversible features of the mutant phenotype, lightly touching the bad mother, before." To answer Berssenbrugge's question about "how a girl makes her identity if her genetics is disorganized as well as the mother's role in her daughter's fate," these sentences could imply that the mother is the source of the cure for the girl grappling with "disorganized" genes. In turn, the notion that the sources for the disease and cure are the same could raise concepts of forgiveness, love and redemption.

Berssenbrugge's visual notes included snapshots photographed deliberately for her poem, e.g. photos displaying scars on her elbow which is referenced in part 5 of her poem as the sentence: "On her fourth birthday, a rash on the elbow indicated enzyme deficiency." Berssenbrugge also includes family photos in her visual space while writing without necessarily anticipating that they will become incorporated into the poem, e.g. the photo of her with daughter Martha. "My process is so cerebral that I try to get things in front of me that hold an emotional element — that's where the family pictures come in," she says.

Nevertheless, while "The Four Year Old Girl" shows Berssenbrugge's mastery in transforming scientific language into poetry, she still considers the poem "experimental" in its use of sentences. In drafting the poem, Berssenbrugge deviated from her usual use of stanzas to what she calls the "sentence format" of a poem, whereby each line is a distinct sentence. It would seem sentences could make more difficult her goal of eliminating "narrative time" in her poetry, given a stanza's potential for seamlessness. Ease, however, is not the point with Berssenbrugge's poetry. She wanted to lessen her dependence on lyricism and stanzas, she feels, enhances the melody of underlying words.

Berssenbrugge focused on the sentence format about two years ago when she collaborated with the artist Kiki Smith to produce *Endocrinology* (U.L.A.E. and Kelsey St. Press, 1997). "I wrote her a poem that started out in stanzas. When I started writing it down I began to form sentences to fit the format of her visual work. The sentence interests me, even though it's awkward and unattractive. I'm trying to work with less continuity, to see if I can make a whole without there being easily-followed connections," she says.

It would not be surprising, however, if the sentence format interests Berssenbrugge specifically because it is "awkward and unattractive." She may want to poeticize the sentence format in the same manner that she feminized scientific language. And when she does master the "continuum" despite the more difficult paths presented by the ungainliness of sentences, then the poem is only more accomplished, as with "The Four Year Old Girl," a poem that begins with two distinctly "scientific" sentences:

The <u>genotype</u> is her genetic constitution.

The <u>phenotype</u> is the observable expression of the genotype as structural and biochemical traits.

The infiltration of these technical, seemingly awkward sentences only work to enhance the resonance of other sentences throughout the poem that generate an emotional pull, such as:

A girl says sweetly, it's time you begin to look after me, so I may seem lovable to myself.

*Or,*

There's an image and a struggle to recognize reception of it.

*Or,*

A moment of seeing can intervene like a suture between an image and its word.

In another example of resonance through the effective making of "a whole without there being easily-followed connections," Part 3 features the following excerpt:

The mother's not looking at her daughter from the place from which the daughter sees her.

She doesn't recognize abnormal attributes.

The daughter resolves this image as fire below in the woods, red silk.

In the waiting room, she hopes a large dog will walk up to her, be kind and fulfill her wishes.

Between what occurs as if by chance and, "Mother, can you see I'm dying?" is the same relation we deal with in recurrence.

It was noted to Berssenbrugge that upon reading the last sentence featured in the above excerpt, there occured a feeling of heartbreak — and that it was an emotion for whose surfacing there was no premonition from previous passages. She responds, "My work — or all poetry — wants to evoke emotion. But I try to do it in a way that's unexpected."

Though Berssenbrugge may spend months researching a poem, she takes only about a week to compose a poem's First Draft. She deliberately keeps the first draft's composition time short because of its arduousness. While composing first drafts, Berssenbrugge says her family knows she is essentially unavailable; she often sleeps in her writing studio which is separate from her residence. "My husband takes over the family and sometimes just takes our daughter to his mother," she notes.

Nowadays, Berssenbrugge typically writes lengthy poems, at least five parts per poem. She also muses that the process of writing her recent poems seem not to have been as difficult as other poems in the past. "They're not getting so hard — I wonder if that's bad," she laughs.

Prior to finishing a poem, Berssenbrugge often shows it to trusted readers; for "The Four Year Old Girl," she showed final drafts to Arthur Sze and Barbara Guest. "Barbara is a poet based in California with whom I've had a dialogue for a long time. I also show all my poems to Arthur; he knows to point out something if he thinks it's too abstruse or awkward."

In addition, Berssenbrugge always reads her poems out loud. "Reading (out loud) is how you notice if a poem doesn't work. By reading, you especially notice if (a section of) a poem is boring."

Berssenbrugge characterizes "The Four Year Old Girl" as a "heartbreaking poem," partly because of its connection to her real-life experiences with her and her mother's illnesses. "I was really trying to mix up the spiritual — considerations of fate — and the hard rock of genetics."

*Heartbreaking.* But this does not mean that "The Four Year Old Girl" is pessimistic about life. Notwithstanding its cerebral style, or the poem's reference to a four-year-old with "disorganized" genes (for which Berssenbrugge's research included photos of toddlers and infants with Down's syndrome and fetal alcohol syndrome), the poem is rather uplifting. As Berssenbrugge puts it, "The poem presents a situation with various kinds of darkness, but it only generates a love. This person has defects and so the person may not survive, but love has its own particular transcendence."

Thus, the poem has a complex, if not ironic, ending, as noted in its last two sentences:

Its materiality is a teletransport of signified protoplasm across lineage or time, avid,
     muscular and compact, as if pervasive, attached to her, in a particular
          matriarchy of natural disaster in which the luminosity of a fetal sonogram
          becomes clairvoyant.

The love has no quantity or value, but only lasts a length of time, different time,
     across which unfolds her singularity without compromising life as a whole.

The following illustrates Berssenbrugge's drafting process for her poem, "The Four Year Old Girl," as shown in the following sections below:

I. Collage of Notes That Berssenbrugge Calls "The First Form Of The Poem"

II. First Draft (July 4-20, 1994)

III. July 24, 1994 Draft and Amended September 20, 1994 Draft (Amendments Show Changes to Version Published in 1995 by *Conjunctions*)

IV. Minor Changes Between Versions Published by *Conjunctions* and *BLACK LIGHTNING* which is publishing Berssenbrugge's Final Draft Dated May 15, 1996

The following lists Berssenbruge's sources. Each source is denoted by a letter of the alphabet as the First Form (below) will reference each source of a passage, along with, if applicable, a page number.

A:       *Quantum Healing* by Deepak Chopra, M.D. (Bantam Books, N.Y. 1990)

B:       *Soul Retrieval* by Sandra Ingerman (Harper San Francisco, 1991)

C:       *Theory of Religion* by Georges Bataille (Zone Books, N.Y. 1988)

D:       *Genetics In Medicine* by M. Thompson, Roderick McInnes and Huntington Willis (W.B. Saunders Co., 1991)

E:       *The Making ± Breaking of Affectional Bonds* by John Bowlby (Tavistock/Routledge, N.Y. 1979)

F:       *Seminar of Jacques Lacan Book II* edited by Jacques-Alain Miller (W.W. Norton, N.Y., 1991)

G:       *Four Fundamental Concepts of Psychoanalysis* edited by Jacques-Alain Miller (W.W. Norton, N.Y. 1981)

H:       *Buddha Nature* by Thrangu Rinpoche (Rangiung Yeshe Publications, Kathmandu, Nepal, 1988)

I:       *Writings, Agnes Martin* edited by Dieter Schwartz (Kunst Museum, Winterthur, edition Cantz)

J:       Taped conversations with Peter Tadd (Berssenbrugge's friend and a psychic)

K:       *Art Forum* article on John Cage

L:        Richard Tuttle (artist and Berssenbrugge's husband)

—ᴍ—

## I.        Collage of Notes That Berssenbrugge Calls "The First Form Of The Poem"

This collage presents Berssenbrugge's taped order of notes after she finished composing the First Draft (note that she envisioned five parts of the poem at this stage, versus the Final Draft's six parts).  Some of the passages may be unclear or include missing words because (i) they were transcribed from lectures and/or conversations, (ii) the original source references since have been lost and/or (iii) they reflect Berssenbrugge's short-hand notes to herself.

*(Editing Marks:  Italicized phrases denote Berssenbrugge's handwritten comments on her drafts.  If a word(s) is underlined or capitalized, it is underlined/capitalized because it was typed as such in Berssenbrugge's draft.)*

### July 4, 1994:  Part 1

B, 53:  the genotype of a person is his or her genetic constitution.  the phenotype is the observable expression of a genotype as a morphological, biochemical or molecular trait

B, 115:  genetic disease is only the most obvious and often the most extreme manifestation of genetic change, superimposed on a background of entirely normal genetic variability

F, 11:  within the conventional unit which we call subjectivities on account of indidividual particularities, what is happening?  (what is resisting?)

F, 11:  (this conviction extends beyond the individual naivete of) the subject who believes in himself, who believes that he is himself — a common enough madness, which isn't complete madness, because it belongs to the order of beliefs   12

F, 53:  when one speaks of subjectivity, the problem is not to turn the subject into an entity.

G, 207:  human psychology cannot be conceived in the absence of the function of the subject defined as the effect of the signifier.

G, 247:  there is between the signifier and the signified, another relation w (than t fraction) wh is the o t effect o meaning.

F, 48:  we do know that consciousness is linked to something entirely contingent, just as contingent as the surface of a lake in an uninhabited world, the existence of our

I, 7:  You wouldn't think of form by the ocean.  You can go in if you don't encounter anything

A, 226:  (for each of the senses, not just sight, impressions are constantly being laid down on our neurons.  although we customarily call the heavier impressions stress, ) in fact all impressions create some limitation.

A, 81: what is at work here is something we can call an impulse of intelligence, which means a thought and a molecule tied together, like a two-sided coin.

apart from our relations to others there can be no moral necessity
Questions of value are implied in human relationships

G, 257: a little girl said to me sweetly that it was about time somebody began to look after her so that she might seem lovable to herself

D, 433: germline  the cell line from which gamettes are derived

the individual by himself must move forward by inspiration in order to live (change genetic by inspiration??)**

A, 87: a cell's memory is able to outlive the cell itself.

A, 87: that memory must be more permanent than matter. . . It is a memory that has built some matter around itself,

## July 7, 1994: Part 2

I, 70: the panic to complete helplessness drives us to fantastic extremes and feelings of helpless-ness drive us to a ridiculousness.

F, 9: (THE SUBJECT) ITS ENTIRE AXIS SPEAKS OF SOMETHING OTHER THAN THE AXIS WE CAN GRASP WHEN WE CONSIDER IT AS A FUNCTION OF AN INDIVIDUAL.

G, 20: the unconscious is structured like a language.

D, 17: nonstaining gaps in chromosomes known as fragile sites are occasionally observed in char-acteristic sites on several chromosomes.  Many such sites are known to be heritable variants 36 PICTURE for Section 2

D, 80: a fragile site in which the chromatin fails to condense during mitosis

G, 9: *we hold to the notion of experience in the sense of the field of a praxis

  while you have a choice that is not inspiration

G, 174: Transference is what manifests in experience the enacting of the reality of the uncon-scious insofar as the reality is sexuality

A, 93: but much of the immune process is highly abstract.  It is conducted almost entirely by the exchange of information

I, 140: those who want to live a true life that is a life that is guided by the consicous mind are surrounded by multitudes that are practically dedicated to ancestor worship (ANCESTOR WOR-SHIP)

D, 432: genetic load . . . the sum total of death and defect caused by mutant genes

G, 257: all the sexual drives as articulated at the level of significants in the unconscious, . . . death as signifier, and nothing but signifier. 258 It is in so far as the object of the voice is present in it that the percipiens is present in it.

it is this that shows us that the time-function is of a logical order here, and bound up with a signifying shaping of the real.

F, 29: if only to note the finality is always implied, in variously embryonic form, in every causal notion.

a gap on the function of cause has always presented to ay any conceptual apprehension ****

purity because it is not tainted by any force or cause, and clarity, a kind of trust and confidence**

I, 37: I don't believe in the eclectic I believe in recurrence

G, 150: the species survives in the form of its individuals. Nevertheless, the survival of the horse as a species has a meaning — each horse is transitory and dies.

## July 8, 1994:  Part 3

F: an image of energy starting from a given point of the real (think of them as being like light, since that is what most clearly evokes an image in our mind — are reflected at some point on a surface, come to strike the corresponding same point in space. The surface of a lake might just as well be replaced by the area striata of the occipital lobe, for the area striata with its fibrillary layers is exactly like a mirror. In the same way as you don't need the entire surface of a mirror —for you to be aware of the content of a field or a room, in the same way as you obtain the same result by using a field or a room, in the same way as you obtain the same result by using a tiny little bit, so any small portion of the area striata can be put to the same use, and behaves like a mirror  *OTHER*

F: All sorts of things in the world behave like mirrors. All that's needed is that the conditions be such that to one point of a reality there should correspond an effect at another point, that a bi-univocal correspondence occurs between 2 points in real space.

D, 301: ( a significant pharmocological problem in which) rational therapy must take into account wide, genetically determined individual differences in response  315 (patients with this condition have relatively normal vision for many years, at least partly because) rhodopsin encoded by the unaffected allele participates normally in the conversion of a light photon into a nerve impulse in the retina.

C, 19:  every animal is in the world like water in water
you see a fire below you

G, 103:  you never look at me from the place from which I see you

G, 126:  (I should see in the unconscious) the effects of speech on the subject, in so far as these effects are so radically primary that they are properly what determine the status of the subject as subject.

D, 42:  Uniparental disomy the presence in a karotype of two chromosomes of a pair both inherited from one parent, with no representative of the chromosome from the other parent.

D, 431:  ecogenetic disorder  a disorder resulting from the interaction of a genetic predisposition to a specific disease environmental factor

G, 126:  the unconscious is the sum of the effects of speech on a subject, at the level at which the subject constitutes himself out of the effects of the signifier . . . .the cartesian subject, who appears at the moment when doubt is recognized as certainty

E, 54:  in the hope that a large dog would come to him, be very kind to him and fulfill all his wishes.

G, 69:  between what occurs as if by chance, (when everyone was asleep) and the element of poignancy, however veiled in the words, father, can't you see I'm burning there is the same relation to what we were dealing with in repetition.

G, 68:  is it not that which is expressed in the depth of the anxiety of this dream — namely, the most intimate aspects of the relation between the father and the son, who emerges, not so much in the death as in the fact that is beyond, in the sense of destiny?

I, 98:  our most anxious and heartfelt obedience is a mother's obedience to the infant and her slavish obedience to her children as long as they are in her care. ...the authority obedience state of being is not a sometimes state but a continous being

disobedience is unhappiness and moving toward unconsciousness
(anti-genetic)

the idea of a space in the body that holds the problem — childhood problem/genetic problem

*obediences & unconscious*

Disobedience moves toward unconsciousness

D, 331: the delivery of the normal gene to appropriate somatic cells (as opposed to the germline) is required. Quite apart from the ethical and technical difficulties involved, it is neither necessary nor desirable to alter the germline of the patient being treated for a genetic disease

D, 331: BY TRANSFERRING FUNCTIONAL COPIES OF THE RELEVANT GENE TO THE PATIENT, PERMANENT CORRECTION OF THE REVERSIBLE FEATURES of the mutant phenotype may be possible.

D, 387: (another use of transgenic mice is to create mouse models of human genetic disease by experimentally disrupting a normal copy of a mouse gene in vitro and then injecting cells containing the newly mutated gene into host blatocysts.) chimeric mice made in this way can then

D, 441: transgenic mice that carry a foreign gene (transgene) in their genome. produced by injection of oocytes with the foreign DNA . . . DNA that is integrated into the mouse genome may be expressed. If the transgene has been incorporated into the germline, it may also be transmitted to the progeny

A, 126: (Every cubic centimeter of space teems with energy, . . .although much of this energy is in) "virtual" form, (meaning it is locked up and plays no active part in material reality.) The power penetrating the universe is much more than what shines through.

A, 129: invisible matter called "virtual" particles as well as to energy fields.

F, 23: the inertia could be intimated by) the ego, which Freud defines very explicitly as the nucleus of resistances in the transference. It is 1 step in the evolution of his doctrine - the ego in analysis that is in a situation which challenges the precarious equilibrium, the constancy, the ego introduces security, stagnation, pleasure. In such a way that the function of the relation of which we spoke a moment ago will not define every subject. The ego, whose main task is to transform everything into secondary energy, into bound energy, won't define every subject, hence the appearance of the tendency to repeat.

J: TADD past life they're not separate and simply a record, are of forces that continue to exhibit through the present parallel realities to the reality now

G, 165: (In the drive) there is no question of kinetic energy, it is not a question of something that will be regulated with movement.

G: (invested as drive ) This investment places us on the terrain of an energy, . . . a potential energy, (for the characteristic of the drive is to be a constant force.)

A, 268: The fact that emotion lies so deep does not mean the cancer patients cannot alter them. (People can be rescued from their feelings of helplessness and despair by) going to a still deeper level. *deep*

A, 81:  Like all of us, the anoreic must fetch thought from the region that lies <u>deeper than thought</u>, and it is there that a cure might be found.  (Becoming a silent witness (of her disease) would disentangle her from the ghost)  (There's no place outside to stand on)    *deep*

G, 205:  (the libido is the essential organ in understanding the nature of the drive.  This organ is unreal.  Unreal is not imaginary )  The unreal is defined by articulating itself on the real in a way that eludes us . . . But the fact that it is unreal does not prevent an organ from embodying itself *also #5*

D, 180:  Rather, the child's chromosome is a patchwork, consisting of alternating portions of the maternal grandmother's chromosome and the maternal grandfather's chromosome.

J:  auric field has layers.  As it comes out about 3 feet from physical body, there is then a shell like an egg shell.  When the shell is strong the person is clear in themselves and feeling unperturbed by the physical environment

J:  The way the auric field is established through the polarity within the central channel of the spine similar to the earth's axis and to the magnetic fields creating the van allen belt, and this huge field

B, 102  she could put herself into a blue egg that would protect her.

this can even use the aura if you can get enough tension in it        *aura comments*


<u>July 10, 1994 - Part 5</u>

our ideas, deductions made from observed facts of life, are of no use in the unfolding of potential

H, 41:  although the true condition of all things is emptiness, they are not merely empty nature. They are also luminous.  In this context <u>luminosity is the potential for phenomena to manifest and be experienced</u> — *connect to light neuron*

H:  because things are a unity of being both empty and luminous. empty and yet arising dependently,

G, 118:  (the moment of seeing can intervene here only) as a suture, a conjunction of the imaginary and the symbolic

G, 50:  why is an act not mere behavior  An act always has an element of structure, by the fact of concerning a (real that is not self evidently caught up in it.

L:  2/94  Instead of denying language, I could symbolize language with the glue and its trailings. R.

F, 18: I myself believe that there are two sorts of relations in time. From the moment that a part of the symbolic world comes into existence it does indeed create its own past. But not in the same way as the form at the intuitive level. In all knowledge once constituted, there is a dimension of error which is that <u>forgetting of creative function of truth in its nascent form</u>

G, 41: (of the unconscious) in order to locate the truth Freud relies on a certain <u>signifying scansion</u>...what justifies this trust is a reference to the real.

H, 53: although the buddhas themselves have realized that suffering has no inherent existence, still they manifest very great compassion for beings who perceive suffering as real.

H, 27: when we say empty we usually mean without any concrete substance or matter

B, 40: (insofar as he is spirit, it is man's misfortune to have the body of an animal and thus to be like a thing, but) it is the glory of the human body to be the <u>substratum of a spirit</u>

983-55  the whole ambiguity of the sign derives from the fact that it represents something for someone.  DAUGHTER///////

H, 59: (enlightened essence) MMMMMMM

H:  intrinsically pure and untainted by the temporary defilements

H:  full of qualities and capabilities

H:  changeless

H:  saturated with compassionate love

G, 25: (discontinuity, is the essential form in which the unconscious first appears to us as a phenomenon) discontinuity in which something is manifested as a vacillation     *unused*

G, 13: there is an entire thematic area concerning the status of the subject when Socrates declares that he does not place desire in a position of original subjectivity but in the position of an object *this could go to desire*

what is a psychoogic genetic

G: since the opposite of the possible is certainly the real, we should be led to define the real as the impossible  167  *unused*

6/8  well, I suppose a factor is why I can't stand to spend much time doing things Martha likes to do.

I, 35:  just a suggestion of nature gives weight

find definition of materiality

D, 352:  there is an underlying continuous variation in liability to the malformation with a threshold marking the point at which the liability is actually expressed as an abnormal phenotype

D, 351:  heritability is the proportion of the total phenotype variance, a (v)
of a trait that is caused by additive genetic variance

C, 31:  (the bringing of elements of the same nature as the subject or the subject) itself onto the place of objects is always precarious, uncertain and unevenly realized.  But this relative precariousness matters less than the decisive possibility of a viewpoint from which) the immanent elements are perceived from the outside as objects.  (in the end we perceive each appearance subject (ourselves) animal, mind, world — from within and from without at the same time, both as continuity with respect to ourselves and as object.

I:  in the night inspiration falls on the world like rain and penetrates our mind when we are asleep.

touching subjects at the navel of dreams, to designate their ultimately unknown center, like the same anatomical navel, that gap of which I have spoken     *gap of course*

E, 84:  searching the external world for signs of the object therefore includes the establishment of an internal perceptual set derived from previous experience of the object   *go to experience here?*

G, 275:  the reduction of the field of god to the universality of the signifies, which produces a serene exceptional detachment from human desire. (pantheism)     *#5*

I, 39:  the materiality of the paintings, . . . contain a stillness which suggests the movement is imminent

you can even have the question, posed by parfitt, re teletransporter as parent to child.

I, 136:  beauty and happiness and life are all the same, and they are pervasive, unattached and abstract

A reaction lasts only a certain length of time.  It could be this whole business has been to teach you a different sense of time

K:  Your concept of silence.  I would just take out the word, concept

F, 34:  a human universe necessarily affects the form of universality, it attracts a totality which is universalised.  That is the function of the symbol

UNUSED NOTES TO BE CONSIDERED:

D, 432: expressivity to extent to which a genetic defect is expressed

F, 144: (insofar as he speaks) it is in the locus of the other that he begins to constitute the truthful lie by which is initiated that which participates in desire at the level of the unconscious. *OTHER*

G, 101: (the function it is said creates the organ *MOTHER*) The function does not even explain the organ

G, 23: *DAUGHTER #5* at first the unconscious is manifested to us as something that holds itself in suspense in the area, of the unborn. That repression should discharge something into this area is not surprising.

G: through the effects of speech, subject always realizes himself more in the other. 188 *OTHER*

of the writing and the heart untying. Love from my need from me to my work.

*This is more comfortable to see the wheat fields of middle & far distance*

G, 129: (One may go so far as to believe that the) opacity of the trauma, its resistance to signification (is then specifically held responsible for the limits of remembering. Significant in the transfer of powers from the subject to the other, to focus on speech, and, potentially truth)

G, 6: PRAXIS CONCERTED HUMAN ACTION . .WHICH PLACES MAN IN A POSITION TO TREAT THE real by the symbolic

—⚭—

**II.**                    **First Drafts Of The Poem (July 1994)**

*(Editing Marks: strikethroughs = deletions; italicized words denote handwritten notations subsequently made to typed text.)*

**Part 1**

July 4, 1994

The genotype is her genetic constitution. The phenotype is the observable expression of the genotype

as morphological or biochemical traits. Genetic disease is only the most obvious or extreme manifestation

of genetic change, superimposed on a background of entirely normal genetic variability. Within the conventional unit which we call subjectivity on account of individual particularities, what is happening?

There is the conviction she is herself, that she believes that she is herself, which isn't complete madness, because it belongs to the order of beliefs.

The problem is not to turn the subject into an entity, the subject defined as the effect of signification of the   gen  signifiers or genes.

There is between her and the displaced gene another relation which is the effect of meaning.

We do know that (consciousness) the meaning she is conscious of is entirely contingent, just as contingent as the surface of a lake in an uninhabited world, the existence of our eyes and our ears.

You wouldn't think of her form by thinking about the ocean.  You can go in, if you don't encounter anything.

~~For each of the senses, not just sight, impressions are constantly being laid down on our neurins.~~

Although we customarily call the heavier sense impressions stress, in fact all impressions create some limitation   -- *insert memory limitation*

The problem is not to turn the subject into an entity, in so far as her expressivity is the extent to which a genetic defect is expressed.

The metaphor would be an impulse of intelligence, which means a thought and a molecule tied together, like a two sided coin.

A little girl said to me sweetly, it was about time I began to look after her so that she might seem lovable to herself.

So that she was inspired to change the genotype at the level of the germline.

Since the cell's memory ~~is able to outlive the cell itself,~~ is more permanent than matter.  It is a memory that has built some matter around itself.

Like something that inevitably befalls a person
the decreed cause of events, like time.

**Part 2**

July 5, 1994 Version:
Lost Ring  (Working Title, 4/30/96)

Her image, the effects of energy starting from given points of real space on her, reflected at some point on a surface,

for the area striata of the occipital lobe with its fibrillary layers is exactly acts like a mirror.

You don't need the entire surface, to be aware of the content of a field or a room, of the figure

Any small portion of the area striata can be put to the same use, and behaves like a mirror., the genotype

All that's needed is that the condition be such that to one point of a reliaty there should correspond an effect at another point, that a biunivocal correspondence occurs between two points in real space

Our ideas, deductions made from observed facts of life are of no use in the unfolding of potential. (see notes on real).

(SUBSEQUENTLY, BERRSSENBRUGGE MOVED ABOVE LINES TO PART 3)

Nevertheless the entire axis of the subjects speaks of something other than the axis we can grasp when we consider it as a function of an individual

The species survives in the form of the young girl asking sweetly.  Note the characteristic short fingers and hypoplastic nails.

The ring with a blue stone, a silver ring and bracelet.

   *insert more clinical*

The four year old affected girl exhibiting the happy puppet syndrome.

There is a deficiency of the chromosomal region on chromosome 15 inherited from the mother, demonstrating that the parental origin of genetic material can have profound effect on the clinical expression of her defect.

holding to the notion of experience in the senses of the field of a praxis.
   *Each species survives in the form of its individuals.*
(Nevertheless the survival of humans *as a species* has a meaning.  Each girl is transitory and dies.)


July 7, 1994 Version With July 8, 1994 Additions

( the nostrils are flared.  The lids of her the eyelids turn down at the edges causing her to appear very alert.  She gives little fantastic cries like a cat)

Each tooth is set far apart from the others
There's a 1/4 inch gap between each of his teeth.  His ears are large, attached low on his skull,

and turned down.  His gaze is innocent (guileless).

Her face is a little unformed, as if gauze were stretched across her face.  The eyes lack
            features are unfinished
            the light of recognition                                        and unfocused.

Her red mouth is large in proportion to the rest of her face.  The eyes also, giving her the look of
a kewpie doll.  Her fingers as she clasps the pole of the merrygoround horse.  (see description of
down's hand)

the gaze of her eyes starts outside of herself, and goes into far distance, so herself is not involved
would not be involved in what she is looking at.

Her nails fingernails hypoplastic painted like little drops of blood on her fingertips.  She
Her fingers are full of small rings.  Silver rings, a ring with a green stone  floral ring with a green
stone.  A silver bangle on her little wrist.

Feelings of helplessness drove me to fantastic and ridiculous extremes.

Nevertheless, the ~~entire~~ axis of the ~~subject~~ (helplessness) speaks of something other than the axis
we ~~can~~ grasp when we consider it as a function of an ~~individual~~ (inheritance)

I constitute her out of these effects, like ancestor worship.  a structure~~d~~ like ~~a~~ linguistic exchange
~~of information~~,

A fragile sight, in which chromatin fails to condense during mitosis.  Many such sites are known to
be heritable variants.

(one of the most striking examples of recombination between misaligned copies of a repeated
sequence.)

(a mechanism by which mutations impair the synthesis processing or molecular associations of
proteins and the consequent effects on protein function.)

Her face is a little unformed, as if gauze were stretched across her face.  The eyes lack the light of
recognition.

The nostrils are flared.  The eyelids turn down at the outer edges, causing her to appear very alert.
When she's excited she emits      She gives little fantastic cries like a cat.

Its entire axis speaks of something other than the axis we can grasp when we xxxxxxxx
            the subject as a function of an individual.

The species survives in the form of the young girl asking sweetly.

We hold to this notion of experience in the sense of the field of a praxis.

While I have the choice, that is not inspiration.

The feeling is what manifests in experience the enacting of reality of the inheritance in so far as the reality is a life force.

And the genetic load (agency) is the sum total of death and defect caused by mutant genes, ~~the gene as signifier~~ thin the sense of death as nothing but signifier.  It is in so far as the object of the voice is present in it that the percipiens is present in it.

<u>FOLLOWING LINES INSERTED ON JULY 8, 1994</u>

in so far as the (time-fate) function is of a logical (real) order here and bound up with a signifying (genetic inherited) embodiment (shaping) of the personal suffering.  (the real)  a deformation

Note the characteristic short fingers and hypoplastic nails.
             Her fingernails painted like little drops of blood on her fingertips.  full of rings
a silver ring, a floral ring with a green stone, a silver bangle on her wrist
                              finality                    always
if only to note that        (the signifier death)       is implied in variously embryonic form, in
every causal notion.

The gap, the function of cause has always presented to any conceptual apprehension (of the rela-
tion) attachment

In her case there is a purity because it is not tainted by any force or cause, (life force or mutation) in the sense of being generic, of a kind of trust and confidence.

holding itself like an organ in the body.  in a case in which, generically, the function is said to create the organ (mother) in this case the function does not even explain the area.

the species survives in the form of its individuals.  Nevertheless the survival of humans as a species has a meaning.  Each girl is transitory and dies.

A ring with _____ stone, a silver ring _____

The four _____-affected girl exhibiting the happy puppet syndrome.

There is _____iency of the chromosomal region on chi_____ inherited from
the mother___demonstrating that the parental origin of _____erial can have
profound _____on the clinical expression of her defect_____

holding _____otion of experience in the senses of the _____praxis.

*Each species is the form of its individuals.*

(Nevertheless the survival of humans has a meaning.  each _____-transitory and
dies.)

She screams and screams at her.

Nevertheless the mother does not believe in the eclectic.  I/she believe in recurrence)
Nevertheless the survival of human as a species has a meaning (relate to signifier) is signified.

Each girl is transitory and dies.

*You could go into cause and then genetic change and then mother and other _____  Buddha*


## Part 3


<u>July 8, 1994</u>

Her red lips are large in proportion to her face. the mouth hangs open at rest.  Very round eyes, also.  ~~She clasping~~  clasping the merry go round pole,

the hands display characteristic dermal patterns of the syndrome, a single flexion crease (simian crease, axial triradius in distal position, a pattern area on the palm between the third and fourth digits, and ulnar loops on all ten digits.

The focus of her eyes starts a little in front of herself, and goes into the far distance, so she herself would not be involved in what she is looking at

~~The forehead xxxxxx is lined with effort to~~

This main idea of having the speech of the other, the signifier identify with the gene.  So that the subject is comprised of the expression of the gene of the mother)

She could have relatively normal vision for many years.  Rhodopsin encoded by the unaffected allele participates normally in the conversion of a light photon into a nerve impulse in the retina. *In this relation she is not looking at the patient from the place from which the patient see her.*

The image, the effects of energy starting from a given point of the real xxxxx  are reflected at some point on a surface.  The surface of a lake might just as well be replaced by the area striata of the occipital lobe, for the area striata with its fibrillary layers is exaclty like a mirror.

You don't need the entire surface to be aware of the content of a field or the figure.

Any small portion of the area striata can be put to the same use, and behaves like a mirror, the genotype.

All that's needed is that the condition be such that to one point of a reality (real space) there should correspond an effect at another point.

There is an image, but there is a struggle to recognize the reception of the image. She *herself* sees the wheatfields and the horizon, as if she herself were water in the water.

~~and mirrors a fire in the valley in the woods.~~

*HANDWRITTEN NOTES SHOW BERSSENBRUGGE WONDERING WHETHER THE PRECEDING PARAGRAPH SHOULD BE MOVED AFTER THE THIRD OR SEVENTH PARAGRAPH.*

The mother does not recognize/*perceive* her abnormal physical attributes. She screams and screams at her.

She resolves manages to resolve the image in this case as the figure of a fire below her in the woods.

      (the red exotic silk of a native dress)

The young girl shows a white reflex in the affected eye when light reflects directly off the (tumor) surface.

~~piecing together                    like black~~

~~he sees some black on a stuffed animal of her hair, and some gold on a bracelet of her ring and some green on a leaf of the jade — the red exotic silk of her native dress~~

one should see relation in the (unconscious) the effects of (speech) on the object, in so far as these effects are so radically primary that they are properly what determine the status of the subject as subject.

as in the case of uniparental disomay, the presence in a karotype of two chromosomes of a pair both inherited from one parent, with no representative of the chromosome from the other forebears, ancestors.

an interaction of a genetic predisposition to a specific relation with an environmental factor. (with chance or fate.) (of chance or fate)

The *personal* relation (*identity* unconscious) is the sum of the effects of the genes on a subject at the level at which the four year old girl constitutes herself out of the effects of the

She waits in the examining room, hoping that a large dog will come to her, be very kind to her and fulfill all her wishes.

Between what occurs as if by this chance (when everyone was asleep) adn the element of poignancy, however veiled, in the words, mother can't you see I'm (burning) there is the same relation to which we were dealing with in repetition

Is it not that which is expressed in the depth of the anxiety of this dream, namely the most intimate aspects of the relation between the mother and the daughter, which emerges, not so much in the death as in the fact that is beyond, in the sense of (chance or) destiny?

Our most anxious and heartfelt obedience is a mother's obedience to and her slavish obedience to her children as long as they are in her care.  The obedience state of being is continuous.

as if a space in her gaze, a white mote in her eye were holding this genetic problem,

while within the scope range even now of her deteriorating sight,

in which sight is will always be her memory,  (in the future)

disobedience ~~moves like a cloudfront~~. moves toward unconsciousness.

her love is what manifests in experience the enacting of the reality of the inheritance in so far as the reality is a life force.


### Part 4


<u>July 9, 1994</u>

*Protoplasm*

The skull is relatively large.  and unmineralized, and ~~was~~ *is* soft to the palpitation.

The thoracic cavity is small, the long bones of the arms and legs are short and deformed, and the vertebral bodies are flattened.  All the obnes are undermineralized.

*There is a blue egg ~~around~~ surrounding her body.  Kind of light, like a blue envelope.*

There is an entire thematic area concerning the status of the (subject) daughter, when she declares that she doesn't place (desire) ~~the daughter~~ her fate in a position of original subjectivity but in the position of an object, removed from perfection ~~even~~ as she is.

The transplantation of the appropriate normal gene to appropriate somatic cells is required.

*In regard to cover(?) hope*
In the luminous x ray, she seems to teem with energy, though much of this virtual energy is locked up and plays no part in material reality.
~~in a blue egg that comes out about three feet from the body~~

by transferring functional copies of the relevant gene to the patient, permanent correction of the reversible features of the mutant phenotype may be possible.  (she won't be so horrible)

One creates a mouse model of human genetic disease by experimentally disrupting a normal copy of a mouse gene in vitro and then injecting cells containing the newly mutated gene into host blastocytes.  Chimeric mice made this way can then . . . (look up)

Transgenic mice carry the foreign gene in their genome, produced by oocytes with teh foreign DNA, DNA that is integrated into the mouse genome may be expressed.  and also transmitted to the progeny (being incorporated into the germline)

~~The~~ *It* is a touch, a single ancestral cell in which the initiating utation has *takes* taken place, resulting in a clone of tumor cells. , for example

The inertia could be intimated by the phenotype,  The mother's ~~picture~~ photograph that is in a situation which challenges the precarious equilibrium, the constancy, the phenotype introduces experiences of pleasure, innocence, kinetic.  ~~The phenotype whose function is to define every~~ *In such a way that to function with relation will not define every subject*
         the phenotype whose main task is to transform everything into kinetic energy, into secondary, into kinetic energy, which define every subject.  *Thus the repeated inherited* _____

a record, but continues to exhibit through the present.  ~~Her genetic bequest~~ So that the mother's life is not separate, and simply
Her genotype is a parallel reality to the/her reality of now

~~not a question of kinetic energy~~.  It is not a question of something that will be regulated with movement.

as if there were long ribbons *constantly* untying wrapping ~~at the molecular~~ at the fated or heart level,
And between them there is a kind of photon wave/ streamers of virtual festive exchange

          (disobedience moves to the unconscious)
     disobedience
the fact that the emotion lies so deep does not mean the cancer patients cannot alter them.
People can be rescued from their feelings of helpless and despair by going to a still deeper level.

The mother stands over her and screams and screams at her, expressivity, the extent of the defect.

          (the drive)
The organ (of exchange is unreal)  Unreal is not imaginary.  The unreal is defined by articulating itself on the real in a way that eludes us.  But the fact that it is unreal does not prevent an organ from embodying itself
          an exchange

so that the child's chromosome is a patchwork, consisting of alternating portions of the maternal grandmother's chromosome and the maternal grandfather's chromosome.

by transfering functional copies of the relevant gene  etc.

~~like a fairy godmother~~, magic wand touching the bad mother *before*

          ~~in a blue egg that~~

**Part 5**

<u>July 10, 1994</u>

She may change her happy ending, here. If the healing is herself, and not her daughter. Then it is a situation of potential or possible.

       which may also resemble the Buddha

(the fact that it is unreal does not prevent the organ from embodying itself)

a sort of grappling with the real at the foetal level, to emerge from the parallel reality.
at the/a psychologic level

              when
About the time of this birthday, a rash on her elbow indicated the advent of this enzyme deficiency, her gaze retreated from ahead of her like an apron

experience note

our ideas  deductions made from observed facts of life are of no use in the unfolding of a potential

       *she folds (recedes) gaze into herself ___ picture*

Although true condition of all things is an emptiness, they aren't of the merely empty nature they are also luminous. In this context, luminosity is the potential for phenomena to manifest and be experienced. Because things are a unity of being both empty and luminous, empty and yet arising dependently.

The moment of seeing can intervene here only as a suture, a conjunction of the imaginary and *the symbolic.* Her imaginary world in herself, moved to the symbolic, shedding brain function

Not that the material ceased to be significant (signifier) (Negative of) An act (no longer has a structure) an element of structure, by the fact of *no longer* concerning a real that is not self evidently caught up in it.

Instead of denying language (the mental) I could symbolize language with the glue (mucuous) (cells) (mitosis) and its trailings

~~(Now the material signification of the birth?)~~

I myself believe that there are two sorts of relations in time (sight) From the moment that a part of the symbolic world comes into existence it does indeed create its own past. But not in the same way as the form at the intuitive level, of her mother's (love) comprehension.

In all (knowledge) comprehension, there is a dimension of error, which is the forgetting of the

creative function of truth in its nascent form.
signification of materiality
material signification in its nascent form

So that when you look into at this gaze, her form of compassion for beings who perceive suffering as real. (a real substratum)

although when we say empty, we usually men without any concrete substance or matter

an opacity, a resistance to signification. resisting signification.

The phenotype is the signification. The genotype is the language, the grammar of the signifiers. the genes, the chromosomal pairs are the signs.

From the moment that a part of the symbolic world comes into existence, it does indeed create its own past, But not in the same way as the form at the intuitive level.

(xxxxx time fate)

(fated, or time)          *or pertaining to matter as distinguished from form*

In the sense that the girl mus thave done something terrible to her mother in a past life

that the mother must have done something terrible to the girl in a past life, to be so berieved.

The whole ambiguity of the sign derives from the fact that it represents something for someone, the girl to her.

intrinsically pure and untainted by the temporary defilements, full of unfolding qualities and capabilities, timeless, suturated with compassionate love.

since the opposite of the possible is certainly the real, we should be led to define the real as the impossible.

her real inability to repeat the primitive game over and over

the parallel woven lines of the rug she lies on go all the way to the ocean.

just a hint of her ferocity gives them material weight.
                    makes them real.

to gene notes
there is an underlying continuous variation in liability to the malformation with a threshold marking the point at which the liability is actually expressed as an abnormal phenotype (perinateal lethal phenotype)

heritability is the proportion of the total phenotypic variance of a trait that is caused by additive genetic variance

The bringing of elements of the same nature as the subject or the subject itself onto the plane of (objects Mother) (child) is always precarious, uncertain and unevenly realized. But this relative precariousness matters less than the decisive possibility of a viewpoint from which the immanent elements are perceived from the outside as objects.  In the end, we perceive each appearamce, subject (ourselves) animal, mind, world — from within and from without at the same time, both as continuity with respect to ourselves and as object,  (like water in water).

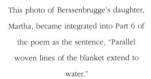

This photo of Berssenbrugge's daughter, Martha, became integrated into Part 6 of the poem as the sentence, "Parallel woven lines of the blanket extend to water."

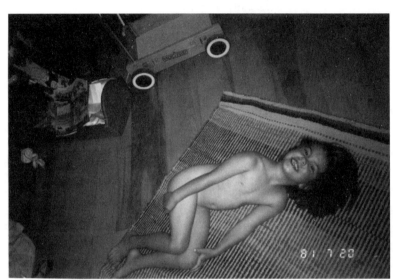

The abstract joyous potentiality of her emotion during the birth  Her gaze completely inward, a compaction of potential to no potential
                    the emotionalized, like heavy matter.

At night, inspiration fell on her like rain, penetrating   touching the subject at the germline (unknown center navel) to the wishes of her love moving the protean germline, like a gap or open place.

She searches the external world for signs of the object, (therefore includes the establishment of an internal perceptual set derived from previous experience of the object (go to exp line)
            the guilty act of the former life.

The reduction of the field of the god (mother) to the universality of the signifier, which produces a serene exceptional detachment from human desire.

abstract as this electron micrograph of a protein deplete human metaphase chromosome, showing the residual chromosome scaffold and loops of DNA

the materiality of the metaphase, a kind of teletransporter of signified 1/2 protoplasm across a lineage or time avid, muscular and compact,

as if pervasive, attached to her and particular.  in a particular family karma matrilinearity (karma) destiny or ultimate natural disaster (big)

in which the luminosity of the sonogram (fetal) becomes a kindof clairvoyance

The love has no quantity measure or value or space between them (insert note about depth) is like a collapsed star, but it only lasts a certain length of time

                    (a singularity in space)

but it only lasts a certain length of time.  It could be this whole busines has been to teach you a different concept of time

~~across which unfolds new life without~~ compromising life as a whole

She would just take out the (word) sign, concept.
                    leave out a signifier at the karmic level.

once at the karmic level she is a signifier for the form of universality, a totality which is universalized.

*HERE GO AGAIN TO ANATIMUCAL DETAILS*

—m—

**III.**                    **July 24,\* Amended September 20, 1994 and 1995 Drafts**

*(\* approximate)*

Both drafts are presented within each section below, for easier comparison by the reader.  The July 24, 1994 version is presented as Berssenbrugge wrote it.  The September 20, 1994 version was written in one-paragraph sections; it was subsequently amended, a process showing Berssenbrugge making her choices for such technical considerations as line breaks, diction and rhythm.  The draft is also shown with Editing Marks that depict subsequent changes made for the poem to become the first published version in 1995 *Conjunctions*).

*(Editing Marks on the September 20, 1994 version:  strikethroughs = deletions; underlined words = added words; back slash = line breaks)*

Part 1

<u>July 24, 1994 Version</u>
genotype is her genetic constitution

phenotype is the observable expression of the genotype as structural and biochemical traits

genetic disease is only the extreme manifestation of genetic change, against a background of normal variability.

Within the conventional unit we call subjectivity from individual particularities, what is happening?

She believes she is herself, which isn't complete madness, because it's a belief.

The problem is not to turn the subject into an entity, the subject defined as the effect of the signifiers or genes.

There is between her and the displaced gene another relation, the effect of meaning.

You know the meaning she is conscious of is contingent, the surface of water in an uninhabited world, the existence of eyes and ears.

You wouldn't think of her form by thinking about the water.

You can go in, if you don't encounter anything.

Each sense, impressions are constantly being laid down on our neurons.

Though we call the heavier sense impressions stress, all impressions create limitations.

I believe the opacity of her subjectivity (trauma), its resistance to signification is responsible here for the limits of remembering.

___ metaphor would be an impulse of intelligence, a thought and a molecule, like a two sided surface.

A girl says sweetly, it's about time you begin looking after me, so I may seem lovable to myself.

She was inspired to change the genotype at the level of the germline, since the cell's memory outlives the cell.

It is a memory that builds some matter around itself, like time, something that inevitably befalls a person.


September 20, 1994 Version, With Editing Marks Depicting Changes to Reach Final Draft:
The genotype is her genetic constitution./ The phenotype is the observable expression of the genotype as structural and biochemical traits./ Genetic disease is ~~just~~ extreme genetic change, against a background of normal variability./ Within the conventional unit we call subjectivity due to individual ~~particularities~~ particulars, what is happening?/ She believes she is herself, which isn't complete madness.~~It's~~ , its belief./ The problem is not to turn the subject ~~into an entity, the sub-~~

~~ject defined as the effect of the signifiers or genes~~. ,<u>the effect of the genes, into an entity</u>./ ~~There is between~~ <u>Between</u> her and the displaced gene <u>is</u> another relation, the effect of meaning./ The meaning ~~she is~~ <u>she's</u> conscious of is contingent, ~~the~~ <u>a</u> surface of water in an uninhabited world, ~~the existence of~~ <u>existing as</u> our eyes and ears./ You wouldn't think of her form by thinking about ~~the~~ water./ You can go in, if you don't encounter anything./ ~~Although~~ <u>Though</u> we call ~~the heavier~~ heavy sense impressions stress, all ~~impressions create~~ <u>impression creates</u> limitation./ I believe ~~the opacity of her~~ <u>opaque</u> inheritance ~~is responsible for the limits of remembering~~ <u>accounts for the limits of her memory</u>./ <u>The mental impulse is a thought and a molecule tied together like sides of a coin</u>./ A girl says sweetly, it's time you begin to look after me, so I may seem lovable to myself./ ~~She was~~ <u>She's</u> inspired to change the genotype, because the cell's memory outlives the cell./ ~~It is~~ <u>It's</u> a memory that builds some matter around itself, like time~~, something that inevitably befalls a person~~.

## Part 2

<u>July 24, 1994 Version</u>
Feelings of helplessness drove me to fantastic and ridiculous extremes.

Nevertheless, the axis of her helplessness speaks of something other than the axis we grasp when we consider it a function of inheritance.

She doesn't believe in the eclectic, she believes in recurrence.

Chromatin fails to condense during mitosis, a fragile site recombines misaligned genes of the repeated sequence.

She is a little unformed, as if gauze were stretched across her face.

Eyes lack the light of recognition.

Nostrils flair out.

Eyelids turn down at the outside so she peers out from her lids.

When she's excited, she emits a cry like a cat.

At four years, she fully exhibits this happy puppet syndrome.

Your entire axis speaks of something other than the axis we grasp when we speak of her as a function of the individual.

The species survives in the form of a young girl asking sweetly.

Note the characteristic short fingers and hypoplastic nails her mother has painted.

The deficiency of the chromosomal region 15, inherited from the mother, demonstrates that the parental origin of genetic material profoundly effects the expression of her defect.

He holds to the notion of experience as the field of a praxis, so while she has a choice that is not inspiration.

The feeling is what manifests in experience the enacting of reality of the inheritance in so far as the reality is a life force.

The agency is the sum total of death and defect caused by mutant genes, in the sense of death as nothing but signifiere.

It is in so far as the object, the voice, is present in it (death) that the percipiens is present (in the womb.

In so far as fate is of a real order here and signifies the embodiment of a deformity.

Note the characteristic short fingers and hypoplastic nails her mother has painted.

The deficiency of chromosomal region 15 inherited from the mother, demosntrates that the parental origin of genetic material profoundly effects the clinical expression of the defect)

Finality is implied in various embryonic forms in every causal notion.

The gap, the function of cause has always presented to any conceptual apprehension of the/her attachment.

In her case, there is a purity because it is not tainted by any force or cause, in the sense of the life force.

A kind of trusting confidence holds itself like an organ in the body.

In a case in which, generically, the function is said to create the mother, in this case the function does not even explain this area.

She screams and screams at her.

Nevertheless, the survival of humans as a species has meaning.

Each girl is transitory and dies.


September 20, 1994 Version, With Editing Marks Depicting Changes to Reach Final Draft:
Feelings of helplessness drove me to fantastic and ridiculous extremes./ Nevertheless, the axis of her helplessness is not the axis I grasp when I consider it a function of inheritance./ Chromatin fails to condense during mitosis, ./ ~~&~~ A fragile site recombines misaligned genes of the repeated

sequence./ She seems a little unformed, ~~as if~~ gauze ~~stretched~~ stretches across her face, <u>eyelids</u> <u>droop</u>.~~/ Nostrils flair out. Eyelids turn down.~~ When ~~she's~~ excited, she cries like a cat~~,~~ <u>and</u> fully ~~exhibiting a happy puppet~~ <u>exhibits the "happy puppet"</u> syndrome./ Note ~~the characteristic~~ short fingers and hypoplastic painted nails./ Your entire axis speaks other than the axis you grasp, when you consider her the function of an individual./ ~~The deficiency on chromosome 15, from the mother, demonstrates that the parental origin of material profoundly effects the expression of a defect. He holds to the notion of experience as the field of a praxis. The~~ <u>Her</u> feeling ~~is what~~ manifests in experience an ~~enacting of the~~ <u>enactment of</u> inheritance, insofar as ~~the~~ <u>its</u> reality is a life force./ ~~The agency is the sum of death and defect caused by mutant genes, death as nothing but signifier. In so far~~ <u>Insofar</u> as fate is of a real order here ~~and signifies~~ <u>, signifying</u> embodiment, the perceived is present in the womb./ ~~Finality is implied in various embryonic forms in every causal notion. The~~ <u>A</u> gap~~, the function of~~ or cause presents to any conceptual apprehension of ~~an~~ attachment./ In her case, ~~there is a~~ <u>there's</u> purity ~~because it is not tainted~~ <u>untainted</u> by ~~any~~ force or cause, like the life force./ ~~A kind of trusting confidence holds itself like an organ in the body. In a case in which, generically, the function creates the other, in this case it doesn't even~~ <u>Where,</u> <u>generically, function creates the mother, in this case it won't even</u> explain ~~the~~ <u>this</u> area./ She screams ~~and screams~~ at her./ A species survives in the form of a girl asking sweetly./ Nevertheless, ~~the~~ survival of the species as a whole has meaning./ Each girl is transitory.


**Part 3**


<u>July 24, 1994 Version</u>
Her focus begins a little ahead of herself and goes into the far distance, so she herself would not be involved in what she looks at.

She could see relatively normally for years.

Rhodopsin encoded by the unaffected allele would normally conver the photon into a nerve impulse in the retina.

The image, the effects of energy starting from a given point of the real, is reflected at some point on a surface, the surface of a lake, or an area of the occipital lobe.

You don't need the entire surface to be aware of the content of a field or a figure.

All that's needed is to one point of a real space, there should correspond an effect at another point.

There is an image, but also a struggle to recognize the reception of the image.

She herself sees the waves and the horizon as if she were water in the water.

In this relation she is not looking at her daughter from the place from which her daughter sees her.

She does not recognize the abnormal attributes.

She screams and screams at her.

She manages to resolve the image as the figure of a fire below her in the woods, a piece of red silk.

The young girl shows a white reflex in the affected eye, when light reflects off the tumor surface.

One sees in the relation the effects of speech on her, in so far as these effects are so radically primary, they properly determine the status of the subject as subject.

It's a case of uniparental disomy in which the presence in a subject of a pair of chromosomes both inherited from one parent, with no representative of the chromosome from another ancestor.

The genetic predisposition to a specific relation interacts with chance.

The identity is the sum of the effects of the genes on a subject at the level at which the she constitutes herself out of the effects of the (signifier).

In the waiting room, she hopes a large dog will come up to her, be kind to her and fulfill all her wishes.

Between what occurs as if by chance and the veiled poignancy in the words, mother can't you see I'm I'm dying, there is the same relation to which we were dealing with in recurrence.

Is it not that which is expresed in the depth of the anxiety of this image, namely, the most intimate aspects of their relation which emerges, not so much in the a(?) as in the fact that is beyond, in the sense of her fate?

Anxious and heartfelt is a mother's obedience to her child, but the obedience is not continous, as if a white space in her eye had been holding this genetic problem, while within the range, even now, of her deteriorating sight, in which sight will be her memory, disobedience moves toward unconsciousness.

Her love for her mother is what manifests in experience the enacting of the reality of the inheritance in so far as the reality is a life force.


September 20, 1994 Version, With Editing Marks Depicting Changes to Reach Final Draft:
Her focus extends <u>from</u> in front of her into ~~far~~ distance, so ~~she is~~ <u>she's</u> not involved in what she looks at./ ~~She could see normally for years~~. Rhodopsin from ~~by~~ the unaffected gene can convert ~~photons~~ <u>photon</u> into retinal impulse, <u>so she sees normally for years.</u>/ The image, the effects of energy starting from a real point, is reflected at some point on a surface, ~~the surface or~~ a lake, or ~~an~~ area of the occipital lobe./ You don't need the ~~entire~~ <u>whole</u> surface to be aware of ~~the~~ <u>a</u> ~~content of a field or the~~ figure, ~~only for one point~~ <u>just for some points</u> of real space to correspond to

~~an~~ effect at ~~another~~ other ~~point~~ points./ There's an image~~, but also~~ and a struggle to recognize ~~the~~ reception of it./ She sees waves and the horizon as if she were water in the water./ The mother's not looking at her daughter from the place from which the daughter sees her./ ~~In this relation, the mother's not looking at the daughter from the place from which the daughter sees her.~~ She ~~does not~~ doesn't recognize ~~the~~ abnormal attributes./ ~~She screams at her.~~ The daughter resolves ~~an~~ her image as ~~the figure of a~~ fire below ~~her~~ in the woods, red silk./ ~~There's a white mote in her eye, where light reflects off the tumor surface. In this case of single-parent disomy, a pair of chromosomes is inherited from only one ancestor. Genetic predisposition to a specific relation interacts with chance. Her identity is the sum of the effects of genes on a subject at the level at which she constittues herself out of the effects of words.~~ In the waiting room, she hopes a large dog will ~~come~~ walk up to her, be kind ~~to her~~ and fulfill her wishes./ Between what occurs as if by chance and ~~the words,~~ "Mother, can you see I'm dying?" ~~there's~~ is the same relation ~~to which~~ we deal with in recurrence./ ~~That which is expressed in~~ Is not what emerges from the anxiety of ~~this image~~ her speech, the most intimate ~~aspects~~ aspect of their relation ~~emerges, in the fact that is~~ beyond ~~desire, her fate~~ death, which is their chance?/ Obedience to ~~her~~ one's child is anxious ~~and~~ , heartfelt, but ~~the obedience is~~ not continuous, like a white mote in ~~a~~ her ~~child's~~ eye./ Within the range of deteriorating sight, in which sight will be her memory, disobedience moves toward unconsciousness.~~/ A child's love manifests in experience the enacting of the reality of the inheritance in so far as the reality is a life force.~~

**Part 4**

July 24, 1994 Version

The skull is relatively large and unmineralized and is soft to touch.

The thoracic cavity is small, the long bones of the arms and legs are short, and deformed, and the vertebrae are flattened.

All the bones are undermineralized.

A bluish light surrounds her body.

There is a whole theme concerning the status of the daughter, when she declares she doesn't place her inheritance (longing) in a position of subjectivity but in the position of an object, removed from perfection as it is.

The X ray teems with energy, though much of this virtual energy is locked outside the material.

By transfering functional copies of the relevant gene to the patient, he corrects the reversible features of the mutant phenotype.

One creates a mouse model of human genetic disease by experimentally disrupting a normal copy of a mouse gene in vitro and then injecting cells containing the newly mutated gene into host blastocytes.

DNA integrated into the mouse genome may be expressed, and also transmitted to the progeny.

It is like a touch, a single ancestral celle initiates therapy.

The inertia could be intimated by the phenotype.

The mother's photograph challenges the precarious equilibrium, the constancy.

The phenotype introduces experiences of kinetic pleasure, innocence, in such a way that the function of the relation will not define every subject.

The phenotype whose main task is to transform everything into secondary into kinetic energy, won't define every subject.

Thus the repeated inherited mutation.

The mother's life is not separate, and simply a record, but continues to exhibit in the present.

Her genotype is a parallel reality to her reality of now.

It is not a question of something that will be regulated with movement, as if long ribbons were continuously untying between them at the fated or heart level, of virtual exchange.

The fact that inheritance (the deformity) lies so deep does not mean she cannot alter it.

people can go to a deeper level.

The other stands over her and screams and screams, expressivity, the extent of the defect.

Their exchange (organ) is unreal.  Unreal is not imaginary.  The unreal is defined by articulating itself on the real in a way that eludes us.

The fact that it is unreal does not prevent an exchange (an organ) from embodying itself.

The child's chromosomes are a patchwork, of alternating portions of the maternal grandmother's chromosome and the maternal grandfather's chromosome.

By transferring functional copies of the relevant gene to the patient, he might permanently correct the reversible features of the mutant phenotype, lightly touching the bad (defective) mother, before.


September 20, 1994 Version, With Editing Marks Depicting Changes to Reach Final Draft:
~~The~~ Her skull is large and soft to touch./  The thoracic cavity small, ~~the~~ limbs short, deformed, and ~~the~~ vertebrae flattened./  All the bones are undermineralized./  ~~A bluish~~ Bluish light surrounds her./  ~~The~~ This theme concerns her status, ~~when she declares~~ since she doesn't place her inheri-

tance in a position of subjectivity, but ~~in the position~~ of an object./ ~~Nevertheless, her~~ <u>Her</u> X ray teems with energy, ~~though this energy is~~ <u>but</u> locked outside ~~the~~ material./ ~~By~~ By transferring functional copies of the ~~relevant~~ gene to ~~the patient~~ <u>her</u>, he ~~corrects~~ <u>can correct</u> ~~reversible features of~~ the mutant phenotype./ One creates a mouse model of human ~~genetic~~ disease by disrupting a normal mouse gene in vitro, then injecting cells containing the mutated gene into host embryos./ DNA integrated into the mouse genome is expressed and transmitted to the progeny./ Like touch, one ancestral cell initiates therapy./ The phenotype, whose main task is to transform everything into secondary, kinetic energy, pleasure, innocence, won't define every subject./ ~~Thus, the repeated inherited mutation.~~ The ~~mother is~~ <u>mother's</u> not simply a record~~, but continues to exhibit in the present~~./ Her genotype makes a parallel reality to her reality ~~of~~ <u>,</u> now./ ~~It's not something regulated by movement, long ribbons untying between them at the fated or heart level, virtual exchange. That deformity lies so deep does not mean she can't alter it. She goes to a deeper level. The mother~~ <u>She</u> stands over her and screams~~, expressivity, the extent of the defect~~./ ~~The~~ <u>That the</u> exchange is unreal, not imaginary~~. It's defined by articulating itself on the real in a way that eludes us. The fact that it's unreal~~ doesn't prevent ~~an~~ <u>the</u> organ from embodying itself./ By transferring functional copies of the ~~relevant~~ gene to her, he might correct reversible features of the mutant phenotype, lightly touching the bad mother, before.

## Part 5 and 6

<u>July 24, 1994 Version</u>
*(In the July 24, 1994 version, what became two separate parts — 5 and 6 — in the Final Draft were written as just Part 5. This version was split into two parts as of the September 20, 1994 version.)*

The fact that it is unreal does not prevent the organ from embodying itself, a sort of grappling with the real at the foetal level, to emerge from the parallel reality.  to an apsychologic level.

About the time of her birthday, when a rash on her elbow indicated the enzyme deficiency, her gaze which spread like cloth ahead of her, folded inward.

We hold to the notion of experience, in the sense of a field of a praxis, but our ideas made from observed facts of life are of no use in the unfolding of a potential.

What she sees folds into herself.

Her true condition is an emptiness that is light.

There's still potential for phenomena to manifest and be experienced.

(A moment of seeing can intervene as a suture between the imaginary and the symbolic.)

Her imaginary world moves to the symbolic, shedding brain function.

Not that material ceased to be significant.  signifier).

An act no longer has an element of structure, by concerning a real that is not self evidently caught up in it.

Instead of denying the material, I could symbolize it with this mucus and its trailings.

From the moment a part of the symbolic world comes into existence, it creates its own scene (past), but not in the same way as form at the intuitive level of her mother's comprehension.

In all comprehension, there is a dimension of error, forgetting the creative function of the material (signification) in its nascent form.

So when you look into her gaze, her form of compassion for beings who perceive suffering as real (a real substratum) in her substratum (with the structural inalterability of the suffering)

although when we say empty, we usually mean without any concrete substance, an opacity, a resisting signification.

_____*(This version was split subsequently at this point to form Part 6)*
From the moment a part of the symbolic world comes into existence, it creates its own past, but not in the same way as form at the intuitive level.

(fated, or time) of or pertaining to matter as distinguished from form

In the sense that the mother must have done something terrible to the girl in a past life, to be so bereaved.

The ambiguity of the sign derives from the fact that it represents something to someone, the girl to her, intrinsically pure, without temporary defilements, full of unfolding capabilities, timeless, saturated with love.

The mother's real inability to repeat the childish game over and over.

Parallel woven lines of the rug she lies on extend to the ocean.

Just a hint of her ferocity gives them weight.

There is an underlying continuous variation in liability to the malformation with a threshold marking the point at which the liability is expressed as an lethal phenotype. (perinatally lethal)

The bringing of elements of the same nature as the subject itself onto the plane of the parent is always precarious, and unevenly realized, but this relative precariousness matters less than the decisive possibility of a viewpoint from which the immanent elements are perceived from the outside as objects.

At night, inspiration fell on her like rain, penetrating the subject at the germline (unknown center navel) to dethe wishes of her love moving the protean germline, like a gap or open place.

The abstract joy of her emotion during the birth, gaze inward, a compaction of potential and no potential, like an emotion that is fully realized.

She searches the external world for signs of the object, (therefore includes the establishment of an internal perceptual set derived from previous experience of the object (to the exp line)
the guilty act of the former life.

The reduction of the field of the (mother) (inheritance) to the universality of the signifier produces a serene exceptional detachment from human desire

abstract as an electron micrograph of a protein deplete metaphase chromosome, showing the residual chromosome scaffold and loops of DNA

The materiality of the metaphase, a kind of teletransporter of signified protoplasm across a lineage or time, avid, muscular and compact, as if pervasive, attached to her and particular.  In a particular matrilinear destiny or natural disaster, in which the luminosity of the fetal sonogram becomes a kind of clairvoyance.

The love has no quantity measure or value (insert note about depth or space between them is like a collapsed star, but it only lasts a certain length of time

It could be this whole business has been to teach you a different concept of time, across which unfolds a singularity without compromising life as a whole.

She would just take out the (word) sign, concept.  leave out a signifier at the karmic level

at the karmic level she nece is a signifier for the form of universality, a totality which is universalized.

September 20, 1994 Version, With Editing Marks Depicting Changes to Reach Final Draft:


## Part 5
On her fourth birthday, a rash ~~at her~~ on the elbow indicated enzyme deficiency./  Her ~~gaze which had spread like cloth in front of her,~~ view folded inward./  ~~Our notion of experience is the field of a praxis, but ideas~~ Ideas about life from experience are of no use in the unfolding of ~~her~~ potential, empty and light~~.  There's~~ , though there's still potential for phenomena to ~~manifest and~~ be experienced./  A moment of seeing can intervene like a suture between ~~the imaginary and the symbolic, and shed brain function.  Not that material ceased to be significant~~. an image and its word./  An act is no longer structured by concerning a real ~~that is self-evidently~~ that's not caught up in it./  Instead of denying material, I could symbolize it with this mucus and its trailings./  The moment the ~~symbolic comes into existence~~ imaginary exists, it creates its own setting, but not the same way as form at the intuitive level of her mother's comprehension./  In all comprehension, ~~there is some~~ there's an error, forgetting the ~~creative function~~ creativity of material in its nascent form./

So, you see in her eyes, her form of compassion for beings who perceive suffering as a real ~~substratum, emptiness, opacity resisting signification~~ substrate.

## Part 6

~~The symbolic world~~ An image creates its ~~own~~ past, but not ~~the same way as~~ like form at the intuitive level~~, in the sense that the~~ ./ ~~M~~mother must have done something terrible ~~to her~~ in past life, to be so berieved./ ~~The ambiguity of the sign~~ Ambiguity of the form derives from its representing ~~something to someone,~~ the girl ~~to her, without temporal defilement,~~ full of ~~unfolding~~ capability ~~and~~ saturated with love./ If the opposite of possible is real, she defines real as impossible, her real inability to repeat the child's game , over and over./ Parallel woven lines of the blanket ~~she lies on extend to the ocean~~ extend to water./ Just a hint of childish ferocity gives them weight./ ~~A threshold marks the point at which underlying continuous variation in liability to the malformation is expressed as a lethal phenotype. Bringing elements of the same nature as the subject onto the plane of the parent is precarious and unevently realized, but matters less than the possibility of viewing immanant elements from the outside as objects.~~ At night, inspiration fell on her like rain, penetrating the subject at the germline , like a navel./ ~~Abstract joy during~~ Joy at birth, a compaction of potential and no potential, ~~like emotion that is~~ is an abstraction that was fully realized./ ~~She searches externally for signs of the object, including an internal perceptual set derived previously from the guilty act of former life. The reduction of the field of the mother~~ Reducing a parent to the universality of the signifier produces a serene ~~exceptional~~ detachment ~~from desire~~ in her, abstract as an electron micrograph of ~~a~~ protein _ deplete ~~scaffold of~~ human metaphase DNA./ Its materiality~~, a teletransporter~~ is a teletransport of signified protoplasm across lineage or time, avid, muscular , and compact, as if pervasive, attached to her, in a particular ~~matrilinear destiny or~~ matriarchy of natural disaster, in which the luminosity of ~~the~~ a fetal sonogram becomes ~~a clairvoyance~~ clairvoyant./ The love has no quantity or value, but ~~it~~ only lasts a length of time~~. It could be this whole business illustrates a~~ , different ~~concept of~~ time, across which unfolds ~~the~~ her singularity without compromising life as a whole. ~~She would just take out the word, concept.~~

— ∿ —

## IV. Minor Changes Between Versions Published by *Conjunctions* and *BLACK LIGHTNING* which is publishing Berssenbrugge's Final Draft Dated May 15, 1996

"The Four Year Old Girl" was first published in 1995 by *Conjunctions* #24 (Bard College). Subsequently, Berssenbrugge made some changes, as follows (*Editing Marks: Strikethroughs = deletion; underlined words = additions*):

Part 2
Sentence 8: Your ~~entire~~ axis speaks other than the axis you grasp, when you consider her the function of an individual.
Sentence 9: Her feeling manifests in her experience ~~an~~ the enactment of inheritance, insofar as its reality is a life force.

Sentence 2:  Rhodopsin ~~from~~ encoded in the unaffected gene can convert photons into retinal impulse, so she sees normally for years.  (This change is a return to an earlier choice made in the July 24, 1994 version which is not shown in this essay.)

Part 4

Sentence 7:  ~~By transferring functional copies of the gene to her, he can correct the mutant phenotype.~~

Sentence 10:  Like touch, one ancestral cell can ~~initiates~~ initiate therapy.

Part 6

Sentence 2:  Mother must have done something terrible in the past ~~life~~, to be so berieved.

Berssenbrugge's most major change was her deletion of Part 4, Sentence 7.  The deletion makes sense as its meaning is captured in a more resonant manner by Sentence 8:  "One creates a mouse model of human disease by disrupting a normal mouse gene in vitro, then injecting cells containing the mutated gene into host embryos."

—m—

The following is Berssenbrugge's Final Draft of her poem written "to overcome fated ill-ness," rooted in the situation of a young girl with "disorganized" genes and which ultimately discovered that "particular transcendence" in love that overcomes heartbreak.

**THE FOUR YEAR OLD GIRL**

1

The *genotype* is her genetic constitution.

The *phenotype* is the observable expression of the genotype as structural and biochemical traits.

Genetic disease is extreme genetic change, against a background of normal variability.

Within the conventional unit we call subjectivity due to individual particulars, what is happening?

She believes she is herself, which isn't complete madness, its belief.

The problem is not to turn the subject, the effect of the genes, into an entity.

Between her and the displaced gene is another relation, the effect of meaning.

The meaning she's conscious of is contingent, a surface of water in an uninhabited world,
        existing as our eyes and ears.

You wouldn't think of her form by thinking about water.

You can go in, if you don't encounter anything.

Though we call heavy sense impressions stress, all impression creates limitation.

I believe opaque inheritance accounts for the limits of her memory.

The mental impulse is a thought and a molecule tied together like sides of a coin.

A girl says sweetly, it's time you begin to look after me, so I may seem lovable to myself.

She's inspired to change the genotype, because the cell's memory outlives the cell.

It's a memory that builds some matter around itself, like time.

2

Feelings of helplessness drove me to fantastic and ridiculous extremes.

Nevertheless, the axis of her helplessness is not the axis I grasp when I consider it a
        of inheritance.

Chromatin fails to condense during mitosis.

A fragile site recombines misaligned genes of the repeated sequence.

She seems a little unformed, gauze stretches across her face, eyelids droop.

When excited, she cries like a cat and fully exhibits the "happy puppet" syndrome.

Note short fingers and hypoplastic painted nails.

Your axis speaks other than the axis you grasp, when you consider her the function of
        an individual.

Her feeling manifests in her experience the enactment of inheritance, insofar as its reality is
        a life force.

Insofar as fate is of a real order here, signifying embodiment, the perceived is present in the
        womb.

A gap or cause presents to any conceptual apprehension of attachment.

In her case, there's purity untainted by force or cause, like the life force.

Where, generically, function creates the mother, in this case it won't even explain this area.

She screams at her.

A species survives in the form of a girl asking sweetly.

Nevertheless, survival of the species as a whole has meaning.

Each girl is transitory.


3

Her focus extends from in front of her into distance, so she's not involved in what she looks at.

Rhodopsin encoded in the unaffected gene can convert photon into retinal impulse, so she sees
        normally for years.

The image, the effects of energy starting from a real point, is reflected at some point on a
        surface, a lake, or area of the occipital lobe.

You don't need the whole surface to be aware of a figure, just for some points of real space
        to correspond to effect at other points.

There's an image and a struggle to recognize reception of it.

She sees waves and the horizon as if she were water in the water.

The mother's not looking at her daughter from the place from which the daughter sees her.

She doesn't recognize abnormal attributes.

The daughter resolves her image as fire below in the woods, red silk.

In the waiting room, she hopes a large dog will walk up to her, be kind and fulfill her wishes.

Between what occurs as if by chance and "Mother, can you see I'm dying?" is the same relation
        we deal with in recurrence.

Is not what emerges from the anxiety of her speech, the most intimate aspect of their relation
        beyond death, which is their chance?

Obedience to one's child is anxious, heartfelt, but not continuous, like a white mote in her eye.

Within the range of deteriorating sight, in which sight will be her memory, disobedience moves
        toward unconsciousness.

Her skull is large and soft to touch.

The thoracic cavity small, limbs short, deformed, and vertebrae flattened.

All the bones are undermineralized.

Bluish light surrounds her.

This theme concerns her status, since she doesn't place her inheritance in a position of
        subjectivity, but of an object.

Her X ray teems with energy, but locked outside material.

One creates a mouse model of human disease by disrupting a normal mouse gene in vitro, then
        injecting cells containing the mutated gene into host embryos.

DNA integrated into the mouse genome is expressed and transmitted to the progeny.

Like touch, one ancestral cell can initiate therapy.

The phenotype, whose main task is to transform everything into secondary, kinetic energy,
        pleasure, innocence, won't define every subject.

The mother's not simply a record.

Her genotype makes a parallel reality to her reality, now.

She stands over her and screams.

That the exchange is unreal, not imaginary, doesn't prevent the organ from embodying itself.

By transferring functional copies of the gene to her, he might correct reversible features of the
        mutant phenotype, lightly touching the bad mother, before.


5

On her fourth birthday, a rash on the elbow indicated enzyme deficiency.

Her view folded inward.

Ideas about life from experience are of no use in the unfolding of potential, empty and light,
        though there's still potential for phenomena to be experienced.

A moment of seeing can intervene like a suture between an image and its word.

An act is no longer structured by concerning a real that's not caught up in it.

Instead of denying material, I could symbolize it with this mucus and its trailings.

The moment the imaginary exists, it creates its own setting, but not the same way as form at
        the intuitive level of her mother's comprehension.

In all comprehension, there's an error, forgetting the creativity of material in its nascent form.

So, you see in her eyes, her form of compassion for beings who perceive suffering as a real
        substrate.


6

An image creates its past, but not like form at the intuitive level.

Mother must have done something terrible in past, to be so bereaved.

Ambiguity of the form derives from its representing the girl, full of capability, saturated with love.

If the opposite of possible is real, she defines real as impossible, her real inability to repeat the
        child's game, over and over.

Parallel woven lines of the blanket extend to water.

Just a hint of childish ferocity gives them weight.

At night, inspiration fell on her like rain, penetrating the subject at the germline, like a navel.

Joy at birth, a compaction of potential and no potential, is an abstraction that was fully realized.
Reducing a parent to the universality of the signifier produces a serene detachment in her,
abstract as an electron micrograph of protein-deplete human metaphase DNA.
Its materiality is a teletransport of signified protoplasm across lineage or time, avid, muscular,
and compact, as if pervasive, attached to her, in a particular matriarchy of natural
disaster, in which the luminosity of a fetal sonogram becomes clairvoyant.
The love has no quantity or value, but only lasts a length of time, different time, across which
unfolds her singularity without compromising life as a whole.

# INDRAN AMIRTHANAYAGAM

Indran Amirthanayagam, a Tamil from Sri Lanka, won the Paterson Poetry Prize for his collection, *The Elephants of Reckoning* (Hanging Loose Press, 1993). A former professor and journalist, he is now a diplomat and currently represents the United States in Cote d'Ivoire. He has published poems and editorials in *The New York Times, New York/Newsday, Grand Street, The Kenyon Review, The Massachusetts Review, BOMB, The Literary Review, Exquisite Corpse* and *Hanging Loose*, among others. His poetry was featured on the PBS television special, "The United States of Poetry," and in several anthologies. He has an M.A. from Columbia University's Graduate School of Journalism and a B.A. from Haverford College. His second poetry collection, *The Last Condors in New Amsterdam*, is forthcoming.

In response to the question, "What advice would you give to a young poet?" Indran Amirthanayagam responds with a poem:

## ADVICE TO YOUNG POETS

I do not know how to multiply bread or fish, but I can write a poem if I set my heart out on the desk; open ears and eyes; concentrate mind.

I must not eat too quickly the swans that fly across my table.

Remember that energy is eternal delight.

Do not be afraid to patch your pockets with assorted lines stolen from the Gods, from Yeats and lesser gods.

Laugh, first. Be humble later, but especially when you leave the privacy of your skull; when you speak to some passing brother or sister.

There are bad poets and good poets. And there are poets who lose their calm and refined sense of judgment when they start hollering "bad bad, good good."

Stay away from delusion. Welcome illusion. Listen to bridge music, some fusion.

Rhyme at all times and especially when you are told not to rhyme.

Define free verse to your mother, best friend, lover and in correspondence to poetry editors.

Discourage any attempts to posit poetry as the highest art, even more difficult than the pole vault;

yet, encourage all such attempts to return the poet to the city, to bring him back as king.

Read *The Republic*, if only to make yourself angry.

Then follow all advice offered by Allen Ginsberg except the hallucinogenics.

Look into your own contradictions, contrary states, employ poetry to resolve them.

Listen to music.

Do not stop listening to music. I lost many years of new poems when I turned off the record player in 1982.

Find out why I turned off the record player, you (......). I can tell you, but I am ashamed to reveal my own rough-stoned path out of eden.

— "But you have, you've written poems," says a journalist. "They speak about a paradise called Sri Lanka and how it's been muddied up with bones and blood" —.

As I've said to the mirror, do not believe your own press.

Fight to keep a space open in your heart, ears, brain, in you, poet, for the music of study guides, the chiming of canned rhymes and pre-cooked verses. This will keep you honest and make the task of writing more difficult. You'll learn to become a good housecleaner, arranger, sorter, extruder.

Do not expect *a* to precede *b* except in the movies. . . in five year plans . . . sometimes in love, war. When the pieces fall easy, let them slide right into the verses you construct.

You do not always have to struggle with the slab. You do not have to sweat while writing.

Finally, first, last, at least on paper, at least in life, love-make.

And if you prefer holy orders, let them batter your heart
like Donne's three-personed god.

# INDRAN AMIRTHANAYAGAM RECKONS
# WITH HISTORY
# AND SINGS FOR ELEPHANTS

*I want poems stained*
*by hands and everydayness. . . .*

*I long for eatable sonnets,*
*poems of honey and flour, . . .*

*Brother poets from here*
*and there, from earth and sky,*
*from Medellin, from Veracruz,*
*Abyssinia, Antofagasta,*
*do you know the recipe for honeycombs?*
*— from "Sweetness, always" by Pablo Neruda*

For the Sri Lankan-born poet Indran Amirthanayagam, 1993 should have been a good year. It was the year Hanging Loose Press published his first book, *Elephants of Reckoning.* But in May 1993, a young man, bombs strapped to his chest, crashed his bicycle into then President Ranasinghe Premadasa. The explosion killed both bomber and president mere days after a leader of the opposition, Lalith Athulathmudali, was gunned down during a campaign rally. Even in a country that had become accustomed to high levels of violence in recent years, the two assassinations were extraordinarily shocking and brutal.

Thus, in May 1993 when Amirthanayagam should have been happily celebrating his book's publication, his attention was focused on calling for an end to the violence in his birthland. In the same month his book was officially released, *The New York Times* published an Op-Ed piece by Amirthanayagam bemoaning "the latest public violations by villains, bogeymen, crazed boys, rogue elephants. Violations. Rape. Murder." As he called for peace and unification among the warring Tamils and Sinhalese, Amirthanayagam raised the image of the rogue elephant as a metaphor:

> The elephant has been cast out of the herd. Perhaps it is mad; perhaps it harbors some wound that does not allow it to graze in peace with its brothers and sisters. So it leaves the herd, or is forced out. And alone in the jungles it eats the dry leaves of loneliness. And when it spots a group of holiday travelers 50 yards down the dirt road — my family in a jeep — it charges.
>
> We were lucky in 1965. The tracker who accompanied us spoke some commands in a tongue that the elephant understood, and the bruised animal stopped its charge. The tragedy of modern Sri Lankans is that far too many of us, living in Colombo or Toronto or New York have forgotten the tongue that will heal our differences.
>
> That tongue is not Sinhalese, or Tamil, or English. It is all of these and much more. It is rooting out the unfortunate link between ethnicity and the bogeymen from the books our children read. We don't need to have a Tamil villain and a Sinhalese hero. And we don't need to reverse the terms either. Let our villains be people who commit

acts against the order of society, whoever they are.

*The New York Times* added a sub-headline to Amirthanayagam's article: "Sri Lanka's expatriates can end the killing." Time has made a mockery of this optimism, with the violence continuing, and highlighting the poignancy of the article's 1993 conclusion:

> "The nightmare rides upon sleep," said Yeats about Ireland. But then we awake, as we must. And we must go about our business, and raise our children, and welcome back the family that has dispersed to Canada, Europe, India, if only for a visit.
>
> And let us have a roaring reunion. Let us have Bharata Nathyam dancers and bell singers and pianos and tables. Let us have Hindu pujas and the rosary and the Four Noble Truths of Buddhism. Let us invite the burghers to return form Australia and the Tamil stowaways from the restaurants of Paris. Let us have a government of national unity. Let us care for the remaining herds of elephants. Let them have jungle and grassland. Let us develop potions to heal the wounds of the rogues.

"It was a bittersweet time. Why did this paradise become bloody? I was in pain. Part of my goal as a poet was to tell the Sri Lankan conflict to the world. When I lived there, it was called Ceylon and it was multi-ethnic and multi-cultural. What was this Sri Lankan conflict? Did I support it? Can I support it? Does it matter if I support it? Who am I?" Armirthanayagam says, recalling some of the questions he faced. "I didn't have a gun in hand, but I did have a pen. Though I had the frustration of not being able to fight physically for either the independent Eelam, or Sri Lanka directly, as I have avoided both choices, I had an emotional anger that I channeled through my poems."

Amirthanayagam was eight years old when he and his family left Ceylon in 1969, partly to seek help for an autistic brother and partly, he says, because "I think my parents saw the darkness in Ceylon's future." *Ceylon.* Amirthanayagam prefers the term to Sri Lanka which he has come to associate with the country's civil war. His family first went to London, then moved to Hawai'i, after which Amirthanayagam attended Haverford College in Pennsylvania and then Columbia University's Graduate School of Journalism. He returned to Sri Lanka for the first time in 1980; after returning to the United States, he began integrating his birthland in his poetry.

"My grandfather was very important to me. That 1980 trip, seeing my grandfather ill, led to a real sense of loss and I wanted with my poems to replace that loss," he says.

Though President Premadasa's assassination heightened the tension in the country, the friction in Sri Lanka goes back to the days when Britain, the colonial power, employed many Hindu Tamils as Amirthanayagam says the British found them motivated and industrious. After independence in 1948, the Tamils suffered at the hands of the majority, the mostly Buddhist Sinhalese. Later, Sinhalese-nationalist governments stirred anti-Tamil feelings to win votes and engaged in heinous practices of colonization, trying to reduce the Tamil majority in the North and East of the island. This colonization along with discrimination in such key areas of life as school admission and jobs in the state sector contributed to the eventual lighting of the tinderbox and the terrible civil war that has raged in the island since 1983.

Amirthanayagam's love for his grandfather and the Ceylon he once knew is evoked in one of the poems in *Elephants of Reckoning*, "Letter from England," which he dedicates to his grandfather, S. Ratnanather:

## Letter from England

You were a hunter of jungle fowl and birds,
a singer of hymns, odes of whiskey verse.
And you were a king! A regal spirit
on a mountain top washing hands in bowls of gold.

I was eight years old when I went with my father
and mother across the ocean,
far away from your mountain chair,
your confident air.

England was pleasant, rainy and full of cricketers,
and "ministries of silly walks" and Irish terriers.
Remember, you came to our house
bearing "The Pagan Love Song" and "Daisy Daisy."

I was growing up,
I learned you were not only a hunter and king,
but a president of a company as well.
And an old man suffering England's winter. Colds. Pain.

I hear you have had a stroke.
You will not read these words.
I hear you walk about the house
in slippers, talking of Jaffna
and Atchuvelli years.
Your childhood. Palmyra. Jungle fowl.

I hear you get up and walk out of the house
unless somebody catches you at the door,
and you say: "Get away, get away, young man,
I am going to Jaffna on my knees and hands,
with my heart and head. My eyes. My breath."

"For me, the idea of living at sea — in exile — away from Sri Lanka without a home in Tamil due to the war, infuses my poetry," Amirthanayagam says. "When I began to write poetry I found a solace for something in me. I found in poetry a salvation."

As Amirthanayagam watched the violence escalate in his birthland, other factors exacerbated the tumultous emotions he was feeling in 1993. Earlier that year he received an acceptance into the American Foreign Service and, thus, knew his days in New York City — just when he felt he had achieved a certain literary success in what he considered a leading center of American poetry — were numbered. But before leaving for Washington D.C. and the rest of the world, he had one last poetry reading scheduled at St. Marks Poetry Project to mark the release of *Elephants of Reckoning*.

Thus, Amirthanayagam wrote the poem, "WORDS FOR THE ENTERPRISE," both to introduce his book during the reading and to reflect on the events then affecting his life. "When I say in the poem that 'Spain is New York', I was trying to evoke the sense of idealism that inspired the world's artists to fight against Franco in the Spanish Civil War. Franco won. Fascism took over. But it was a noble fight and Federico Garcia Lorca was one of its victims," he says. "Though it was 1993 and not 1935, I was trying to evoke that sense of bravado. That, as we look towards the Millenium, we should gather ourselves and assume the heroics and idealism that infused earlier generations.

"Because I wrote the poem as an introduction to my book, I was acting as a cheerleader to the audience," he continues. "I wanted to rouse the audience to get the elephants out. Elephants are a symbol for many things in my book, including the best of ourselves — the best of human potential. That, too, is the role of the poet: to enter the hearts and minds of people and ask them to realize their own potentials."

Tellingly, Amirthanayagam adds that he concocted the poem's title partly in reference to the popular television and movie series, "Star Trek." He explains, "I was actually thinking of the U.S.S. Enterprise because that starship had all of the world's races represented as they went out there to boldly go where no man has gone before."

Finally, Amirthanayagam says, he considered "WORDS FOR THE ENTERPRISE" a response to what he found disappointing in contemporary poetry.

"So much of American poetry takes place in workshops and M.F.A. programs — I felt a certain frustration with that. So I wanted to say to the M.F.A.-ers to go out there and build roads and houses," he recalls. Or, as the poem states: ". . . let the Master/ of Fine Arts require building/ of roads or houses, breaking/ eggs for sweet cakes and meats,/ watching eggs break/ and chicks blind-hungry/ jump for worms, fly oceans."

For Amirthanayagam, part of the "ENTERPRISE" is what he calls "the literary tradition of being political and social, where the social is equal to caring" — a tradition practiced by such admired poets as Garcia Lorca and Pablo Neruda. For him, it translated into a new career: diplomacy. Shortly after reading at St. Marks Poetry Project, Amirthanayagam moved to Washington D.C., then later to postings in Argentina, Belgium and currently Cote D'Ivoire.

"It was a tortured decision. I was comfortable in New York, but felt I needed a new challenge to grow further as a poet. That Op-Ed piece (in *The New York Times*) was significant. I had this romantic idea that through diplomacy I could do this (social role) on a planetary scale, as Neruda did in Mexico when he squired away David Siqueiros who had been accused of trying to kill Trotsky."

"I don't know how long I'll be a diplomat and when I'll go back to the poetry circuit or teaching. But I was inspired by Neruda's role as a diplomat and poet. I thought this was a noble way of taking care of my family and not have to rely on the M.F.A system of dependency in the United States," he says.

Featured below are illustrations of Amirthanayagam's process of drafting "WORDS FOR THE ENTERPRISE." The similarity between the First Draft and the Final Draft exemplifies the effect of the emotions Amirthanayagam was feeling at the time he birthed the poem.

"The stronger the emotion or clearer the idea when I'm writing a poem, the more apt I am to get it at the first draft or have less revision," he says about his poetic process. "The more diffuse the emotions or ideas, the more revisions it'll take. When I feel an emotion or idea clearly, I can usually get it down — it's a meditation of the heart. Though one does have to strike a balance between heart and intellect, I do a lot of work in my head."

—๛—

The following presents early drafts of "WORDS FOR THE ENTERPRISE," with Amirthanayagam's thoughts about some of the changes presented after each draft. *(Editing Marks: strikethroughs = deletions; underlined words = additions)*

I.  First Draft

**WORDS FOR THE ENTERPRISE**

Lorca called it The Deep Song,
Neruda told us to go out
and sell light on the roads,
the grandmother of my friend said
that he reminded her of the boys
that went to Spain; today Spain
is New York, and tonight I ask
you to ride all your elephants out,

Ride with Allen
and a hundred billion
others out of the hydrogen
jukebox, remember
my father as you read
"Outside The Window," the words
are here on the first page
of *The Elephants of Reckoning*

Tonight and tomorrow New York
is Spain and the bayonets
are out, the firing squads
out, and we shall dance
at the end of 20 centuries,
at the end of 20 centuries
I ask you to honor the peace
that comes dropping slow,

At the end of 20 centuries,
I recall with you the briars
binding our joys and desires,
I insist that the purveyors
of the televisions of our eyes
rewind and re-spool, reel
William Shakespeare out of school

and let him bring his protean

observations and hundred
billion sensations, let the master
of fine arts require building
of roads and houses, breaking
eggs for sweet cakes and meats,
watching eggs break
and chicks hungry-blind
jump for worms, fly oceans,
blind an hungry rea (sp?)
for the worm at nest,
the chick come blind
and hungry for the worm,
let us roll again in earth,

planting bulbs
Tonight, let us welcome back
the Deep Song and Lightseller
Shakespeare and the Howler,
tonight, let us study
the world again and return
to our desks and write songs
songs of these days
at the end of 20 centuries.


    The first stanza refers to Lorca's poems, which use the form of *cante jondo* (deep song), an Andalusian lyric, and Neruda's work, "EXTRAVAGARIA." Amirthanayagam says he wished to honor the two poets' lyricism as well as their political lives. At age 38, Lorca was killed by fascists during the Spanish Civil War and his body thrown into an unmarked grave. Neruda was a diplomat — and Amirthanayagam says that he considers one of his "points of connection" with the Chilean poet to be the fact that Neruda wrote poems that became his collection, *Residence On Earth*, while he was posted in Sri Lanka.

    "For me, I think of Lorca's *duende* — his darkness and soul that infuses a poem, his deep song like gypsy ballads. They resonated with me, for what it asked in me: depth and song. I shy away from poetry that is prosaic, or with prose-like rhythms versus song-like rhythms," he says. "Poetry is a mnemonic device. Homer's *Odyssey* was written so that people would remember it with the help of refrains. The idea of a poem as a device to improve memory is one with which I strongly empathize. I've always had a poor memory and I lost Tamil as a language. Today, despite having learned Spanish and French, I continue to have a degree of insecurity about language. So the use of poetry as a way to remember speaks to my insecurity — not just in subject matter (about the lost Ceylon) but as a way of writing to be a way of remembering."

    In the second stanza, Amirthanayagam recalls Allen Ginsberg and an opera by Philip Glass entitled "Hydrogen Juke Box." For Amirthanayagam, Ginsberg is special partly because he once visited the Amirthanayagam family when he attended a colloquium at Hawai'i's East/West Center organized by Amirthanayagam's father. "I was in high school and Ginsberg stayed at our home. I remembered Bob Dylan telephoning him at our house — that was a dazzling, thrilling moment. Ginsberg was very nice to me. I showed him my poems. He corrected them, saying something that's come to be quite useful to me, 'Cut 50% of what you do during revision.' I doubt he did it himself but it was nice advice," he recalls. "That week he stayed with us was an important push in my work. I feel that Ginsberg — with poems like 'Kaddish' and 'Howl' — has blessed poetry: he inspired and led me and others."

The second stanza also references *The Elephants of Reckoning* as well as one of his father's poems, "Outside The Window." Amirthanayagam uses his father's poem as an epigraph to the book's contents. "The references bring up the tension between autobiography and trying for accessibility — the tension between private versus public metaphors," Amirthanayagam acknowledges.

But if there was a battle between the "private versus public metaphors," it was easy for Amirthanayagam to choose to retain the references as they honor his father, Guy Amirthanayagam, a poet and former Sri Lankan diplomat to whom he partly dedicates the book. His father 's life was saved by friends during the civil violence that erupted in 1958, a violence that foreshadowed the later, more extreme conflagration of 1983. Guy Amirthanayagam's poem displays a resonance similar to what is evoked by some of Lorca's and Neruda's poems:

**Outside The Window**

The road is dark, and stained with damp grey leaves.
The scissored lightning cuts against the sky.
Now I would accept love's hazard with a sigh
And pass my blind hands gently over her face.

The weather stayed:  the impulse cleared,
A stir of the heart, afraid for its loneliness:
The drapes too tattered for the menace which peered
Too frail the window for the waiting darkness.

Though Guy Amirthanyagam's poem could foretell the "darkness" that wreathed Sri Lanka after 1983, it is also a poem that transcends the particular reference to his family's birthland.

Finally, the third stanza in "WORDS FOR THE ENTERPRISE" references another lyrical poet admired by Amirthanayagam, William Butler Yeats. The stanza's last line, "that comes dropping slow" references Yeat's poem, "The Lake Isle of Innisfree," from which an excerpt is as follows:

"I will arise and go now, and go to Innisfree,
. . .
And I shall have some peace there, for peace comes dropping slow,
Dropping from the veils of the morning to where the cricket sings;
There midnight's all a glimmer, and noon a purple glow,
And evening full of the linnet's wings."

**WORDS FOR THE ENTERPRISE**

Lorca called it The Deep Song,
Neruda told us to go out
and sell light on the roads,
the grandmother of my friend said
that he reminded her of the boys
that went to Spain; today Spain
is New York, and tonight I ask
you ~~,~~ ~~to~~ ride all your elephants out,

Ride with Allen
and a hundred billion
others out of the hydrogen
jukebox ~~, remember~~ ; Remember
my father as you read
"Outside The Window," the words
are here on the first page
of *The Elephants of Reckoning*

Tonight and tomorrow New York
is Spain and the bayonets
are out, the firing squads
out, and we shall dance
at the end of 20 centuries,
at the end of 20 centuries
I ask you to honor the peace
that comes dropping slow,

At the end of 20 centuries,
I recall with you the briars
binding our joys and desires,
I insist that the purveyors
of the televisions of our eyes
rewind and re-spool, reel
William Shakespeare out of school

and let him bring his protean
observations and hundred
billion sensations, let the ~~master~~ Master
of ~~fine arts~~ Fine Arts require building
of roads ~~and~~ or houses, breaking
eggs for sweet cakes and meats,
watching eggs break
and chicks ~~hungry blind~~ blind-hungry

jump for worms, fly oceans,
~~blind an hungry rea (sp?)~~
~~for the worm at nest,~~
~~the chick come blind~~
~~and hungry for the worm,~~
~~let us roll again in earth,~~

~~planting bulbs~~
Tonight, let us welcome back
the Deep Song and Lightseller
Shakespeare and the Howler,
<u>Willliam Blake and William</u>
<u>Butler Yeats,</u> ~~the usual sometimes~~ Mahadeviakka
<u>Sappho and Sylvia Plath,</u>
~~forgotten infamous~~ <u>the wizards and witches</u>
~~who~~ <u>gathered outside the</u> ~~gates~~ <u>window</u>

[New P] At ~~of~~ the ~~Garden~~ <u>gates</u> of Paradise
~~and waited~~ <u>waiting for</u> ~~Eve and~~ <u>Adam and Eve</u>
to come ~~flying, the witches~~ <u>fleeing out</u>
~~who brewed the resurrection of the woman garden~~
~~of Paradise wa (sic) suspects~~
tonight, let us study
the ~~world~~ <u>earth</u> again and return
to our desks and write songs
songs of these days
at the end of 20 centuries.

*(a melange of older recent*
*sometimes forgotten infamous)*

The last two stanzas as well as a parenthetical note to himself at the bottom of the poem illustrate Amirthanayagam's call for "a moment of assessment, to review where we are before the millenium." He repeats the line, "at the end of 20 centuries" four times in the poem, his own way of using form to honor Lorca's "deep song" — the *cante jondo* whose structure and melodic configuration includes the repetition of a dominant note.

As Amirthanayagam considered the impending millenium, he says, "For me at that time, these poets' names came up. Still, there comes a question of honesty: why Sylvia Plath and not Elizabeth Bishop. Or Li Po? Thinking about it, I could have used Li Po if I found the rhythm. That's the problem with lists. They still have to fit the song."

Nevertheless, Amirthanayagam says he wanted to acknowledge South Asia, and so included Mahadeviakka, a wandering poet in India who was devoted to Lord Vishnu. "Mahadeviakka wrote love songs that I read in translation by A.K. Ramanjan in his book, *Speaking of Shiva* (Penguin). I wanted to reference South Asia because I meant the poem to be a touchstone for getting all sorts of discussion going about the state of the world, state of minorities and state of women — that is, if the reader wants to extrapolate that way and if the reader believes a poem can have that type of function," he adds.

"But perhaps I was being cynical. Sappho may not necessarily mean anything to me but I recognize that Sappho means something to the outer world," says Amirthanayagam who has served on various committees assessing other poets' works for various grants and fellowships. "Sometimes, one is writing with an imaginary committee in mind, which becomes silly. So you quit and you go to the foreign service. When one is operating for this group of unnamed committee members, leaving Eden — New York in the poetry world — can be a release."

Amirthanayagam's references to "wizards and witches" reflect his belief that poets are like wizards. "I see poets as engaged in mystic arts. They're like magicians and inventors in their ability to conjure up things," he says.

"The wizards also relate to an ancient druidic idea which Dylan Thomas picked up a bit. I guess I wanted to evoke that sense of history . . . .I met a poet recently who said she only reads living poets, that she doesn't have time to read dead poets. I'm the other way: I tend to read more the poets who are dead. I feel a certain debt to those in the past. I don't want them to be forgotten."

III.    Final Draft

Despite Amirthanayagam's multi-layered inspiration for "WORDS FOR THE ENTERPRISE," he would be the first to note if the poem collapsed under its references and failed to live up to his determination of what he believes a poem to be: "For me, poetry goes back to Ezra Pound — if music moves away from dance and poetry away from music, that moving away lessens the effect. Stay close to the song."

As examples of staying "close to the song," Amirthanayagam changed in the last two stanzas "Eve and Adam" to "Adam and Eve," linked the similar sounds of "Yeats" and "Blake" and changed the word "world" to "earth." Amirthanayagam says he often mutters the poems out loud as he revises his drafts.

*Song.* As Pound once said, "Poetry, as regards its function or purpose, has the common purpose of the arts, which purpose Dante most clearly indicates in the line where he speaks of: *That melody which most doth draw/ The soul unto itself.'* "

Here is Amirthanayagam's final draft for his call to everyone to seek out the elephants, with the elephants in this poem symbolizing, he says, "what is best within human beings."

**WORDS FOR THE ENTERPRISE**

Lorca called it The Deep Song,
Neruda told us to go out
and sell light on the roads,
the grandmother of my friend said
that he reminded her of the boys
that went to Spain; today Spain
is New York, and tonight I ask
you, ride all your elephants out,

Ride with Allen
and a hundred billion

others out of the hydrogen
jukebox; Remember
my father as you read
"Outside The Window," the words
are here on the first page
of *The Elephants of Reckoning.*

Tonight and tomorrow New York
is Spain and the bayonets
are out, the firing squads
out, and we shall dance
at the end of 20 centuries,
at the end of 20 centuries
I ask you to honor the peace
that comes dropping slow,

At the end of 20 centuries,
I recall with you the briars
binding our joys and desires,
I insist that the purveyors
of the televisions of our eyes
rewind and re-spool, reel
William Shakespeare out of school

and let him bring his protean
observations and hundred
billion sensations, let the Master
of Fine Arts require building
of roads or houses, breaking
eggs for sweet cakes and meats,
watching eggs break
and chicks blind-hungry
jump for worms, fly oceans,

Tonight, let us welcome back
the Deep Song and Lightseller
Shakespeare and the Howler,
William Blake and William
Butler Yeats, Mahadeviakka
Sappho and Sylvia Plath,
the wizards and witches
gathered outside the window

At the gates of Paradise
waiting for Adam and Eve
to come fleeing out

tonight, let us study
the earth again and return
to our desks and write songs
songs of these days
at the end of 20 centuries.

—⁓—

Amirthanayagam's *Elephants of Reckoning* — for which Amirthanayagam intended
"WORDS FOR THE ENTERPRISE" to be an introduction — begins with a poem titled "The City,
with Elephants." In this poem, Amirthanayagam says the elephants are homeless people on the
streets whose "aching homelessness is similar to my desire to be housed in America."

He stresses, "I want to be called an American poet — I am a convert similar to converts
being more religious than those born to a religion. As an immigrant and then a representative of
America abroad, I've developed a texture that I want to explore: the America like New York
which is multicultural and with freedom in expressions of art, expression and styles. I like the
freedoms I've been enjoying in America and recognize that these do come at a cost."

Interestingly, Amirthanayagam concedes that American freedom of expression poses cer-
tain implications about poetics. "I think the democratic tradition in the United States invites a lot
of voices into poetry. There's nothing wrong with that, but be conscious of what you're doing.
You don't have to write everything down in a poem. But when you do write a poem, make sure
every word counts. I like lyrical poetry but I don't want to be a Stalinist. Let everyone in, includ-
ing those with prose rhythms. There's nothing wrong with a lot of voices, but whatever voice you
choose as a poet, let every word fit. Do the work. Lose flaccidity in lines. If you don't, some
fascist out there will shoot you down. If you don't care enough for the *enterprise*, then don't fight
the war."

Finally, Amirthanayagam recalls, "I was once in MacDowell (Artists' Colony) where I
wrote some poetic prose about what it means to be a Sri Lankan poet in the diaspora. I saw red
foxes, chipmunks, the New England flora and fauna for the first time and I was conscious of them
in comparison to the Sri Lankan jungle. I was also in this cabin used by Thornton Wilder to write
'Our Town." And there I was writing my own poems about America. That search for ideal — that
return to the Garden of Eden — I found it for a few weeks in New Hampshire: peace. I look for
that peace in America. I'll always keep looking for it."

As an *American* poet, Amirthanayagam writes the following as a sample of the poems
that he meant "WORDS FOR THE ENTERPRISE" to introduce:

**The City, with Elephants**

The elephants of reckoning
are bunches of scruff
men and women picking up
thrown out antennae
from the rubbish
bins of the city

to fix on their tubular

bells and horn about
by oil can fires
in the freezing midnight
of the old new year

We ride by their music
every hour in cabs on trains
hearing the pit pat
of our grown-wise pulse
shut in shut out

from the animals
of the dry season
the losers and boozers,
we must not admit our eyes
into the courtyard

the whimsy of chance
and our other excuses —
dollars in pocket —
to write beautiful songs
is all I ask, God

to do right with friends
and love a woman
and live to eighty
have people listen
to the story of my trip to America

The elephants of reckoning
are beaten and hungry
and walk their solitary horrors
out every sunrise slurping
coffee bought with change

while in some houses
freedom-bound lovers
embrace late and read Tagore
about the people working
underneath the falling of empires.

*The elephants of reckoning are beaten and hungry . . . underneath the falling of empires.*
This evokes an excerpt from one of Dylan Thomas' most loved poems:

**I SEE THE BOYS OF SUMMER**

I see the boys of summer in their ruin
Lay the gold tithings barren,
Setting no store by harvest, freeze the soils;
There in their heat the winter floods
Of frozen loves they fetch their girls,
And drown the cargoed apples in their tides.

. . .

I see you boys of summer in your ruin.
Man in his maggot's barren.
And boys are full and foreign in the pouch.
I am the man your father was.
We are the sons of flint and pitch.
O see the poles are kissing as they cross.

In turn, Thomas' poem may be applied to the turbulence in Sri Lanka where women and children have served as cannon fodder. Amirthanayagam honors Tamil women in one of the poems in *The Elephants of Reckoning*, "The Flight of Boys," excerpted below:

Women protect the men/ as *boys* hidden/ in the folds of their sarees/ hand-held as baby/ brothers in the middle/ of the caravan/ the more women there are/ the safer for the *boys*/ as the new-made families/ talk to the checkpoint guards/ . . .we are on a pilgrimage/to the shrine at Kattaragama/ . . . please, sir, let us go/ let us continue our walk/ (on the finest roads/ in the whole of Sri Lanka/ spanking and fast/ to speed armored carriers/ and troop convoys/ on their journey to the war)

—◊◊◊—

Three years after writing "WORDS FOR THE ENTERPRISE," Amirthanayagam says he can now "recognize a certain foretelling in that poem," with regard to his diplomatic career. "The main thing right now for me is to be engaged in the larger enterprise of diplomacy. I don't want to lose touch with the political and social life of a poet," he says.

For Amirthanayagam, this means defining his role as a diplomat as one of also expanding the world of poetry. When he was based in Argentina, he helped bring an Argentinian poet, Ariel Schettini Quilmes to the Iowa Writing Workshop. When he was based in Belgium, he helped bring American poets over to Belgium, serving as the United States' last Assistant Cultural Attache to that country. "It's the small things one can do that makes me feel good," he says.

As Amirthanayagam travels the world as a diplomat representing the United States, he is clearly searching as well for the peace that he once found in Thornton Wilder's cabin — the peace denied to his beloved *Ceylon*. Most assuredly, we will be hearing him sing of what he will experience during this search. As he says, a poet must *stay close to the song*.

# MEENA ALEXANDER

Meena Alexander's earliest volumes of poetry were published in India: *The Bird's Bright Ring* (Calcutta: Writers Workshop, 1976); *Without Place* (Calcutta: Writers Workshop, 1977); *I Root My Name* (Calcutta: United Writers, 1977); and *Stone Roots* (New Delhi: Arnold Heinemann, 1980). Her first volume of poetry published in the United States is *House of a Thousand Doors* (Colorado: Three Continents Press, 1988). This was followed by two chapbooks, each a long poem: *The Storm: A Poem in Five Parts* (New York: Red Dust, 1989) and *Nightscene: The Garden* (New York: Red Dust, 1992). The latter was choreographed and performed Off-Off-Broadway by the Medicine Show Theatre Ensemble. Alexander's most recent volume of poetry is *River and Bridge* (New Delhi: Rupa, 1995/ Toronto: TSAR Press, 1996). She has also published novels *Nampally Road* (San Francisco: Mercury House, 1991) (which was a VLS Editors Choice) and *Manhattan Music* (Mercury House, 1997); a memoir, *Fault Lines* (New York: Feminist Press, 1993) which was part of Publishers Weekly Best Books Selection for 1993; and a book of essays and poems, *Shock of Arrival: Reflections on Post-Colonial Experience* (Boston: South End Press, 1996). She is also the author of two critical works: *The Poetic Self: Towards a Phenomenology of Romanticism* (New Delhi: Arnold Heinemann, 1979/ New Jersey: Humanities Press, 1981) and *Women in Romanticism: Mary Wollstonecraft, Dorothy Wordswroth and Mary Shelley* (London: Macmillan, 1989).

She has received awards from the Arts Council of England, CSIR (India), National Endowment for the Humanities, American Council of Learned Societies, Lila Wallace Foundation, New York State Council on the Arts and Altrusa International Foundation. She has been a Frances Wayland Collegium Lecturer at Brown University and a MacDowell Fellow. Selected works have been translated into German, Italian, Spanish, French, Malayalam, Hindi, Arabic. She is Professor of English and Women's Studies at the Graduate Centre and Hunter College, City University of New York.

In response to the question, "What advice would you give to a young poet?" Meena Alexander responds:

> Whatever you do, do not lose heart. Remember that the lines you work with, work through, need the quietness that only you can give so that the act of composition might fulfill itself. Once I heard Joseph Brodsky speaking. It was at Columbia University just after he got the Nobel Prize. And this is what I recall him saying: "I'm a poet. I send something out and it comes back to me. I send it out again and again. There is no certitude here." To which I would like to add, this is the palimpsest of time through which we make ourselves as poets. Going the long road. There are no shortcuts. Remember that the poem on the page is only the tip of the iceberg. Most of what endures, turning into the soil of the poem, is carried within, unseen, even worldless. An act of meditation without cease. Poetry is a small scale art, an art of exquisite detail and this is its power. It can be recited, shared, sung. It need not be bought and sold.

# GOLD HORIZON: The "Unquiet Borders" Of Memory

*The ocean twanging away there*
*and the islands like scattered laundry—*

*You can feel so free, so free,*
*standing on the headland*

*where the wild rose never stands still*
*— from "The Parting: I" by Adrienne Rich*

*But questions persist: Where did I come from? How did I become what I am? How shall I start to write*
*myself, configure my "I" as Other, image this life I lead, here, now, in America? What could I ever be but a*
*mass of faults, a fault mass?*
*. . . That's all I am, a woman cracked by multiple migrations. Uprooted so many times she can connect noth-*
*ing with nothing. Her words are all askew. And so I tormented myself on summer nights, and in the chill*
*wind of autumn, tossing back and forth, worrying myself sick. Till my mind slipped back to my mother—*
*amma—she who gave birth to me, and to amma's amma, my veliammechi, grandmother Kunju, drawing me*
*back into the darkness of the Tiruvella house with its cool bedrooms and coiled verandas: the shelter of*
*memory.*
*— from "Fault Lines" by Meena Alexander*

I hid from Meena Alexander for nearly a year. I interviewed her in the summer of 1996 for this poetry-in-progress essay. Then, for months, I failed to follow up with her and might have continued avoiding her if we hadn't bumped into each other in a ladies room at Rutgers University during a poetry conference in April 1997. We stood on a long line (of course), surrounded by others who had just witnessed her impressive performance on a panel discussing the theme of "Poetry, Feminism(s), and the Difficult Wor(l)d." Almost as if a year had not lapsed and we were just continuing our discussion from the previous summer, she proclaimed as others stared at us, "My Muse has found her feet!"

I left the conference mentally clutching her statement because I was nervous I would forget her words. Her pronouncement inexplicably allowed me to return to our poetry-in-progress project. To paraphrase a line from Sam Hamill's poem, "What The Water Knows," *my heart poured out in waves* and I wrote the first draft of her article in one sitting. The last time I spoke with Alexander, we had focused much of our conversation on why she long felt her Muse's feet were cut off at the ankles. A year later, Alexander was telling me that she had achieved some sort of resolution, and I no longer had to hide from her and a bleeding Muse who walked with much difficulty.

It was not until after I finished the first draft that I realized I had interviewed Alexander while she was in the midst of a turbulent transition. During our interview, she was finishing what came to be three books published within months of each other: a collection of essays and poems, *The Shock of Arrival* (South End Press, 1996); a poetry collection, *River and Bridge* (Tsar Press, 1996); and a novel, *Manhattan Music* (Mercury House, 1997). All the books mine what she has described as her singular, specific focus: the borders of migration, crossed but never left. By her own admission, Alexander was undergoing a period of uncertainty about her life and work during that summer of 1996. And, with hindsight, I realized I found it difficult to write the article because her transitional phase resulted in the image of a feetless, suffering Muse whose distress so touched me. When Alexander revealed that her Muse had "found her feet," then and only then could I begin to write the article: I was relieved Alexander had accepted having to straddle the "unquiet borders" of her concerns and that her Muse was no longer bitter — or "cut off at the ankles" — about Alexander's choices.

Alexander says she carries within herself the memory of a fragment she once read from the *Milindapanha* (from the section on Theravada Buddhism in *Sources of The Indian Tradition*, Vol. I., ed. Theodore de Bary). The sage Nagasena is in dialogue with the King Milinda who asks: "Reverend Nagasana, when a man is born does he remain the same or become another?"

In the course of the dialogue the sage asks the King if he is still the baby he once was. When the King replies that he is no longer the baby, that the baby was another self, the sage drives his point home: "If that is the case your Majesty, you had no mother or father and no teachers in learning manners or wisdom . . . is the boy who goes to school one (being) and the young man who finished his education another? Does one person commit a crime and another suffer mutilation for it?"

Nagasena's point, hard, elusive but so true, Alexander says, is that even as the body continues till death, it might be said that one self comes into being and another passes away. Still, in self-conscious existence the multiple selves can be seen as parts of a whole.

The sage's point resonates for Alexander because "as a writer and poet, what I'm moving towards is that territory that deepens what it is that migration or dislocation does." Her concerns are backed by the facts of her history: Alexander was born in India, raised in India and Sudan, educated in Sudan and England, and currently lives in New York. While growing up in Africa, she had returned each summer to her grandparents' home in India, a pattern of travel that continues as she returns as frequently as she can with her two children from New York to India during summer holidays.

Her growth personally and as a writer is a journey across "unquiet borders" that she never leaves behind. Alexander also calls these unquiet borders "thresholds" in her writing. This permanent state of residing on the threshold highlights why she so values memory.

"Memory is very important to me. Memory is also memory of ancestry. And it's part of the trajectory of people who migrate. . . ." For example, she says immigrants may come to behave differently in their adopted country, but still would retain memories of more appropriate behavior as determined in their birthlands. For immigrants, this is a perpetual "struggle inside." No matter how many years they may come to reside in their new country, Alexander says, these immigrants forever live on a "threshold" — that space of the boundary or border that they intended to cross.

For Alexander's attempts to transmute her migration experience and concerns into her poetry, her Muse, too, must cross this "very difficult border." It's not an easy passage, as shown by Parts I and II of her three-part poem, "GOLD HORIZON." The poem depicts a dialogue between Alexander and a ghost-woman in Parts I and II who becomes her Muse in Part III. In Part I, Alexander envisions her to be a woman with her "feet cut off at the ankles/ severed from her thighs."

**GOLD HORIZON**

I.

She waited where the river ran

that summer as the floods began
stones sinking, fireflies murmuring
in paddy fields, herons on stumps of trees
the axe planted where little else would work
and everywhere the mess of water.

'So you have entered a new world'
her voice was low, growling even.
There was nothing humble in her voice.
Sometimes the dead behave in that know-all-way
ploughing the ruts of disaster,
their unease part of our very pith —
what the axe discovers marrow and meat to us.

'So what's it like there?' she asked.

I replied: 'As the Hudson pours
the river wall clings tight with glinting stones.
Yet what's so bright makes for odd imaginings.
Sometimes I feel as if a metal bowl had split
dented by blows from a woman's fist
and bits of spelling lessons, shards of script
struck from a past locked into privacy,
— this is the immigrant's fury, no?
who understands my speech, further what is my speech? —
dropped, pounding as rice grains might.'

'You think that bowl's your head
your words a crypt!  Look at your feet!
How can you stand addressing me?'
I heard her laughing bitterly.

'What's with you?'  I shot back
'What's with the dead, sheer jealousy?'

Her fingers waved a whitened scrap
paper or cloth I could not tell.
She held it out to me:  'Take!  Eat!'

I saw the sari that bound her
dropping free, feet cut at the ankles,
severed from her thighs, slicked with red earth.
Water poured in short streams
over her mutilated parts.
She stood, shored by a single elbow
against a mango branch.

"GOLD HORIZON" was written while Alexander was developing a group of prose pieces in the voice of a woman from her grandmother's generation — a woman who has never traveled beyond her birthplace, who lived there forever and would never imagine doing anything else. Alexander further notes that she long had thought that if she were male, she would have felt more free to wander out of the familial home to travel. But by being female, she says, "I always thought I had one foot on the ancestral threshold. I was tied to it and if I took a step, I'd return to it. It's like the ghost woman (in "GOLD HORIZON") — she had her ankle cut off and although she was allowed to leave, she couldn't move very well. It's an ancestral thing that relates to crossing borders to get to America. She's bitter about my going into a new world."

Part II of "GOLD HORIZON" continues as follows:

II.

Place names splinter
on my tongue and flee:
Allahabad, Tiruvella, Kozhencheri, Khartoum,
Nottingham, New Delhi, Hyderabad, New York,
— the piece work of sanity,
stitching them into a corruscating geography —
why a single long drawn breath
in an infant's dream might do,
ruined by black water in a paddy field.

We wrestle on wet ground,
she and I, living and dead,
stripped to our skins,
naked, shining free in
the gold of a torn horizon.

Our thrashing is not nice.
Her ankle stumps shove against my eyes.

Words bolt, syllables rasp
an altered script,
theatre of memory I could never have wished.

Breathless I search for a scene
mile long city blocks,
iron bridges scraping back short hills,
asphalt pierced with neon plots,
the rage of sense:
bodegas in the Barrio, Billy's topless bar,
Vineeta's Video Store crammed with cartoons
of Nutan and Madhuri
— 'Kya, kya hum kon hai? Idher hum kon hai' —*
'Namal ivide ara? Ivide namal ara?' —*

The mixed up speech of newness,

flashing as a kite might,

pale paper on a mango branch.

(* *The English translation of both lines, the first in Hindi and the second in Malalayam is: "Who are we here? Here, who are we?"*)

When asked about the inspiration for "GOLD HORIZON,' Alexander replies, "I come from Kerala. It provides the landscape of my childhood with paddy fields, very green and lush. There's an image I can still see today: a shadowy figure and she was in white and in this paddy field. It's very watery and moist because the grass needs a lot of water. And I also think it's about monsoon time, and when it rains the world has a lot of rain. (The ghost woman) was standing there, wearing white as women in Kerala usually do. She wasn't coming any closer at the beginning but then she wouldn't go away. At nights I dreamt her. She just wouldn't go away. Somehow, the very first draft had this landscape in it and she didn't approve of what I was doing, which is also very much a sense I get from some people in India about going to America. They say, 'You think it's such a great thing, but what is it? Where does America come from. We're the people who count. We're the bearers of this world, this nation's ancient culture.' So I'm not saying there's too much of this in the poem, but there is a bit of this idea — of being asked how I can write anything real if I'm out here in America that's not my place."

"But the other play on this is that she's dead while I'm in this other life. So I'm playing between the borders of life and death as well as the borders between nations — and cultures," Alexander notes.

In the fourth stanza of Part II, Alexander references "Barrio, Billy's topless bar,/Vineeta's Video Store." It is a change she made towards the end of her drafting process. "What (the contemporary references) do to the poem is that it places it here in the United States. Somehow, I needed to do that and I think it was a way for me to say, 'This is my world. It may not be so great but my world is here'."

Alexander says she considers the migrant "passage a tearing which is why the horizon is torn. But it is also a birthing where something has to tear for something to come out. It is a kind of difficulty for which we don't ordinarily have words."

*A kind of difficulty for which we don't ordinarily have words* — yet the difficulty posed by what Alexander calls a "threshold place from which she can't depart" is also what drives her as a poet. She reverts again and again to exploring this threshold — "that territory that deepens what it is that migration or dislocation does." In an earlier poem, "Passion," Alexander names the threshold as only a master poet can:

**Passion**

I.
After childbirth
the ten month's passion

a bloodiness
still shifting at her core
she crawls on the mud floor

past the empty rice sacks
blown large with dust,
rims distended like sails.

Her skin scrapes a tin bowl
with water from the stream,
a metal frame

bearing a god
whose black blue face
melts into darkness, as a gem might

tossed back
into its own
implacable element.

She waits,
she sets her sari to her teeth
and when the chattering begins

fierce, inhuman joy,
monkeys rattling the jamun tree,
bellies distended, washed with wind

she screams
and screams
a raw, ungoverned thing.

II
There are beetles scrabbling
in the open sacks,
chaff flies in the half light
a savage sound in her eyes
struck free

the human realms of do and don't
the seemingly precise, unalterable keys
dashed to a frenzy
and still the voice holds.
. . .

IV
I am she
the woman after giving birth

life

to give life
torn and hovering

as bloodied fluids
baste the weakened flesh.

For her
there are no words,
no bronze, no summoning.

I am her sight
her hearing
and her tongue.

I am she
smeared with ash
from the black god's altar

I am
the sting of love
the blood hot flute
the face
carved in the window,
watching as the god set sail

across the waters
risen from the Cape,
Sri Krishna in a painted catamaran.

I am she
tongueless in rhapsody

the stars of glass
nailed to the Southern sky.

Ai ai
she cried.

They stuffed
her mouth with rags
and pulled her
from the wooden bed

and thrust her

to the broken floor.


I, I.


A passionate sensibility — "a raw, ungoverned thing" — finds its way in "GOLD HORI-ZON," not only because of Alexander's overall poetic concerns but, because she wrote the poem after a traumatic period that involved returning to India when her father there became very ill. As she spent time in the hospital and during her subsequent plane trip back to New York, Alexander read Homer's *The Odyssey*.

"Because *The Odyssey* is a kind of return, it came into my poem. And a necessary part of the return is to confront the dead. So the whole part of *The Odyssey* of being in the underworld and borrowing those lines were in my head as I wrote the poem," Alexander recalls.

Specifically, Alexander was remembering *The Odyssey*'s Book XI, "A Gathering of Shades" wherein Odysseus tells the ghost of Akhilleus:


"But was there ever a man more blest by fortune

than you, Akhilleus? Can there ever be?

We ranked you with the immortals in your lifetime,

we Argives did, and here your power is royal

among the dead man's shades. Think, then, Akhilleus:

you need not be so pained by death."


To this

he (Akhilleus) answered swiftly:


"Let me hear no smooth talk

of death from you, Odysseus, light of councils.

Better, I say, to break sod as a farm hand

for some poor country man, on iron rations,

than lord it over all the exhausted dead."

**— *from Homer's* The Odyssey, *translated***
**by Robert Fitzgerald, (A Borzoi Book, Knopf, 1992)**


In addition to hoping her father would recover — for, similar to Akhilleus' attitude, there could be no consolation for her father's death — Alexander recalls, "I wanted that ferociousness displayed by Akhilleus, which is also about a vitality in living, to come through in the poem."


—⁓—


While developing "GOLD HORIZON," Alexander was also writing a prose poem titled "Translated Lives."


**TRANSLATED LIVES**


The past that we make, presumes us as pure invention might — our being here compels it: an eye cries out for an eye, a throat for a throat, we muse on Rimbaud's lips caked with soil, his Parisian whites stiffening: *'Quick: are there other lives?*

Who shall fit her self for translation — word for word, line for line, eyes flashing at squat gulls on this mid-Atlantic shore, sail boats rudderless, the horizon scrawled in indigo? What water here, or air? A terrible heat comes on, birds scurry, swallowing their own shadows and lovers coupling on hard rock turn grotesque, forced to grope at the sea's edge.

Neon mirages mock the world Columbus sought. In Times Square, selling the National Debt, electronic numbers triple on the light strip — and where the digits run, pure ciphers — OOO mark heaven's haven. Into that nothingness, a poverty of flesh, track tanpura and oudh, the torn ligaments of a goat's throat, still bloodied, strummed against sand.

As boats set sail through our migrant worlds, faxes splutter their texts into the crumpled spaces in our skin, and the academies bow low, white shirts, threadbare elbows scraped into arcane incandescence, shall we touch each other stiffened with sense, bodies set as if in Egyptian perspective, full frontal, necks craned to the glint of the horizon? Will a nervous knowledge, a millenial sense be kindled? Must the past we make consume us?

————————

*(Note: On a draft of this poem I have scribbled a note: Rimbaud's Saison en Enfer' is much in my mind and also the condition of these immigrant lives we lead and what it means to write (= to translate) across a border — a trip wire — How to summon this and say 'This is my past. Our past. This is the great challenge as I see it.' MA July 15, 1996*

"I think Translated Lives' is also about making up a past to live by and yet knowing that, having made it up, it becomes what you have. I remember when I was growing up in Khartoum reading Wallace Stevens' poem, 'NOTES TOWARD A SUPREME FICTION.' And he said something in there about how, once you've invented a fiction, it becomes hard. You know you've made it up, but it's what you have to live by. And this, too, relates to the issue of migration."

It is easy to see Alexander's empathy with "NOTES TOWARD A SUPREME FICTION" which includes the following excerpt:

What am I to believe? If the angel in his cloud,
Serenely gazing at the violent abyss,
Plucks on his strings to pluck abysmal glory,

Leaps downward through evening's revelations, and
On his spredden wings, needs nothing but deep space,
Forgets the gold centre, the golden destiny,

Grows warm in the motionless motion of his flight,
Am I that imagine this angel less satisfied?

Are the wings his, the lapis-haunted air?
Is it he or is it I that experience this?
Is it I then that keep saying there is an hour
Filled with expressible bliss, in which I have

No need, am happy, forget need's golden hand,
Am satisfied without solacing majesty,
And if there is an hour there is a day,

There is a month, a year, there is a time
In which majesty is a mirror of the self:
I have not but I am and as I am, I am.

These external regions, what do we fill them with
Except reflections, the escapades of death,
Cinderella fulfilling herself beneath the roof?

. . .

———————

Soldier, there is a war between the mind
And sky, between thought and day and night. It is
For that the poet is always in the sun,

Patches the moon together in his room
To his Virgilian cadences, up down,
Up down. It is a war that never ends.

Yet it depends on yours. The two are one.
They are a plural, a right and left, a pair,
Two parallels that meet if only in

The meeting of their shadows or that meet
In a book in a barrack, a letter from Malay.
But your war ends. And after it you return

With six meats and twelve wines or else without
To walk another room . . . Monsieur and comrade,
The soldier is poor without the poet's lines,

His petty syllabi, the sounds that stick,
Inevitably modulating, in the blood.
And war for war, each has its gallant kind.

How simply the fictive hero becomes the real;
How gladly with proper words the soldier dies,

If he must, or lives on the bread of faithful speech.

In writing "Translated Lives," Alexander also recalled Arthur Rimbaud because he had migrated to Africa. She borrowed the line, *"Quick: are there other lives?"* from a line in the Symbolist poet's *Season in Hell* to capture the poetic sensibility she desires. "He went to Ethiopia and Egypt and lived a turbulent, violent life. But he also wrote extraordinary narrative and just had an amazing sense of life."

Rimbaud's "extraordinary narrative and . . . sense of life" is captured in this excerpt featuring the line Alexander borrowed:

> Light will my days be and I shall be spared repentance. I shall not have known the torments of the soul half dead to good, whence like funeral candles a grave light ascends. The fate of the sons of good families, the premature coffin covered with limpid tears. Certainly debauch is stupid, vice is stupid; all that is rotten must be cast aside. But the clock will not have succeeded in no longer striking only the hour of pure pain! Am I to be carried off like a child, to play in Paradise forgetful of all sorrow?
>
> Quick! Are there other lives?. . .The keys of knowledge are the gifts of divine love alone. I see that nature is but the display of goodness. Farewell chimeras, ideals, errors!
>
> The reasonable song of angels rises from the saviour ship: it is divine love. Two loves! I can die of earthly love, die of devotion. I have abandoned souls whose pain will be increased by my going! Among the ship-wrecked you choose me; those who remain, are they not my friends?
>
> Save them!
>
> Reason is born to me. The world is good. I will bless life.
>
> **___from A SEASON IN HELL by Arthur Rimbaud,**
> **Translated by Louise Varese (New Directions, 1961)**

"Rimbaud also has this other wonderful line, *'Je est un autre.* I is Another' — and that's it: it captures for me not only what it's like to be (an immigrant) writing poetry in America but also just writing poetry. I is Another," Alexander adds.

"Translated Lives" ends by asking, "Must the past we make consume us?" By the nature of the question, the door opens to the possibility that *the past need not consume.* And it was only after the writing of "Translated Lives" that Alexander says she was able to complete "GOLD HORIZON" with its Part III. Unlike earlier versions of the poem which show the ghost as a woman with her legs cut off at the ankles, the Final Draft depicts a more optimistic ending — depicting, too, perhaps Stevens' *Angel* as he described it in "NOTES TOWARD A SUPREME FICTION": "The fiction of an absolute—Angel,/ Be silent in your luminous cloud and hear/ The luminous melody of proper sound."

III

*She waited where the river ran,*
*that summer as the floods began.*

Is this mere repetition,

or the warm sprawl of time,
inscribed in limestone?
Who can cry back into a first world
a barefoot child on a mud forking path,
fields gold with monsoon water,
haunt of the snail and dragonfly?
What makes the narrative whole?

Beneath my cheek I feel her belly's bowl
thick with blood, the woman who waits for me.
Are these her lips or mine?
Whose tongue is this
melting to the quick of migrancy?
I touch raw bones, a skull's precise asymmetry.

As rivers north and rivers south soar
into tongues of mist parting our ribs
I hear voices of children whisper from red hills:
'An angel, you have caught an angel!'

Part III's resolution in the struggles between the "I" and the woman/ghost of Parts I and II
illustrates, Alexander says, the surfacing of "the voice of the poet." In Part III, the ghost, after a
struggle that mirrors the difficulty of transmigration, becomes her Muse, the woman who waits for
her. It is a resolution that mirrors Alexander's acceptance of the United States as her world in the
face of people in India who question this residence.

"There's a little bit of this issue in the poem. I think inside of me, deep down, I think
there's some guilt. I think deep, deep down there's some conflict there. And yet I know that this
is the place where I have to be because it's the only place where I can bring all the parts of my
life together as a writer. In that sense I'm American — because this becomes the landscape, the
suturing of all these pieces. I need it and therefore I'm American. That's the justification of my
citizenship here."

For Alexander, part of "America" means its receptivity to a variety of poetic styles. "My
first books of poems were written in a very tight form. I think that the tightness of the form was
hurting me. It was something I'd learned from the British model — the kind of controlled lan-
guage. Whereas, one of the most exhilirating things about coming to America and writing poetry
here is that it's much more open about the possibilities of what a poem can be and I just find that
wonderful as a writer," she says.

It is no wonder that in her poem, "Muse," which she wrote concurrently with "Gold
Horizon," Alexander displays a feeling of protectiveness towards her Muse:

**MUSE**

She walks towards me, whispering
Dried petals in her hair
A form of fire

But her skin,
like finest Dacca cotton
drawn through a gold ring, spills

Over bristling water.
Something has hurt her.
Can a circlet of syllables

Summon her from the Vagai river?
She kneels by a bald stone
cuts glyphs on its side, waves to me.

Our language is in ruins —
vowels impossibly sharp,
broken consonants of bone.

She has no home.

Why gossip about her
shamelessly — you household gods,
raucous, impenitent?

For Alexander, "openness" to what a poem may be is particularly important given her multi-layered style that transcends traditional forms. She references different time periods and geographical locations in the same poem in a style that she has called "stitching together" or "suturing together" — an aesthetic, too, that she relates to Indian goddesses with many arms. "When the British went to India, they thought that those gods were monsters and very grotesque. But I consider the model of beauty more to be the women with so many arms and legs dancing as opposed to the tight-waisted European model of beauty. I think it's important for artists not to be trapped in any narrow model of beauty."

Alexander's exploration of her migratory history also manifests itself in form which includes prose as well as poetry. 'Sometimes I know the form, sometimes I don't. I think that, as a writer, you sort of have your hand open to catch what it is that comes. I do believe that there is an organic shape to each piece and that one must simply have the emotional courage to let it take the shape that it takes. If you look at ancient Indian aesthetics, there was *kavya* which offered no distinction between prose and poetry. You can have highly charged prose which are like narratives or you can have poetry which is tighter. But there's no compartmentalization and, for me, that's a very important way of looking at it.'

In addition, Alexander is not fearful of layering references within her works that would not be understood by all readers. For example, in "GOLD HORIZON," she deliberately sought to make the poem "denser" by inserting a line in Hindi and another in Malalayam, as well as including references to Nutan and Madhuri, film stars in India. Similarly, in "Translated Lives," Alexander inserted references to the musical instruments "tanpura" from India and "oudh" from North Africa.

"I work with the Indian landscape and the details of it because they're very emotional to me. But to reference a particular community does not make it less universal. What does 'universal' mean anyway? Is it the Greek and Roman cultures? What I'm doing is building a community of voices. That's the thing about 'art.' It only becomes universal as a paradox — to the extent to which there is intensity in the particular. The struggle of the poem is to make that emotion play such that readers who don't know the local elements (e.g. Indian references) can still feel it."

Alexander says that once when she read her works for an audience at Columbia University in 1988, the audience was almost equally-divided between Indians and Anglo-Americans. "It was fascinating because the questions were different: the access was different," she notes. "Similarly, I don't need to understand all the details in Czeslaw Milosz's writing to respond to it because there's some resonance emotionally in the shape of it that moves me. Poetry is a complicated play."

—w—

## The Drafting Process of Gold Horizon

The following features most of Alexander's drafts as she wrote the poem. After each draft is a discussion about some of her thoughts as she developed the poem. *(Editing Marks: strikethroughs = deletions; underlined words = insertions/additions; [Del L] - deleted line breaks; [New L] = new line breaks; [Del P] = deleted stanza breaks; [New P] = new stanza breaks; all-capitalized, italicized words denote editorial comments that were not part of the original manuscripts.)*

A)      June 17, 1996 Drafts

Alexander began the poem with three drafting attempts on June 1, 1996. The version below will show a composition of the three drafts with the use of Editing Marks:

### Her Ghost

Her ghost waited where the river ran
~~I told him that~~ She spoke to me in the summer before
the floods began. It was hard ~~:~~ ~~It was~~ —
~~the~~ stones ~~rising~~ sinking, ~~the~~ fireflies in paddy ~~fields~~
herons on stumps of mango trees
the axe planted where ~~nothing~~ little else ~~could move~~ would work.
~~move if voices could move!~~

'So you have entered a new world' she said
her voice low, growling even. No,
there was nothing humble in her voice
after all the dead behave in that know-all-way
ploughing the ruts of disaster~~, their~~
unless ~~that's the wrong end first and~~
the unease is part of our very pith —
what the axe discovers marrow and meat to us.

*THIS ENTIRE STANZA WAS DELETED AND ITS MIDDLE THOUGHT MOVED DOWN LATER INTO THE POEM:*
~~Though how far can that take us? The dailiness~~

~~of bed and bowl something to succour,~~
~~the spirit, though~~ \sometimes its as if a metal
bowl had bent itself, dented perhaps by
blunt knocks from an axe or hoe
the heart fearful of hoarding itself,
~~or else fit to burst as grapes on the vine~~
~~in an electric storm or passion fruit~~
~~spurting its seed.~~

Though how far can that take us?

So what's it like there, she asked
Does it rain as hard as it rains here?
And I, not knowing what to say, replied,
"The wind blows. The Hudson River is fine
in summer."

THIS STANZA WAS SUBSEQUENTLY DELETED:
the sexual homing ~~all come~~ brilliant with heat
~~into a kindred fishing pool, the nets raised~~
~~with hot hands,~~
and he, feet in water, as if on a black hook
trembling.

Sometimes its as if a metal
bowl had bent itself, dented perhaps by
blunt knocks from an axe or hoe
the heart fearful of hoarding itself,
And I, not knowing what to say
I had no real answer
Nothing spoke to me firmly as speech

June 18, 1996 Journal Entry

The day after beginning the poem, Alexander wrote the following thoughts in her journal about the poem:

**GHOST POEM**

What I see now, the draft of the ghost poem in front of me, is that she is offering me something, paper, scrolled leaf, something to write on. And her hand wavers as if it had passed through mist to get me. And vaporises at the wrist. But I catch the thing that crumbles in my fingers and I write on it.

Something else too. I see: this is like the overture of the long piece I had in mind for her, for me, for the coast of Kerala, for the telling that will be the child's story. And perhaps I can weave this in with some Kerala history.

And then, set it here, in all the dailiness I so want and need, streaming in. Will this be possible? Possible this summer? I must spend this summer writing poetry. Shall I also take some Malayalam classes?

What does she have, this ghost to give me? Perhaps when I see the dance performance tonight, of Indian dance in the Hunter Playhouse, what she is will clarify. Perhaps the dancer will come close to me, with something in her hand. Approaching. As Radha approached Krishna. As the mouths open and the land cries out with all its name (and make here a litany of names as Derek Walcott does in this poem 'Names.") The land of Kerala — the lands outside Sudan — they will cry out in their voices to me. And the lands outside the mining towns of Nottingham. And the lands here, where I am poised. What do they cry to me? What?

The fourth paragraph of the journal entry references "a litany of names as Derek Walcott does in this poem 'Names'." Commencing with the July 22, 1996 draft (shown below) of the poem, Alexander would insert such a litany: "Allahabad, Tiruvella, Kozhencheri, Khartoum/ Nottingham, Delhi, Hyderabad, New York." However, it would oversimplify Alexander's references to say that Walcott's poem alone inspired the litany; in Alexander's memoir, *Fault Lines* (The Feminist Press, 1993), she also lists places, a litany that would reflect logically her history of migration and its effect on her poetry:

Where was my town? If I could not invoke the god of my town, how would the bandages drop from my mouth? How would I be freed to speak? Far, far from Tiruvella and Kozencheri, Allahabad, Pune, Delhi, Khartoum, far even from Nottingham, on that lovely cold island, the words I had carried around for so long echoed in my inner ear. I wanted to be more than a tympanum, a pale, vibrating thing that marked out the boundaries between worlds. More than a mere line in the dry earth. I wanted to give voice to my flesh to learn to live as a woman. To do that, I had to spit out the stones that were in my mouth. I had to become a ghost, enter my own flesh.

Alexander says she wrote the "GHOST POEM" journal entry shortly after seeing a performance of a dance troupe from Bangalore. The performance made her recall another famous dance about Krishna (god of love) and Radha (Krishna's lover). "Radha approached Krishna and he says 'come come come' and I think I was thinking that the ghost would give me something, like a letter or something, that perhaps the dancer will come close to me with something in her hand in the way Radha had approached Krishna."

In the subsequent (June 29, 1996) draft of "Gold Horizon" shown below, the poem ends with the words: "There was something/ scrolled so tightly in her hand, white paper/ rolled in palm leaf."

When asked what that "something" was that Alexander wished the dancer to offer and that she references in her poem, she replies, "I wanted the answer to my life. But the answer has to come from inside me. It's as Toni Morrison once said: we write the books we wish to read."

**HER GHOST**

Her ghost waited where the river ran.
She spoke to me that summer ~~before~~ when
the floods began.  It was hard —
stones sinking, fireflies in paddy fields
herons on stumps of mango trees,
the axe planted where little else would work
and everywhere the mess of water.
'So you have entered a new world'
she said, her voice low, growling even.
There was nothing humble in her voice
after all the dead behave in that know-all-way
ploughing the ruts of disaster.
Is their unease part of our very pith —
what the axe discovers marrow and meat to us?
'So what's it like there?' she asked
'Does it rain as hard as it rains here?'
And not knowing if my tongue could shape
~~translated~~ syllables she could understand, I muttered ~~ever so slowly~~:
~~'I like the~~ The river in summer, it simmers ~~grey green~~
shot with leaves, ~~wild~~ grasses, mixed flowers
by a river wall, stones packed tight
~~shot free of moss~~, glinting in sunlight.
Yet what's so bright makes for odd imaginings.
Sometimes I feel as if a metal bowl had bent
dented by knocks from axe or hoe
~~blunt blows from hand or fists:  crude agency~~
and bits of reading lessons, shards of scripts
~~knocked loose~~ struck from a ~~past~~ voice locked into privacy,
(this is the immigrant's fury — no?
who understands my speech, further what is my speech?)
echoed, pounding as the ~~water pounds~~ rain can pound on roof and wall.
~~Then~~ Listen I saw the bricks of ~~a house stood~~ the apartment jagged, broken free
~~I saw~~ a girl in a sari tugging at a rope,
an infant crawling forwards in the mud, more mirrored than memory
bits and pieces of desire, ~~a~~ still a landscape unreal
with luminosity ~~and closer at hands, closer~~ .
~~than I could have wished~~, a mango stump,
an axe leant there, red earth, water pouring
in streams, syllables of speech splattering.
'Your feet, were they your feet?" I faced her firmly
'Listen, red earth pouring over your feet?'
I heard her laughing, bitterly.  I heard

the sound as if my tongue ~~burnt~~ <u>scraped</u> with chillis
my ears sodden with the cries of crickets in
the swollen paddy fields. 'What's up with you?'
I cried. 'What is it with the dead? Sheer jealousy?'
        There was something
scrolled so tightly in her hand, white paper
rolled in palm leaf

As she  wished the "ferociousness" of Akhilleus in *The Odyssey* to infuse the poem, Alexander says she had translated the reference of "break sod" (in Akhilleus statement, 'Let me hear no sweet talk of death from you.  Better I say to break sod as a farmhand for some poor countryman on iron rations than lord it over all the exhausted dead.") to the poem's dented metal bowl.

"A bowl is a very female thing; you cook in it and carry it.  Then what happens in the end (in drafts featured below) is that I see her belly as a bowl so that there's a return of it but in a different form." she says.

Alexander combined the thoughts about the bowl with her observations of the Hudson River which her apartment overlooks.  "The Hudson is held in by river walls.  In the lines, 'river wall, stones packed tight/ glinting in sunlight' I am thinking of when the sun hits the stones and the brightness makes me think of a metal that's been hit.  And the *hitting*, too, comes from the ghost woman because she's inside me trying to get out.  It's like my past is held inside this bowl. And it is dented by the velocity of this image.  This, too, is 'the immigrant's fury . . .who understands my speech, further what is my speech.'  And I'm appealing to the (ghost) image to be a fellow migrant.  But (at this stage of the poem) she doesn't buy that yet."

C)     <u>July 12, 1996 Draft</u>

### ~~HER GHOST~~ The Ghost Who Speaks To Me

Her ghost waited where the river ran.
She spoke to me that summer before
the floods began.  It was hard —
stones sinking, fireflies in paddy fields
herons on stumps of mango trees,
the axe planted where little else would work
and everywhere the mess of water.

'So you have entered a new world'
she said, her voice low, growling even.
There was nothing humble in her voice <u>.</u>
~~after all~~ <u>Sometimes</u> the dead behave in that know-all-way
ploughing the ruts of disaster.
Is their unease part of our very pith —
what the axe discovers marrow and meat to us?
'So what's it like there?' she asked

'Does it rain as hard as it rains here?'

~~And not knowing if my tongue could shape~~
~~my native syllables,~~ I like the Hudson, I muttered ever so slowly:
~~'I like the Hudson',~~ it simmers grey-green
shot with leaves, grasses, br__ a river wall, its
stones shot free of moss, glinting in sunlight.
'Yet what's so bright makes for odd imaginings.
Sometimes I feel as if a metal bowl had split
dented by knocks from ~~axe or~~ a hoe or blunt blows
even from a woman's fist, and bits of spelling lessons,
shards of script struck from a past locked into privacy
(this is the immigrant's fury — no?
who understands my speech, further what is my speech?)
echoed, pounding as ~~grain~~ rain might in ~~the~~ a granite mortar.'
[Del P]
I heard her voice again, the ghost who speaks to me:
'You think that bowl's your head, do you, and your feet?
where are they? ~~Where do you~~ How can you stand, addressing me?'
I heard her laughing, bitterly.  I heard the sound,
my ears sodden with the cries of crickets
my tongue burnt with red chillis from my lost mother's kitchen.
'What's up with you?' I cried.  'What is it with the dead?
Sheer jealousy?' ~~I saw~~ Her ~~right~~ hand waved a whitened scrap,
paper or cloth I could not tell.  She held it out to me:
I have torn it/this off
~~so you can~~ for you to write.  Take!'

I saw the silken thing that bound
her dropping ~~loose~~ free and then I saw her feet,
cut off at the ankles parted from her thighs,
They now slicked with red earth.  Water poured in short streams,
over her mutilated parts ~~yet~~ and there she was so delicate,
shored by a single elbow against a mango branch.

Among the changes Alexander made above was the new title, "The Ghost Who Speaks To Me."  She explains this as a way to increase the intensity of the line. "It's like a theater where the self splits into two and the 'Me' becomes a voice that I both can hear and also absorb inward."


D)    July 17, 1996 Draft


~~The Ghost Who Speaks To Me~~
**FIELD OF DREAMS**

~~Her ghost~~ She waited where the river ran.

~~She spoke to me~~ that summer ~~before~~ as before [Del L] the floods began ~~:~~

~~It was hard~~ — [New L] stones sinking, fireflies <u>murmuring</u>

[New L] in paddy fields, herons on stumps of ~~mango~~ trees,

the axe planted where little else would work

and everywhere the mess of water.

[Del P]

'So you have entered a new world'

~~she said,~~ her voice <u>was</u> low, growling even.

There was nothing humble in her voice <u>.</u>

Sometimes the dead behave in that know-all-way

ploughing the ruts of disaster.

~~Is~~ their unease part of our very pith —

what the axe discovers marrow and meat to us <u>?</u>

'So what's it like there?' ~~she asked~~

~~'Does it rain as hard as it rains here?'~~

[Del P]

I ~~like~~ <u>live by</u> the Hudson, I muttered ~~ever so~~ slowly:

~~'It simmers grey-green with rain,~~ <u>when the</u> [Del L] river wall ~~its~~ <u>rises, the river wall</u>

~~that binds it in packed~~ <u>is tight with</u> [Del L] stones ~~[New L]~~ [Del L]~~shot free of moss,~~

      glinting in sunlight.

<u>:</u> Yet what's so bright makes for odd imaginings.

~~Sometimes~~ <u>Sometimes</u> I feel as if a metal bowl had split

dented by ~~knocks from a hoe or blunt~~ blows [Del L] ~~even~~ from a woman's fist,

[New L] and bits of spelling lessons, {Del L} shards of script

[New L] struck from a past locked into privacy

(this is the immigrant's fury — no?

who understands my speech, further what is my speech?)

~~echoed,~~ <u>fell</u> pounding as ~~monsoon~~ rain might ~~in a granite mortar~~.'

[Del P]

~~I heard her voice again, the ghost who speaks to me.~~ ~~What rot!~~

'You think that bowl's your head ~~, do you, and your~~

[New L] <u>your speech a cipher slyph.</u> <u>Look at</u> ~~Your~~ <u>your</u> feet ~~?~~ <u>!</u>

~~where are they?~~ How can you stand ~~,~~ addressing me?'

I heard her laughing, bitterly. ~~I heard the sound,~~

~~my ears sodden with the cries of crickets~~

~~my tongue burnt with red chillis from my lost mother's kitchen.~~

'What's ~~up~~ with you?' I ~~cried~~ <u>shot back, turning aside</u>

[New L]. 'What is it with the dead? [Del L] Sheer jealousy?'

[New L] Her ~~hand~~ <u>fingers</u> waved a whitened scrap,

paper or cloth I could not tell.

[New L] She held it out ~~[New L] to me: [Del L] I have torn it this off [Del L] for you to~~

      ~~write.~~ [Del L] <u>to me.</u> Take!' <u>Write!</u>'

[Del P]

~~I snatched at my pen and then~~ I saw [Del L] ~~I saw~~ the ~~silken thing~~ <u>the sari</u> that bound

      [Del L] her

[New L] dropping free, ~~[New L] and then I saw~~ ~~her~~ feet ~~,~~ [Del L] cut ~~off~~ at the ankles

[New L] parted from her thighs, [Del L] slicked with red earth :
[New L] <u>two feverish monuments.</u>  Water poured [Del L]
[New L] in short streams, [Del L] over her mutilated parts .
~~[New L] and Yet there she was so delicate, [Del L] shored~~
[New L] <u>She stood shored</u> by a single elbow against a mango branch.

<u>Now place names splinter</u>
<u>on my tongue and flee from the flooded</u>
<u>field of dreams:  Manhattan</u>

<u>trees by the paddy field of dreams</u>
<u>manga guava love apple breadfruit</u>
<u>quick skins tearing</u>
<u>and the burnt plum of longing</u>
<u>erasing me . . . the terrible quick</u>
<u>of self (help me who can help? who can I cry to?)</u>
<u>Newness flashing as the firefires</u>
<u>flit</u>
<u>as the river a gash of blue pours</u>
<u>upwards to our mortality.</u>

For this draft, Alexander amended the title once more to "FIELD OF DREAMS," noting that she concluded that the previous title was "too bald. And I wanted to put the emphasis on the landscape — the two landscapes of the United States and India."

The July 17, 1996 draft also features many revisions, including some additions that she subsequently deleted. For instance, the added phrase, "two feverish monuments" never made it to the poem's Final Draft because Alexander felt the phrase "too stark" to capture the essence of a ghost.

In addition, at this stage, Alexander says that the first half of the poem contained something with which she had not yet come to terms. "I was still working through the catastrophic part of the beginning. The way the catastrophe comes together in the imagination is very interesting. It's like a shock, as I describe in my book (*Shock of Arrival*, 'Reflections on Postcolonial Experience, and published by South End Press in 1996). The shock is what the poem is about in a way. That I've made it but the *it* where one arrives also makes me. That's what 'GOLD HORIZON' is about — the process of assimilation and not in a readily translatable way."

Or, as Alexander writes in *Shock of Arrival*:

The shock of arrival is multifold—what was borne in the mind is jarred, tossed into new shapes, an exciting exfoliation of sense.  What we were in that other life, is shattered open.  But the worlds we now inhabit still speak of the need for invention, of ancestors, of faith.  In a time of literally explosive possibilities, we must figure out how to live our lives.

The shock of arrival forces us to new knowledge.  What the immigrant must work with is what she must invent in order to live. . . .

What multifoliate truth is stirring here?

What buried voices, quickening?

<u>E)</u>    <u>July 22, 1996 Expansion of the Last Three Stanzas Added in July 17, 1996 Draft</u>

Place names splinter on my tongue and flee:
Allahabad, Tiruvella, Kozhencheri, Khartoum
Nottingham, Delhi, Hyderabad, New York
the piece work of sanity flooded by a stream,
black water rising from the flooded field
where she and I wrestle, two women
wounded, mortal, skins naked, shining
in ~~that fever in the quick~~ the ~~hot pour~~ gold of a horizon
burnished ___ by disaster, the moon torn
from its axis, the carved teak of a threshold,
a ~~broken~~ bit of roof, window ledge, floating
by the mango tree.  The thick of thought
bolted up, struggling for release moved me:
~~I felt~~ her ankle stumps pressed against my throat
~~the new world with its mile long city block~~
~~silver bridges, asphalt studded with cries~~
~~burnt my throat, a speech~~

I cried out for my ~~new~~ world: ~~its~~ mile long
city blocks, silver bridges, asphalt studded
with neon plots, bodegas, bars, video stores
the mixed up speech of newness — the tenderness
of dogs flashed as a wing might, a silver heron
on a mango branch.  <u>Then</u> I felt her belly thick with blood
the woman who had waited for
the river pouring upwards . . .
through the rocks

and the voices whispering from red hills:
'an angel, you have caught an angel!'

the new world with its mile long city block
silver bridges, asphalt studded with cries
burnt my throat, a speech

and ~~from my~~ in the distant ~~and in the~~ hills
blue mist and red earth ~~whisper~~ ~~murmur~~ whispering to me. . .

"I was still struggling here with the ending," Alexander recalls. "I was working towards settling the landscape and the struggle was on how to crystallize the landscape versus the narrative tension. (For example,) how much of the new world should I put in?"

~~THE WOMAN WHO WAITS FOR ME~~

**GOLD OF A TORN HORIZON**

She waited where the river ran

that summer ~~before~~ as the floods began

stones sinking, fireflies murmuring

in paddy fields, herons on stumps of trees

the axe planted where little else would work

and everywhere the mess of water.

'So you have entered a new world'

her voice was low, growling even.

[New P]

There was nothing humble in her voice.

Sometimes the dead behave in that know-all-way

ploughing the ruts of disaster,

their unease part of our very pith —

what the axe discovers marrow and meat to us.

'So what's it like there?' she asked.

'~~When~~ As the Hudson ~~rises~~ ~~fills~~ pours ~~'I replied'~~ the river wall

is tight with stones, glinting in sunlight.

Yet what's so bright makes for odd imaginings.

Sometimes I feel as if a metal bowl had split

dented by blows from a woman's fist

and bits of spelling lessons, shards of script

struck from a past locked into privacy,

(this is the immigrant's fury — no?

who understands my speech, further what is my speech?)

dropped, pounding as ~~rain~~ rice grains might.'

[New P]

'You think that bowl's your head

your words a crypt!  Look at your feet!

How can you stand addressing me?'

I heard her laughing bitterly.

'What's with you' I shot back, ~~turning aside~~

'What's with the dead, sheer jealousy?'

Her fingers waved a whitened scrap

paper or cloth I could not tell

She held it out to me:  'Take! Eat!'

I saw the sari that bound her

dropping free, feet cut at the ankles,

parted from her thighs, slicked with red earth,

~~two feverish monuments~~.  Water poured [Del L] in short streams over her mutilated

          parts.

She stood shored by a single elbow against a mango branch.

[New P]

Place names splinter on my tongue and flee:

Allahabad, Tiruvella, Kozhencheri, Khartoum

Nottingham, ~~New York,~~ ~~New~~ New Delhi, Hyderabad, New York , corruscating
  geographies ~~coruscating a wilderness of geographies geography~~, the piece
  work of sanity ~~flooded~~ ruined by ~~a stream, dream, streets~~ [Del L] ~~black~~
  water rising

[New L] in ~~the~~ a ~~flooded~~ paddy field [Del L] where ~~she and I~~ we wrestle, she and I,
  two women

~~one~~ the living, the dead, ~~one living,~~ ~~both~~ naked ~~shining slipping shining~~ ____free

~~through~~ in the gold of a torn horizon,

*INDENTED LINES SUBSEQUENTLY DELETED:*

  The ~~settled world — from its axis~~ household lives hang from a kitchen hook, a
    hold
  kitchen counter knives, fresh folded sheets, spill to the paddy field
  ripe tomatoes, burnt chilllis, sliced ginger
  ~~spurt~~ knocked from neat mounds by our thrashing.

Our thrashing is not nice. [Del L] Her ankle stumps

[New L] ~~pressed~~ press against my eyes .

~~breath bolted, hungry for new life~~

Words ~~bolted~~ ~~inside~~ bolt, ~~old~~ syllables ~~scrolled~~ ~~mangled~~ scroll [Del L] ~~into~~ a scratched
  out script

[New L] ~~my own~~ memory rasps ~~against~~ on, a theatre I never wished.

Breathless I ~~cried cry~~ reach out ~~to~~ for ~~my~~ a ~~world~~ scene — ~~its~~ mile long [Del L] city
  blocks,

[New L] ~~painted~~ [New L] ~~silver~~ [Del L] iron bridges ~~buckling~~ ~~peeling~~ scraping back the
  ~~sky~~ hills,

[New L] asphalt ~~studded~~ ~~pressed~~ pierced [Del L] with neon plots, ~~the~~ a rage of sense :

[New L] bodegas in the Barrio, Billy's topless bar, [Del L] Vineeta's

[New L] Video Store [New L] ~~video stores~~ crammed with cartoons of Nutan and Madhuri:

'Kya, kya hum kon hai? Idher hum kon hai?'

[Del L] ~~the~~ [New L] The mixed up speech of newness ~~, sore tenderness~~

~~of pain gain~~ flashing as a ~~wing~~ heron might, [New L] ~~as twilight turns a silver heron~~
  [Del L] ~~and~~ against its ____ on a mango branch.

[New P]

She waited where the river ran, that summer as the floods began.

[New L] ~~Underneath~~ ~~Under~~ Beneath my ~~cheek~~ ~~chin~~ cheek I feel her belly thick with blood
~~underneath my cheek the woman who waits for me.~~ Whose tongue is this?

~~My tongue It~~ What melts in the terrible quick of migrancy ~~.~~ ?

I feel raw bones, the skull's precise asymmetry.

~~As rivers~~ Rivers north and rivers south ~~pour~~ soar ~~upwards~~

~~in~~ into tongues of mist ~~through~~ parting both our ribs,

~~I hear~~ as children's voices ~~whispering~~ whisper from red hills:

'An angel, you have caught an angel!'


Alexander's poetic resolution of the tension between the "I" and the ghost woman led to the ending of children whispering, "An angel, you have caught an angel!"

"I was thinking about Jacob and his struggle with the angel in the Bible — a story I grew up with in childhood," Alexander says. "It was a terrible struggle and that's why the poem's angel is a muscular angel, not one of these things on Christmas trees. And the struggle with the angel is similar to a struggle with psyche, with God. It, too has to do with the terrible tension of self-invention, so that the struggle is also with the Muse."

Alexander adds humorously, "I thought if Jacob can have an angel, why can't I have an angel? But it's a female angel, of course, because it's part of myself, just as Jacob's angel was male. But it's still a muscular angel."

In addition, she says that "it was very important to me that I had these voices of children" in order to allow her Muse to surface. "There's a kind of innocence about children's voices which may or may not be the truth, but it may be the truth — maybe it's the only truth," she says. "You see, the early part of the poem was powerful and scary with the woman tearing off a piece of her sari and saying, 'Take. Eat.' She doesn't say 'Take. Write.' "

As is typical of Alexander's multi-layered poetic approach, there is yet something else happening with the ending of the poem. "In the ending, and I was aware of this, in a way both bodies dissolve. After they wrestle together, they rise up together. A great influence on my writing is (William) Wordsworth's "Prelude" — there is a sea of mist and also the real sea, a doubling in the landscape that allows for the imagination to rise up. It's like having these two bodies — our ribs are parted. Creation coming after a terrible struggle which seems almost a battle to the death."

The following relates to Book Thirteenth from (the 1805 version of) "Prelude" that Alexander recalls. The section depicts Wordsworth's ascent of Mount Snowdon, made when he was twenty-one, and a "youthful friend," Robert Jones:

### *from* **The Prelude**

In one of these excursions, travelling then
Through Wales on foot and with a youthful friend,
. . . It was a summer's night, a close warm night,
Wan, dull, and glaring, with a dripping mist
Low-hung and thick that covered all the sky,
Half threatening storm and rain; but on we went
Unchecked, being full of heart and having faith
In our tried pilot. Little could we see,
Hemmed round on eery side with fog and damp,
And, after ordinary travellers' chat
With our conductor, silently we sunk
Each into commerce with his private thoughts.
Thus did we breast the ascent, and by myself
Was nothing either seen or heard the while. . .
                With forehead bent
Earthward, as if in opposition set
Against an enemy, I panted up
With eager pace, and no less eager thoughts,
Thus might we wear perhaps an hour away,
Ascending at loose distance each from each,

And I, as chanced, the foremost of the band —
When at my feet the ground appeared to brighten,
And with a step or two seemed brighter still;
Nor had I time to ask the cause of this,
For instantly a light upon the turf
Fell like a flash. I looked about, and lo,
The moon stood naked in the heavens at height
Immense above my head, and on the shore
I found myself a huge sea of mist,
Which meek and silent rested at my feet.
A hundred hills their dusky backs upheaved
All over this still ocean, and beyond,
Far, far beyond, the vapours shot themselves
In headlands, tongues, and promontory shapes,
Into the sea, the real sea, that seemed
To dwindle and give up its majesty,
usurped upon as far as sight could reach.

Alexander's process is also reflected in the evolution of the titles of her poem, which are (in chronological order) "Her Ghost," "The Ghost Who Speaks To Me," "The Woman Who Waits For Me" and "Gold Of A Torn Horizon," before culminating in "Gold Horizon." The title's evolution reflects how Alexander arrived at a title without referring to a ghost only after she was able to write Part III where the ghost changes to become her Muse.

Alexander adds, "If I had just used 'Ghost' it would have been too scary for me. I'm scared of ghosts. There's some savagery in the ghost — it's inspiring but terrifying and confusing and yet at the end I come out of it."

G)    July 23, 1996 Draft With Revisions To Achieve Final Draft

Alexander initially considered a July 23, 1996 draft to be the poem's final version. Subsequently, she made additional changes featured below. (The Final Draft, dated as of August 20, 1996, is interspersed within the text above.) One of her changes was to divide the poem into three parts, a technique that Alexander felt would facilitate the reader's understanding of the narrative progression of the poem, given its "back-and-forth" flow across thresholds of time and place.

**GOLD HORIZON**

I.

She waited where the river ran
that summer as the floods began
stones sinking, fireflies murmuring
in paddy fields, herons on stumps of trees
the axe planted where little else would work
and everywhere the mess of water.

[New P]
'So you have entered a new world'
her voice was low, growling even.
There was nothing humble in her voice.
Sometimes the dead behave in that know-all-way
ploughing the ruts of disaster,
their unease part of our very pith —
what the axe discovers marrow and meat to us.

'So what's it like there?' <u>she asked.</u>
[New P]
I replied: 'As the Hudson pours
[New L] the river wall [Del L] clings tight with <u>glinting</u> stones ~~, glinting in sunlight~~.
Yet what's so bright makes for odd imaginings.
Sometimes I feel as if a metal bowl had split
dented by blows from a woman's fist
and bits of spelling lessons, shards of script
struck from a past locked into privacy,
— this is the immigrant's fury — ¸ no?
who understands my speech, further what is my speech? —
dropped, pounding as rice grains might.'

'You think that bowl's your head
your words a crypt!  Look at your feet!
How can you stand addressing me?'
I heard her laughing bitterly.
[New P]
'What's with you?'  I shot back
'What's with the dead, sheer jealousy?'
[New P]
Her fingers waved a whitened scrap
paper or cloth I could not tell.
She held it out to me:  'Take!  Eat!'
[New P]
I saw the sari that bound her
dropping free, feet cut at the ankles,
severed from her thighs, slicked with red earth.
Water poured in short streams
over her mutilated parts.
She stood, shored by a single elbow
against a mango branch.

[New P and Part II]
<u>II.</u>

[Delete indent] Place names splinter

on my tongue and flee:

Allahabad, Tiruvella, Kozhencheri, [Del L] Khartoum,

[New L] Nottingham, <u>New</u> Delhi, Hyderabad, New York,

~~corruscating geographies,~~ — the piece work of sanity — ,

stitching them into a ~~paradise without cease~~, <u>corruscating geography</u>

why a single long drawn breath

[New L] in an infant's dream [Del L] might do

[New L] — ruined by black water in a paddy field.


We wrestle on wet ground,

[New L] she and I, [Del L] ~~the~~ living and dead,

[New L] stripped to our skins,

naked, shining free [Del L] in

[New L] the gold of a torn horizon.

[New P]

Our thrashing is not nice.

[New L] Her ankle stumps [Del L] shove against my eyes.

[New P]

[New L] Words bolt, [Del L] syllables rasp

[New L]an altered script,

theatre of memory I ~~would~~ <u>could</u> never have wished.

Breathless I search for a scene

[New L] — mile long city blocks,

iron bridges scraping back ~~the~~ <u>short</u> hills,

asphalt pierced with neon plots,

[New L] the rage of sense:

bodegas in the Barrio, Billy's topless bar,

[New L] Vineeta's [Del L] Video Store crammed with cartoons

[New L] of Nutan and Madhuri

— 'Kya, kya hum kon hai?  Idher hum kon hai' —

<u>'Namal ivide ara?  Ivide namal ara?'</u> —

[New P]

~~the~~ <u>The</u> mixed up speech of newness,

[New L] flashing [Del L] as a kite might,

[New L] ~~white~~ <u>pale</u> paper on a mango branch.


[New Part III]

### III.


*She waited where the river ran,*

*that summer as the floods began.*

[New P]

Is this mere repetition,

[New L] <u>or</u> the ~~backward~~ <u>warm</u> sprawl of time,

~~echoing~~ <u>inscribed</u> in limestone?

Who can ~~slip~~ <u>cry</u> back into ~~her~~ <u>a</u> first world

a barefoot child on a ~~muddy~~ mud forking path,
~~paddy~~ fields ~~green~~ gold with monsoon water,
haunt of the ~~goldfish~~ snail and ~~fireflies~~ dragonfly?
What makes the narrative whole?
[New P]
Beneath my cheek I feel her belly's bowl
thick with blood, the woman who waits for me.
Are these her lips or mine?
Whose tongue is this ~~;~~
[New L] melting to the quick of migrancy?
I touch raw bones, a skull's precise asymmetry.


As ~~Rivers~~ rivers north and rivers south soar
into tongues of mist parting ~~all~~ our ribs
~~and childrens' voices~~ I hear voices of children whisper from red hills:
'An angel, you have caught an angel!'

—◆◆◆—

Aptly, Alexander delivered a speech titled "Unquiet Borders" during the April 1997 confer-
ence on "Poetry and the Public Sphere" sponsored by Rutgers University. After delivering her
speech as part of a roundtable on "Poetry, Feminism(s) and the Difficult Wor(l)d," co-panelist
Adrienne Rich announced that Alexander's words — and the image Alexander described of
Mirabai, a woman in "tattered oriental clothing" — are the best way to end the discussion on the
topics at hand. It seems appropriate, as well, to end Alexander's poetry-in-progress project with
her words:

## UNQUIET BORDERS

The unquiet borders of poetry: I muse on Mirabai, poet mystic of the bhakti
movement in India, she who left home and princely husband and roved across thresh-
olds, borders. Leaving the confines of domesticity her saris were torn; her hair matted,
lacking the oil that Indian women prize. Her feet were dry, chapped.

And she roved, she sang of Krishna continually, that perpetual absent, her
beloved.

Was Mira's body covered with dirt, like that of Akkamahadevi, another great
woman poet, such that she might have been said to wear a skin of dirt?

And what of menstrual blood? How did she wash it off? Or did it mix in with
the mud?

I ask all this quite deliberately, here, now at the tail end of this century, on this
North American continent and I ask, what would it mean if Mirabai were alive, here, now
in America? How would she write? What sense would our complex, multifarious world
we women writers inhabit make to her?

I will try and answer by pretending I can see into her soul. We poets do that a
lot and failing short stand dismayed at our own shortfalls. Still . . . first her body. She let
her body show. It was warm in Rajasthan in most seasons. Her skin was brown. It was

not enough crouched in the hot alleyway to sing of Krishna — *I am your knife, you my noose* — sing of palaces that did not offer food for the soul, dirt shacks, soiled thresholds.

She crossed a border, never to return. I imagine her, here, now. But what do they make of her, a brown skinned woman in tattered oriental clothing at the edge of Broadway in Manhattan. Or by the railroad tracks in New Brunswick? Is she hunched on the sidewalk? Is she rooting in the garbage for food?

Then again we might find Mira like many other Asian immigrant women working in a sweat shop in the lower east side, her rhythms of poetry beaten to the tracking needle, silks spinning out of her skin, English syllables edgy, forced, brajbhasha flowering only in dreams.

The hidden language that flowers only in dreams torn from the body.

Frantz Fanon who Mirabai did not need to read — in his work women are so much cast aside — in a crucial section of *Black Skins, White Mask* imagines people crying out 'Look, a negro!' So she might find the fingers pointing — 'Look, a brown woman!' The shame, the torment, the turning, beseeching others. Stumbling, falling, the body splintering into a thousand shards. The body split open.

'I burst apart' Fanon writes. 'Now the fragments have been put together again by another self.'* What is this other self? What might this putting together of a racialized body mean? A body not male, but female, haunted by its femaleness, earth it cannot shed. Will Krishna put her together again? Or is this the secret of her genius, the impossible sense that Krishna who lies in wait for her, under the waters of sleep will not stitch her back again, piece together the broken bits?

So who will put together a body torn by border crossings, skin marked by barbed wires, bandages hastily knotted, the body of a pariah woman?

Why do I conceive of the female poet like this? Perhaps because I think that she needs to slip her flesh in order to sing, yet it is only by being drawn back into a larger, more spiritual body, the mouths of many others, the hands that labor in the sweat shops, on the street corners, in the market places and, yes, in the academies, that she can write.

A few points to conclude this reverie. Our world is filled with unquiet borders It would be a terrible error — too grave to be borne — to think that our capacity for words can lose us our bodies. Bodies banned, beaten, jailed, twisted in childbirth, bodies that are the sites of pleasure, of ecstasy. Female bodies that can babble, break into prophetic speech, rant.

Any aesthetic implications I hear someone ask. None except what I have called elsewhere *'a back against the wall aesthetic**. The woman poet who faces the borders her body must cross, racial, sexual borders, is forced to invent a form that springs out without canonical support, a rough and ready thing, its order crude, its necessity beyond the purchase of self-invention. There is something in this species of play, the body in pain or pleasure, crying out for a sense that a multicultural feminism might learn from.

And I try to learn from Mirabai, from her nakedness. The most delicate play of words is what we aspire to in the face of terrors that confront us. The beloved perpetually lost, the body fragmented, its bits and pieces spelling out a map that a new Fanon, female now and a poet, might make, crossing unquiet borders.

*NOTES TO ALEXANDER'S SPEECH, "UNQUIET BORDERS"*

*Mirabai, c 1498-1565, a princess who left her royal home to wander, singing the praises of Krishna. She is considered one of the major figures of the devotional movement of bhakti in which love of the deity often takes intense, erotic form. Mirabai wrote in both Gujarati and Brajbhasa, the latter a dialect of Hindi in which a great deal of devotional poetry was composed.*

*The line, 'I am your knife, you my noose' is Alexander's rendering of what she imagines Mirabai to have sung. Alexander is playing with lines from her poem: 'He's left me wearing,/ dainty and small/ a noose . . . . Why not straight to/ Kashi? One touch/ of the knife, one end?' (See* In the Dark of the Heart, Songs of Meera *translated by Shama Futehally (New Delhi: Indus, 1994)*

*\* Frantz Fanon,* Black Skin, White Masks *(New York: Grove Press, 1967)*
*\*\* 'Skin With Fire Inside: Indian Women Writers' in Meena Alexander,* The Shock of Arrival: Reflections on Postcolonial Experience *(Boston: Southend Press, 1996)*

# SESSHU FOSTER

Sesshu Foster is the author of the poetry books, *Angry Days* (West End Press, 1987) and CITY TERRACE *Field Manual* (Kaya Production, 1996). His poetry has appeared widely in such journals as *BOMB, Fuel, The Coe Review, Forkroads, Crossroads* and *The Asian Pacific American Journal* as well as the anthologies *Premonitions: the Kaya Anthology of New Asian North American Poetry* (Kaya Production, 1996) and *The Party Train: A Collection of North American Prose Poetry* (New Rivers Press, 1996). He also co-edited the 1990 American Book Award winner, *Invocation L.A.: Multicultural Urban Poetry* (West End Press, 1989). He currently teaches at Francisco Bravo Medical Magnet in Los Angeles.

In response to the question, "What advice would you give to a young poet?" Sesshu Foster responds:

> In a corollary of the dictum, "Pessimism of the intelligence, optimism of the will," patiently endure your frustrations and try to write as much as you can; save as much time as you can for writing — give readings whenever asked: they're instant, free workshops. A lot of people are looking for happiness in life, but why bother to do that in poetry? Go for *revenge*. It has to taste sweeter when you're young.

# Sesshu Foster's Coming-Of-Age:
## CITY TERRACE Field Manual

*"hagamos profesion terrestre/ toquemos tierra con el alma"* (1)
— *Pablo Neruda*

*". . . then there's the terrible lucidity of your eyes. How do we account for something so transparent as the eye seeing?*
— *Gabrielle Glancy*

*"I'm going to study so hard
that when I explain myself,
I'll be talking geography."*
— *Pablo Neruda*

I think of a huge soap bubble, rainbows staining its undulating curves, floating a belly-dance through the air — and me holding my breath as if that would prolong its fragile existence. The light dappling the face of a pond. A piano's high notes tinkling in the distance then threading their way through my veins. The shimmer of a heat wave. The sheen on a lover's neck. It's also like that dude in Panama swimming after deflowering a virgin on a hot day — afterwards, he goes for a walk, "a little warm beer in (his) hand, a little sip in the stunning light."

That dude in Panama is one of the characters in Sesshu Foster's second book, *CITY TERRACE Field Manual* ("*CTFM*") (Kaya Productions, 1996), a collection of prose poems and vignettes set in or about East Los Angeles. *CTFM* displays Foster's intimacy with East L.A.: its geography, its people, its despair, its dreams. But East L.A. is not poetry; the poetry is Foster's words — how he crafts the poems to seem so weightless that I sometimes sense a stillness in my body as I read them, as if a movement could disturb the poems into flying off the page. The poems make me recall the fragility of a soap bubble as well as certain memories that conjure in me the same resonating response. I am awed that in a poem about some dude deflowering a virgin, what mostly lingers is that brief slide of warm beer: "a little sip in the stunning light."

Or, how about a poem about, basically, a corpse — including the corpses of "kids (who) grow up thinking this life is their fault. Take its fucked-up sadness into themselves, left off at foster homes and distant relatives." Here's an excerpt:

> I don't know, but I think deep in the ground a heart beats like a train, it's a heart that pumps molten rock and courses like wolves across the ice. It listens as our naked footfalls mark the contemplative earth, ascending toward noon. Silence rings from it like circles in disturbed water.

Even when Foster's poems are more direct in their references to incidents and characters in East L.A., the poems are not burdened by their subject matter — as in this poem:

> **I SAW** their bodies steaming, lying on the avenue. The motorcycle was crammed up under the car. Their bodies were unmoving and gray under the streetlights, and I could not see what they were looking at. I had not seen that before. The bodies were steam-

ing on the ground.  People were coming out onto the street to look at them.  The people were not shining like the car dealerships.  I kept going, driving down skid row at midnight, looking for my brother.

*CTFM* contains mostly one paragraph poems.  They possess a rhythm that allows for a reading without strain; often, they are lyrical.  One can read them out loud and fall into natural pauses without the need for line breaks.  In the first four sentences of the above poem, for example, I found such natural pauses indicated by "/" as follows:  "I saw their bodies steaming,/ lying on the avenue./  The motorcycle was crammed up under the car./  Their bodies were unmoving/ and gray under the streetlights,/ and I could not see what they were looking at./  I had not seen that before."

In another poem, this internal melody is more obvious because of its Spanish words — recalling Ezra Pound's statement about poetry sharing "its media with music in so far as words are composed of inarticulate sounds."  For this non-Spanish speaker, the music remains in the following:

> Ay, woman I been traveling south, . . . I coiled a black highway in my hands like a cinturon, reading *Las Cinco Cartas* por Hernan Cortez y las mentiras del periodismo, I seen women with hair black as yours but I'm still thirsty, refresco de tunas but still thirsty, humming like a colibri La maldicion de Malinche to chavalos y ancianos as the train pulls out, pulling daylight itself through the back of my skull like a bullet hole in an empty can, querida, when I see you on campus next month I will spit a small stone of dawn into the palm of your hand.

Foster does not always write in a prose poem structure.  But it is a form that, he says, reflects a maturity in his poetic development, just as *CTFM*'s subjects partly relate to his coming-of-age experiences in East L.A.  *CTFM* is a landmark work for Foster who acknowledges that he previously enforced limitation on his words, constraints that may be a metaphor for, in the past, simplifying his persona to others.

"For years — maybe decades — I felt that I'd been avoiding the form of the prose poem because I felt that it was middle-of-the-road:  not fiction and not poetry.  But I have always been interested in it because I'm a continual reader and writer of both fiction and poetry.  The prose poem was a voice that kept calling.  So I decided to use this form for *CTFM*," he says.

"Prose poems allow me to use a voice and voices to structure lines and language.  Rather than have paragraphs and chapters in prose or lines, phrases and diction in poetry, I could work all the voices more directly.  I could have a variety of voices, a community of voices.  This is important," he notes, "because *CTFM*'s poems take on the voices of people I knew growing up (although) some are fictionalized because I didn't want a portrait gallery.  I wanted to create something like a human landscape.

"*CTFM* has a personal basis," Foster continues.  "I have a background that I often have had to simplify for people.  When people first meet me, they ask, 'Who are you?  What's your background?'  I have a white Dad and Nisei mom and grew up in a Chicano barrio.  I grew up with Asians, Chicanos and people with mixed heritage — but I've always had to simplify for people who come from outside that experience."

Consequently, Foster says he wanted to ensure that he didn't dilute the multi-layered landscape of East L.A. in both subject matter and language.  He notes, "If you only talk about one aspect of anything, it becomes a reduction. In *CTFM*, I gave myself permission to deal with complications."

With such permission, *CTFM* released Foster from his historical reluctance to work in the style of prose poetry. In addition, he says he "gave (him)self license in *CTFM* to use language that might be a very interior or personal or regional language — regional as in Chicano or Spanglish."

Foster adds that "there might be a typecasting about prose styles in that prose is conceived to be less pure as a poetic language." As Foster explains why he disagrees, one senses that this issue, too, may be a metaphor for how he believes those whom he considers — and has called in his poetry — "my people" are perceived by others. "The typecasting might include that the prose style is conceived to be for the less-educated, and that people limited by class backgrounds are expected to be less idiosyncratic, less nuanced or possess less of a viewpoint. I definitely wanted to avoid that (by not simplifying *CTFM*). I have never found that people of less education or lower class backgrounds are less complicated people. I was interested in allowing the language to capture that subtlety and nuance beyond the stereotypes."

Indeed, Foster does not use complicated language or literal devices in the earlier poem about the car accident but only describes the incident. Yet, the poem resonates, as does this example where he simply observes a neighbor:

> . . . and mom's looking good sunbathing out in the yard. Radio on, lying on her book, straps untied. Her kids are out in the streets, shooting into traffic between parked cars, lighting summer fires on the hillside, watching lizards dry up inside bottles on the wall. I vote her kids least likely to succeed — somebody's gonna try and kill them before they grow. I carry my trash cans down the driveway to get a better look. She gives me her best smile and I like it.

*CTFM*'s subjects also include the anti-war activists Foster met during the 1970s and 1980s. "This is another added complication that I told myself I should allow to happen. Gary Soto wrote *Neighborhood Odes* — about Chicano children growing up. I could have done something like that whose stock is coming of age stories and childhood incidents. But coming of age in East L.A occured during tumultous and historical times," he says.

Foster is referring to a period in America's history which could be called aptly "Angry Days," which happens, too, to be the title of his first poetry collection (West End Press, 1987). Some of the poems in *CTFM* contain a heat — ever simmering, often breaking through the surface. They reflect the context of their subjects: the 1970s with the nation in turmoil over the Vietnam War, student activism, riots in the streets, the difficult birth of the Chicano movement, Blacks calling for empowerment, community activists fighting drug dealers and trying to stop gang killings. With the 1980s arrive more wars: El Salvador, Nicaragua and more of the same social, political and cultural battles — the faces are different but the fall of bodies familiar.

In some ways, Foster was too young to be directly affected; for example, he was too young to be drafted in the Vietnam War. But, always, he recalls, he observed and now feels those days inseparable from himself and what he addresses in his poetry.

"I've been writing for as long as I can remember. My first publication was in a Little Tokyo newspaper published by activists called *Gidra* (a Japanese cartoon of monster). *Gidra* was published by community activists fighting the urban renewal of Little Tokyo in which Japanese capital pushed the Issei (first generation Japanese immigrants) out of Little Tokyo. The New Otani Hotel replaced buildings where Issei retirees lived. And these activists' newspaper was where I was first published. And so that was what I knew as I grew up. On the one hand, I grew up with the Vietnam War and its associations, the continual turmoil in the country; on the other hand, I grew up in a neighborhood where activists were dealing with community issues. In East L.A., there were student activists protesting the wars, dealing with drug dealers and trying to stop gang killing.

"And because I grew up in a Chicano barrio, part of my coming of age was the Chicano movement, reflecting a change in consciousness among the community. The Chicano movement came in part from anti-Vietnam activism. The 1970 Chicano Moratorium mobilized thousands of people in the streets protesting and calling for an end to the draft. Because it was primarily the poor who were being drafted, blacks and Chicanos were dying disproportionately in Vietnam versus their percentage of the U.S. population. The protesters were attacked by sheriffs and three people were killed, including a Chicano journalist, Ruben Salazar. Vietnam provided a main impetus and example to the anti-war activists. In *CTMF*, there is a deliberate blurring of which war is being addressed by some of the poems — whether Vietnam, El Salvador, Nicaragua, urban renewal or community-related wars — because many activists became involved with one war and then another, right on up to the Gulf War.

In addition, Foster recalls, "There was a nationalism going on at the time. The Chicano movement was founded on the idea that Southwestern United States was part of Mexico that was taken over by the U.S. and so should constitute its own separate nation. Blacks were calling for Black Power and Black Liberation."

Nationalism, however, also resulted in factionalism — another source of tension to Foster's coming-of-age. "East L.A. was right across the river from Little Tokyo — I went back and forth; I had family and friends in both places. But because there was a nationalism going on at the time, there were feelings of exclusiveness and the fact that I was going back and forth bothered some of the people I knew. But I could never not deal with people just because they were of different ethnicities. I could never deal with turning Little Tokyo into a Bosnia, its own enclave."

Consequently, Foster concludes that "the politics of the 1970s always seemed too simple." It is a conclusion bolstered by his personal history of living in East L.A. which has long been an area of mixed heritages, encompassing Latin Americans, Jews and Asians.

Nevertheless, Foster stresses, that the politics of the activists "did not keep me from admiring people I knew who were politically active. I felt at the time that it was important to oppose war, what forces brought us into war, what forces there were that might bring it about again. This is part of the notion of *CTFM* — that exclusivity turns out to be both political and personal dead-ends. But I look at that sympathetically. I never would have told these people, 'Don't get involved; it'll just bring you grief.' I felt somebody had to be doing that stuff whether or not I agreed with their politics."

In Part II of the excerpts from *CTFM* featured below, Foster presents the story of Xiomara and Rigo, two anti-war activists based on real-life people. Their stories end in tragedy, reflecting the "dead-end" of "exclusivity." Yet Foster notes, "I'd hesitate to say that Xiomara and Rigo paid a special price. I mean, I think that commitment takes a certain cost. Commitment in anything, whether in relationships or to a political or social idea. If it's a real commitment, then that requires a certain effort. And efforts don't always pay off. You lose sometimes."

Foster adds, "William Carlos Williams suggested you can't have an American literature when you don't stay in one place long. Part of the function of East L.A. for me is it's a place where I came of age, but part of coming-of-age is becoming conscious about how people's histories bear on them, how they respond to their own history. That they're not just reactive, as my grandparents were when they were brought here to work in the fields of Central California. People attempt to create their own history and decide what kind of life they want to lead. I feel that I have a certain window into East L.A. and my narratives of its history are also about me."

—ɷ—

*CTFM*'s complicated background only enhances Foster's poetic accomplishment: the subject matter does not burden poetic style. In part, this results from Foster's drafting process — how he distills a poem. His typical writing process involves typing into his computer several separate versions of the same idea, which he later cuts and recombines.

Featured below are illustrations of Foster's drafting process towards some sample poems from *CTFM*. Part II reflects Foster's typical writing process; the distillation of his ideas can be seen by reading some of the early drafts that eventually resulted in the three sample poems below. Part I is unusual in that it features a journal entry as the first draft of the excerpt; Foster says he writes frequently but doesn't keep journals (though he keeps copies of all his writings, e.g. letters, to help form his works.)

The early drafts are presented as they exist in Foster's files, thus including spelling errors or other idiosyncracies during Foster's creative process. *(Editing Marks: strikethroughs = deletions; underlined words = additions)*

**Part I**

Featured below are (A) a First Draft that takes the form of a Journal Entry; (B) the Journal Entry distilled to highlight the poem's underlying mood; (C) an Intermediate Draft with Editing Marks depicting subsequent changes by Foster and Kaya's editors; and (D) the Final Draft which appears in *CTFM*.

A.     First Draft/Journal Entry:
Foster's journal entry is written in a stream-of-consciousness style, reflecting thoughts that never made it to subsequent drafts of the poem, but which clearly influenced the mood of subsequent drafts.

this month there's a storm over l.a. it's slapping up against the san gabriel mountains with the sloppy exhuberance of sex in a steamy bath tub all night it was coming down on the skylight with tapping like the crow who kept attacking his own image seen as a reflection on the other side i haven't seen that crow since though i was thinking about it as i looked across the field through the screen of thin eucalyptus ragged against the breeze the distance between me and arizona and between me and the sun and between me and another human being and between me and my people intervening years of dust intervening years of afternoon light and warmth interludes of fateful chaos you sort out later interludes like summers after which people turn up dead or fade away and disappear i'm sending out an idea like a satellite to voyage in the black spaces between planets and broadcast items such as hard breathing after two miles jogged such as some woman who used to feel you up under the table when she was thirteen years old and you were fifteen and couldn't handle it didn't know what to do tried to talk your way out of it now she is a nice person and has she forgotten her disgust and her own breathlessness there in the kitchen with the rest of the family walking in and out such as the close of another year in wet weather like california dipping into the ocean into its oceanic cetaecian dreams warm gaseous bubbles undulating like farts rising toward the surface and what a surface it always turns out to be the raw interface with fate and its raw deals and absurd ironies like some game it has to play even if no one is gonna play with it because we all got too much work to do trying to survive this vertical red tidal wave of the moment pounding through the blood each one as necessary as the last each one in its way more necessary for the next like a tornado of sweat whipped up into a sky the color of black blood thundering over our heads the color of the avenues that return to life after each police cruiser departs the teenagers who feed the life of the streets their own moments like stripped kindling in some savage bonfire of excess entirely expunged of spirit of cerebral decorum or any intellectual party their forays into the vast wastes of this daily nation not even footnotes in tossed out pornographic magazines where their smiles end up (eyes half closed and early promise evaporated following all too numerous drugs and other responsibilities) cluttering the intersections of houseparties and front offices of public services emergency rooms and other waiting areas like leaves in a canyon stream are embedded in a tangle of bleached driftwood where the water itself pours out below through sand and boulders where in the usual afternoon you make the loudest noise simply in your foot steps i took the strongest leash in the pocket of my raincoat and let akai out in the drizzle knowing it was likely my running shoes were going to be soaked before i got back to the house before we got around the far side of the soccer field it was already pouring but akai was having fun grinning and running full out across the field and reading the scents in the wet grass and marking out each tree he found time for and for once the streets were relatively empty and quiet in midday because it was raining shakespeare brecht ngugi wa thingo susan sherman peter mathiessen lorna dee cervantes all sleeping on the shelf ignored while i go out for a walk instead with my big red malemute in the first real rain this winter the first rainy day as the year ended in this wet curtain wrapped about my shoulders my hands stuffed into my pockets as my pantlegs soaked stiff sooner than i thought possible we walked into alhambra over one freeway and down toward monterey park under another and i knocked on naomi quinonez's door and victor hernandez cruz opened it and she recognized me from the upstairs window shouting down come on up but he was standing at the door saying we're sleeping and your dog is all wet what's going on? so I said maybe some other time and walked down the street to granada park and akai ran around grinning like crazy and slipping and sliding ont eh wet grass i looked at the monterey highlands through the curtain of wet and at the empty children's playground the the bright green baseball diamond shining in the cool darkness of the day the el sereno hills where i walked during the seventies in winter rains like this thinking about the coup in chile and poetry and stories and what should i do while casualties rained down on us like asteroids on a lunar plain hendrix and santana guitars blaring in my ears made it hard to say all that much about it you could feel the bass thrumming in your guts the rhythm of every foot step echoless adn too weighty for words now under the big oaks in the park watching the rain come down on the picnic tables that on other weekends will be reserved for birthday parties and family barbeques vans crammed with kids and plump middle-aged women pillars of these affairs pinatas toddlers carne asada ribbons ice chests boomboxes each happy family the same each unhappy family a different story akai would like to meet friends and get into fights with dogs on the other side of fences all the way back it must be exciting like the last day of work those girls must have been expectantly waiting for the bell to ring outside my door when it finally did the kids were rushing out and they hurried in to say goodbye their cute last minute courage set the precedent so that all the sweet girls who would like to be hugged could following their example get their hugs too and there was a brief line where every girl who wanted one could get theirs but no boys they all ran away and after awhile the girls did too and i was trying to sort it through and pack up what i needed to take home with me after i was done with another semester and walk out of the buildings through the emptied and lit-tered corridors toward a skyline the color of flesh and cold bones hair after a shock closed eyelids boyle heights eight years later our lives just another east l.a. barrio bisected by two different freeways where the people fly through in their steel vehicles like space travelers and catch videos of conversation violence graffitti-style personalities my soaked clothes are warm after walking back i had wanted to run and had missed working out but this was better than nothing

B.      Distilled Journal Entry

Certain words, for me, seem to rise to the surface of the Journal Entry and help illustrate Foster's meditative mood, redolent with memories:

"... there's a storm over l.a. ... all night it was coming down on the skylight ... tap-ping like the crow who kept attacking his own image ... i looked across the field through the screen of thin eucalyptus ... the distance between me and arizona ... me and the sun ... me and my people ... intervening years ... interludes of fateful chaos . . . like summers after which people turn up dead or fade away .... hard breathing after two miles jogged such as some woman who used to feel you up under the table ... she was thirteen years old and you were fifteen and couldn't handle it ... the close of anoth-er year in wet weather ... california dipping into the ocean ... warm gaseous bubbles undulating like farts rising toward the surface and what a surface it always turns out to be . . . its raw deals ... we all got too much work to do trying to survive this vertical red tidal wave ... the color of the avenues ... after each police cruiser departs ... teenagers who feed ... streets their own moments like stripped kindling in some savage bonfire of excess entirely expunged of spirit of cerebral decorum ... not even footnotes in tossed out pornographic magazines where their smiles end up ... like leaves in a canyon stream ... embedded in a tangle of bleached driftwood ... the streets ... quiet in midday because it was raining ... this wet curtain ... walked into alhambra ... and i knocked on naomi quinonez's door and victor hernandez cruz opened it ... she recog-nized me from the upstairs window shouting down come on up but he was standing at the door saying we're sleeping and your dog is all wet what's going on? so I said maybe some other time ... walked down the street to granada park ... i walked during the seventies in winter rains like this thinking about the coup in chile and poetry ... and what should i do while casualties rained down on us ... santana guitars blaring in my ears ... you could feel the bass thrumming in your guts the rhythm of every foot step .. . too weighty for words now ... the last day of work ... the kids ... they hurried in to say goodbye ... cute last minute courage set the precedent so that all the sweet girls

who would like to be hugged could . . . but no boys they all ran away . . . and i was try-
ing to sort it through and pack up what i needed . . . and walk out of the buildings
through the emptied and littered corridors toward a skyline the color of flesh and cold
bones . . . my soaked clothes are warm after walking back . . . missed working out but
this was better than nothing


<u>C.</u>    <u>Intermediate Draft with Subsequent Revisions</u>

In the draft submitted to Kaya, Foster deleted many incidents that otherwise would have
weighed down the poem:  the 1970s, the casualties, the adolescent experience of being felt up
under the table, the books ignored on his shelf, Naomi Quinonez and the last day of school with
shy female students mustering their "cute last minute courage" to get farewell hugs.  Not only do
the deletions lighten the poem but the resulting focus also strengthens the voice of the protago-
nist.

In addition, dropping the reference to the last day of school avoided an element of sweet-
ness that would have diluted the poem's partly moody, partly resigned tone.

Foster also added notions of calling in sick to work and having paychecks reduced.  By
grounding the poem in contemporary time, these references solidified the Journal Entry's idea of
life's "raw deals . . . we all got too much work to do trying to survive this vertical red tidal wave."

The Editing Marks were made by Foster and editors at Kaya who, by tightening the draft,
partly improved the rhythm of the poem.


Light rain like Spring, L.A. can do that in the ~~W~~ <u>w</u> inter.  Maybe they can do that in
Casablanca or Chile or desert cities in Central Asia.  I wake up and the whole house is
quiet, the city flowing around me like the Amazon ~~around an island~~.  I call in sick, I'm
not going to go to work today.  The hell with it.  What a bunch of shit.  They keep cut-
ting my pay.  Now we're going ~~to go~~ on strike again, the second time in ~~3~~ <u>three</u> years.
Nobody has to stand for that.  They can pay me to stay home today.  Outside, everything
looks ~~light~~ <u>lime</u> green in the rain.  I put on my shorts and ~~T~~ <u>t</u> -shirt and run a mile
through the neighborhoods, run till my ~~running~~ shoes are soaked.  And keep running.
My breath is hot, my hair plastered on my face and neck.  When I reach the park, I do
forty squat kicks under the <u>partial</u> shelter of <u>the trees.  It's raining harder now.  I do
twenty side-kicks and twenty front- kicks.  I take a breather under </u>the ~~eves~~ <u>eaves</u> of the
restroom and then I'm out in the rain again.  Five quick katas, some not so good.  Now I
can <u>truthfully</u> say to the sensei ~~, truthfully,~~ that even in the rain I was practicing.  ~~Then~~ I
run <u>the mile back</u> home across the park, the ~~mile back with the~~ rain pouring down on
me.  ~~Inside the house,~~ I take a hot shower and I'm ready to run some errands.  To the
post office, to the store, to Lupita's for breakfast at noon.  When I get home I notice how
clean the rain makes everything smell.  I love the smell of the hot engine of my vehicle
on a day like this.  Maybe I'll call in sick tomorrow <u>,</u> too.  The kids are all in school.
The street is deserted, except for the ghost of your smile.  ~~I see the lemon tree, peaking~~
~~peeking out from the side of the house where someone else is living now.  The tree is~~
~~full of lemons.~~


Kaya's editors deleted the reference to a lemon tree.  The lemon tree was significant to
Foster as it was located in the backyard of Sixto Tarango, one of Foster's friends who died at age

"Sixto was a friend I grew up with who was a student activist, a photographer for the radical community Chicano newspaper, *La Raza*, and also the student body president at Cal State University, Los Angeles. He got burnt out of the radical politics of his time and opted to become a family man, to lead a quiet life. That is, it was a quiet life on one level but he was working two jobs and putting his wife through school. But he worked with carcinogenic solvents in a rubber-stamp plant for about 10 years and developed the leukemia which killed him. I guess the meaning I got out of that incident was — politics or not — life is kind of dangerous. Even when you opt for a 'quiet life' — a family-oriented life — life doesn't become less dangerous."

Foster says he allowed the reference to be deleted as it didn't mean anything to the Kaya editors — which means the same could occur with the poem's readers. Nevertheless, a reference to his friend remains in the ending, "The street is deserted, except for the ghost of your smile." This wise change opened up the poem to more possibilities of interpretation, thus response, by its readers — particularly those who would not know the tale of Foster's friend. For example, the protagonist now could be referring to a lover, the person whose smile lingers in the memory — resulting in a romantic ending.

D)      Final Draft

**LIGHT** rain like Spring, L.A. can do that in the winter. Maybe they can do that in Casablanca or Chile or desert cities in Central Asia. I wake up and the whole house is quiet, the city flowing around me like the Amazon. I call in sick, I'm not going to go to work today. The hell with it. What a bunch of shit. They keep cutting my pay. Now we're going on strike again, the second time in three years. Nobody has to stand for that. They can pay me to stay home today. Outside, everything looks lime green in the rain. I put on my shorts and t-shirt and run a mile through the neighborhoods, run till my shoes are soaked. And keep running. My breath is hot, my hair plastered on my face and neck. When I reach the park, I do forty squat kicks under the partial shelter of the trees. It's raining harder now. I do twenty side-kicks and twenty front-kicks. I take a breather under the eaves of the restroom and then I'm out in the rain again. Five quick katas, some not so good. Now I can truthfully say to the sensei that even in the rain I was practicing. I run the mile back home across the park, the rain pouring down on me. I take a hot shower and I'm ready to run some errands. To the post office, to the store, to Lupita's for breakfast at noon. When I get home I notice how clean the rain makes everything smell. I love the smell of the hot engine of my vehicle on a day like this. Maybe I'll call in sick tomorrow, too. The kids are all in school. The street is deserted, except for the ghost of your smile.

## Part II

Part II includes some of the drafts that led to three poems involving Xiomara and Rigo. The drafts are presented in sequential order, after which the final drafts of the poems are featured. Evident is the paring down process that Foster says occured with most of *CTFM*'s poems — many of the one-paragraph poems were birthed in five or more full pages of drafts. Foster says his original manuscript was about 250 pages, versus the published version of 167 pages.

It is interesting to note the frequency of words relating to darkness in the first two drafts; the words are shown in bold-face below. Their frequency implies a certain tone which Foster was trying to develop, or in which he found himself as he wrote the drafts. This darkness seems apt, given the nature of the subjects, and recalls one of Pound's views: "Intense emotion causes pattern to arise in the mind — if the mind is strong enough."

Most of the drafts featured below are in the voices of Xiomara and Rigo, or in the narrator's voice about them.

First Draft:

I sleep in a gravel desert, I curl in a fetal position in silos, I wait in a universe of nerve gas. The steel youth who no longer remembers his or her own identity, they have been bound and gagged in the **dark** so long, they no longer know the day or date, they may no longer know the year. They have been raped and abused with electrodes, they have been beated and spit on and humiliated. But their identity is no longer of any importance, the authorities have other political criteria to consider in the formulation of their social policies. Mexico did not inherit the gods of this empire: millions climb the Pyramid of the Moon inside ornamental skulls to offer their hearts up to any sun. Millions more march the Avenue of the Dead. Coatlicue's* skull racks are busy with vermin and insects. The calender wheel burns in epochs of **darkness**, smolders with **black** pitch under the earth. The stones are worn down by the penitent knees, the air **smoky** and stained with mumbling, wailing.

(* Coatlicue is the name of an Aztec goddess)

Second Draft:

I woke and it was already midday. I looked out of the window, and there was the **black** mountain with rain on it. I looked out the front door and there was the **black** road with rain on it. My dogs barked at me, wanting to come, as I went out and got in my vehicle. Then the earthquake struck, everything shook with a deep rumbling, rolling across the land. I got out and stood on the shivering ground. The mountain was gone, the **black** road, the dead fat **black** mule with its legs stiff up to the sky, all gone. The rain clouds were gone. It was sunny now. A morning had flown in with the birds. It was a new day. Some people might've lost their lives, some bridges might be down. A smell of Mexico drifted in the air. Did I still have to go to work? I sat in my truck and turned on the radio.

In the middle of the Second Draft, Foster inserts "It was sunny now" — a transition that serves to lift some of the darkness. The poem continues to lighten with "A morning had flown in with the birds. It was a new day." Yet Foster avoids the easy ending of simply obviating the poem's earlier dark mood, maintaining instead an ambivalence with the tone of "Some people might've lost their lives, some bridges might be down." Finally, the almost matter-of-fact tone of the last two sentences results in a version crafted to end in an open-ended manner.

<u>Third Draft :</u>

In the morning I look at myself in the mirror. I open my mouth: like flies come out. My eyes like rocks in a cold surf. I'm drowning. I barely make it to the kitchen table. Hot water for coffee. I haven't been able to make any money. But there is still instant coffee. My friends put some day jobs my way. It pays for this closet space. On cold mornings, it feels wet in here like the dew of the fields sweating through plywood walls, or the ocean secreting itself into my life. I go out, hit the streets. My hair sticking up. Women look at me nasty. It makes me feel nasty: I'm not evil, but it makes me feel evil. It makes me want to kill something. It makes me want to finish off this life. So when I'm hanging out, I'm likely to say shit about killing cops. It's all bullshit, but I can't help it. This bullshit feels at times more real than anything I ever had, than all our lives: friends, all their wives, kids, girlfriends and lives. All their better jobs, and me, still moving furniture, cleaning yards. This is no real life, it's all bullshit, but it's real. This shit is more real than anything. I'm lucky if I get something indoors, painting. This was all right for us as kid. Now, I got no interest in seeing anyone. No one has fresh proposals for me. Me and my pocketful of change like a soft erection. Sometimes I watch TV, and laugh. Sometimes the phone rings, sometimes it doesn't and sometimes I watch lots of TV, hour after hour of TV, and sometimes I laugh.

The first half of the Third Draft might as well be a punch in the softest part of the belly, culminating with the sentence, "So when I'm hanging out I'm likely to say shit about killing cops." The reference evokes the visceral significance of cop-killing which television has taught us is the type of crime most likely to receive the most attention by law enforcement authorities. The elemental emotion underlying this reference heightens the helplessness of its ending which begins with ". . . my pocketful of change like a soft erection." The whole of it is a heartbreaker.

<u>Fourth Draft:</u>

Xiomara wanted the Steering Committee Report. I tried to talk her into a beer. She's always on the move, all big brown eyes, bony hands and mane of dark hair. The victory was to get her to have some iced tea. You can't jog in and out of a house, flip through a report and skim the conclusions, talk and listen all at the same time with me on your heels and a full cup of ice tea in your hands. She had to stop on the porch, and I got her to sit on the bench. Impressed by the report, she closed the file folder, and said sadly, Rigo's left town again. He'll be back, I said. This makes me feel guilty, she said, but I was relieved to see him go. He'd been harassing me, calling me at work, or waiting on my doorstep when I got home. If it had been anybody else I would've called the cops, but you know Rigo and the cops. Remember what the sheriffs did to him. Now he's gone to Honduras. He said he was going to infiltrate across the border and fight with the Mayan guerillas. That's what comes from talking about the Revolution all the time, all that shit about CIA contracts on everybody from Robert Kennedy to the Black Panthers. And every time he messed with the cops and you got him out, he wanted to stay at my place because, he said, of "the surveillance." Don't sweat Rigo, I said, if he can survive carrying a rotting sixty-pound canvas rucksack full of moldy tortillas and plastic bags and ten or twenty pounds of plastic M-16 and bullets in a nylon poncho up and down the mountains in the jungle in the pouring rain, following a bunch of kids who've lived there their whole life barefoot in those mountains in that war, he'll be back. She looked at me doubtfully, and I felt a twinge that I knew Rigo felt: the warmth of her eyes on me. Don't worry about Rigo, I said, L.A.'s gonna be the death of him and the rest of us as well. If the marching and malaria don't get him, he'll be back soon enough with lots of war stories to tell. That way L.A. will get another chance at him, too. You don't think you get away from L.A. that easy, do you?

In the Fourth Draft, the insertion of ". . . and I felt a twinge that I knew Ringo felt: the warmth of her eyes on me" is well-placed after the discussion ranging from the CIA to Black Panthers to jungle wars in South America. It personalizes the effects of history and heightens the poem's emotional content.

Fifth Draft:

East L.A. can have a smell like Mexico: out of the corner of your eye a black volcano rises, a dead mule on the side of the black highway lifts big dead legs. A swarm of sparrows brings clear sunshine from somewhere to the south. You think you see a ristra of red chiles hanging against a wall, but it's a child's jump-rope with red handles. You might hear Victor Jara singing, "alli donde llega todo, y donde todo comienza, canto que ha sido valiente . . ." from a secondstory window in the projects. It doesn't matter if you fucked over Akemi and treated her wrong, or if Xochitl did the same to you. East L.A., with its stray rooster crowing in the dark and its radio towers with red lights. The El Sereno hills where kids light big grass fires every long summer doesn't care if they killed that Chilean singer with their machine guns. It don't matter if you were naughty or nice, on a warm and sunny day like today, there's gonna be a major earthquake. The earth will roll in its own bed of thunder. Your pickup truck will wiggle and jiggle like a good time you once had. After the earthquake, turn on the radio: Do you have to go to work today? What do you think? Naturally, when it's all over, I mean when all of it is over, (when Mexico is gone, the volcano, the dead black mule, Victor Jara, the sparrows), you will get back into that pickup truck and drive to work again. Naturally, when the earthquake is over, again and again. You will forget Mexico and everything else.

The Fifth Draft presents fine examples of imagery, as in "a rista of red chiles . . . but it's a child's jump-rope with red handles" and "a dead mule on the side of a black highway lifts big dead legs." It also features an interesting mix of stream-of-consciousness writing with very specific images and references.

Akemi and Xochitl were friends of Foster. Victor Jara was a *nueva cancion* (new song) folksinger killed by the military in the Sept. 11, 1973 coup in Chile. His song referenced above is translated as "There, where everything arrives and everything begins, the song that has been courageous."

Sixth Draft:

Tobacco dust . . . spiraling, outlines gas depository tanks . . . Whiskers from the razor fly up in the mirror sunlight . . . barrels along the loading dock . . . white linen in his hand as he wipes his mustache . . . Certain portions of the document appear altered or damaged . . . a photograph creased by the fold of a wallet, smelling of hair oil, tuberculin handkerchief . . . Sweat stains on the back and under arms . . . fish oil on paving stones . . . tears spread city lights west on Broadway into the dark . . . wires, tongs, the baby on the lawn is faded by sunshine . . . Hello, We're Open . . . bus 118 . . . The color line simplifies the whole thing, there's whites and there's the others . . . We're early for the services, waking up in a car outside Evergreen Cemetary, time to get ready . . . ice water at the Tokyo Grill . . . a passport of two hands pressed together, opened outward . . . Alberta Buell(7), still a teenager, played keyboards accompanying films in the silent movie theater on Broadway . . . her future husband an L.A. cop. . . the trolley and train tracks are torn up . . . both Barbary Coast sons would marry Japanese Americans, Niseis, their Sansei grandchildren Anglo, Jewish, Creole, Chicano . . . at noon an overcast day, at 9 months, Citlali Anati Foster sleeps, sighs and sleeps.

The Sixth Draft ends with a gem: the image of an infant (Foster's daughter) sleeping. The softness of this image is a deft end to a series of disparate images — many of which are so vivid, especially "fish oil on paving stones" and "a passport of two hands pressed together, opened upward."

Seventh Draft:

I fall like a shadow into a cracked mirror. The room is dark, better with yellow shades down than dusty light from the alley. I don't know if I care anymore whether people see my room. Garage-sale decor I've known my whole life. Who sees it any more? Since I was laid off at the restaurant I haven't found anything else. Sometimes Arturo finds me a day job, moving, painting. Sometimes Jesse lends me his truck, I can do some hauling. Some cold mornings, nothing is up. I'm looking at a whole day of no money, no work. I can't blame Mayra for moving out. Sometimes I call her up and tell her to leave the Salvadoran guy. Move back in here. But she won't. She says she's pregnant by him, but I think it could be me. I boil water for instant coffee. Mayra was sick of this, my excuses. It's just luck, I tell her, but she looks at me like I'm evil. Mayra and my friends, my ex-friends, they all make me feel like a criminal. Their girlfriends, wives, jobs, stereos, kids, health clubs; I'm practically homeless and broke. In this remodeled garage behind an apartment complex, with my electric plate kitchen. Temporary exile, till I get on with the city or the county, roadwork or something. Anything. Anything but my eyes buzzing like red flies, my tongue cold as mud in my mouth. This was how it was when I was growing up, when I grew up I thought I could get out of it. I'm still here, with just a pocketful of change like a soft erection. I don't want to think about an agenda for the day, but the coffee is starting to work. Today the day old bread store, maybe the church foodline. The park, el Gato Negro, First Street. I'll have to take the bus over to Xiomara's house, I don't want to think about that, that's for later. Xiomara hates to see me on her doorstep when she gets home from work. I hate to be there, especially if she doesn't show. Rigo, she says, looking at me for a long time, Rigo, Rigo. Rigo. She doesn't want me to come in, but I'll tell her a story about how I need a letter of reccomendation from her for, or to use her phone number, or that the cops are keeping my place under surveillance. I'm a gentle person, I never hurt anyone. But Xiomara doesn't want my stories any more. She's scared of me like everyone else.

The Seventh Draft is a later version of the Third Draft. In comparing both versions, one can see the effects of intervening drafts through the Seventh Draft's more heightened mood and multi-layered references.

Eighth Draft:

I called Xiomara. I didn't recognize the voice that answered, except that it was her. Yes, hello? she said. I told her who it was. —Oh my god, how are you? I could not tell if she were about to laugh or was apprehensive. I'm sorry, I said, I tried to call you last year but I had the wrong number. Is something wrong? she asked. No, no . . . everything's all right. Same as it ever was. How about you? Oh, everything's fine. You know how it is with us: the town may be burning down, the country might go to war, we might see little kids die in car crashes and earthquakes, but nothing happens to us. We go on, we survive. Yeah, I laughed. How long has it been: she asked, twelve years? Something like that, I admitted. You son of a bitch, she said, you mean you haven't called me in twelve years? I meant to—I did. . . I thought about you a lot. I didn't tell her about how hot the sun made her black hair and how I longed for that scent on diesel afternoons, with the clatter of transmissions and the roar of pipes. Instead, I talked about people we both knew. She grew impatient before I did, as always. I'll let you go if you promise to keep in touch, she said. Promise! she said. I promise, I said, knowing she'd never write, never call. It had always been up to me. The trouble was, I didn't know about me, either. I promise, I said.

The Eighth Draft is a brilliant mood piece illustrating sheer helplessness — Rigo's ability to understand he lacks control over his life. It evokes frustration and resignation at the same time.

Ninth Draft:

Black telephone hands, eucalyptus corridor of boulevards stretching east into the navel fo the past, Mayra will not be there to pick up, your hair sticking out of your head like wires is as close to becoming an astronaut as you will get, today or any day, outer space thoughts falling to the ground like fleas,                    secret codes dictate how
many teaspoons                    of instant coffee require fresh light
growling like a stomach in the window above your head,                    oatmeal and
masa farina                    still in the box from the church basement
on the table next to the radio, KPFK Radio Pacifica                    midmorning commu-
nity calender,                    you liked to see Mayra do the dishes because that was
the only altar in your home, her candlelight of eyes before shadow lashes closed.

The Ninth Draft seems to serve partly as an exercise for Foster to attain the image found in its ending: "her candlelight of eyes before shadow lashes closed." This powerful image (evoked earlier in the Fourth Draft) echoes another poem in *CTFM* that begins with "LOS ANGELES" which ends with the question, "Are your eyes beautiful in the dark?" Similarly, it surfaces again in a poem that begins with "I'M ALWAYS" which ends with "I'm following something like honey. I think it drips from brown eyes."

Within the prose poem format, *CTFM* uses poetic devices of image, metaphor, symbolism and heightened language.  As featured in the Ninth Draft, Foster also inserts blank spaces within the paragraphs.  He considers the spaces "functional caesuras, just as line breaks would be."

## Final Drafts

**I AM** this fetus:  a worm in a womb of earth, root, stone.  You can look up and see Chinese ideograms etched in baby's breath across the crystalline firmament, flame-dark pre-Columbian constellations over dusty streets of Aztlan.  A youth who no longer knows who he or she is, ~~they've~~ been bound and gagged in the dark so long, raped and abused with electrodes, beaten, spit on and humiliated.  A calendar wheel burns in ~~the~~ epochs of darkness, stones worn down by penitent knees, the air smoky and stained with mumbling, wailing. . . They tell me you've been looking for me.  I know you are coming.  I know you want help studying your kanji, katas, calo, your future-tense English.  I know I told your mother I would.  The years are falling down, but I just can't be there for you today.  I will, I will, but . . . there is ~~still~~ too much light.

(The Editing Marks above depict some of the last changes made before the poem was published.)

—⁓—

**XIOMARA** wanted the Steering Committee Report.  I tried to talk her into a beer.  She's always on the move, big brown eyes, bony hands, mane of dark hair.  Victory was to get her to have some iced tea.  You can't jog in and out of a house, flip through a report, skim the conclusions, talk and listen all at the same time with me on your heels and a glass of iced tea in your hands.  She had to stop on the porch, and I got her to sit on the bench.  Impressed by the report, she closed the file folder, and said sadly, Rigo's left town again.  He'll be back, I said.  This makes me feel guilty, she said, but I was relieved to see him go.  He'd been harassing me, calling me at work, or waiting on my doorstep when I got home.  If it had been anybody else I would've called the cops, but you know Rigo and the cops.  Remember what the sheriffs did.  Now he's gone to Honduras.  He said he was going to infiltrate across the border and fight with the Mayan guerrillas.  That's what comes from talking about the Revolution all the time, all that shit about CIA contracts on everybody from Robert Kennedy to the Black Panthers.  And every time he messed with the cops and you got him out, he wanted to stay at my place because, he said, of "the surveillance."  Don't sweat Rigo, I said:  he'll be carrying a rotten sixty-pound canvas rucksack full of moldy tortillas, plastic bags, ten or twenty pounds of plastic, M-16 and bullets in a nylon poncho up and down the mountains in the jungle in the pouring rain, following a bunch of barefoot kids who lived their whole lives there.  If he survives his own cooking, he'll be back.  She looked at me doubtfully, and I felt a twinge that I knew Rigo felt:  the warmth of her eyes on me.  Don't worry, I said, L.A.'s gonna be the death of him and the rest of us.  If marching and malaria don't get him, he'll be back soon enough with lots of war stories to tell.  L.A. will get another chance at him.  You don't think you get away from L.A. that easy, do you?

Interestingly, this poem was deleted from inclusion in *CTFM*. Since the poem's subjects are covered by other poems, this poem may have been considered dispensable. (Or perhaps the book didn't have enough pages to include this poem.) But it's also note-worthy that this poem contains a stronger narrative than many other poems in *CTFM*; perhaps its story in this poetic format is, as Foster says in his journal entry in Part I, "too weighty for words now."

Or perhaps the ending (seen earlier in the Fourth Draft) jarred (unconsciously) with Foster: *You don't think you get away from L.A. that easy, do you?* Reading *CTFM* is to feel Foster's love for his home town, and one could imagine Foster replying, *Why would you want to?*

—∿—

**XIOMARA**, she treats me well. Men look at me and see the calavera in hysterical rigor mortis beneath my flesh, a skull splintery and dried, but she never makes fun of me for it. I see death in men and they see it in me. We watch each other across a wary distance of handshakes, camaraderie and compromises. Xiomara, she dispenses with that. She allows the nerves their weakness, their spinal moments of aftermath, small happinesses like a breeze. I wander with her like water through an estuary in the morning fog. With her birds, her rushes, her long grass. With her, I can go out on the dunes in that sun. She sees me in the world and the world in me, and still, in spite of it, lets me stay. With the sound of the sea beyond the day.

This poem is among the most lyrical in Sesshu Foster's *CTFM*. It also may be revealing to see this poem in the following format where line breaks are based on the pauses that occured from my reading:

Xiomara,
she treats me well.
Men look at me
        and see the calavera in hysterical rigor mortis beneath my flesh,
a skull splintery and dried,
but she never makes fun of me for it.
I see death in men and they see it in me.
We watch each other across a wary distance of handshakes,
camaraderie
and compromises.
Xiomara,
she dispenses with that.
She allows the nerves their weakness,
their spinal moments of aftermath,
small happinesses like a breeze.
I wander with her like water through an estuary in the morning fog.
With her birds,
her rushes,
her long grass.
With her, I can go out on the dunes in that sun.
She sees me in the world

and the world in me,

and still,

in spite of it,

lets me stay.

With the sound of the sea

beyond the day.

(I show the fourth line to be indented to note that in different readings, I was sometimes compelled to read the third and fourth line as a single line.)

The above form of this poem exemplifies Foster's wise use of the prose poem structure. He proves for *CTFM* the inappropriateness of poetic forms that rely on line breaks; such forms might even encourage an unnecessary shortening of some of the longer lines. This ratifies Foster's decision to utilize a prose-based form because he wanted to "use language to evoke imagery, peoples' lives, metaphors and only use poetic decisions as (he) saw fit."

Besides, the prose paragraphs look better, physically more pleasing to the reader. Sometimes, this matters. To paraphrase Gertrude Stein, one can hear with the eyes as much as with the ears.

—⚏—

*Humor.* Finally, there's humor. *CTFM* shows the breadth of Foster's love for his *Home*, East Los Angeles. Only someone with that love can manage to find, not only the passion and compassion evidenced in the above poems but also, the laughter amidst the tribulations of East L.A.:

"**THURSDAY** Richard says to me, 'You know I'm going to tell her we should lighten up a little,'" Sara tells Betti as the RTD zooms toward Marengo & Soto, General Hospital rising like a castle over the freeway & railroad tracks, "Friday he goes, 'You know what, I told her I think we should see other people," and Betti, who has already dropped Kathleen off at Headstart, is chuckling appreciatively as Sara adds, "So I go, 'Richard, it's really none of my business, but you should be nice to your girlfriend because obviously she's one of the only people you know who cares what you do,'" and Betti cracks up, Sara laughs too, leaning away from the twisted old dude, the skinny bent guy with the gnarly grizzled face whose neck is bent the opposite way from his body, who teeters toward them unsteadily, in danger of spitting all over them, gripping his cane in his warped fingers as he barks out in a gravelly voice heard throughout the whole bus: "BUNCHA FUCKIN' GODDAMN PAYASOS RUNNIN' THIS CITY STUPID ASS ALATORRE I CALL HIS OFFICE EVERY DAY ASK HIM ABOUT MY BUS PASS THEY OWE ME FROM SOCIAL SOCIALSOSOSOSOCIAL SECURITY BUNCHA FUCKIN' GODDAMN PAYASOS I BET YOU VOTED FOR THAT ASSHOLE ALATORRE HUH?" Sara just sniffs in disdain, looks at Betti and goes on, "So then Richard goes . . ."

It is a search all the more successful because, as shown in the above poem, Foster also listens to his neighborhood. "I'm interested in voices — especially in the rhythm of the spoken language," Foster told the poet Amy Uyematsu in an interview(2) after *CTFM*'s publication. "To me, that's a kind of poetry; that's an important part of this aesthetic of how working people talk.

It's important to me to listen to these people's voices and to allow their rhythms of speech to inform the language, and often these kinds of rhythms dictate the forms of the pieces."

Foster continued, "There are all kinds of combinations of spoken dialect and tones of writing; there'll be language that's obviously media-driven language, journalistic kind of language, fictional or literary kinds of description mixed in with spoken expression. I was looking at the juxtaposition and interplay of all these different types of language in (*CTFM*).

"One of the things that interests me is that something is happening with those kinds of tones. Definitely there's a recycling of combined tones of language throughout all the (prose poems). I feel that's reflective of an urban experience, that we're continually enveloped in media-driven language and street expressions and workplace discourse. We're continually thinking on all these levels, and I feel like one of the ways my writing can evoke the city is by evoking these rhythms. Those kinds of technical things, that's what I like to do when I'm writing. If there aren't interesting technical questions happening all the time when I write, I get bored."

Yes, it's a "technical" consideration — but consistent with the love he displays towards East L.A. I firmly believe that East Los Angeles is fortunate to have Sesshu Foster walking its streets.

—m—

**POSTCARD**(3) to Sesshu Foster, East Los Angeles, CA 90063

Neruda once sang, "Mientras escriboy estoy ausente/ y cuando vuelvo ya he partido:/ voy a ver si a las otras gentes/ les pasa lo que a mi me pasa,/ si son tantos como soy you,/ si se parecen a si mismos/ y cuando lo haya averiguado/ voy a aprender tan bien las cosas/ que para explicar mis problemas/ les hablare de geografia."

Si, Sesshu, sometimes I go through the same things you do — and will continue for as long as you sing your poems. "Entonces cantare en silencio."

Muchas Gracias,

ET

Footnotes:

(1)     "let us make a profession of being earth-bound/ let us touch the earth with our beings" from "Sonata with some pine trees" by Pablo Neruda as translated by Alastair Reid (*EXTRAVAGARIA*, University of Texas Press, originally published as *Estravagario*, 1958, by Editorial Losada, S.A. Buenos Aires; translation copyright 1969, 1970, 1972 and 1974 by Alastair Reid)

(2)     Amy Uyematsu's interview of Sesshu Foster was published by *dIS*Orient Journalzine* (Volume Five).

(3)     Postcard reference: The first paragraph references Pablo Neruda's "We are many" — translated as "While I am writing, I'm far away;/ and when I come back, I've gone./ I would like to know if others/ go through the same things that I do,/ have as many selves as I have,/ and see themselves similarly;/ and when I've exhausted this problem,/ I'm going to study so hard/ that when I explain myself,/ I'll be talking geography." The last sentence is from "Autumn Testament" — translated as "Then I will sing in the silence." Both poems are featured in *EXTRAVAGARIA*.

# LUIS CABALQUINTO

Luis Cabalquinto writes in English, Bikolano and Pilipino. He is the author of three books of poetry: *The Dog-eater and Other Poems* (1989), *The Ibalon Collection* (1991) and *Dreamwanderer* (1992) (all published by Kalikasan Press, Manila). His works have appeared in publications in the United States, Philippines, Australia, Hongkong, France and the Czech Republic, including *American Poetry Review, Prairie Schooner, Manoa, Greenfield Review, Manila Review, Caracoa, Philippines Free Press, Asiaweek, Heritage, Contact, River Styx, Portable Lower East Side, Trafika, International Quarterly, Frank* and *Poetry Australia*. His works have been anthologized in *Gems in Philippine Literature* (National Bookstores, 1980); *Breaking Silence: Anthology of Asian American Poets* (Greenfield Review Press, 1983); *New Worlds of Literature* (W.W. Norton & Co., 1989); *A Day in the Life: Tales From the Lower East Side* (Autonomedia Press, 1990); *Fiction by Filipinos in America* (New Day Publishers, 1993); *Brown River, White Ocean — Anthology of 20th Century Philippine Literature in English* (Rutgers University Press, 1993); *Returning A Borrowed Tongue* (Coffeehouse, 1996); *Flippin': Filipinos On America* (Asian American Writers Workshop, 1996 First Printing and 1997 Second Printing); *LITERATURE: Fiction, Poetry, Drama, and the Essay* (HarperCollins, 1996); and *Contemporary Fiction by Filipinos On America* (Anvil, 1998).

His awards and fellowships include a Fulbright-Hays grant; writing fellowships at the University of the Philippines at Diliman and Siliman University (Dumaguete City, Philippines); Bread Loaf Conference (Vermont); New York University's Academy of American Poets poetry prize; the New School for Social Research — Dylan Thomas Poetry Award; and the New York Foundation for the Arts fellowship award in poetry. He has studied poetry and fiction writing at workshops conducted by Galway Kinnell (his biggest influence in poetry writing), William Matthews, Philip Levine, David Ignatow, Charles Simic, Carolyn Forche, E.L. Doctorow, among others.

He is now retired after working 12 years for Pfizer International as a customer service representative in charge of coordinating exports to Southeast Asia. His current projects include *Bridgeable Shores* (a collection of new stories and poems); *Depths of Fields* (100 selected poems);and *Pamamangka Sa Di Lamang Dalawang Ilog* (a collection of poems in Pilipino; the title in English is *Paddling A Boat In More Than Two Rivers*).

In response to the question, "What advice would you give to a young poet?" Luis Cabalquinto responds:

1 — Read all you can, everyday if possible, especially the works of writers you admire and want to emulate. Even reading newspapers can draw out the most creative writing ideas.

2 — Write all you can, everyday if possible, even if it's only a one-sentence entry in your journal. If you're like me, once that crucial first line is written, you won't be able to stop.

3 — Listen to what other writers (including this one) tell you, then go your own way; follow your own instincts and hunches. If you were born to write, you'll become a writer no matter what. Any road you take will bring you ultimately to Xanadu.

# Luis Cabalquinto Finds A Home In Poetry

*The skinny waterfalls, footpaths*
*wandering out of heaven, strike*
*the cliffside, leap, and shudder off.*

*Somewhere behind me*
*a small fire goes on flaring in the rain, in the desolate ashes.*
*No matter, now, whom it was built for,*
*it keeps its flames,*
*it warms*
*everyone who might wander into its radiance,*
*a tree, a lost animal, the stones,*

*because in the dying world it was set burning.*
*— from "Lastness" by Galway Kinnell*

*It's utter sublimation,*
*A feat, this heart's control*
*Moment to moment*
*To scale all love down*
*To a cupped hand's size,*

*Till seashells are broken pieces*
*From God's own bright teeth,*
*And life and love are real*
*Things you can run and*
*Breathless hand over*
*To the merest child.*
*— from "Bonsai" by Edith L. Tiempo*

*It is in these rare seconds*
*When our bodies are stilled*
*by afternoon rivers*
*like the Seine:*
*When we momentarily look out*
*from the banks,*
*When we come upon finest sheen,*
*upon a sudden space*
*From tight spirals in our lives.*
*— from "AFTERNOON BY THE SEINE" by Luis Cabalquinto*

There's the sense of a man speaking from the peak of his wisdom when Luis Cabalquinto says, "If I die now, I'll die happy."

Born on January 31, 1935, Cabalquinto says he doesn't have a death wish. But he does possess the knowledge that, so far, at 62 years of age, he can consider his life "well-lived," primarily because he has come to devote his life to poetry.

Cabalquinto lived the first half of his life in the Philippines where he was born in Magarao, Camarines Sur. When he was 21 years old and in the middle of college at Ateneo de Naga, he took and passed a civil service exam which elicited a job offer to become a community development officer with the then Office of the Presidential Assistant on Community Development ("PACD").

"I had to make a choice, take the job or finish my college studies. I was not from a wealthy family, though we managed; I also was anxious to have the feel of the 'real world,' having experienced life only in school and in my home province," he recalls about his decision to accept the job. "I was assigned to Marinduque, far from my province and enjoyed it. For the first time, I dealt with a different type of people, mostly people older than myself. As part of my job, I had to drink a lot with the local people, which is when I learned how to drink; I got to be a very good drinker. I had a nice job, had access to wonderful social situations."

Six years later, Cabalquinto was reassigned to Manila to work as an editor at the PACD's headquarters. He then earned a degree in communications at the University of the Philippines Institute of Mass Communication, after which he transfered to the University of the Philippines College of Forestry in Los Banos where he worked as an instructor and head of the Publications & Information Section.

"In hindsight, I could sense that there was something hollow in me — an inner need for something to do that would make me feel: 'This is it! This is my life. This is what I should be doing with my life — something meaningful in the most fundamental sense.' " he recalls. "But I was very vague about my interior life back then and, as a socially-engaged person, I could always distract myself with a wide variety of activities and relationships."

It wasn't until Cabalquinto received a Fulbright-Hays grant in 1968 and left the Philippines to attend Cornell University for further studies in mass communication that he found what he needed — not poetry immediately, but what triggered it: the *isolation* whose benefits many poets before him have realized.

"At Cornell, the detachment from the culture in the Philippines put me on an iceberg by myself and I started looking at my life in ways that I had not considered because I didn't have the time and focus, what with being too busy drinking, womanizing and traveling," he concedes. "There was this intense isolation I felt at Cornell, a feeling that made me ask myself what I really wanted to do with my life."

Though Cabalquinto had been writing poetry sporadically since high school, he says he began writing seriously in his mid-thirties while at Cornell. "The isolation was healthy for me. Living by myself on a very interior level brought out the real me," he says.

At Cornell, Cabalquinto enrolled in writing workshops conducted by A.R. Ammons, William Matthews, James McConkey and others in the university's English Department. He returned to the Philippines in 1971 to teach and work as a journalist, but never stopped writing poetry. In 1975, Cabalquinto returned to the U.S. to work as a customer service representative for Pfizer International ("Pfizer"), coordinating their exports to Southeast Asia. While working at Pfizer, he studied poetry and fiction writing in workshops conducted by Galway Kinnell. He considers Kinnell his "biggest influence in poetry writing," dedicating to him his first poetry collection, THE *DOG-EATER and OTHER POEMS* (Kalikasan Press, Manila, 1989).

In 1990, Cabalquinto retired to become a full-time writer and, he notes, "I have not looked back since. I have never been happier or more content. I write four to six hours a day, five to six days a week. I write because I feel driven to do so. I'm obsessed. I feel like a fish out of water when I'm not writing. When I'm writing I don't feel there is anything else I would

rather be doing.  My mind and my body are totally engaged, at the exclusion of everything else —
as in making love."

Cabalquinto also relishes having found his "voice," which he says he developed after
years of exposure to other poets' works and being asked in some poetry workshops to borrow
other poets' styles.  Cabalquinto offers the following poem, "Prelude," as an example of a "failed
poem" for him because it was written in someone else's voice:

### PRELUDE

On a barren, desert-like plain
it's early evening.  The sun
removes itself from the horizon
and perches on the branch of
a leafless tree, solitary
at mid-landscape.  The sun
is an orchid of fire.  It shoots out
sepals of flame in red, putting
the sky and earth to mad vermilion.
Slowly, out of the ground, rise
what appear to be two enormous spheres:
one is dark, the other pale.

"I was in a class taught by David Ignatow when I wrote 'Prelude'," Cabalquinto recalls.
"What makes me uncomfortable with poems like this — and I've written a lot of them — is that it
demonstrates my early tendency to imitate somebody whose poetry impressed me.  I'd try to imi-
tate what I liked about their poems, whether it's language or the use of abstraction; I did this
unconsciously.  The surrealistic imagery in 'Prelude' is not me; it's David.

"It wouldn't surprise me if a critic would like this poem.  But this poem doesn't work for
me because it violates my basic concerns in writing poetry — to stay as close as possible to the
poem that comes from within, that wells up from the subconscious without one's bidding,"
Cabalquinto continues.  "With 'Prelude,' I was sitting in a poetic chair, wearing my poetry cap and
self-consciously writing poetic lines.  But writing a poem for me is like a woman carrying a child
through a gestation period.  When it's fully-formed, it comes out on its own."

He considers his poetic sensibility more similar to Kinnell, as well as to Filipino poets
Nick Joaquin and Edith Tiempo.  "I want to evoke an unspoken rapport with the reader by using
the simplest language possible," he explains.  "After all the workshops and readings, I have decid-
ed that I am more into communicating (with my audience).  I don't want to limit my connections
to critics and the avant garde — I don't want to be this type of writer, especially because what I'm
trying to say in my poems are things that are better said in the simplest diction.  No matter how
complicated my feelings and thoughts are, there's always a way to express them simply."

By trying to develop a rapport with his audience, Cabalquinto says he is manifesting his
goal of "becoming as close to nature in a holistic way, as in the Buddhist concept that every bit of
the universe is related to every other bit of the universe."

Thus, he says he wants his poetry to evoke the same type of emotions he feels when he
watches a flamenco dance, sees certain movies and views certain paintings.

"One of my most defining moments as a poet occurred in Madrid in 1971 when, for the first time, I saw flamenco," says Cabalquinto. "There was this explosive energy and emotion, but also control and artistry in the movement — there was this wild thing that was almost getting out of hand but it was being kept under leash and, in the process, producing an exciting piece of art. I couldn't believe what I was seeing; but I also felt it was the kind of effect I wanted to produce in my writing."

He adds, "Picasso and Lucian Freud are my two biggest influences in the visual arts. When I see their works, I feel I have to write the way they paint: with intense resonance but also a masterful control of the elements that go into composition, the intelligence and sensuality at the same time. It's the same resonance I perceive when watching movies by Kurosawa, the New Wave of Italian films (like "La Dolce Vita") — a resonance that comes from life fully and deeply understood: a depth of emotion evoked by complete and profound human compassion."

Resonance explains Cabalquinto's empathy for Kinnell's poetry. "Galway is always magical, beyond verbal," he says. "When he uses a word or statement, aside from their literal values there are extra-literal nuances. There's something else that radiates, that possibility for other layers of meaning which only someone with the same sensibility can appreciate.

"In fact, that's another reason why I stayed in poetry. Poetry has helped me arrive at that plateau of consciousness where things are beyond structures and rituals," adds Cabalquinto, noting that he was raised as a Catholic. During his younger days, he says that he "lacked that special awareness which I've since learned from reading and writing poetry."

Cabalquinto cannot separate two words — emotion and control — whenever he discusses his poetry. He puts it another way, "I have nothing against sentiment; I have a lot against sentimentality."

Such control, says Cabalquinto, is one reason why he so admires Tiempo who, along with her husband, the novelist Edilberto K. Tiempo, were the guiding lights of the prestigious Silliman University Writers' Workshop in the Visayas region of the Philippines. Cabalquinto twice attended the Tiempos' workshop.

"When it comes to poetic craft, she had more influence on me than even Jose Garcia Villa," Cabalquinto recalls. Born in the Philippines circa 1911, Villa has been a seminal influence on many poets in the Philippines and edited several anthologies of Philippine poets under his nom de plume, "Doveglion." An associate editor at New Directions Books from 1949 to 1951, he has had poetry and short stories anthologized widely and studied throughout the world.

"I loved Villa when I was young because he had accomplished so much and I loved his verbal acrobatics," Cabalquinto says. "But when I started to write, I felt more kinship with Tiempo. She uses simple language. There is a very intelligent resonance in her treatment of simple themes and simple topics. It is an elevated intelligence with breadth and depth. There's a lot of feeling, but the feeling is controlled and restrained and dry. It's not mushy, which was an early danger in my writing that I had to make a lot of effort to control."

Featured below are three of Cabalquinto's most widely-anthologized poems: "THE DOG-EATER," "ALIGNMENT" and "DEPTHS OF FIELD." The first two poems were written in the 1980s while he was studying under Kinnell. "DEPTHS OF FIELDS" was written in 1995. All poems evoke a sensibility similar to the poems by Kinnel and Tiempo (as exerpted above). But by Cabalquinto's own admission, "DEPTHS OF FIELDS" is more accomplished, which may explain why it is the title poem of his one hundred *Selected Poems* which he expects to publish in the Philippines.

" 'DEPTHS OF FIELDS' is an example of progression from both poems. The language is more simple, more nuanced. Every word, every phrase and every line carries more weight than any given word, phrase or line. And the feelings captured in 'DEPTHS OF FIELDS' are feelings that I found more difficult to capture in the earlier poems," he says.

Cabalquinto's poems often do not undergo many drafts because he begins to write poems only when he is emotionally compelled to do so — even when he long has been mulling the underlying inspirations to a poem(s). "Usually I will have thoughts about a poem and I will simply put these in the back of my unconsciousness to simmer until the poem boils over and I try to catch the overflow," he says.

—⁓—

Featured below are examples of Cabalquinto's drafting process, from beginning entries to the final drafts, for three poems: "THE DOG-EATER" which was first published in *The American Poetry Review* (and later in *Trafika*); "ALIGNMENT" which was first published in *Contact II* (and later in *Trafika*); and "DEPTHS OF FIELDS" which was first published in *Heritage Quarterly* (and later in the anthology, *Returning A Borrowed Tongue* (Coffee House Press, 1996)).

Many of his editing changes exemplify Cabalquinto's search for simplicity to maximize the poem's accessibility to a reader. "Usually, whenever I revise words to a simpler word, it's because the original word sounds pretentious, or doesn't say anything specific; perhaps the original word(s) is just there because it sounds good or was written to impress the critic — even though I may have done so unconsciously," he says.

(*Editing Marks*: strikethroughs = deletions; underlined words = added words; back slash = line break; [Del L] = delete previous line break)

## I.     THE DOG-EATER

Cabalquinto says he thought of "THE DOG-EATER" while taking a walk one day through a snow-clad street in New York. "It was a moonlit winter night and I noticed an almost perfectly-round yellow spot on almost pure-white snow. It could have been beer; I didn't actually know if it was dog piss. But the visual sight made me recall an incident from my youth," he says.

When he was about six years old, Cabalquinto lived in a town in Magarao. On some evenings, he noticed an old man walking down the street. The man was known in the village as one who ate dog meat, a practice that was not yet common in Magarao. "He was a strange man who kept to himself. It was his habit to walk up and down the street late at night. We'd see him go by and my mother would say, 'There he is again — that dog-eater'," he says. "The sight of him made quite an impression on me."

In his mind, Cabalquinto says, he theorized that the old man ate dogs partly to undergo "a communion with the animal world."

But because dog-eating was not yet a common practice in Magarao and dog-meat, as a delicacy, was more expensive than other animals' meat, Cabalquinto recalls that the old man symbolized, for him, someone more sophisticated than many people in his village. As such, the old man became unforgettable to him, such that, years later, Cabalquinto developed "THE DOG-EATER" while taking a poetry workshop taught by Kinnell at the 92nd. Street Y in New York City. The poem also subsequently inspired the title of Jessica Hagedorn's critically-acclaimed novel, *Dogeaters* (Penguin, 1990).

The only surviving preliminary draft of the poem is shown below with Editing Marks depicting subsequent changes. In the third stanza, Cabalquinto's replacement of the phrase, "growing to a crescendo" with "rising in volume" exemplifies his search for the simplest way to show his thoughts. The changes made to the last stanza are also well thought out in preserving a certain resonance that otherwise could have been interrupted by the reader reacting negatively to the image of "piss."

### THE DOG-EATER

It was the piss on the snow
On a sidewalk in New York
That brought up the ~~memory~~ thought of a moon
In his childhood : ~~; a moving moon~~ in a cloudless sky ,
~~Clear and mothless~~ A clean sphere like a huge new lamp
Under which, for the first time, ~~he~~ the boy saw the dog-eater

It was said in the barrio of San Miguel that the man Jose
Ate dog's meat each day of the week
And the village dogs could tell this from his scent ,
That eating dog's meat occasionally was all right
But to do it every day makes you smell like a dog yourself .
But they said Jose knew that too and he was a man
Who knew who he was and what he was doing

On ~~a~~ the moon-lit night he saw the dog-eater
~~The boy~~ He heard the barking and howling, first from a distance
Softly, then ~~growing to a crescendo~~ rising in volume like an accompaniment
To something ~~coming~~ ~~approaching~~ coming that was dangerous to someone —
Though not to the boy who eagerly waited .

~~The boy saw the dog-eater~~ He saw him from the window of his house :
A small dark man in a dark shirt who walked
Easily, as if oblivious to the noise and commotion
That followed him, as all the dogs in all the houses
(All houses in the boy's village had dogs
And the boy's house had three) came out
To complain, barking and following the dog-eater
Though they dared not come close enough to do him any harm

The dog-eater, the light of the moon on his ~~thin~~ white hair
And on his thin clothes, walked by with his head tilted
To the ground ~~as if casually looking for something~~
~~He had lost.~~ [Del L] He never lifted his head
Even when ~~another passerby~~ somebody called out his name
And said something the boy did not understand

He kept his eyes to the gravel road, walking
Until his body disappeared at ~~a~~ the bend

When the dog-eater was gone the boy looked up :
He saw again the bright moon ~~moving~~ in the cloudless sky
He stared at its huge and perasive presence —
Its color like the color ~~of piss which~~ that many years later
~~later he~~ He would see on a patch of snow
On a sidewalk in New York

The following is the <u>final draft</u> of "THE DOG-EATER."

### THE DOG-EATER

It was the piss on the snow
On a sidewalk in New York
That brought up the thought of a moon
In his childhood: in a cloudless sky,
A clean sphere like a huge new lamp
Under which, for the first time, the boy saw the dog-eater.

It was said in the barrio of San Miguel that the man Jose
Ate dog's meat each day of the week
And the village dogs could tell this from his scent,
That eating dog's meat occasionally was all right
But to do it every day makes you smell like a dog yourself.
But they said Jose knew that too and he was a man
Who knew who he was and what he was doing

On a moon-lit night he saw the dog-eater
He heard the barking and howling, first from a distance
Softly, then rising in volume like an accompaniment
To something coming that was dangerous to someone —
Though not to the boy who eagerly waited.

He saw him from the window of his house:
A small dark man in a dark shirt who walked
Easily, as if oblivious to the noise and commotion
That followed him, as all the dogs in all the houses
(All houses in the boy's village had dogs
And the boy's house had three) came out
To complain, barking and following the dog-eater
Though they dared not come close enough to do him any harm.

The dog-eater, the light of the moon on his white hair

And on his thin clothes, walked by with his head tilted
To the ground.  He never lifted his head
Even when somebody called out his name
And said something the boy did not understand.
He kept his eyes to the gravel road, walking
Until his body disappeared at the bend.

When the dog-eater was gone the boy looked up:
He saw again the bright moon in the cloudless sky.
He stared at its huge and pervasive presence —
Its color like the color that many years later
He would see on a patch of snow
On a sidewalk in New York.


## II.    ALIGNMENT

Cabalquinto says "ALIGNMENT" was inspired by the movie, "Swept Away," directed by Lina Wertmuller.

"There was something about the movie that roused something in me that I wanted to approximate as a feeling in the poem — a feeling that has to do with creating a unity from all my previous experiences around the world and answering the question of why I exist," he says.  "As I've gotten older, I realized that my concerns in writing are *extra-literary*.  Through my writing, I think I'm trying to tie together everything that I used to associate with religion and determinations of why I exist.  (Through poetry, I realize that) my body and mind are of the same universe and each have found their orbit around each other.  Poetry is my defining activity, my defining preoccupation:  poetry is me."

In the revisions depicted below, Cabalquinto shows how he gave a lot of thought to the rhythm of the poem in addition to continuing his search to state his thoughts as simply as possible.

The following is Cabalquinto's first draft, complete with notes — e.g. questions to himself — depicted in parenthesis, presented as they were written on the draft:

### *ALIGNMENT*

It happened again this afternoon
while watching a Wertmuller movie
In the East Village:
This alignment that comes ~~deep~~
Like a magnet's work on iron filings
When most things of the mind
As well as of the body are turned
Toward the one direction
Where all must come from
And where all must one day begin
Again:  it comes unsummoned, a shift

Now familiar, a quick
Turning over of an (the?) event.
It comes as a small wind in Central park
As a distant hammering (at noon?) from a Philippine village
      (an echo of someone hammering in the hometown village?)
      (as a hammering echo in a Philippine village?)
      (as a mountain hammering heard in a Philippine village?)
It is the afternoon walk on a rain-wet street in Agra
The neon lights seen from a hotel at midnight in Tokyo
Sometimes it comes as a passage of Mozart,
A dance by Baryshnikov and Makarova.
It came once from the bend of a woman's body in Rome,
From a late flamenco show in Barcelona.
Also it came on the Monterey road
Riding the Greyhound from San Francisco
And again in the odd light of an old man's eye
Photographed in New Mexico.
When it happens a strong grip takes over
In the body: the head becomes light.
The hair stands on end, the pores open
And currents run down to the palms and feet:
Aware at this moment of a new knowledge
that makes the old truths untrue.
Still, each time this happens,
The clarity lasts only seconds:
Before full possession can take place
Something changes the air, rewards the body:
The mind is dislodged, recalled
To an accustomed disorder.


The following draft is an intermediary draft with Editing Marks depicting some of Cabalquinto's thoughts on revising the poem:


### ALIGNMENT

~~Again,~~ It happened ~~again~~ again this afternoon
while watching a Wertmuller movie
(indent this line?)   In the East Village:
This alignment that comes
like a magnet's work on iron filings
When most things of the mind
As well as(/and?) of the body are turned
Toward the one direction
Where all must come from

And where all must one day (line break here?) begin

Again: (new line break here?) it comes unsummoned, a shift

Now familiar, a quick

Turning over of the event.

It comes as a _____/(in/with a clutch of) wind in Central Park,

As a ___ hammering from (with an echo from?) a Philippine village/mountain.

It is the ~~afternoon~~ walk on a rain-wet street in Agra,

The view of neon lights from a hotel at midnight in Tokyo.

Sometimes it comes as a passage of Mozart,

A dance by Baryshnikov and Makarova.

It came once from the bend of a woman's body in Rome

From a ~~the~~(/That?) late flamenco show in Barcelona.

Also it came in the Moneterey road

Riding the Greyhound from San Francisco

And (again) in the odd light (glint?) of an old man's eye

Photographed in New Mexico.

When it happens a strong grip takes over

In the body:  the head becomes light.

The hairs stand on end, the pores (line break here?) (break?) open

And currents run down to (new line break here?) the palms and feet;

Aware at this moment of a new knowledge

That makes the old truths untrue.

Still, each time this happens

The clarity lasts only seconds:

Before full possession can take place

something changes the air reworks the body —

The mind is dislodged, recalled

To an accustomed disorder.

The above reflects Cabalquinto's thought process through four drafts of the poem; at this point, all his drafts except for one were in long-hand.  He then typed a fresh draft as depicted below; although the draft all starts in lower-case letters, he had handwritten a question to himself about whether he should "use conventional caps."  The Editing Marks reflects changes made to reach the poem's final draft; all lines in the final draft do start with capitalized words.

At this phase, Cabalquinto's changes included deleting the lines related to Mozart, Bach, Baryshnikov and Makarova.  He says he did so because (i) the references seemed like name-dropping and (ii) to pare down the enumerations, the inadvertent list-making.

### *ALIGNMENT*

~~many times in my life it has happened~~

~~as~~ it happened again this afternoon

<u>while</u> watching a Wertmuller movie

in the East Village <u>:</u>

this alignment that ~~occurs~~ <u>comes</u>

like a magnet's ~~control of~~ <u>work on iron</u> filings

when ~~all essential preoccupations~~

~~of body and~~ [Del L] most things of the mind ~~are exposed~~

As well as of the body are turned

~~to face~~ Toward the ~~assigned~~ one direction

where ~~we~~ all must come from

and where ~~we all~~ all must one day begin

again: it ~~occurs~~ comes unsummoned, a shift

~~a~~ now familiar , a quick ~~shift yet undefined~~

~~unsurpassed~~ turning over of an ~~events~~ event

it comes ~~in a clutch of~~ as a small wind ~~at~~ in Central Park

~~As a~~ The noontime hammering heard (~~I heard~~?) ~~echoes from~~ in a Philippine

mountain

~~a~~ It is ~~an that~~ an afternoon walk on a rain-wet street in Agra ,

~~The~~ neon lights seen ~~the view~~ from a hotel at midnight in Tokyo

~~sometimes it comes as a passage of Mozart of Bach~~

~~a dance by Baryshnikov or Makarova~~

it came once from the bend of a woman's body in Rome ,

From a late Flamenco show in Barcelona .

also it came ~~to me~~ on the ~~Monterrey~~ Monterey road

riding the Greyhound from ~~Frisco~~ San Francisco —

and ~~once~~ ,again , in the odd light of ~~that~~ an old man's eye

photographed in New Mexico

when ~~this happens I feel a tight clasp~~ it happens a strong grip takes over

~~of~~ in the body ~~, a lightening of the head~~ : the head becomes light.

~~against common advice I allow my hairs~~

~~to stand on end, the pores to open~~

The hairs stand on end, the pores open

and currents run down to ~~my~~ the palms and feet :

~~as if certain at this moment of new matters~~

~~all the old concepts now assailable~~

~~still, each time it happens, though like~~

~~a prophet's foreknowledge of things to come~~

Aware at this moment of a new knowledge

That makes the old truths untrue

Still, each time this happens,

the ~~utter~~ clarity lasts only seconds :

before ~~I can assume fullest~~ full possession can take place

something changes the air, reworks the body :

~~my~~ The mind is dislodged, recalled

~~again~~ to an accustomed disorder

The following is the <u>final draft</u> of "ALIGNMENT."

### *ALIGNMENT*

It happened again this afternoon
While watching a Wertmuller movie
In the East Village:
This alignment that comes
Like a magnet's work on iron filings
When most things of the mind
As well as of the body are turned
Toward the one direction
Where all must come from
And where all must one day begin
Again:  it comes unsummoned, a shift
Now familiar, a quick
Turning over of an event.
It comes as a small wind in Central Park,
The noontime hammering heard in a Philippine village.
It is an afternoon walk on a rain-wet street in Agra.
Neon lights seen from a hotel at midnight in Tokyo.
It came once from the bend of a woman's body in Rome,
From a late Flamenco show in Barcelona.
Also it came on the Monterey road
Riding the Greyhound from San Francisco —
And, again, in the odd light of an old man's eye
Photographed in New Mexico.
When it happens a strong grip takes over
In the body:  the head becomes light.
The hairs stand on end, the pores open
And currents run down to the palms and feet:
Aware at this moment of a new knowledge
That makes the old truths untrue.
Still, each time this happens,
The clarity lasts only seconds:
Before full possession can take place
Something changes the air, reworks the body:
The mind is dislodged, recalled
To an accustomed disorder.

### III.    DEPTHS OF FIELDS

Cabalquinto says "DEPTHS OF FIELDS" was inspired by a mixture of conflicting emotions that he was feeling while visiting Magarao during one of his vacations from Pfizer.  "It was during one of my home leaves and the idea of 'depths of fields' became a metaphor for the many feelings I was feeling at the time," he says.

"I was feeling wonder at the natural beauty of the simple rural life; affection towards my parents, but also a sadness at the surrounding poverty; unfulfilled lives and ugly politicking going on at the time," he recalls.

In drafting this poem, Cabalquinto experimented with three types of beginnings. The drafts below will feature versions based on each of the beginnings, presented in chronological order.

The following is Cabalquinto's first draft, complete with Editing Marks and notes — e.g. questions to himself — depicted in parenthesis; this first draft begins with the line, "About a hundred paces from the old house." The word, "poblacion," in the second stanza refers to the center of town.

## DEPTHS OF FIELD

About a hundred paces from the old house
where I was raised (born?), where they're absent now —

~~my~~ the father ~~and~~ , the mother, two brothers , ~~and~~ a sister —
our poblacion ends and the vast space of rice

fields fall into view ~~, there where on home~~ where during home
leaves (visits? vacations?) I'm drawn to watch on evenings such

as this, when the moon is full and given
to a neverending show of its extravagant light
        (to a never-stopping show of its most extravagant glow?)

that transmutes everything: it now changes me,
an alien visiting from a (his very?) distant planet

assessing and reporting everything the first time.
This is a land of the most exquisite tenderness.

From the susurrus of wind in crowns of singly-grown
coconuts to the broad patches of moon-flecked water —

newly-planted with seedings — to the small huts
of farmers, windows framed by the flicker of kerosene

lamps, an unearthly calm (here?) appears to be the rule:
beauty unreserved holds down a country's suffering,

Disclosed in this one superb (high-pitched?) moment:  a long-held
secret displaced by ambition and need:  a country

boy's deep attachment to his hometown lands
that remains intact in a lifetime of wanderings.

As I look alone, engulfed by depths of a pristine
loveliness, I'm permanently returned to this world (fold?)

to all the meanings it has saved for me.  If I die now,
in the bosom of my (this?) childhood land, I'll miss nothing.
           (change bosom to clasp?, grasp? heart? arms? bands? embrace?)


     Cabalquinto's subsequent drafts begin with the first line, "Walking a hundred paces from
the old house."  As with the above, this version includes Editing marks and notes depicted in
parenthesis.  Among the changes Cabalquinto made in this version, versus the above first draft,
was the deletion of the reference to "poblacion" which he said he did because it sounded awk-
ward.  "It broke the poem's rhythm so that the musical flow wasn't quite right."
     Cabalquinto also deleted the word "susurrus" as part of trying to achieve the simplest way
of expressing his thoughts, as well as the word "alien" whose resonance jars with the overall
mood of the poem.
     In addition, Cabalquinto changed the reference, "a country boy's deep attachment" to "a
country boy's pained enchantment" with his childhood land — a "pained enchantment . . . that
remains intact."  Cabalquinto concedes that he had some "rough times while growing up in the
Philippines but that I don't dwell in pain and suffering.  To me, everything has a solution that will
transcend the negative.  There's a lot of life to be enjoyed.  Everyday is a gift — I try not to waste
it.  I believe people can have a good amount of control in their lives."


### DEPTHS OF FIELD

Walking a hundred paces from the old house
where I was raised, where many're absent now,

the vast ricefields sweep into view:  there where
during home leaves I'm drawn to watch on evenings

such as this, when the moon is fat and much given
to the free spending of its rich cache of light

which transmutes ~~all~~ things:  it changes me ~~now~~,
like someone visiting a very separate universe.
           (like someone coming to view/to preview his next life?)
           (like someone restored to the newness of his life?)

From the wind's shuffle in the crown of tall coconut
trees to the broad patches of moon-flecked water —

newly-rowed (freshly-rowed?) with seedlings — to the grass huts of
croppers, windows framed by the flicker of kerosene

lamps, an unearthly calm pervades all that is seen;
beauty unreserved holds down a country's suffering.

Disclosed in this high-pitched hour is a long-held
secret displaced by ~~old~~ ambition and need:  a country

boy's pained enchantment with his hometown lands
that remains intact in a lifetime of wanderings.

As I look again, embraced by depths of an old
loneliness, I'm permanently returned to this world,

to the meanings it has saved for me.  If I die now,
in the grasp of childhood fields, I'll miss nothing.


This next version begins with the line that remained intact for the poem's final draft:  "I
walk some hundred paces from the old house."  The only other change made for the first pub-
lished draft of the poem was changing "there" to "here" in the second stanza.

### *DEPTHS OF FIELD*

I walk some hundred paces from the old house
where I was raised, where many are absent now,

and the ricefields sweep into view:  ~~there~~ here where
during home leaves I'm drawn to watch on evenings

such as this, when the moon is fat and much given
to the free spending of its rich cache of light

which transmutes all things:  it changes me now,
like someone restored to the newness of his life.

Note the wind's shuffle in the crown of tall coconut
trees; the broad patches of moon-flecked water —

freshly-rowed with seedlings; the grass huts of
croppers, windows framed by the flicker of kerosene

lamps:  an unearthly calm pervades all that is seen.
Beauty unreserved holds down a country's suffering.

Disclosed in this high-pitched hour:  a long-held
secret displaced by ambition and need, a country

boy's pained enchantment with his hometown lands
that remains intact in a lifetime of wanderings.

As I look again, embraced by depths of an old
loneliness, I'm permanently returned to this world,

to the meanings it has saved for me.  If I die now,
in the grasp of childhood fields, I'll miss nothing.


    The following is the final draft of "DEPTHS OF FIELD."  Cabalquinto recalls that after the
poem's first publication, he changed the title by pluralizing "FIELDS."
    "There are so many things going on in the poem that I wanted to clarify that more than
one field of rice was involved," he says.  "The pluralization of the word also brought in more res-
onance, expands the range of the poem."


### *DEPTHS OF FIELDS*

I walk some hundred paces from the old house
where I was raised, where many are absent now,

and the ricefields sweep into view:  here where
during home leaves I'm drawn to watch on evenings

such as this, when the moon is fat and much given
to the free spending of its rich cache of light

which transmutes all things:  it changes me now,
like someone restored to the newness of his life.

Note the wind's shuffle in the crown of tall coconut
trees; the broad patches of moon-flecked water —

freshly-rowed with seedlings; the grass huts of
croppers, windows framed by the flicker of kerosene

lamps:  an unearthly calm pervades all that is seen.
Beauty unreserved holds down a country's suffering.

Disclosed in this high-pitched hour:  a long-held
secret displaced by ambition and need, a country

boy's pained enchantment with his hometown lands
that remains intact in a lifetime of wanderings.

As I look again, embraced by depths of an old
loneliness, I'm permanently returned to this world,

to the meanings it has saved for me.  If I die now,
in the grasp of childhood fields, I'll miss nothing.

—⁓—

In discussing his joy at living a poet's life, Cabalquinto says, "If I die now, I'll die happy."
It is perhaps apt that Cabalquinto describes his joy while referencing death.  It recalls a 1976 inter-
view of one of his most influential teachers, Kinnell, published by the *Sam Houston Literary
Review 1*.  During this interview, Kinnell said:

> The most difficult thing for the human being is the knowledge that he will die;
> everything else can be dealt with, or could be, were it not for that knowledge.  And so
> we develop, one after another, some manner of accounting for death, or for turning it
> aside, or of making it more tolerable. . . .
>     . . . . we do grasp that there's an element beyond our reach, from which we
> came, and into which we will dissolve, which is the mother and father of all the life of
> the planet, to use terms which may apply better than we think.  Our happiness in this life
> — our capacity to sense this element — makes us able, when the time comes, to die will-
> ingly, to return to it without bitterness or the feeling of having been betrayed.

*If I die now, I'll die happy.*  It is the same sentiment with which "DEPTHS OF FIELDS" —
the title poem for his collection of *Selected Poems* — concludes.  To find himself — what he calls
"the real me" — required leaving his birthland and its distractions.  Yet, as Cabalquinto ultimately
says of himself in "DEPTHS OF FIELDS,"  "*. . . a country/ boy's pained enchantment with his
hometown lands/ that remains intact in a lifetime of wanderings./ As I look again, embraced by
depths of an old/ loneliness, I'm permanently returned to this world/ to the meanings it has saved
for me.  If I die now,/ in the grasp of childhood fields, I'll miss nothing.*"

# JESSICA HAGEDORN

Jessica Hagedorn is a poet, multimedia artist, screenwriter and novelist who was born and raised in the Philippines and moved to the United States in her teens. Her first novel, *Dogeaters,* (Pantheon, 1990) was nominated for the 1990 National Book Award. She also has written a second novel, *The Gangster of Love* (Houghton Mifflin, 1996). Her other books include *Danger and Beauty* and, as editor, the critically-lauded anthology of fiction and poetry by Asian Pacific American writers, *Charlie Chan is Dead: An Anthology of Contemporary Asian American Fiction.* Her poetry has appeared in numerous publications, including the anthologies *Flippin': Filipinos on America* (Asian American Writers Workshop, 1996); *Premonitions: the Kaya Anthology of New Asian North American Poetry* (Kaya Productions, 1995); and *Returning A Borrowed Tongue* (Coffeehouse, 1995).

In response to the question, "What advice would you give to a young poet?" Jessica Hagedorn responds:

Treat language as music — music that is beautiful, rhythmic, sometimes harsh, ugly and powerful.

# Jessica Hagedorn Sings:
## Listen To   "PICTURE THIS"

*in/ ourselves/ there/ is/ the/ world/ & in this place where music stays*
*/ you can let yrself in . . . / i know where music expects me/ & when she finds me*
*/ i am bathed in the ocean's breath/ & the soft glory of my laughter*
*— from "an invitation to my friends" by Ntozake Shange*


*The Lesser and Greater Antilles like/ Keys on a saxophone/ An acoustic shoot*
*/ Each playing their note./ Did he blow?/ A high sea note/ Crescendo-waves/ Coastal blues.*
*/ An air of leaves,/ A percussion of branches/ In the melody/ The sound of green.*
*—from "Atmospheric Phenomenon" by Victor Hernandez Cruz*


*. . .*
*in brazil/ the women samba/ only with their legs/ their faces are somber*
*/ and their upper torsos/ never move*
*. . .*
*her dreams were filled with ghosts/ perched on her bony wrists/ grinning gargoyles*
*/ who menaced her every step/ and wouldn't/ let her go*

*she longed to be/ her mother/ in a silver dress/ some softly fading memory*
*/ lifting her legs/ in a sinuous tango*
*— from "THE WOMAN WHO THOUGHT SHE WAS MORE THAN A SAMBA" by Jessica Hagedorn*


In 1992, James Rosenquist painted a series that he titled "Gift Wrapped Dolls."  The works portray close-ups of the faces of dolls from the 1950s — mass-produced dolls with generic features offering blank stares.  Rosenquist wrapped the dolls in plastic, photographed them and, from the photographs, created his paintings.  The paintings are also huge, all 60" by 60" squares.  The paintings disconcert and perhaps repel; but, ultimately, they seduce the viewer into fascination.

Rosenquist's paintings were shown from September 10-October 9, 1993 at the Feigen Gallery in Chicago.  During the preparations for the show, Jessica Hagedorn received a call from writer and friend Lawrence Chua who had been contacted by Rosenquist's wife, Mimi Thompson.

"It turns out that Mimi, who's also a painter, knew of my work and had called Larry to try to track me down.  And she had thought that it would be nice for this particular show not to do just a catalogue essay by an art critic or a scholar but also to have another artist contribute a piece that would be reacting to the show," Hagedorn recalls.  "I was intrigued — I'm certainly an admirer of James Rosenquist's) works."

Hagedorn visited the Feigen Gallery in New York and looked at some of the paintings there; she returned home with slides and polaroids of the series.  After perusing the images as well as considering the notion of being "commissioned" to write a poem, Hagedorn says,"I really thought about it and decided I would try it.  I react to images very powerfully.  Images are inspirational to me.  When I was an adolescent, I used to go to a lot of art shows, wander through galleries, and really look at paintings.  My mother was a painter.  I was influenced by paintings and comforted by them and I would often write poems after seeing paintings."

Consequently, Hagedorn says she considered the commission "natural, not an odd thing.

In fact, it made a lot of sense to me — it's an interesting approach — but no one had thought to ask me before. That's why I wanted to do it. I thought, 'Oh, this painter whom I truly admire, who is alive, who is a 20th century painter has asked me to do this: how wonderful! And what a challenge to me — am I up to this? And what is this relationship going to be? And how is *He* going to respond. Because I didn't know him. I still don't know him. We finally did meet but way after my job had been done. It was an interesting collaboration — or a lack of collaboration. The paintings had been done. Then I come in. He gives me carte blanche. He says for me to write whatever I want."

After Hagedorn finished her poem which she titled, "Picture This," she sent it to Rosenquist for his response. "Of course I was really nervous," she recalls about waiting for Rosenquist's reaction. In addition, Hagedorn deliberately had avoided discussing the paintings with Rosenquist. "I didn't want too much information and I think they didn't want me to have too much information because then I would be taking the position of the scholar or the critic which I was totally not interested in doing."

To Hagedorn's relief, she said that Rosenquist subsequently told her, "I don't know if I understand it but I like it."

The following is the poem Hagedorn wrote in response to Rosenquist's paintings and first published in the brochure for Rosenquist's show at the Feigen Gallery:


**Picture This**
(after a series of paintings titled *Gift Wrapped Dolls*, by James Rosenquist)


A woman hurled.  Hurled out.
A woman
Hurls herself out the window
exits out
the window
expects to            crashland
on the sidewalk
crashland
bones and skin
into sidewalk
below

surprise                *(surprise)*

there she is        buoyant
in mid-air
in limbo
screeching the screech of a bitch eagle:
*my grrrls!*
*my lost daughters*

hurls herself        she
hurts herself

tries to catch up

with her lovely lost
placid girls
Hey dollface
Hey babydoll
*Sugar sweet*
*sweet thang*

I reach out          palms up
stigmata     oozing     divine blood     of pig     and rooster
*Down, down     come down*
*down with me*               now

enough of this burning house
this ruin
this dream
*cobalt blue*
*pure love*
*electricity*

my daughters defy me
pastel virgin brides
saran wrap serene
perpetually puckering
swollen lips
bloody          divine

(kiss.  kiss.  don't buy into it.  bite into it.)

*hey mama     hey dollface     hey baby*     (hey) face
*wrap me up*
*wrap me tight*
*in your embrace*

*like a mummy*
*Mommy*

*tight*

I hurl myself
hurt myself
screech
the screech of a bitch eagle;

*into     the rubble     it is time     now*

unfurl from my broken spine

calla lily    cobra lily    mud

shrouded in cellophane    *(upkeep: minimal; shelf life: eternal)*

feral and glossy

bouquets


profane

immaculate

conceptions

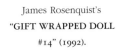

James Rosenquist's
**"GIFT WRAPPED DOLL**
**#14" (1992).**
Oil on canvas, 60" x 60"
(Copyright 1997 James Rosenquist
/Licensed by VAGA, New York, N.Y.)

"In thinking about dolls, I kind of thought of how sinister they can be. I considered the way that he had them wrapped — you know saran-wrapped and cellophaned. I found them beautiful yet, in some instances, really menacing. You know, like some of the dolls looked like they were set on fire. And, yeah, they're frightening, they're quite frightening, the way he has them in extreme close-ups," Hagedorn recalls.

Though Rosenquist has said that he painted the dolls from the photographs, the paintings mix elements of realism with pop, abstraction and superrealism — partly due to the effects of the cellophane folding and wavering around the dolls' faces. The wrapping blurs colors, lines and perspectives; additionally, the paintings are quite confrontational because the dolls' eyes stare right at the viewer. The images are of dolls, but they have a human look: a dead look.

Hagedorn says she had a "violent" response to the paintings, which she considers "interesting. You look at a doll and it's an intensely female reaction. I was looking at dolls as a woman, as a mother, and as a person who has to run around buying dolls for my daughters because they demand them. So I'm very conscious of what these dolls are and the kind of images presented by the dolls. This is a dialogue I have with myself all the time. So I thought, how do you translate all these ambivalent feelings into this poem and still address the poem?"

As a result of her "ambivalent feelings," Hagedorn believes that she "became a doll" in writing the poem, as much as she considered the other dolls to be her daughters. "I think that when (the woman hurls herself out of the window) to catch up with those placid girls, it's with this awareness of some of the paths that her daughters might go down, paths not approved by the mother. So she's trying to catch up with them and control (them) but they're out of her control, of course."

Just as Rosenquist's paintings transcend realism, Hagedorn's poem goes beyond narrative; it is as complex, indeed, as mother-daughter relationships can be. Hagedorn begins the poem with a woman hurling herself out of the window. "It's very suicidal, but it's also the woman who hurls herself out — she takes control of her own death. Except, then the surprise is that she flies through the air. And she becomes this eagle. An eagle is a majestic image — fierce, not victim-ey but rather one who is in control and magnificent but can also be terrifying," Hagedorn says. "This is how I often think about the mother image, and in a positive way — this magnificent image, very animal, very grand and all-encompassing and capable of these surprises and miracles. And it's not necessarily a comforting image all the time — it can be this terrifying image."

The poem's eighth and ninth stanzas are

> my daughters defy me
> pastel virgin brides
> saran wrap serene
> perpetually puckering
> swollen lips
> bloody    divine
>
> (kiss. kiss. don't buy into it. bite into it.)

Hagedorn says she considered the "swollen lips" to be "this sort of religious imagery that's also very destructive, and that goes back to violence — the idea of the kiss as something that's seductive, but I say, 'don't buy into it.' I see dolls as part of the consumer culture — the dolls that James Rosenquist deliberately chose to paint are those that, it seems to me, he purposely picked because they're mass-produced. I remember dolls like those when I was growing up. They had these little fat faces. They were chubby baby dolls with curls. When I was younger and in the Philippines, we had no Barbies. What we had was a variation of this fat Goldilocks thing."

*Barbie.* It would be difficult to discuss dolls without referring to that American icon. Hagedorn calls Barbie "another kind of creepiness. I tell you, my five-year-old Esther is much more fascinated by Barbie than baby dolls. But Barbie — it's a fantasy land of ridiculous things like these high heels. And we talk about it. I really had to think a lot about whether I should buy into this."

It's not a stretch to consider the possibility that the line, "kiss. kiss. don't buy into it. bite into it." mirrors Hagedorn's experience with Barbie and her daughters. To deal with Barbie's relationship with Esther, Hagedorn says she speaks about "Barbie very irreverently and I allow my daughter to dismember the dolls. I think that by dealing with them that way, I allow her to demystify the damn thing by herself; and not too get caught into this feeling of 'I MUST BECOME THIS DOLL'."

Though Rosenquist picked a different type of doll from Barbie, Hagedorn says she thought he picked dolls that are similar to Barbies in how they mirror what society considers to be the ideal feminine look. "They are a little less obvious than Barbies but they're still mass-produced and are just as much models of what women should be, or a baby doll — a little girl — should be. So that's my thing about 'don't buy into it.' It's that two-pronged thing about the other side of sweetness being the danger — of love, hate —so don't buy into it, 'bite into it' — destroy it."

Hagedorn says the same thoughts recur in the eleventh stanza, " ' like a mummy/ Mommy.' It's the idea of being suffocated and smothered. In a way, I am dealing with the commodified sweetness — that fake and artifical notion of childhood as a Disneyland version of how we should live; that fakeness and unrealness that I find very destructive and I find dishonest and plastic. In my text, I'm trying to achieve the same thing that I think James Rosenquist did by wrapping the dolls in plastic and the distressing of them, making them even more sinister. That's his visual commentary. With my words, I purposely go against the sweet. The words are meant to be fiery.

— ɯ —

James Rosenquist's
**"GIFT WRAPPED DOLL
#5" (1992).**
Oil on canvas, 60" x 60"
(Copyright 1997 James Rosenquist
/Licensed by VAGA, New York, N.Y.)

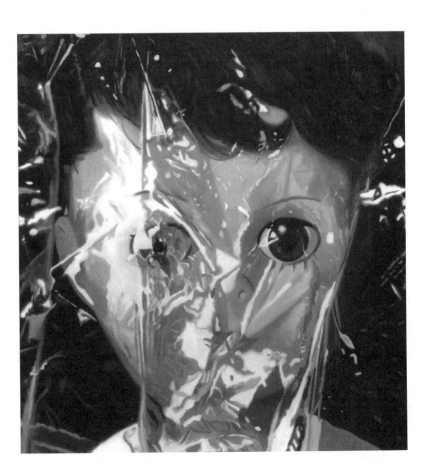

Though "Picture This" reflects the inspiration of Rosenquist's paintings, Hagedorn says she didn't write the poem any differently because it was a commissioned poem, noting, "My main worry from the beginning of writing the poem was to do it justice. And I really wanted to be disciplined about it: make the images be the force that moved the poem but then within that have (poetic) freedom. And I think Mimi and James were looking for someone who was not attached to the idea of just writing about these dolls."

The poem is as much song as storytelling, reflecting Hagedorn's poetic technique. Part of Hagedorn's music occurs through her word plays: the combination of "hurl" with "hurt" and "mummy" with "Mommy" as well as spelling words the way that she says she hears people speak them, as in spelling "girls" as "*grrrls!*" She considers the latter "as adding another layer to the word itself."

"I can hear the poem. I actually hear it as I write it. I hear voices in my head. When the poem takes control of me or takes over me, it's writing itself. It's like with any creative writing I do. It's as if these voices, spirits, take over and they're busy and they're speaking in different rhythms and I try to capture that. When I finally write the first couple of lines, the rest of the poem just comes," she says.

As regards the italicized words in her poems, Hagedorn says, "I do italics instinctively. Some of them I did because they're in the voice of the dolls. Some of them were because they're meant to be in another voice than the poet's. It's just a way to differentiate. I tend to write them as if I'm writing them to be performed; it's a way to suggest another voice."

Among the influences for her poetry, Hagedorn cites Victor Hernandez Cruz, Ntozake Shange, Frederico Garcia Lorca, Serafin Syquia, French surrealist poets whose styles she "found liberating" and the American Beat Poets whose "take on America is very appealing." Hagedorn notes that Cruz and Shange, in particular, were important in her "getting comfortable with my poetry."

Shange returns the compliment in her poem, "talking to myself." In this poem, Shange pretends to interview herself and, in response to a question about who helped her understand her poetic craft, Shange says the following:

> *tz: some people think lorraine hansberry influenced you; since she didn't, who did help you understand your craft?*
>
> around 1966/ abt the time i went to barnard i thot leroi jones (imamu baraka) waz my primary jumping-off point. that i cd learn from him how to make language sing & penetrate one's soul, . . . then i found myself relating technically to ishmael reed, particularly in terms of diction & myth, . . . then i discovered the nostalgia david henderson can make so tangible; our immediate past as myth. & here comes pedro pietri, allowing language to create a world that can't exist outside his poems. i find victor hernandez cruz shows me how to say anything i thot i saw.
>
> jessica hagedorn on the other hand puts the worlds we both share in a terribly personal & cosmopolitan realm. . . . (she) says to me that complicated notions can be explicated by rhythm. we can approach difficult concepts with ourselves; there is no need to go the route of iowa to get a sophisticated poem. . . .

Hagedorn also cites the influence of nineteenth-century French poet Stephane Mallarmé , specifically "the way his poem looked on the page." Like many of her other poems, "Picture This" incorporates blank spaces, about which Mallarmé wrote in a preface to his final work, "UN COUP DE DES (A THROW OF THE DICE)" (as featured in *COLLECTED POEMS*, Translated by Henry

Weinfield, University of California Press, 1994).

The "blanks," in effect, assume importance and are what is immediately most striking; versification always demanded them as a surrounding silence, . . . The paper intervenes each time an image, of its own accord, ceases or withdraws, accepting the succession of others . . . . This copied distance, which mentally separates words or groups of words from one another, has the literary advantage . . . of seeming to speed up and slow down the movement, of scanning it, and even of intimating it through a simultaneous vision of the Page: the latter is taken as the basic unit, in the way that elsewhere the Verse or the perfect line is. The fiction rises to the surface and quickly dissipates, following the variable motion of the writing, around the fragmentary interruptions of a central phrase, a phrase introduced from the title and continuing onward. Everything that occurs is foreshortened and, as it were, hypothetical; narrative is avoided. Add that from this stripped-down mode of thoughts, with its retreats, prolongations, flights, or from its very design, there results, for whoever would read it aloud, a musical score.

—◊—

As a novelist, Hagedorn wrote *Dogeaters* (Pantheon, 1990) which was nominated for the National Book Award and won a Before Columbus' American best book of the year award. Her second book, *The Gangster of Love*, was released in 1996 by Houghton Mifflin Company. Consequently, she is frequently asked whether there is a difference between the way she writes poetry versus prose. The answer is simply that she considers herself a *poet* and writes all her works the way she would write poetry.

Her poems sometimes generate images that eventually find their way into her novels. Indeed, the last three lines of "Picture This" — "profane/ immaculate/ conceptions" — resulted in the following excerpt from *The Gangster of Love*:

Milagros trips on the curled-up edge of a rug, a woman suspended in a red void. Her daughters float in the sky above her. She reaches out, her legs spread, the palms of her hands up in a gesture of . . . supplication? beseeching? blessing? Is she screaming or laughing? Where is her son? She imagines her children into existence. She can imagine anything into existence, she is that powerful. Profane immaculate conceptions.

In addition, in the excerpt just before the above paragraph that references "profane immaculate conceptions," Hagedorn writes:

Milagros wears a black crepe skirt, which she has forgotten to zip all the way up, and a glittery moth-eaten sweater. On her stockinged feet are scruffy slippers, bought for $2.99 at Walgreen's. She peers into her dining room, expecting to find her guests. They're late. How she hated when anyone was late, especially for one of her dinner parties. Seagulls, Milagros suddenly thinks. Seagulls pecking at my brain. *Pensamiento, pentimento, pimiento, punieta.*

What to do when the English no longer makes sense? *Ay, puta. Ay naku. Buwisit. Putang ina mo. Que asco. Que barbaridad. Que horror.*

In the italicized last lines of the above paragraphs, one can sense Hagedorn's "poetic" perspective in choosing words for their underlying music in addition to their meanings.

Finally: *What to do when the English no longer makes sense?* Much has been written about Hagedorn's language, with words like "post-colonial" and "creating a New American Literature" attributed to her works. For Hagedorn, the issue is simpler, reflecting primarily her early exploration to write in English in a way that she felt comfortable with, versus the styles of other Filipino writers to whose works she was exposed as a young student in the Philippines.

"I think part of it was when I was trying to figure out how to write and be myself and not imitate French surrealists. I was thinking of who I am when it comes to language. Well, I'm most at home with the language of English. But how can I make it my English? I recall when I grew up in the Philippines that a lot of novels I used to read by Filipino writers were written in this stiff colonialist English; I was put off by how stilted the language sounded. So I was floundering around — was my poet's voice e.e. cummings or Lorca's? I was groping in the dark, and I guess my voice as a writer coming up in the 1970s was influenced and inspired by the Black vernacular. Back then, that particular music was most comfortable to me. I also met other Filipino poets who were equally Afro-centered because, for them, the playful wit of the urban Black vernacular was similar to the innovations of Taglish (a combination of Tagalog and English)."

Nevertheless, talking about the work can never replace listening to the work. As Shange says in her poem, "takin a solo/ a poetic possibility/ a poetic imperative,"

> my basic premise is that poets address themselves to the same issues as musicians/ but that we give the musicians more space to run with/ more personal legitimacy than we give our writers. . . .we assume a musical solo is a personal statement/ we think the poet is speakin for the world. there's something wrong there, a writer's first commitment is to the piece, itself. how the words fall & leap/ or if they dawdle and sit down fannin themselves. writers are dealin with language/ not politics. that comes later. so much later. to think abt the politcs of a poem/ before we think abt the poem/ is to put what is correct before the moment.

It may be enough to say about Hagedorn's poetry, her words don't *sit down fannin themselves.*

—⁓—

Following Rosenquist's show, "Picture This" was published in a chapbook of poems by Hagedorn and her daughter, Paloma Hagedorn Woo. Titled *VISIONS OF A DAUGHTER, FORETOLD*, the chapbook was published in 1994 through the Woodland Pattern Book Center and Light and Dust Books in Wisconsin. The project was part of the National Literary Network Tour funded by the Lila Wallace-Reader's Digest Foundation through which writers visit various literary centers around the country. As part of her visit to Milwaukee, Hagedorn was asked whether she had a new book of poems available for publication.

"But I was in the middle of the novel and I didn't want to give them old poems. I did have a few new poems, but not enough for a book. So I thought of showcasing a young poet and thought of my oldest daughter, Paloma, who had been doing poems — not for any particular reason but I thought she came out with some good stuff without thinking much of doing them. So I showed the press a poem titled 'Paloma/The Poet: Visions of a Daughter, Foretold' which is a very private poem and never been published.  I wrote it in 1979, way before I had a daughter but I've always loved that name and thought that if I ever had a daughter I would name her Paloma."

"Picture This" became part of the chapbook project because of its applicability to the theme of a mother/daughter relationship.  The chapbook begins with "Paloma/The Poet:  Visions of a Daughter, Foretold," features Paloma's poems in the middle and ends with "Picture This."

"It's a great order because 'Picture This' is also an open-ended poem:  it's an ending to a chapbook but also the beginning of a life with the mother/daughter tension," says Hagedorn.

Fittingly, the chapbook also contains "Lullaby," a poem that Hagedorn wrote in response to the unexpected death of a former lover:

### Lullaby
### (for Paloma)

*I cry big fat tears*
*stir up the phantoms*
*of dread*
*baby, baby*
*there are so many dead*

*You crawl inside my head*
*make it all better*
*sing*
*"hush, mama, hush . . .*
*food to break the sadness . . ."*

*Bring me a lime green dog*
*a pumpkin with moustache*
*mold a face out of clay*
*stick a flag*
*in one eye*
*paint a flying girl*
*dance up a storm*
*inside me*
*banish the demons*

*Sing*
*"eat, mama, eat . . .*
*food to break the sadness . . ."*

Hagedorn never discussed the paintings with Rosenquist but, in subsequent interviews about his works, Rosenquist said that "Gift-Wrapped Dolls" are partly about his concerns about AIDS.  In a February 25, 1993 interview with independent curator David Whitney, Rosenquist said that he was thinking "of all kinds of so-called beauty gift wrapped.  I began to think of people falling in love, like a child does with a doll and then yet, people having to make a business relationship with love because of AIDS.  This seems to be the complete antithesis to passion.

Recently, I heard Claude Debussy's little piece called 'Serenade for the Doll' and it sounded melancholy. It was written for his three year old daughter. I happen to have a daughter, Lily, who was three years old when I heard it. So, I continued to paint more gift-wrapped dolls' heads."

It was suggested to Hagedorn that "Lullaby" — indeed, the very title — could be related to Rosenquist's thinking: the nature of growing up in an environment with AIDS, including the constraints on sexual and/or romantic experimentation.

Hagedorn agrees, saying, "I had written 'Lullaby' when an ex-lover had died suddenly and unexpectedly and not in a pretty way. I was pregnant at the time with Esther. The death was not AIDS-related but it was the cap to an accumulation of deaths, many of which were of friends who died from AIDS. So I was depressed and I remember not wanting to eat dinner and seven-year-old Paloma trying to make me eat one night. Some of these lines — 'Bring me a lime green dog/ a pumpkin with moustache' — were from her."

Interestingly, two of Paloma's poems also fit within the themes raised by Rosenquist and Hagedorn: dolls and death.

Here is a poem about dolls that Paloma wrote when she was nine years old:

### WEDNESDAY NIGHT

A YOUNG BABY'S TEAR LYING ON A PHOTOGRAPH
HANGING ON THE WALL, THAT SAME BABY
WALKING TOWARD YOU WEARING PLASTIC HIGH-HEELS
AND PUSHING A DOLL STROLLER FULL OF DOLLS
TWO SECONDS LATER YOU HEAR THE TELEVISION GO ON
IT'S YOUR FATHER HE IS WATCHING THE NEWS
THEN YOU HEAR THE WATER RUN, IT IS YOUR MOM
SHE IS PLANNING TO TAKE A NICE HOT BATH
WELL THIS IS WHAT MY HOUSE IS LIKE ON
### WEDNESDAY NIGHT . . .

Here is a poem about death that Paloma wrote when she was ten years old:

### Pearl's Problem

it is green. an old green, 1930's mint.
a red felt, it reads photo album.
inside—black pages with husbands from your mother's twin.
husbands one, two, and three—all in one book.
filled with pictures of her ocelot and her parties—all in one
book.
husband number one—jail. convicted of a murder, you
know he's innocent
husband number two—cheated. a young woman— half her
age. of course she had a sleazy name, tonya.
and husband number three—died. a disease they didn't
know jack about. we still don't know what it is.

all three husbands gone.
she is too.

Hagedorn says she wrote the poem, "Paloma/The Poet: Visions of a Daughter, Foretold" long before she became pregnant with Paloma or before Paloma would show an interest in writing poems. But, finally, it also is an *ars poetica* poem. Listen to the song of her first three stanzas:

she used to say:
as long as i can dance
as long as i can
still dance . . .

her concerns
were simple
although there were
times
she would waken
from a deep sleep
with the taste
of metal
in her mouth

dark and lush
like a jungle garden
her fears
were somehow alleviated
by the knowledge
that there are
poets in the world
whose first language
is music
and whose second language
english

In her introduction to her 1993 collection of stories and poems, *Danger and Beauty* (Penguin Books), Hagedorn writes about her art: "It will never end, I hope—whatever 'it' is. The gift, the quest, the visions, the dreams in secret languages. The songs and the storytelling. It will never end; it is still writing itself."

# MARILYN CHIN

Marilyn Chin is the author of *DWARF BAMBOO* (The Greenfield Review Press, 1987), nominated for the 1987 Bay Area Book Reviewers Award; and *THE PHOENIX GONE, THE TERRACE EMPTY* (Milkweed Editions, 1994), winner of the PEN, Oakland Award for the best book of 1994. She is currently on the faculty of the M.F.A. program at San Diego State University. She has received a Stegner Fellowship, two National Endowment for the Arts Writing Fellowships and a Mary Robert Rinehart Award. She has held residencies at Yaddo, the MacDowell Colony, Centrum, Virginia Center for the Creative Arts and the Djerassi Foundation. In the late 1970s she was a translator for the International Writing Program at the University of Iowa where she co-translated *THE SELECTED POEMS OF AI QING* (Indiana University Press, 1985). She majored in ancient Chinese Literature at the University of Massachusetts at Amherst and received her M.F.A. in Poetry from the Iowa Workshop in 1981. Her poetry has appeared in numerous journals including *The Iowa Review, The Kenyon Review, Parnassus* and *Ploughshares* as well as is included in *THE NORTON INTRODUCTION TO POETRY* and 1996 *Best American Poetry*. She was featured in Bill Moyers' PBS series, "THE LANGUAGE OF LIFE."

In response to the question, "What advice would you give to a young poet?" Marilyn Chin responds:

> My advice to young poets is to cultivate a strong stomach for rejection. The dominant society will tell you that you may not enter the canon, because what you have to say does not matter to them. Your mother will tell you that writing poetry is a useless enterprise and that you should do something practical like become a brain surgeon or at least a computer wiz . . . because, face it, you can't make a living off of poetry. Your father wants you to get married. Secretly, your boyfriend thinks and/or hopes that you're not really cut out for it, and that poetry is just a passing fancy. Everybody thinks that you're not really good enough. Even your own muse rejects your work over and over, relegating most of it to the trash. There would be plenty of disparaging self-doubt . . . You have to be a steadfast disciple, keep reading and writing, keep growing in your craft . . . don't become lazy and facile, publish only your best . . . I promise you, if you're good to your art, it will be good to you . . . for me, my art is the last true promise land . . .

# MARILYN CHIN'S FEMINIST MUSE
## ADDRESSES WOMEN,
## "THE GRAND VICTIMS OF HISTORY"

*They teach us to walk headbent in devotion,*
*to honor the five relations, ten sacraments.*
*Meanwhile, the feast is brewing elsewhere,*
*the ox is slaughtered and her entrails are hung*
*on the branches for the poor. They convince us, yes,*
*our chastity will save the nation—Oh, mothers,*
*all your sweet epithets didn't make us wise!*
*Orchid by any other name is equally seditious.*

*— from "A PORTRAIT OF THE SELF AS NATION, 1990-1991" by Marilyn Chin*

In the 1980s, Marilyn Chin visited Taiwan to study classical Chinese. While there, she visited the Tai-Chung University library and stumbled across some notes taken by an Imperial Gardener discussing one of the Imperial Consorts in the Ming Dynasty. The concubine, like others, had bound feet and was unable to walk for lengthy periods of time. The gardener often observed the concubine in the terrace or courtyard and, in his notes, reflected on her beauty. Suddenly, Chin was transported into another world, another era.

"What was strange about the excerpts from the gardener's notes is something he said about the Royal Consort 'dying of sorrow' — a passage that ends the notes but without any further explanation about what happened to the woman. I thought this intriguing," Chin recalls. "There could be many reasons for her death: for example that the Emperor was overthrown and all his wives and concubines were murdered with him. I wonder about this woman and many women like her who have disappeared due to political viccissitudes. They were grand victims of history."

Chin's concern, combined with a line from a poem by Li Bai, resulted in her poem, "The Phoenix Gone, The Terrace Empty."

"As a person, I'm bubbly and happy and easy to get along with. But my Muse is very strident. She knows her history and she's a feminist. She voices what she wants and needs in the poem and guides me through. This poem is a softly-feminist poem," says Chin. "Some people say (my Muse) is an academic feminist, that I've read Helene Cixous and, therefore, I want to write with bodily references. I certainly am influenced by important feminists like Adrienne Rich and Cixous, as well as the postcolonial criticism of Said Bhaba and Spivak. I love reading polemical stuff — it fires me up. There's a new batch of Asian American feminist critics: Sauling Wong, King-Kok Cheung, Amy Ling, Michelle Yeh, Lisa Lowe and Elaine Kim, to name a few — and I know that there is also a young generation of dynamite critics coming up — whose work fires up my imagination. My Muse's major concern is the suffering of women, the suffering of my mother, first and foremost. My feminism is born out of personal and familial experiences. The feminist and political discourse informs my work as added leverage."

Nevertheless, Chin is reconciled with her Muse, saying "the Muse is much wiser than the poet. She is far more wise as I can be as a person. If she were not wise, I wouldn't be a good poet."

For her Muse's "political voice," Chin acknowledges the influence of her family history, especially the "tragic tale" of her mother. "My father left her and she never recovered and I think

I need to repair her pain through my poems. My mother died because she simply stopped eating. She drove herself into madness. My family knew she died from slow suicide though we never voiced it," Chin says. "To destroy one's self is the final cry of despair."

Her approach is also consistent with her views on the role of minority poets. "The American lyric is dominated by self and that doesn't satisfy me. I hate to generalize for all minority poets but we have an agenda. We have to be greater than self," she stresses. "I think poetry has a mission. It may be foolish to think so but I think it has to teach, to illuminate, to make the world a better place. Otherwise, why write poetry? I'd write for 'Hard Copy' and at least make some money."

Chin's poetry also depends on highly-rigorous craft. She required four years, from 1988 to 1991, to write "The Phoenix Gone, The Terrace Empty," the title poem to her 1994 book published by Milkweed Editions. As with all her poems, Chin first wrote several drafts in a No. 2 pencil. "I can't compose on a computer. I believe the first draft is from God and is connected from my fingertips to the pencil," she says.

Chin calls her hand-written stage the "First Stage" for the poem which, for "The Phoenix Gone, The Terrace Empty," was written "furiously" and "very very long. After I finished the first draft, I started chipping at it for about two months. By the time the poem entered the 'Second Stage' it had gone through a number of revisions," she says. "I knew I had something and I knew it was a good poem but it took me a long time to finish it."

By "Second Stage," Chin refers to the drafts typeset into her computer. "Once a long poem enters the Second Stage, I like to let it sit for another year. Then I start changing small things that could be line breaks or a turn of phrase. I love the ambitions in long poems; I'm really challenged by a poem that takes me years to compose."

Chin notes that, as with most of her poems, she wrote "The Phoenix Gone, The Terrace Empty" for the "eye" versus "for voice." She says, "I never just write for voice. I think how a poem lines up on the page is important. I must write for the page first and if it sounds great in recitation that's good, too, but it's an afterthought. Part of my mission is to bring the poems to the world. I address myself to the question, will I survive in the end? And, even though there's video and cellular tape, I still believe that we will survive through words on the page."

Chin's concern is particularly appropriate for "The Phoenix Gone, The Terrace Empty" which contains many places, time periods and voices. "I wanted to write a political, post-colonial poem with personal, familial and historical layers. Poems such as 'A Portrait of the Self as Nation' and 'The Phoenix Gone, The Terrace Empty' take a while for the reader to get through and figure out what's going on," she says. "They are poems to read over and over and each time one should find something new."

—⧋—

Second Stage: First Draft

Featured below is the first draft of "The Phoenix Gone, The Terrace Empty" during the poem's "Second Stage." Chin's notations on the page are shown as all-capitalized notations; underlined words denote words added after the featured draft; words "striked-through" denote words eliminated after the featured draft; "[New P]" denotes new stanza breaks; "[Del P]" denotes deleting existing stanza break; "[New L]" denotes a new line break; and "[Del L]" denotes the deletion of an existing line break.

The first draft is shown with alphabetical notations by the poem's left margin for purpose of Chin's discussion of her drafting process (which follows the poem's draft).

These stairs are steep/deep                 **A**
shallow river, shallow river
      (REVERSE ORDER OF FIRST TWO LINES?)
one foot, another/the other
I pull/gather up the hem
of my terrycloth robe
quietly
gingerly
as if
an inch
could sing
for miles
past the courtyard
past the mulberries
the marble ox
the terracotta horse
dead horses
hoisted from the dead/grave/earth
(can't whinny)                       **B**
and Buddha
<u>fragrant with jossticks</u>
beneath the Bodhi tree
whose laughter
is unmerciful
the porcelain bowl/birdbath            **C**
mocking the ocean
the frog's terrain
is my face
shimmering
gaunt, sallow —
Narcissus                          **D**
is thirty-three
today, five
in dog years-
a twinkle
in the life of
a star
Walk,
one step, another
so not to disturb
<u>They say you must not leave the courtyard</u>     **F**
<u>You must not see</u>
the nasturtium

so not to ruin

the irises

they/you planted

and in the rock garden

the flagstones

~~are archipelagoes~~ <u>lead the way</u>

my feet

fit/hug them tenderly<u>/they will deliver me</u>

I think

who in the netherworld

walks on my feet

as I walk?

And opens her black mouth

when I cry?

whose lutestrings

play my sorrow.

whose silence

rings out

              LIKE THE GREEN MOSS OF APRIL

~~for ten thousand years~~/<u>millenium of bells</u>

This banister

painted with red lacquer

my grip turns white

the Wutung trees

facing west

(a symbol)s mocks                                   **G**

of my loneliness

the plum blossoms

and peach trees

(stock images)

for her ripeness

She thinks about

death

or the warm blear

her mother

or he—the hard shape

her father

they, slowmoving,

mugworts

            NO—BISON NO—WATERBUFFALO NO—BISON

discuss

your future/dowry

<u>How many taels for a new ox donkey/</u>               **H**

<u>How many      </u>

<u>How many for a Maytag or a      </u>

in a fulcrum

of angry gestures
Interpret, interpret:
hands clenched
hard roses
open, slap
a frond of young palmetto
loud wails of a lullaby

       LINES FROM "INTERPRET, INTERPRET"
       TO "LOUDWAILS OF A LULLABY" ARE
       SUBSEQUENTLY CROSSED OUT

an ancient falsetto
dry heaves
taking in all
the earth can give
<u>What is the color of the womb?</u>
Do you remember                    **I**
remember
the shanty town
the hills of Macao
tin-roofs
crying into the sun
do you remember
Ah Lan/Auntie Jade
throwing (her) kerosene lamp
into a hovel
Do you remember
the hills ablaze
the dry rushes crackling
the debris
turning to ash and thin air
~~Interpret, interpret~~
<u>narrow your eyes obtuse Chinese worm</u>
the man crouched
on the dirty linoleum/his restaurant floor
fingering dice
He said
Meiling, don't cry
Meiling
I can change my life
with one strike.
Do you know the stare
of a dead man?
your uncle Ox
sitting on a ridge
at the Quay
Auntie Jade

remembers
"Hunger
has spooned
the flesh
from his cheeks."
His tuff/shock
of black hair
was his only movement.
That Chinaman
had no ideals
no beliefs
his dreams
were robbed
by the Japanese,
his home was plundered
by the nationalists
the communists
seared their home
Misery has propped
him there
when you pray
to your ancestors
you are praying
to this hollowness
and child                                            **J**
they cried
"Ten thousand years of history and you have come to this?
four thousand years of tutelage and you have come to this.

Should I walk
into the next world
in last year's wardrobe?

grief is no longer in fashion.                       **K**
terror is mundane—

So you've come home
finally
with a new/your boyfriend                            **L**
what is his name?
Ezekiel
odd name for a boy
Your mother can't pronounce it
and she didn't like
his dismeanor
too thin, too sallow

he does not eat beef
in a country
where beef is possible
he cannot or does not sing
in a country
where rapture is music/passable/legal
He cannot/does not smile
perhaps/~~because~~ he is hiding
bad intentions
<u>That moon that evening</u>                          **M**
moon won't drink
and is (naughtily) shaped
like a woman's severed/white ear
or the golden lotus
(her foot), the blood dried/pricked
on the arch
where the toes meet the bridge
Once in the courtyard
the monogamous ducks promised
everything


The snake bites her own tail                          **N**
meaning harmony
at the year's end
or doesn't it mean
she is eating herself
into extinction


Look:  mother says                                    **O**
yellow crowfeet in the pond
not lotus, not lily


<u>Discussion on Second Stage:  First Draft</u>


**A**

To begin the poem, Chin says, "(I) put myself in a trance.  I entered the consciousness of the courtesan going down the stairs but I use the reference to 'terrycloth' robe to keep myself in the mundane present, even as I follow the woman into the past."

As shown by the third ("another" vs. "the other"), fourth ("pull" vs. "gather") and seventeenth ("dead" vs. "grave" vs. "earth") lines, Chin often writes synonyms or alternate word choices next to each other throughout all the drafting stages of the poem.  She returns to the options later to refine how she wishes to deal with such issues as sound and diction.

**B**

Chin says she realized immediately that "can't whinny" would not be the "right sound" for the poem but she inserted this 18th line because she felt it would be important later to remind herself of horses whinnying.  In the Final Draft, this section becomes

> Saunter,
> my pink horses,
> my tiny soldiers.
> heartbeat, hoofbeat,
> softly, gingerly

**C**

The reference to "the porcelain bowl/birdbath/ mocking the ocean/ the frog's terrain" refers to a Chinese folk saying about a frog in a pond who thinks he's in the ocean.  "I wanted to have that reference but thought of the birdbath as the possible prop," she recalls.

**D**

Commencing with the reference to "Narcissus," Chin says she wished to feature both the downward walk through the stairs and the notion of a "spiritual walk" with the lines' meditative descent.

**E**

With the line, "They say you must not leave the courtyard," Chin says she was trying to imagine what others say about the Royal Consort whose story first inspired the poem.  The reference also works to continue the "long walk back in the journey of time through the past."

**F**

Chin changed "for ten thousand years" to "millenium of bells" because she thought the first reference a cliche.  It also is part of the same refining of word choices first noted under "A."

**G**

As Chin continued her "walk" through time, her insertion of "(a symbol)" reflects her realization that she was in the midst of writing a poem.  "I became aware that I'm in the midst of this profound literary endeavor.  I know I'm in the process of writing."  Chin says she returns to the poem again with the references to her parents that begin with the line "She thinks about."

**H**

Looking back at the lines, "How many taels for a new ox donkey/ How many ____/ How many for a Maytag or a ____," Chin muses that these are "strange inserts.  I knew I'd take them out later but I was writing an associative poem and the lines were telling me something.  So I thought I'd leave them in then and later return to them."

Indeed, Chin wrote the subsequent lines from "Interpret, interpret" to "loud wails of a lullaby" but then deleted them later. Given the associative nature of her poem, Chin says she continues to write down what she is compelled to write for a later deliberation. In this section of the poem, it's not until the lines that reference Macao ("Do you remember/ remember/ the shanty town/ the hills of Macao") that she says she realized what her Muse was telling her. "I was writing in the voice of a sixteenth century courtesan but my Muse wanted me to enter Macao and to bring in my (real-life) family," she recalls.

## I

With the poem reverting to Macao, Chin references "Ah Lan/Auntie Jade." However, she says, "I really wanted to talk about my mother and how, perhaps, she once had a lover in Macao. This is my conjecture and also one of those family secrets. So perhaps 'Auntie Jade' was a way to disguise my mother."

As Chin interweaves the notion of her family, the poem continues on to the lines "the man crouched/ on the dirty linoleum/his restaurant floor/ fingering dice." Chin concedes the reference to her father, saying, "My father always enters my poems in a disparaging way. I've often likened my father to disgusting animals. He was a terrible man and is always a dark image in my mind. He was also an obsessive gambler, and he and other cooks at the restaurant would throw dice on the linoleum floor — it was an image that repelled me in the past."

The poem continues on to reference "Uncle Ox" which, just as Auntie Jade was her mother, was meant to refer Chin's father. The poem, however, begins to rationalize the behavior of Chin's father — hence, the references that "his dreams/ were robbed/ by the Japanese,/ his home was plundered/ by the nationalists/ the communists/ seared their home." Chin says that by the time she reached this part of the poem, she "knew some absolution has happened. So I absolved him."

## J

Chin frequently travels through time in her poems and she says she often references her childhood to bring herself "back to self." Thus, she introduces the reference to "and child" for this purpose, while still back in the past as she introduces a saying in a couplet form that she envisions some old Chinese sage would say to try to sum up the previously described events: "Ten thousand years of history and you have come to this?/ Four thousand years of tutelage and you have come to this?"

## K

Chin writes "grief is no longer in fashion./ terror is mundane—" as a reminder of what she wants to talk about, a device that she uses particularly as she drafts a long poem. "The words were cliches but they are reminders and act as scaffolding that later I will take off," she says.

**L**

To expand on the theme of grief becoming unfashionable and terror mundane, Chin references her youth when she began to date. "I had all kinds of boyfriends with names like Bob — not very interesting names. Ezekiel references a prophet in the Bible, a prophet who smeared his own shit all over his body. There's something about all the men I dated — they were all weird," Chin recalls.

**M**

With the reference to "That moon that evening," Chin is recalling once more the poet Li Bai whose poem partly inspired the poem. "Li Bai was always drinking to the moon," she says.

**N**

With the line, "The snake bites her own tail," Chin says she begins to move the poem to closure. She notes the image of the snake biting its own tail is one of the Chinese symbols that means harmony. "I thought it appropriate to try to end the poem on that note because it raises the question of whether she's also 'eating herself/ into extinction.' So, this symbol is not only about harmony, it's about self-annihilation."

**O**

Finally, Chin ends the poem with referencing personal family as well as the bound feet of the Royal Consort. "Crowfeet is a flower as well as the wrinkles behind our eyes. I name the lotus and lily because they are epithets for bound feet," she says.

—⁓—

## Changes Between "Second Stage: First Draft" and "Second Stage: Sixth Draft"

The draft featured below will show Chin's drafting process as she amended the "First Draft" to a "Sixth Draft" in the poem's "Second Stage." Chin's notations on the page are shown as all-capitalized notations; underlined words denote words added after the featured draft; words "striked-through" denote words eliminated after the featured draft; "[New P]" denotes new stanza breaks; "[Del P]" denotes deleting existing stanza break; "[New L]" denotes a new line break; and "[Del L]" denotes the deletion of an existing line break.

Shallow river, shallow river,                    FIRST TWO LINES REVERSED
these stairs are steep ~~deep~~,
one foot, another ~~the other~~,
I ~~pull~~/ gather the hem
of my terrycloth robe .
~~q~~ Q uietly,                                              **A**
gingerly ~~;~~
<u>as</u> if [Del L] an inch [Del L] could sing

~~I would sing~~
for miles —
past the courtyard ,
past the mulberries ,
~~the marble ox~~
~~the terracotta horse~~
~~dead horses~~
~~hoisted from the dead/grave/earth~~
~~(can't whinny)~~
~~past the~~ <u>and</u> Buddha
fragrant with jossticks ,
~~past~~ <u>beneath</u> the Bodhi tree
whose laughter
is unmerciful.
~~the porcelain bowl/birdbath~~
~~mocking the ocean~~
~~the frog's terrain~~
~~is my face~~
~~shimmering~~
~~gaunt, sallow —~~
~~Narcissus~~
~~is thirty three~~
~~today, five~~
~~in dog years~~
~~a twinkle~~
~~in the life of~~
~~a star~~
~~Walk,~~
~~one step, another~~
~~so not to disturb~~
~~They say you must not leave the courtyard~~
~~You must not see~~
~~Gallop,~~ Saunter, gallop,
<u>my pink horses,</u>
<u>my tiny soldiers.</u>
~~One~~ heartbeat, hoofbeat, (another,)
<u>softly,</u>
<u>gingerly,</u>
<u>do not disturb</u>
the nasturtium,
~~so~~ <u>do</u> not ruin
the irises
they ~~you~~ planted ,
<u>And in</u> ~~In~~ the rock garden
the flagstones
~~leads the way~~

**B**

290

~~caress~~ my feet,

~~fit/hug~~ kiss them tenderly.~~/they will deliver me~~

~~I think~~

"Who in the netherworld

walks on my ~~feet~~ soles

as I walk?

~~And~~ ~~Who~~ And opens her black mouth

when I cry?

Whose lutestrings

play my sorrow?

Whose silence

~~rings out~~

undulates

a millenium

[New L] of bells?

~~For whom shall~~ ~~in which all of~~

~~all history shall wallow?~~

~~[New P]~~ [Del P]

This banister

~~painted with red lacqer~~

where my grip turns white.

~~the Wutung trees~~

~~facing west~~

~~(a symbol)s mocks~~

~~of my loneliness~~

~~These~~ the plum blossoms,

and peach trees

~~(stock images)~~ stock signifiers,

~~mocking my own~~ for her ripeness

~~She thinks about~~

~~death~~

~~or the warm blear~~

I cannot taste

~~Flesh remembers~~

~~what the mind resists~~

I think of

love

or the warm blur,

my ~~her~~ mother —

I ~~think~~ remember of death/hate,

~~or he~~ — the hard shape,

~~her~~ my father.

They, slowmoving,

mugworts,

no, water bison,

discuss [Del L] ~~her~~ my future/~~dowry~~

~~How many taels for a new ox donkey/~~
~~How many ____~~
~~How many for a Maytag or a~~
in a fulcrum
of angry gestures.
~~Interpret, interpret.~~
~~hands clenched~~
~~hard roses~~
~~open, slap~~
~~a frond of young palmetto~~
~~loud wails of a lullaby~~
*They shall come,*
*they shall come,*
*they shall come*
*for our tithes.*
She, my grandmother,
oiling her shuttle, cock
sings a lullaby
in an ancient falsetto
~~dry heaves~~
~~taking in all~~
~~the earth can give~~
~~What is the color of the womb?~~
*In the east, a pink sash,*
*a girl has run away*
*from her mother.*
He, my grandfather,
itinerant tinker,
heaves
his massive bellows.
His ember of hope
~~flickers~~ flickering
~~in the village's~~
~~eternal sulperere.~~
at the horizon

[New P] Do you remember,
~~remember~~
the shanty towns,
on the hills of ~~Macao~~ Wanchai,
tin-roofs
crying into the sun?
Do you remember
~~Ah Lan/Auntie Jade~~
mother's first lover
~~throwing (her)~~ hurling a kerosene lamp

into a hovel?
[Del P]
Ooooh, I can smell
the charred sweetness/rancor
in his raven hair.
~~Do you remember~~ The hills ablaze
~~the dry rushes crackling~~
~~the debris~~
~~turning to ash and thin air~~
~~narrow your eyes obtuse Chinese worm~~
with mayflies
and nightblooming jasmine.

[New P] Open the gate,
open,
the gilded facade
of restaurant "Double Happiness."
The man crouched
on the dirty linoleum ~~his restaurant floor~~
fingering dice
is my father.
He ~~said~~ says:
"Meiling, child,
Meiling, don't cry,
~~Meiling~~
I can change ~~my~~ our life
with one strike."

[New P]
Do you know the stare [Del L] of a dead man?                     **D**
My ~~uncle Ox~~ father, the ox,
without his yoke,
sitting on a ridge
~~at~~ of the Quay.
Auntie Jade
remembers:
"Hunger
~~has~~ had spooned [Del L] the flesh
from his cheeks.
His tuft ~~/shock~~
of black hair
was his only movement.
That Chinaman
had no ideals,
no beliefs,
his dreams

were robbed
by the Japanese,
his fortune
was plundered
by the nationalists,

[New P] the communists
seared ~~their~~ his home.
Misery ~~has~~ had propped
him there.
When you pray
to your ancestors
you are praying
to ~~this~~ his hollowness."
Amaduofu, amaduofu—                                    **E**
~~and~~ child, child,
they cried,
"Ten thousand years of history and you have come to this.
Four thousand years of tutelage and you have come to this!"

~~Should~~ Shall I walk
into the new world
in last year's ~~wardrobe~~ pinafore?
Chanel says:
"black, black
is our century's color.
Proper and elegant,
slim silhouette,
daywear and nightwear,
for parties and death,
and deep, deep regret.

~~grief is no longler in fashion.~~
~~terror is mundane —~~

"So you've come home
finally
with ~~a new~~ your new boyfriend.
What is his name?
Ezekiel !
Odd name for a boy.
Your mother can't pronounce it.
And she doesn't like [Del L] his dismeanor.
Too thin, too sallow,
he does not eat beef
in a country

where beef is possible.
He cannot ~~or does not sing~~ play the violin
in a country
where rapture is ~~music/~~ possible ~~/legal.~~
He ~~cannot/does not~~ beams a wry/tawdry smile,
perhaps he is hiding
bad intentions.
And that moon ~~that evening~~
that/which accompanied his arrival,
that Moon won't drink,
and is ~~(naughtily)~~ shaped naughtily
like a woman's severed ~~/white~~ ear."
~~or the golden lotus~~
~~(her foot), the blood dried/pricked~~
~~on the arch~~
~~where the toes meet the bridge~~
~~Once in the courtyard~~
~~the monogamous ducks promised~~
~~everything~~

Something is known,
I said, something
is always
[New L] about to be known
if that something
[New L] is knowable.
"George, perhaps/George, (you should) let her go
~~go walk~~ down to the watermargin.
Let her discover
that which is not there/meaningful
that which is not beautiful.

She can't/won't stray far—
          NOTATIONS DENOTE DELETION OF FIRST 4 LINES
she knows her boundaries,
and besides there is a new fence
now to replace that crumbling wall—
a good lamb won't cross
[New L] ~~to~~ where a pasture
she cannot see; a good lamb
obeys the herd
[New L] and their tendencies.

You are not they,
how do you know
that they are not happy.

295

You are not I,
[New L] how do you know
that I don't know
[New L] that they are unhappy.
You, who is neither fish nor butterfly.

The snake bites her own tail
meaning harmony
at the year's end;
or ~~doesn't~~ does it mean
she is eating herself
into extinction.

O dead prince, O hateful love,
shall we meet again
on the bridge of magpies?
will you kiss me tenderly
where arch meets toe meets ankle,
where dried blood warbles.
Once in the courtyard
the monogamous ducks
promised everything

      NOTES DENOTE DELETION OF
      LAST 3 LINES OF STANZA

"Little bird, little bird,
something escaping . . ."
something escaping."

"The phoenix gone, the terrace empty.
Look, ~~mother says~~ Mei Ling,
yellow crowfeet in the pond,
not lotus, not lily.

Discussion on Changes Between Second Stage: First Draft" and "Second Stage: Sixth Draft:

**A**

Further into her drafting process, Chin begins to consider and reconsider line breaks. She says she uses line breaks to achieve "controlled entropy" in her work. In the case of "The Phoenix Gone, The Terrace Empty," she wanted to provide the "illusion of a natural flow of a river" which meant keeping the lines irregular, just as a river's flow might be interrupted every so often. Chin specifically envisioned the motion of a river gathering waterlilies in its path, so that she deleted previous line breaks between three lines to create a single, "if an inch could sing." Prior to the change the two prior lines and the subsequent lines were all composed of three syllables and Chin wanted to break them up with a new, six-syllable line. The revised section is as follows:

Quietly,

gingerly,

if an inch could sing

I would sing

**B**

Chin deleted the following lines during this stage:

~~the porcelain bowl/birdbath~~

~~mocking the ocean~~

~~the frog's terrain~~

~~is my face~~

~~shimmering~~

~~gaunt, sallow~~

~~Narcissus~~

~~is thirty-three~~

~~today, five~~

~~in dog years~~

~~a twinkle~~

~~in the life of~~

~~a star~~

~~Walk,~~

~~one step, another~~

~~so not to disturb~~

~~They say you must not leave the courtyard~~

~~You must not see~~

The frog reference also evokes a frog poem by Basho:

| | |
|---|---|
| Ancient pond | *Furu ike ya* |
| A frog leaps in, | *Kawazu tobikomu* |
| the sound of water. | *mizu no oto* |

"Basho's poem was the quintessential zen haiku. I liked the reference but I also thought the poem was becoming too cluttered. To make the reference resonate, it must be done perfectly for that zen moment and it didn't work here," she says. "My spirit was embodied in the spirit of the courtesan's walk downward on bound feet and it was too burdensome for her to stop there by the birdbath."

In addition, Chin says she made Narcissus' age to be thirty-three to mirror her age at the time she was writing the poem. "Psychologically, I needed to put the information down to indicate my position in the universe at that point in time; it was a piece of scaffolding that I eventually deleted as I later realized it was not necessary for the poem," she explains.

**C**

In another example of "scaffolding" that she would later deem unnecessary, Chin eliminated the lines shown below referencing "ox," "donkey" and "Maytag":

~~How many taels for a new ox donkey/~~
~~How many _____~~
~~How many for a Maytag or a~~
in a fulcrum
of angry gestures.
~~Interpret, interpret.~~
~~hands clenched~~
~~hard roses~~
~~open, slap~~
~~a frond of young palmetto~~
~~loud wails of a lullaby~~
*They shall come,*
*they shall come,*
*they shall come*
*for our tithes.*
She, my grandmother,
oiling her shuttle, cock
sings a lullaby
in an ancient falsetto
~~dry heaves~~
~~taking in all~~
~~the earth can give~~
~~What is the color of the womb?~~
*In the east, a pink sash,*
*a girl has run away*
*from her mother.*
He, my grandfather,
itinerant tinker,
heaves
his massive bellows.
His ember of hope
~~flickers~~ flickering
~~in the village's~~
~~eternal sulpercre.~~
at the horizon

"Ox is in my Chinese lexicon for working class Chinese which is my people, my family. The ox is a toiling animal, a beast of burden. I needed to dissolve from the courtesan image toward village vignettes with my family as characters — a transition from 'high art' down to folks. But sometimes, we put words as 'markers' which I find I don't need later. This is the same idea with Maytag reference which I had used to switch from historical to familiar," says Chin.

Nevertheless, though the "markers" were deleted, Chin says they served their use of helping to make a seamless transition from the courtesan image to the village folk reference. "I believe transitions should be seamless unless you wish to make a bang," says Chin.

In addition, the insertion of *"They shall come,/ they shall come,/ they shall come/ for our tithes."* exemplify Chin's use of an "incantatory rhythm" in writing her poems. She also wanted to vary the rhythm in the poem to give it musical texture.

**D**

In her earlier draft, Chin had written the poem by trying to camouflage references to her mother and father with, respectively, an aunt and an uncle. In this stage of drafting, she changed the references to mother and father.

"In poems like this with a big historical drama, there is a symbolic or mythical level. In Shakespeare's 'high tragedy' the heroes were all princes and overlords, just as in Chinese drama the characters were usually in the emperor's family and references were made to court intrigues and members of the court. But as a socialist ideal I move the focus to the village. When I put in the aunt and uncle references, I was trying to work out the narrative of the poem. But I realized that no matter how I try to disguise them, the references were really versions of my mother and grandmother. Even the courtesan is a version of my mother; she is someone who is victimized by social and political circumstances. We all try to overcome the damages that happen in early childhood," she says. "Students — especially Asian or Asian American students — tell me that it's difficult for them to write about their parents, especially if their parents are still living. That's where courage comes from. At some point in our art, we need to address the people we need to address."

**E**

*"Amaduofu, amaduofu"* is a reference to Buddha and a Buddhist chant. The reference, along with the parallel couplet, "Ten thousand years of history and you have come to this./ Four thousand years of tutelage and you have come to this!" also work to provide the incantatory flow that breaks the smooth rhythm of the piece.

—⁓—

Changes from Second Stage:  Sixth Draft and Final Draft

The draft featured below shows some of Chin's process as she adjusted the "Second Stage: Sixth Draft" to reach the "Final Draft" that was the title poem in her 1994 book. Underlined words denote words added after the featured draft; words "striked-through" denote words eliminated after the featured draft; "[New P]" denotes new stanza breaks; "[Del P]" denotes deleting an existing stanza break; "[New L]" denotes a new line break; and "[Del L]" denotes deleting an existing line break.

Shallow river, shallow river,

these stairs are steep,

one foot, another,

I gather the hem

of my terry-cloth robe.

Quietly,

gingerly

~~as~~ if an inch could sing

I would sing

for miles —

past the courtyard,

past the mulberries,

~~and Buddha~~

past the Bodhi tree

fragrant with jossticks,

past the Buddha

~~beneath the Bodhi tree~~

whose laughter [Del L] is unmerciful.

Saunter, ~~gallop,~~

my pink horses,

my tiny soldiers.

heartbeat, hoofbeat, ~~(another,)~~

softly,

gingerly,

do not disturb

the nasturtium,

do not ruin [Del L] the irises

they planted.

~~And in~~ In the rock garden

the flagstones

caress my feet,

kiss them tenderly.


[New P]"Who in the netherworld [Del L] walks on my soles

as I walk?

And opens her black mouth

when I cry?

Whose lutestrings

play my sorrow?

Whose silence

undulates

a millenium

of bells

in which

all of history
shall wallow?

[New P] This banister
painted with red lacquer
where
[New L] my grip turns white.
These ~~The~~ plum blossoms,
~~and peach trees~~
stock signifiers,
mocking my own ~~for her~~ ripeness
I cannot taste .
Flesh remembers
what the mind resists.
I think of
love
or the warm blur,
my mother —
I remember of ~~death/~~hate,
the hard shape,
my father.
They, slow-moving,
mugworts,
no, water bison,
discuss my future
in a fulcrum
of angry gestures.
*They shall come,*
*~~they shall come,~~*
*they shall come*
*for our tithes.*
She, my grandmother,
oiling her shuttle, ~~cock~~
sings a lullaby
in an ancient falsetto .
*In the east, a pink sash,*
*a girl has run away*
*from her mother.*
He, my grandfather,
itinerant tinker,
heaves
his massive bellows.
His ember of hope [Del L] flickering
in the village's
eternal sepulchre.
~~at the horizon~~

[Del P] Do you remember ~~;~~
the shanty towns ~~;~~
on the hills of Wanchai,
tin-roofs
crying into the sun?
Do you remember
mother's first lover
hurling
[Del L] a kerosene ~~lamp~~
into a hovel?
Ooooh, I can smell
the charred sweetness~~/rancor~~
in his raven hair.
The hills ablaze
with mayflies
and night-blooming jasmine.

Open the gate,
open,
the gilded facade
of restaurant "Double Happiness."
The man crouched
on the dirty linoleum
fingering dice
is my father.
He says:
"~~Mei Ling,~~ Mei Ling, child,
~~Mei Ling,~~ , Mei Ling, don't cry,
I can change our ~~life~~ lives
with one strike."

Do you know the stare
[New L] of a dead man?
My father ~~;~~ the ox,
without his yoke,
sitting on a ridge
of the ~~Quay~~ quay.
Auntie Jade
remembers:
"Hunger
had spooned
[New L] the flesh
from his cheeks.
His tuft
of black hair
was his only movement.

That Chinaman
had no ideals,
no beliefs,
his dreams
were robbed
by the Japanese,
his fortune
was plundered
by the nNationalists,
[Del P] the ~~The~~ communists
seared his home.
Misery had propped
him there.
When you pray
to your ancestors
you are praying
to his hollowness."
*Amaduofu, amaduofu*—
child, child,
they cried,
"Ten thousand years of history and you have come to this.
Four thousand years of tutelage and you have come to this!"

Shall I walk
into the new world
in last year's pinafore?
Chanel says:
" black, black
is our century's color.
Proper and elegant,
slim silhouette,
daywear and nightwear,
for parties and death,
and deep, deep regret.

"So you've come home
finally
with your new boyfriend.
What is his name?
Ezekiel!
Odd name for a boy.
Your mother can't pronounce it.
And she doesn't like
[New L] his demeanor ~~dismeanor~~.
Too thin, too sallow,
he does not eat beef

in a country
where beef is possible.
He cannot play the violin
in a country
where rapture is possible.
He beams a ~~wry~~/tawdry smile,
perhaps he is hiding
bad intentions.
And that ~~m~~Moon
~~that/~~which accompanied his arrival,
that Moon won't drink,
and is shaped naughtily
like a woman's severed ear."

~~Something is known,~~                                          **B**
~~I said, something~~
~~is always~~
~~about to be known~~
~~if that something~~
~~is knowable.~~
~~"George, perhaps/George, (you should) let her go~~
~~down to the watermargin.~~
~~Let her discover~~
~~that which is not there/meaningful~~
~~that which is not beautiful.~~

~~She can't/won't stray far —~~
~~she knows her boundaries,~~
~~and besides there is a new fence~~
~~now to replace that crumbling wall —~~
~~a good lamb won't cross~~
~~where a pasture~~
~~she cannot see; a good lamb~~
~~obeys the herd~~
~~and their tendencies.~~

~~You are not they,~~
~~how do you know~~
~~that they are not happy.~~
~~You are not I,~~
~~how do you know~~
~~that I don't know~~
~~that they are unhappy.~~
~~You, who is neither fish nor butterfly.~~

The snake bites her own tail

meaning harmony [Del L] at the year's end ~~;~~ .
~~or~~ Or does it mean
she is eating herself
into extinction ~~.~~ ?

~~O~~ Oh dead prince, ~~O~~ Oh hateful love,
shall we meet again
on the bridge of magpies?
~~W~~will you kiss me tenderly
where arch meets toe meets ankle,
where dried blood warbles ~~.~~ ?
~~Once in the courtyard~~
~~the monogamous ducks~~
~~promised everything~~

~~—~~" *Little bird, little bird,*
*something escaping* ~~——"~~
*something escaping~~—"~~* . . .

~~—~~" *The phoenix gone, the terrace empty.*
*Look, Mei Ling,*
*yellow crowfeet in the pond,*
*not lotus, not lily.*

## Discussion on Changes Between "Second Stage: Sixth Draft" and Final Draft:

**A**

Chin added an epigraph in Chinese characters which is translated into English as "The river flows without ceasing."

"While I was studying classical Chinese in Taiwan, I wrote down my favorite lines and this epigraph must have come from the *Book of Songs*. What I loved about this epigraph is that the three simple strokes (of the Chinese character for river) evoked a pictograph of a river," she explains.

Chin adds, "It's hard to do a pictograph of a poem in English. It's too corny, like when we had that 'concrete poetry' stage or Robert Indiana's 'Love' — the shape of the piece literally spells out the poem. But in the shape of the Chinese epigraph I was trying to show the flowing of a river and this is very easy because there is a visual element to all Chinese characters, anyway."

Though epigraphs sometimes move Chin to "bring forth a wonderful poem," she also has a "store-room" of beloved lines that Chin keeps and which she looks to include in her work — as was the case with "The river flows without ceasing." "Poetry is about precision and I think things in a poem should snap together beautifully. I chop away at lines and boldly get rid of all excess. But I tell my students, don't throw away the good lines; use them at a later date."

**B**

Towards the end of the poem, Chin added the following lines during the "Second Stage: Sixth Draft" which she subsequently deleted for "Final Draft":

> Something is known,
> I said, something
> is always
> about to be known
> if that something
> is knowable.
> "George, perhaps/George, (you should) let her go
> down to the watermargin.
> Let her discover
> that which is not there/meaningful
> that which is not beautiful.
>
> She can't/won't stray far—
> she knows her boundaries,
> and besides there is a new fence
> now to replace that crumbling wall—
> a good lamb won't cross
> where a pasture
> she cannot see; a good lamb
> obeys the herd
> and their tendencies.
>
> You are not they,
> how do you know
> that they are not happy.
> You are not I,
> how do you know
> that I don't know
> that they are unhappy.
> You, who is neither fish nor butterfly.

"George is my father. I directly named him to move the poem towards a personal direction, away from a historical image of the patriarchal oppression of the courtesan. On the familial level, the poem is about my father oppressing my mother. Once you name a person, the mystery is dispelled. But this was another type of marker. He's like the 'Maytag'," Chin explains, before laughingly adding. "It's terrible to compare my father to 'Maytag' or 'donkey' but he is taking a lot of beating in this poem."

Chin deleted the next stanza containing the reference to "a good lamb" because she considered it a "regressive voice." She explains, "My Mother was passive and I recognized that same passivity in myself that I despise."

The next stanza is from one of Chin's favorite philosophers, Chuangtzu. "One of the anecdotes about him is where one of his acolytes says, 'Chuangtzu, you are not a fish; how do you know how a fish feels?' And he replies, 'You are not Chuangtzu; how do you know how Chuangtzu feels?' "

"So here, I'm dwelling on my parents' happiness but it's also about consciousness," Chin continues. "How do we really know how our mothers feel? As poets, aren't we taking poetic license?

"This is the basic thesis of my work: my mother was destroyed by my father — the poet needs to address and reconcile with this truth. As writers, we also embody other voices. It was a moment of questioning the poem's role as a conduit of other women's voices. I want the integrity of voice, the gathering of lilies, but we know that all the voices are really my mother's. So I question consciousness — whether we really know what other people's voices are," Chin says, "given that our personal urgencies often dominate the Muse."

The second-guessing — the questioning of poetic license — seems appropriate. It displays the same care that created a Muse concerned about the suffering of women, the kind of sensitivity displayed in both Chin's subjects and technique.

—◊—

The following is the poem's Final Draft:

**The Phoenix Gone, The Terrace Empty**

# 川　流　不　息
*The river flows without ceasing.*


Shallow river, shallow river,
these stairs are steep,
one foot, another,
I gather the hem
of my terry-cloth robe.
Quietly,
gingerly
if an inch could sing
I would sing
for miles —
past the courtyard,
past the mulberries,
past the Bodhi tree
fragrant with jossticks,
past the Buddha
whose laughter is unmerciful.
Saunter,

my pink horses,
my tiny soldiers.
heartbeat, hoofbeat,
softly,
gingerly,
do not disturb
the nasturtium,
do not ruin the irises
they planted.
In the rock garden
the flagstones
caress my feet,
kiss them tenderly.

"Who in the netherworld walks on my soles
as I walk?
And opens her black mouth
when I cry?
Whose lutestrings
play my sorrow?
Whose silence
undulates
a millenium
of bells
in which
all of history
shall wallow?

This banister
painted with red lacquer
where
my grip turns white.
These plum blossoms,
stock signifiers,
mocking my own ripeness
I cannot taste.
Flesh remembers
what the mind resists.
I think of
love
or the warm blur,
my mother —
I remember of hate,
the hard shape,
my father.
They, slow moving,

mugworts,
no, water bison,
discuss my future
in a fulcrum
of angry gestures.
*They shall come,*
*they shall come*
*for our tithes.*
She, my grandmother,
oiling her shuttle,
sings a lullaby
in an ancient falsetto,
*In the east, a pink sash,*
*a girl has run away*
*from her mother.*
He, my grandfather,
itinerant tinker,
heaves
his massive bellows.
His ember of hope flickering
in the village's
eternal sepulchre.
Do you remember
the shanty towns
on the hills of Wanchai,
tin-roofs
crying into the sun?
Do you remember
mother's first lover
hurling
a kerosene
into a hovel?
Ooooh, I can smell
the charred sweetness
in his raven hair.
The hills ablaze
with mayflies
and night-blooming jasmine.

Open the gate,
open,
the gilded facade
of restaurant "Double Happiness."
The man crouched
on the dirty linoleum
fingering dice

is my father.
He says:
"Mei Ling, child,
Mei Ling, don't cry,
I can change our lives
with one strike."

Do you know the stare
of a dead man?
My father the ox,
without his yoke,
sitting on a ridge
of the quay.
Auntie Jade
remembers:
"Hunger
had spooned
the flesh
from his cheeks.
His tuft
of black hair
was his only movement.
That Chinaman
had no ideals,
no beliefs,
his dreams
were robbed
by the Japanese,
his fortune
was plundered
by the Nationalists,
the Communists
seared his home.
Misery had propped
him there.
When you pray
to your ancestors
you are praying
to his hollowness."
*Amaduofu, amaduofu—*
child, child,
they cried,
"Ten thousand years of history and you have come to this.
Four thousand years of tutelage and you have come to this!"

Shall I walk
into the new world
in last year's pinafore?
Chanel says:
black, black
is our century's color.
Proper and elegant,
slim silhouette,
daywear and nightwear,
for parties and death,
and deep, deep regret.

"So you've come home
finally
with your new boyfriend.
What is his name?
Ezekiel!
Odd name for a boy.
Your mother can't pronounce it.
And she doesn't like
his demeanor.
Too thin, too sallow,
he does not eat beef
in a country
where beef is possible.
He cannot play the violin
in a country
where rapture is possible.
He beams a tawdry smile,
perhaps he is hiding
bad intentions.
And that Moon
which accompanied his arrival,
that Moon won't drink,
and is shaped naughtily
like a woman's severed ear."

The snake bites her own tail
meaning harmony at the year's end.
Or does it mean
she is eating herself
into extinction?

Oh dead prince, Oh hateful love,
shall we meet again
on the bridge of magpies?

Will you kiss me tenderly
where arch meets toe meets ankle,
where dried blood warbles?

*Little bird, little bird,*
*something escaping,*
*something escaping . . .*

*The phoenix gone, the terrace empty.*
*Look, Mei Ling,*
*yellow crowfeet in the pond,*
*not lotus, not lily.*

# GARRETT HONGO

Garrett Hongo was born in Volcano, Hawai'i where he completed a memoir titled *Volcano* (Knopf, 1995). He has written two poetry collections, *Yellow Light* (Wesleyan, 1982) and *The River of Heaven* (Knopf, 1988); the latter was the Lamont Poetry Selection of the Academy of American Poets and a finalist for the Pulitzer Prize. His other awards include fellowships from the National Endowment of the Arts, the Rockefeller Foundation and the Guggenheim Foundation. He edited *The Open Boat: Poems from Asian America* (Anchor, 1993); *Songs My Mother Taught Me: Stories, Plays and a Memoir By Wakako Yamauchi* (The Feminist Press, 1993); and *Under Western Eyes* (Anchor, 1995). He is currently professor at the University of Oregon where he was director of the Program in Creative Writing from 1989-1993.

In response to the question, "What advice would you give to a young poet?" Garrett Hongo responds:

> Seek learning, treasure inspiration, find a teacher to help you question what is base and be loyal to the heavenly.

# Garrett Hongo: *Feeling* Knowing, Knowing *Feeling*

*I will arise a go now, for always night and day*
*I hear lake water lapping with low sounds by the shore;*
*While I stand on the roadway, or on the pavements gray,*
*I hear it in the deep heart's core.*
— *William Butler Yeats*

Garrett Hongo wishes he has more time for poetry.

"The person who writes poems," says Hongo, "is the type of person I want to be.  But I don't have the life that allows me to be a poet most of the time.

"It's not easy.  To try to remember to be the type of person who writes poetry is more work than the act of writing poetry."

When Hongo refers to how a busy life in academia imposes time and other constraints on his preferred endeavor, one is reminded of why he loves to visit Hawai'i, far from many elements that distract him from his poetic "soul" and whose beauty inspires passion.  In his memoir, *Volcano* (Knopf, 1995), he describes one return:

I stepped off the plane, and when the full blast of the island's erotic and natal wind hit me, when I caught sight of Mauna Loa's purple slopes disappearing into clouds, a sob of gratitude filled my chest and choked my throat.  I wept and felt like falling to my knees in daedal mimicry of my soul's Icarus. . . .I tell you, my heart gave itself over to the roiling cloud of feeling at that moment.  I think I gave up detachment.

For Hongo, it is easier to be a poet when he has given up "detachment" for his poetry is about *feeling*.  Featured below are the original journal entries that birthed four of Hongo's poems.  What is interesting about these works is how resonance — what Hongo calls *feeling* — already shimmers from the raw passages.

Despite their unfinished state, the works glow with what Hongo describes (in *The Open Boat:  Poems From Asian America* ("OB") (Anchor Books, 1993) as poetry's nature:  "If there is something to me that I would call the salient characteristic of poetry — contemporary or otherwise, Donegal or Singapore English, songs from a Kearny Street Pinoy or sonnets from a South Hadley, Massachusetts Yank — I'd say it was this *sprezzatura* of consciousness and sound I feel in my bones and in my throat and my breast and my loins when I hear or read the work that moves me and turns me gay, yet fills my eyes with tears."

"For (my) . . . voice I've tried to train. . ., it has been a *feeling* for language and its beauty that has brought me to poetry and kept me at it.  I enjoy the sound of the language raised in quiet passion, the finish of sentient attention on a line of free or formal verse, the rich patina of elegant syntax and coloraturas of dense accentuals sliding into the syncopated rhythms of common speech. . . . Like musicians and traditional singers, the poets I admire most love to make a sound and perhaps love making it as much or more than any creation of what used to be called meaning."

Hongo is expanding on a theme he learned years ago as a young student of the poet Bert Meyers.  In his memoir, Hongo describes in a chapter titled "Self-Portrait" his first day of studying with Meyers at Pomona College:

A man with long blond hair and puckered face that gathered down to a ginger beard introduced the topic of Walt Whitman and his homosexuality. A woman with long, braided brown hair, smelling of patchouli oil, cited some critics and a few discussions she'd been involved in at a writers' conference in Vermont that past summer. I felt awe at how complicated their acquaintanceship with the subject was, how *socialized.* I'd barely begun to *read* poetry, let alone discuss it with adults in a public place.

(Meyers) said 'That's bullshit,' then proceeded to provide us with an extended critique of this particular *journalistic* and decidedly unliterary approach to the discussion of Whitman. He said that Whitman was a *poet* who may have been gay, who may not have been gay, who might have been multi-sexual or bisexual or nonsexual, but what was important about him was that he had this *feeling* for humankind, for the wounded dying in the Union hospitals, for the *workers* and *builders* and *teamsters* and for *women* that compelled him to write a strange, prosaic, but chantlike nonmetric verse, slightly imitative of what he thought *Indian* vedic scripture was like, slightly imitative of what he thought Native American *storytelling* and cermonial *chant* were like, and taking off on what he'd vaguely heard about as *vers libre* from the French; borrowing certain common American *religious* ideas; joining all of them to what he felt was the elite fashion of literary Transcendentalism; and from *that,* he Walt Whitman, a newspaperman and profound sentimentalist, had accomplished the building, along with Emily Dickinson, a spinster, of what had come to us as our *American* poetry. Homosexuality was *not* the issue, nor was *heterosexuality.* It was *poetry* that was the issue and he, Meyers, would not allow our discussions to be turned over to whatever fashionable or scholarly controversies had arisen to divert attention away from what was important. *Poetry was poetry,* he said, and although gay rights and women's rights and minority rights were important, it was *poetic content* and *poetic style* and *poetic tradition* which we would emphasize, and not the social controversies, not the debunking and not the dismissing.

*Feeling.* Hongo is a man who feels passionately, as evidenced by what inspires his poems and how, in subsequent development, he enhances resonance with technique. With his poetry-in-progress works below, Hongo explores the *feeling* behind four stories that have touched him: what could have happened in Seattle's Astor Hotel on the day the Japanese bombed Pearl Harbor; a man remembering his father and grandfather; a house in the Hawai'ian town of Volcano; and the tale of one Filipino immigrant and his family during the early 20th century.

There is a poetic synergy between Hongo's topics and poetic desire to explore *feeling.* That he cares clearly about his stories enhances the passion of his craft. Indeed, during the early 1980s (at about the time he wrote the first poem mentioned below), he said in *Breaking Silence, An Anthology of Contemporary Asian American Poets* (The Greenfield Review Press, 1983), "For me, poetry has been a way towards self-definition and the engagement of an imagined community. More and more, though, I'd like it to become a way of mystery and syncretic metaphysics, beautiful to write, read and hear spoken aloud. . . ."

*BLACK LIGHTNING* presents four examples of Hongo's poetic efforts to be the type of person he really wants to be — a poet:

- "On The Last Performance of *Musume Dojoji* at the Nippon Kan of the Astor Hotel, Seattle, Washington"

- "O-Bon: Dance For The Dead"
- "Volcano House"
- "*Pinoy* at the Coming World"

The final version of the first poem may be read in Hongo's 1982 book, *Yellow Light* (Wesleyan, 1982); the final versions of the other poems are included in his 1988 book, *The River of Heaven* (Knopf, 1988).

*(Editing Marks: strikethroughs = deletions; [New L] = new line break; capitalized instructions describe Hongo's notes to himself in his journals)*

**I.**    **On The Last Performance of *Musume Dojōji* at the Nippon Kan of the Astor Hotel, Seattle, Washington**

Hongo recalls that he wrote this poem after meeting an elderly *Nisei* (second generation Japanese immigrant) woman who was once an *odori* dancer. The dancer told Hongo that she happened to be in the middle of a dance when the Japanese bombed Pearl Harbor. Hongo visited the Astor Hotel to try to imagine what it would have been like during the last performance of *Musume Dojōji* , a 14th century Noh play (in which a jealous woman pursues a monk and turns into a snake) which has been transformed into a play featuring the "odori" style of Japanese dance. From his visit, he imagined a story that he developed through a poem.

January 26, 1980 Original Journal Entry:

On the Last Performance of Musume Dojōji at the Nippon Kan
of the Astor Hotel, Seattle, 1941

dedicated to Tama Tokuda

Something still remains
from the fall of '41
~~in the old Astor Hotel~~
in the theater of the Astor Hotel,
~~boarded~~
in its windows shuttered with planking,
in the floorboards greening with mold;
in a stable of old programs ~~yellowing~~ yellowed
in the darkness of a backstage dressing room,
in a photograph of the cast
curling and peeling loose from its paper.
~~The w~~
The bouquet of ~~yellow~~ mauve and violet chrysanthemums
[that] the ~~young grocer~~ thin butcher brought for the girl
who danced the legend at <u>Musume Dojōji</u>
~~has withered long ago and turned to dust~~
has withered and turned to a chalky dust,

forgotten on a small mirror-stand
beside an open tray of make-up
~~that petrifies~~ petrifies white greasepaint.
that itself ~~has petrified long ago.~~
~~When you come in, with lead by the~~
When you come in probing your way
by the long ~~yellow~~ tube of yellow light
~~from your flesh,~~
streaming out from your hand you smell the years
rocking back from their graves
in the pile of broken chairs
stacked against the back wall
under the overhang of the balcony.
Small puffs of gray ~~dust &~~ powder bloom
under your shoes, ~~with each step~~
~~you take and~~ roll away behind you
~~like soft~~
like a tribe of ~~gentle~~ dust-devils
swirling into life and dying back
~~into nothing~~
into the nothing you begin to hear
~~speak to you as you approach the stage~~
speaking as you approach the stage.

A flute whistles, a tensed hand smacks
at the tuned hide of a small drum,
and voices strum through the plastered walls
in ~~the~~ a plain song of ~~a~~ the slow adagio
~~rolling out from all you know~~
~~of the past and what it never~~
rolling out from all you never knew
of the past and its privacy.

you begin to ~~sing~~ hum your own ~~song~~ tune,
a tentative blues from Brahms
or maybe something you picked up
in a piano bar on King Street
late at night [after the ~~Obon Festival~~ Festival For The Dead]
and drinking <u>sake</u> with friends*, (MOVE BRACKETED WORDS TO AFTER "FRIENDS")*
and it's better now because
you've gotten up the steps downstage,
~~and stand against the world~~
~~and~~
stand facing the cinderblock wall
~~behind the~~
~~behind the curtain splotched with mildew~~

~~scarred with names and dates~~
~~and forgotten jokes that no one understands~~
~~and arcane~~
~~an~~
scarred with a huge arcana of names
and dates and old jokes
~~no one ever laughed about even theirs~~
no one cared to laugh at even theirs.

This is okay, you say to yourself,
this doesn't mean any more
than Minoru Izumi, 1938
than Sanford Hayase Kisses Ass,
than Japtown Is My Town China Stay Out;
and the dead don't mind
that ~~I've~~ you've never washed a gravestone
~~or left flowers for them~~

~~when it mattered or~~

or left flowers or lit incense
or paid for a priest to chant
~~for them~~ when it might have mattered.

~~Listen~~

~~What's here~~

She comes from the wings on

She comes gliding on cloth slippers
of blue silk, stepping out from behind
~~the damask curtain in the other side~~
~~the damask~~
the flag of damask cloth curtain
~~that curtains the wing theater's far wing.~~
that curtains the ~~other wing of the stage~~.
Her hair trails out behind her,
~~in a long black~~
in a long tangle like ~~black surf~~ jet-black surf
spilling ~~from~~ over the white of her neck
~~and down~~ and over the folds of her robe
~~foaming~~
~~churning on the sand colored~~
~~churning~~
~~rippling on the sands of the stage.~~

~~Her image~~
~~The~~
~~churning~~
rushing over the dry shore of the stages
Something howls in the throat
of history as she snakes out
of the layers and ~~layers~~ latticework

Of her gown ~~and stands standing~~ and stands before you
~~naked as a~~
naked as a matchflame flickering
~~in the warm air of your breathing,~~
~~claiming~~, under the warm breath from your mouth,
~~and claims you as her son.~~
claiming you and all you own as hers.


"Mimosa Izume - 1938," "Sanford Hayase Kisses Ass," and "Japtown Is My Town China Stay Out!" refer to Hongo's observations of graffiti written on the walls behind the stage of the Astor Hotel.


Final Version

The poem's final title is "On the Last Performance of *Musume Dojōji* at the Nippon Kan of the Astor Hotel, Seattle, Washington."  Given the reference to 1941 on the second line of the first stanza, Hongo felt the title no longer need reference the year.

The Final Version contains 82 lines compared to the 76 lines of Hongo's journal entry.  To determine diction and where the final line breaks should occur, Hongo says that he reads a poem to an audience (e.g. Cynthia Thiessen and Wakako Yamauchi during the 1980s) to work out the final rhythm of a poem.

"It never works to just read a poem to yourself.  I read it out loud to friends to sense their reactions, too," Hongo says.

As an example, the poem's last stanza in the Final Version reads as follows — in a more punchy version than Hongo's journal entry:

She glides on slippers of blue silk,
stepping from behind the flag of damask
that curtains the theater's far wing.
Her hair trails behind her,
spilling over the white blaze of her neck
and down the folds of her robe
in a long tangle across the stage.
Something howls in his throat,
choirs like memory as she snakes
out of her gown
and stands before him, naked
as the match flame flickering out
under the warm breath of a word.

## O-bon: Dance For The Dead

The poem was originally titled "O-Bon: Remembering The Dead." Hongo said he changed the title because "remembrance" is self-evident in the poem. In addition, he says, the new title "sounds better." Hongo calls the change an example of "rhythmic revision" — just as, Hongo suggests, when William Butler Yeats experimented with the following three passages in trying to determine the appropriate rhythm for the first line of his poem, "The Lake Isle of Innisfree."

> "I will rise and go to Innisfree."

> *then,*

> "I will rise and go now and go to Innisfree."

> *then what became the final version,*

> "I will arise and go now, and go to Innisfree."


September 22, 1986 Original Journal Entry

> I have no memories or photograph
> of my father coming home from war,
> thin as a caneworker, a splinter of flesh
> in his olive greens and khakis and
> > spit-shined G.I. shoes,

> Or of my ~~mother~~ grandfather in ~~her~~ his flower-print
> half-tone trousers and idiogrammed ~~skirt~~ shirt
> and ~~rotted white furoshiki holding back~~
> tied to hold back ~~her glossy hair~~
> ~~as she hoed the~~ the sweat
> as ~~she~~ he bent ~~to hoe and weed the garden~~ in the garden to weed
> ~~in the vegetable garden~~ that Sunday
> ~~as the~~
> as swarms of planes manouevered overhead;

> I have no memories of the radio that day
> Or the clatter of machetes in the Filipino camp,
> The long wail of news over the mountains,
> > ~~from Honolulu,~~
> or the glimmerings and sheaths ~~of fear~~
> > of fear in the village.

> I have no story to tell about lacquer shrines
> or filial ashes, about a small brass bell

and incense smoldering in a jade bowl,

about the shining black face of Miroku,

[Buddha of Apocalypse] gleaming w/ detachment,

the crown of anthuriums ~~behind his~~ in the stone vase,

hearts and red wheels of fire behind her.


And though ~~I~~ I've mapped made the ~~long~~ strike march

from North Shore to town in 1921,

and though I've never sang psalms at festival,


~~sprinkled w/~~

or dipped the bamboo cup ~~ladle~~ in the stone bowl,

on the Day of the Dead though

I've never ~~pitched a coin through the slit~~ pitched a coin or took my turn

~~of the cedar box~~, folded ~~while~~

at the taiko drum, ~~a~~ paper fortunes

and strung them on the *hala* tree;


Though I've made a life ~~in exile~~

and raised my house oceans ~~to the east~~

                              east of my birth,

though I've craned my neck and cocked my ear

for the sound of flute and *shamisen*

jangling its tune of bitterness and woe—

more than ~~the memory of men~~ memory or the image of

                    ~~memory and~~ the slant of grey rain

pounding ~~on the of thatch~~ the coats and ~~hats peaked~~

                              peaked hats

of townsmen racing across a blond

                    arch of the bridge,


more than the past and its aches and brocade

~~its dry month of people and~~

of tales and ritual, its dry month of repetition,


~~I have always loved the word~~

I want the cold stone in my hand

to pound the rice, I want the splash

of cool or steaming water to watch my feet,

I want the ~~corpse to rise and sing its song~~ dead beside me when I dance,

~~snicker and to tell it it's all right~~

to help me flesh the notes of my song,

to tell me it's all right.

<u>Final Version</u>

Some of the changes Hongo made to reach the Final Version included line breaks in the first stanza to affect rhythm:

I have no memories or photograph of my father
coming home from war, thin as a caneworker,
a splinter of flesh in his olive greens
and khakis and spit-shined G.I. shoes.

The second stanza required more work to narrow its focus and ended up as follows:

Or of my grandfather in his flower-print shirt,
humming his bar-tunes, tying the bandana
to his head to hold the sweat back from his face
as he bent to weed and hoe the garden that Sunday
while swarms of planes manoeuvered overhead.

A comparison of the two versions of the second stanza also depicts Hongo's change in reference from "mother" to "grandfather" — a move that reflects Hongo's real-life circumstance at the time when his father and grandfather died within a month-and-a-half of each other.


**III.**                **Volcano House**

Hongo dedicated "Volcano House" to Charles Wright who was one of his poetry teachers when he attended University of California at Irvine in 1978-1980.  In his memoir, Hongo describes Wright as a favorite teacher among the students and "as a gentle and soft-spoken imagist."

"Charles is a white Southern poet and a great landscape poet.  I understood something about Charles and his love of landscape while I was in Volcano.  I felt a connection to something that his poems are about:  a certain calming feeling, not violent, but a calming feeling," Hongo recalls.


<u>September 25, 1986 Original Journal Entry</u>:

Mists [swaddle]/in the lantern ferns, green wings
furling against the [chill]/cold and a mountain wind
starts its low moan through ~~the~~ 'ōhi'a trees.
The lava land blazes in [fuschia,] primrose, and thimbleberry,
~~lasiandra~~
~~swaying(?) their fleshy bells in the soft rain~~
~~their~~ scented fires of pink and blue
racing through the ~~underbrush and~~ jungled underbrush.
I'm out feeding chickens, slopping a garbage _____
of melon seeds ~~[New L]~~ and rind [New L] over the broken stones and woodrot of the forest
path.

*DELETE THIS SECTION*

Kilauea steams and vents through its sulphurous roads

~~in _____ (?) in the distance~~

miles in the distance, huts and rumblings

       *END OF DELETED SECTION*

I'm ~~singing~~ humming ~~some~~ a [dumb] blues, some old song about Chinese Nights

~~and a lover back in my/the hometown~~

and ~~ridi(ng)~~ boarding a junk, taking me from my village.

Miles in the distance, Kīlauea steams and vents

through its sulphurous roads; And Sunlight spills

through a faultline in the clouds, ~~gathering~~ glazing

~~on the cracked~~

on the slick wet beaks of the chickens, shining

~~on the falling~~

~~on the falling rain like _____ (?) pearls~~

in their eyes like ~~the phosphorescence~~

            the phosphorous glow from a cave

tunneled miles through the earth. What was my face

before I was born? The white mask and black teeth

~~glimmering~~ at the bottom of the [lotus] pond?

~~Who said the sea and who shapes the whole~~

~~that flings itself~~

What is the ~~first question~~ mind's insensible ~~and~~ the gateless gate?

Through [the] overgrowth at and the drizzle through

the pile and [the] dump of tree fern and the indigoed snare

of lasiandra shedding its collars of sadness

by the broken [bamboo] fence, I make my way

down a narrow path to the absolute

and the house of my last days, a ~~script~~ dazzle of light

~~shimmering~~ scripting on the leaves *[New L]* and on the weeds,

tremours in the shivering trees.


In his memoir, Hongo remembers his return to Volcano, the town in Hawai'i where he was born. He describes the "relentlessly spectacular landscape" below the summit of the Kīlauea volcano, including the " ʻŌhiʻa " tree, which he references in his poem:

Of all the plants I was trying to get familiar with, it was the ʻŌhiʻa , a species of myrtle with the scientific name *Metrosideros* polymorpha ("heart of iron with many forms"), that was the most important tree in Volcano's rain forest. ʻŌhiʻa . . . was everywhere around me — out in the front and back yards in little stands of saplings, as mature trees sixteen to more than eighty feet tall in the deep forests forming their upper canopies, as seedlings in little perched botanical colonies in a patch of butchy green hair among mosses and worts colonizing on the wet stump of a fallen tree or growing epiphytically at the top of the trunk of a host *hāpuʻu*. . . .

I loved the way ʻōhiʻa looked, whether carved or corded, living or in senescence and dieback, in silvery branches stretching up to a blue cerulean canopy of sky by Volcano's dump and transfer station, remnants of a five-acre burn in '87. 'Ōhi'a like the long digits of powder-white finger coral fronding up from a black reef. I liked the wind-shimmered leaves of 'ōhi'a in the sunny three o'clock afternoons, green coins mullioned in the slanting light of a mustard-yellow sun, and I liked the gray Rip Van Winkle beard of aboveground roots balling and shrouding down from an old sentinel trunk alongside Crater Rim Drive near Kilauea Iki.

Hongo's memoir contains the real-life inspiration for many poems in *The River of Heaven*, including "Volcano House." It is particularly worth reading "Lasiandra: A Tale" in *Volcano* which expands on one of the lines in the poem, "of lasiandra shedding its collars of sadness."

The tale discusses how a visiting marine betrayed a teenage country girl, resulting in the girl's neighbor (and Hongo's grandfather) forcing the marine to drink a quart of whiskey before the marine drove down a mountain. Halfway down, "he hit a shallow bump and bounced, just a little, up off the seat, and, as he came down, cranked the wheel sharply toward his knee. The jeep veered off the road into the wall of lava rocks and the marine was thrown thirty feet or so, his head and shoulders bouncing against the black face of the road. He died instantly, drunken, his heart full of revenge, his loins satisfied. A purple oil dripped and pooled under the wrecked jeep from the broken pan. Petals from a violet flower fluttered away from a roadside hedge and mired themselves in the rivulet of oil below the jeep. The woody stem of the same flower had been stuck through one of the buttonholes of his green jersey. The flower's name is lasiandra. . . . Petals of a velvet indigo, yellow anthers full of pollen, and stamens the color of pink coral — filaments encircled by a sexual girdle of oceanic flesh. . . .The beauty of sadness encountered and then forgotten, shaded in rage, in disgrace, for me only a whisper from the trees, the gesture-free bounce of a fragrant conscience-troubled wind against the withering cups of passion's flower."

Final Version

The poem remained a single stanza with a number of indentations. Hongo says the indentations denote the continuation of a long line that comprises a single unit of rhythm.

Despite the active images of the Volcano landscape, the poem is contemplative, as in the middle section of the Final Version:

Miles in the distance,
        Kīlauea steams and vents
                through its sulphurous roads,
and a yellow light spills through
        a faultline in the clouds,
glazing the slick beaks of the feeding chickens,
        shining in their eyes
        like the phosphorous glow
        from a cave tunneled miles through the earth.
What was my face before I was born?
        the white mask and black teeth
at the bottom of the pond? What is the mind's insensible,
        the gateless gate?

Hongo wrote the poem after listening to an oral history available in *Hanahana: An Oral History Anthology of Hawai'i's Working People*, compiled by the Oral History Project of the University of Hawaii at Manoa.

The poem presents the tale of one man who joined the exodus of Filipino immigrants to the United States earlier in the century; by the late 1920s, about 100,000 Filipinos had arrived in Hawai'i. The *Pinoy* in Hongo's poem is one who, after much struggle, believes he is finally "going to the top" only to be felled by the spread of the flu, a phenomenon he cannot control. The flu eventually kills his youngest daughter, "so weak in years that English is her only tongue."

June 2, 1986 Original Journal Entry

Glory Across the River

Pinoy at the Coming World

I thought, when I left the fields

~~for this~~

~~for the~~

and hauling cane and hoeing out the furrows

for this job of wanting and writing

~~and palaver in the pidgin of~~

and palaver in the rough, sing-song English of the store,

~~I had~~

I had it made and would [relax a little] scheme a little for wealth

so long as ~~the~~ I ~~made~~ hit the balance

                at the end of the day

and nobody squawked ~~I cheated~~

                ~~or sassed them~~

                to the bosses

that I cheated or sassed ~~at~~ them.

~~Or made them speak a level of English~~

~~or made them ashamed for their~~

And I [never tried to shame ~~anyone either~~ nobody,] shamed no one

reading the paper or some [cheap] cowboy, dime-novel,

showing off my literacy as they shuffled into the store

dressed in their grimed khakis,

                ~~muttering~~

and gloves sticky w/ juice

and nettled head to toe w/ cane fiber.

I spoke Ilocano, a pidgin Visayan,

the Tagalog that was intended by Rizal,

~~the hero of national independence~~

~~our~~ the ~~national~~ hero of national independence and of our hearts,

to be our ~~common language~~ lingua franca.

And the insults — <u>bayow</u>, <u>salabit</u>, <u>bagoong</u>!
no matter if affectionate or joking,
never entered my speech again
from the day I left the ditches

       *WRITTEN IN THE MARGIN OF THE PAGE AS A RECONSIDERATION OF*
       *THE ABOVE LINES FROM "I SPOKE ILOCANO,…LEFT THE DITCHES"*

I would speak Ilocano, ~~my native tongue,~~
like a king or a muleteer,
a Visayan pidgin,
a Portugese,
a Chinese,
a Puerto Rican.
Simple words
for service.
But for jokes
for talk story we used the English,
chop-suey at first
then year by year,
more better,
smooth as love between old partners.

       *END OF MARGINALIA*

and walked behind
tied on the apron, and stepped behind this counter.
No more '<u>manong</u>,' no more 'rat-eater' or 'fish-brain,'
       ~~no more~~
no more garbage-talk to anybody.
[We all live on the same mountain,
on our way to
on the way to heaven or hell —
it doesn't matter to me,
I speak you all the same.]


~~We all pulling a load across this same river to glory.~~


How I see it, we all pulling a load,
glory across [this] the same river. [to glory.]


So, when I brought the wife in
and the babies start to coming —
American citizens every one
       <u>born</u>, not smuggled, here,
I had every ~~right~~ reason to figure
'<u>Pinoy</u>, no worry, you going to the top.'


~~I was surprised when the strike came~~
~~and the black market start to cut me out.~~

Even when the strike me and the black market
start to cut me out, I wasn't surprised.
The union had told me to stay on,
keep open even though they picket.
When they need cigarettees, sugar, coffee
when they need box matches for light
            torches for the labor rally, [the rally torches]
they still come to me, only
                        call from the back door,
and I sell in secret out of pity
and, for the plantation, of a convenient profit ~~for the plantation~~.
Nobody lose.  And I had the goodwill,
fish or vegetables or papayas whenever anyone had extra.
They came to the back, just as during the strike,
~~in a bag or a hat or a pretty cloth,~~
~~which I always kept, depending,~~
~~through the back door~~
            *CUT THIS SECTION*
in a rice sack or a hat woven from the hala tree
and, sometimes, from the Japanese,
even in a pretty cloth
            *END OF DELETED SECTION*
knowing things through the door in an old rice sack
~~but~~ and smiling, bowing if they were Japanese,
and running off down the street past the ~~cypress~~ cedar trees
w/out too much to say ~~besides "Here, you take."~~
                        , bowing each they glanced back,
~~to see if I~~
slightly comic, framed in the green monkey-tails of the trees.


But none of us ~~were~~ was ready for the flue that hit,
first the Mainland and all the reports of dead
on newspapers wrapped around all the canned meats
~~photographs~~ drawings of mourners joining hands in long processions
like a black parade on an unholy day,
~~the saint~~
then here ~~by cargo and troop ship~~
            at Pearl by cargo and troop ship,
through the military and the workers at the docks,
finally to all of us here on the plantations
diggers and <u>lunas</u> and storekeepers all alike,
sick w/ it, some of us writhing on the beaches
sleeping naked and in the running wash from the waves,
to try and cool
shivering, trying to cool our fevers down.

My boys were worse w/ it at first,
all of them groaning like ~~starved cattle~~ diseased cattle,
~~penned in a~~
helpless and open-eyed all through the night.
But they slipped the worst punch
and came back strong, eating soup
and fruits and putting the weight back on.

The oldest even went back to school
and took over for us behind the counter
times when my wife ~~left~~ needed to nurse the sick
and I left ~~by~~ on the stage for Honolulu,
hoping to fetch medicines from the wholesalers
and maybe a vaccine from the doctors at Pearl.

But it's my youngest now that has it bad,
so weak in years English is her only language,
fevers all the time and a mask of sweat
~~covering her~~
always on her face.  It's worse because
she doesn't groan or call out or say anything,
only cries and coughs and rasps in her breathing
like a dull saw cutting through rotten wood.
We pray bathe her face and ~~arms~~ neck and arms
in a cloth soaked w/ alcohol or witch hazel
we took from the store, light a few candles
and call on the saints and the Immaculate mother
to cure her and to ease her pain,

~~but I wish more than this that she'll be delivered somehow,~~
~~no matter~~ under my skin,
but, I know it's near her time
and that no faith or doctor of traveling hilot,
our old ~~village~~ healers expert in herbs and massage
will bring her back from this last sickness.
I wish only, now, that she'll be delivered somehow,
~~know, if only for a moment, of our love~~
know, for a moment at least that the choir
~~she might hear from inside the church at the end of our street~~
~~we hear~~ she might hear from inside the church at the end of the street
~~is only an echo, a murmurous sign~~
singing its soft requiem to our village ____
rolling through the green sea of sugar canes,
is only an echo, a ~~murmurous~~ humming remnant
of some other ~~initial~~ song of praise and holy joy
recommending us to the coming world,

~~and that we, ourselves~~
for which we ourselves are some shadowy forecast.


~~Last night~~
~~Evening, when~~
~~Tonight where all there's left is to wait,~~
Last night, when waiting was all there was to do,
I dressed myself in khakis again
and a pair of work boots so new
~~they~~ the laces were still full of wax
       ~~they~~ and the soles like iron
against ~~my~~ the soft heels of my feet.
I walked past the mill and the raw sugar ___
~~the past the locomotive~~
by past the union hall used for a morgue
~~and~~ [the Scottish church that was a hospital,]
and past the locomotive bedded down for the night.


I ~~walked~~ wanted to walk completely off plantation grounds
and get all the hay out of town
to where sugar cane can't grow ~~and~~
and no moon or stars rose over pineapple fields.


I wanted to get up on a ridge ~~somewhere~~ someplace
where the Hawaiian kings and their holy men
~~sacrificed to their dead and buried~~
might have sacrificed [to their ~~dead unholy~~ dead]
or buried, in secret, ~~some child of royalty~~
         ~~the bones of~~
         some intruder's unholy bones.
I wanted rain to fall, and streams to churn,
and waterfalls to glow as they fell
(from clifftop across mossy stone
         [and jungle fern
to the smooth black lava rocks below
     ~~that was their beds~~
     that were their beds below]
with the homely yellow light of mourning,
our candles lit for the souls of the dead and the dying;
I wanted the roar from the sea, from the falling water,
and from the harrowing wind
*THIS LINE SUBSEQUENTLY INSERTED* : the mounds and stones of the
                Filipino graveyard
over graves and the gravestones
themselves only a faint echo of
to be the echo of my own grief keening w/in,

~~purifying my heart~~
making pure my heart for the death I know is to come.


The poem's references include (i) *Pinoy* means Filipino; (ii) *Ilocano, Visayan* and *Tagalog* are three Filipino dialects; and (iii) *Rizal* refers to Jose Rizal, considered a "National Hero" of the Philippines for his activities against Spanish colonial rule, for which he was executed by the Spaniards.


Final Version:

The poem's Final Version was more simply titled "*Pinoy* at the Coming World." Hongo also compressed the text in several places, such as the 20-line section from "I spoke Ilocano, a Pidgin Visayan" to "glory across [this] the same river. [to glory.]" and associated marginalia into the following 14-line section; it is interesting to note how Hongo sacrificed the "meaning" of *Rizal* for the "sound" (rhythm) of the finished text shown here:


> I could speak Ilocano like a king or a muleteer,
> a Visayan pidgin, a Portuguese,
> a Chinese, and a Puerto Rican.
> Simple words for service.
> But for jokes, for talk story,
> we used the English — chop suey at first —
> then, year by year, even better,
> smooth as love between old partners.
> And the insults — *bayow, salabit, bagoong!*—
> no matter if affectionate or joshing,
> never entered my speech again
> from the day I left the ditches,
> tied on the apron, and stepped behind this counter.
> No more "*manong*," no more "rat-eater" or fish-brain."


Similarly, Hongo compressed the Original Journal Entry's last stanza into what became the second half of the Final Version's last stanza, as follows:


> . . .I wanted to get up
> on a ridge someplace where kings
> and their holy men might have sacrificed
> or buried, in secret, some intruder's
> unholy bones. I wanted rain to fall
> and streams to churn and waterfalls, as they fell
> from the *pali* across mossy stone, to glow
> with the homely, yellow light of mourning, our candles
> lit for the souls unwinding in their shrouds
> and shrieking off the cliff-coasts of these islands.
> I wanted the roar from the sea, from wailing water,
> and from the wind over mounds and stones

to be the echo of my own grief, keening within,
making pure my heart for the world I know is to come.

—⁂—

When Hongo is not writing poetry, he sometimes writes <u>about</u> poetry. He is known for presenting the view that literature — as *art* — need not be defined by a social, political and/or cultural context. However, as shown by the four sample poems, this is not a dismissal of social, cultural and/or political references for such are what comprise history. Just as he would castigate those who would attempt to silence certain writers' styles of writing, he battles those who would censor or silence the stories of ethnic and minority peoples — including the stories he presents through his sample poems featured above. As a poet, Hongo presents his stories from what he described in *Under Western Eyes* ("*UWE*") (Anchor, 1995) as his "principles as a writer — a verbal music, a simplicity and directness, the idea of cherishing the smaller things . . . (but also) an acknowledgment of history and its wanton acts."

Hongo, a *Sansei* (third-generation immigrant) knows about the repression of history; he feels keenly the "silence" of members of the *Issei* (first) and *Nisei* (second) generations about their experiences in relocation camps during World War II. Through such silence, the *Sansei* were "denied, not just the facts, but the emotional experience, the report, the *parenting* of knowing about our parents' and grandparents' lives," Hongo says in <u>UWE</u>.

"To be without history, to be without an emotional life, to be without the ability even to imagine the emotional lives of the people who came before you, is an incredibly damaging thing, an ache that hurts in a way that you don't even realize hurts."

—⁂—

"OBon: Dance For The Dead," "Volcano House" and "*Pinoy* at the Coming World" are all contained in Part One of <u>The River of Heaven</u>. It was noted that there is a sadness flowing through all of the poems in Part One, appropriately introduced by a few words from Li Po:

> . . . Shall goodwill ever be secure?
> I watch the long road of the river of stars.

When asked if there was some real-life incident(s) that would explain the melancholy of his poems during those times, Hongo recalls his father's and grandfather's deaths.

"My father died on January 25, 1984 and my grandfather on December 7, 1983," he says. "These were heavy losses."

—⁂—

In his memoir, Hongo explains the significance of the moment when he recalls how the beauty of the Hawai'ian landscape so affected him that he then "gave up detachment." He says,

> What radiates as knowledge from that time is that there is a beauty in belonging to this earth and to its past, even one locked in mystery and prohibition, unstoried, that exceeds all the passion you can claim for it.

Hongo says that "every singer of . . . magnificence in every land knows" of this "beauty in belonging to this earth and to its past." Yeats (for whom Ireland was the core of inspiration) puts it another way in "The Lake Isle of Innisfree," his poem that Hongo knows so well:

> I will arise and go now, and go to Innisfree,
> . . .
> And I shall have some peace there, for peace comes dropping slow,
> Dropping from the veils of the morning to where the cricket sings;
> There midnight's all a glimmer, and noon a purple glow,
> And evening full of the linnet's wings.

Hongo ends his memoir with a message for his readers: "I wish you knowing. I wish you a land." It is a poet's message about what Hongo — and Meyers, Whitman, Wright and Yeats — realized through poetry: the joy of knowing *feeling*, the joy of *feeling* knowing.

# DAVID MURA

David Mura has published two memoirs, *Turning Japanese: Memoirs of a Sansei* (Anchor, 1991), which won the PEN Josephine Miles Book Award, and *Where the Body Meets Memory: An Odyssey of Race, Sexuality and Identity* (Anchor, 1996), and two books of poetry, *The Colors of Desire* (Anchor, 1995), which won the Carl Sandburg Literary Award, and *After We Lost Our Way* (Carnegie Mellon University Press, 1989), winner of the National Poetry Series Contest.

With writer Alexs Pate and director Arthur Jaffa, he created a short film, *Slowly, This,* for the PBS Series Alive TV. His writing has received numerous awards including a Lila Wallace Reader's Digest Writers' Award, a U.S.-Japan Creative Artist Fellowship, two NEA Literature Fellowships, two Bush Foundation Fellowships, and a Discovery/*The Nation* Award. He has also received a Jones Commission, a Multicultural Collaboration Grant, and a McKnight Advancement Grant for playwrighting from the Playwrights' Center. His poems have appeared in *The American Poetry Review, The Nation, The New Republic, Crazyhorse,* and the *New England Review,* as well as numerous anthologies, including *The Open Boat: Poems from Asian America, The Language of Life* (ed. by Bill Moyers from the PBS Series), *The New American Poets of the '90's* and *Western Wind.* His plays and peformance pieces include *Relocations, Secret Colors* (with Alexs Pate), *After Hours* (with Kelvin Han Yee & Jon Jang), and *The Winged Seed* (an adaptation of Li-Young Lee's memoir). He has served as the Artistic Director of the Asian American Renaissance, a Minnesota community arts organization, and is now an Artistic Associate at Pangea World Theater.

He also has written numerous essays about race and multiculturalism for such publications as *Mother Jones, The New York Times, The Utne Reader,* and *The Graywolf Annual V: Multi-Cultural Literacy.* His criticism has appeared in *The Boston Review, The Poetry Flash, AWP Chronicle,* and *The Hungry Mind Review.*

He has an MFA in creative writing from Vermont College and has taught at the University of Minnesota, St. Olaf College, the Loft, and the University of Oregon. He gives readings and speaks on the issues of race and multiculturalism throughout the country. He lives in Minneapolis with his wife, Susan, and their three children, Samantha, Nikko and Tomo.

In response to the question, "What advice would you give to a young poet?" David Mura responds,

> This is the usual but undeniable: Read widely and constantly — the great poets from all countries and cultures and times, their criticism and other writings too. Some criticism has been particularly instructive for me — T.S. Eliot, William Gauss, Czeslaw Milosz (everything he's written), Richard Hugo's *The Triggering Town.* Travel. Ask yourself large questions, find out what the large questions are. Revise not simply by line or word choice but by re-envisioning the whole poem or your whole approach to language or your whole writing process. Experiment, don't settle for the first answer, move beyond the boundaries (of your genre or discipline, of society, of your family, your culture, your times, your own conceptions of yourself). Joseph Campbell's *The Hero's Journey* is a useful palimpsest. Journeys are required.

# HOW HISTORY STAINS THE COLORS OF DESIRE

*"One of the changes in my own writing in the last few years is that I understand to a much better degree what it means to be an African American in this country, and therefore I think I have a better sense of how a Black audience will react to my work . . . And that question has come more and more to provide a context for the way in which I think about my work. I believe that my Japanese American identity is (also formed in relation to) African Americans."*
— *David Mura (from an interview by Stewart David Ikeda for CREATING ASIAN AMERICA, University of Wisconsin Asian American Studies)*

*"Alexs (Pate, an African American friend) thought our jobs were different. (Pate said,) 'What I want to do is to say, 'No there is a gentle spirit in African America.' Humanizing the African American male. For you, your work is about exposing the madness that is in the civilized caricature of Asian America."*
— *David Mura (from WHERE THE BODY MEETS MEMORY: AN ODYSSEY OF RACE, SEXUALITY & IDENTITY)*

I think I was eight years old when this incident occured. I was holding on to a family friend's hand as we walked down a street in Baguio City, Philippines where I grew up. We passed by a group of *loko-lokos* hanging out by the street corner. I don't remember them smoking but in my memory of them today, I smell (what my memory presumes to be) their stolen Marlboros.

I kept my head bowed as we walked by, but couldn't keep from darting a glance sideways before we crossed the street. One of the more boisterous teenagers, caught my eyes. I swiftly looked down at the tips of my shoes. But I heard him whistle and shout, "White Legs, White Legs" before the streetlights changed and we escaped.

Across the street I asked our family friend what "White Legs" meant. But she only sniffed and muttered, "Those *loko-lokos*!"

Years later, just before 1997 was about to end, I was in a plane landing in San Francisco. During the six-hour flight from New York City, I read David Mura's book, *WHERE THE BODY MEETS MEMORY: AN ODYSSEY OF RACE, SEXUALITY & IDENTITY* (Anchor, 1996) ("WTBMM"). And rather than seeing the California skyline through the window, I was seeing myself as a girl, confused over what that *loko-loko* meant when he proclaimed: "White Legs!" I had forgotten about this incident and hadn't thought about it for years. I only remembered it after reading Mura's meditation about race, identity, memory and, yes, the ramifications of a body's physicality.

I telephoned my mother to ask about that childhood incident. After her surprise at the question, my mother explained that "White Legs" was intended as a compliment. The Philippines was still enamoured with Americans and their culture (e.g. Marlboros). Thus, my mother explained, the paler a woman's complexion, the more she was prized. I replied in (dare I say) post-colonial amazement: "Those *loko-lokos*!"

Then my mother called the next day. She said she was mistaken about the roots of the phrase, "White Legs." She said the compliment goes all the way back to the Philippines' history as a former colony of Spain for nearly 400 years. She said that the phrase stemmed from bastard-children of Spanish friars trying to proclaim their superiority over the *kayumangi-* or brown-skinned Malay natives. And that the natives acceded to their claims because the Spaniards were persistent and consistent in proclaiming the superiority of their culture over that by the local *Indios*.

And I replied with silence even as my mind remained in the turmoil caused by Mura's memoir and how it evoked yet another example of the long reach of history as well as how the mind, the psyche, can be so affected by the body. Later, I recalled this childhood incident once more as I discussed with Mura the title poem to his most recent poetry collection, *The Colors of Desire* (Anchor, 1995). This unexpected recollection from the depths of my memory — of something that occured nearly two decades ago — seems a logical response to Mura's wide-ranging explorations of self and history. Mura's path is admirable, not only for its courage but also, for how he places no limits to his exploration that crosses geographical, time, cultural, social and physical boundaries. One result is Mura's controversial conclusion that his "Japanese American identity is (also formed in relation to) African Americans."

Thus, Mura's poem, "The Colors of Desire" which was triggered by a black-and-white 1930s photograph of a lynching ends up being a meditation on race, sexuality, history and identity. The poem opens with this photograph before connecting to Mura's viewing of the pornographic film, *Behind the Green Door*, where a black man makes love to a white woman, and the way that image focused on the taboo of miscenegation. Later, the poem continues to the image of Mura's father stepping onto a segregated bus in Jerome, Arkansas, confronting the line between the white and black passengers. "How did he know," the poem asks, "where to sit?" And the poem continues to engage other images before ending with Mura standing in the nursery of his first daughter, helpless with love for her, with fear on her behalf at the world she is inheriting and a question that perhaps remains unanswerable for all time: "And if what is granted erases nothing,/ if history remains, untouched, implacable,/ as darkness flows up our hemisphere,/ her hollow still moves moonward,/ small hill on the horizon, swelling,/ floating with child, white, yellow,/ who knows, who can tell her,//oh why must it matter?"

For Mura, "The Colors of Desire" is "historical" — not only in tracing the elements of American history but also Mura's personal history. The poem would not exist without Mura's troubled past, which includes years of sexual promiscuity and addiction to pornography, exacerbated by feelings of racial inferiority that manifested itself in being attracted in the past primarily to Caucasian women. As he puts it in his poem, "I married a woman not of my color./ Tell me: What is it I want to escape?" Mura depicts this past honestly — and brutally so — in his poems and memoirs such as *A MALE GRIEF: NOTES ON PORNOGRAPHY AND ADDICTION* (Milkweed Editions, 1987); *Turning Japanese* (Anchor, 1991); and *WTBMM*. Mura spent his twenties mired in obsessive sexual behavior. Then, in 1985, Mura read Frantz Fanon's "great" book, *BLACK SKIN, WHITE MASKS* (Grove Press Inc., 1967) in which Fanon examines a black neurotic, Jean Veneuse, who uses his blackness as the sole explanation of his psychic condition. Mura describes the effect of Fanon's book in *WTBMM* as follows:

> Trapped in feelings of inferiority, Veneuse clings to the sense that his skin color is a flaw; a loner, he accepts the separation imposed on him by the color line. At the same time, he wants 'to elevate himself to the white man's level,' and his 'quest for white flesh' — he constantly seeks out white women — is part of that attempt. Veneuse's acceptance of the color line dooms him, says Fanon. It keeps Veneuse from seeing that the world must be restructured and, with it, his own psyche....
>
> I came to the passages on the black man who constantly sleeps with white women, how he has the illusion that his sense of inferiority will be erased by doing so. Somehow crossing the color line sexually will prove himself as good as a white man.
>
> In an instant I understood what I'd been doing all those years....
>
> I'd elevated whiteness, I'd inculcated its standards of beauty, I'd believed on some deep level in the myth of white superiority. That was part of my sickness, part of

the colonizing of my sexuality. I felt that every white woman who rejected me somehow reaffirmed both my sense of a color line and my sense of debasement.

Subsequently, when he traveled to Japan, Mura "realized that my reading of Fanon helped deepen my experience there, my questioning of identity. It wasn't just that I was encountering various aspects of Japanese culture or that my experience there enabled me to imagine more deeply the lives of my grandparents and therefore the lives of my parents. The presence of Japanese faces and media images made me much more aware of how culture shapes how we see our bodies and the bodies of those around us."

In Japan, Mura recalls a "telling instance" of when he watched the movie "Out of Africa":

> I suddenly found myself looking at Meryl Streep, Klaus Maria Brandauer, and Robert Redford and the characters they play — Karen Blixen (a.k.a. the writer Isak Dinesen), her husband, and her lover — in an entirely different light. The moment occured when Blixen is taken by her husband for the first time to their farm in Kenya and all the African servants come out to greet them. It's night, and the movie tries to impart a sense of the heroine traveling into an unknown space. Always the focus is on what the Meryl Streep character is going through....
>
> (But) What I wanted to know about, what I knew little about, were the minds of the Africans around Blixen, the Kenyans who, two decades later, would organize the Mau Maus and the revolt which gained independence for Kenya. What was the interior life behind those black faces? I found I couldn't keep both the Meryl Streep character and the black faces at the center of my attention .... I had to choose. Indeed, I had been choosing all my life. Only now I was withdrawing attention, affection, curiosity from the white face at the center of the picture and giving it to the black faces. I was striking a new balance. And the world looked differently. I saw that this was a form of cultural and political power, the almost unconscious and instantaneous granting of priority to faces of one skin color over another.

After returning from Japan, Mura attended an African American literary conference, the first time he says he was surrounded by a group of black writers. He recalls being pleasantly surprised by their agreement with the aesthetic, "Art is political" — a question he had been arguing at the time with white writers in Minnesota (where he lives). It was also an incident that made him question why there was such a discrepancy between the white Minnesota writers and the black writers at the conference. Consequently, he began writing work that was more explicit about his sexuality as well as trying to articulate connections between sexuality and race. One of the results was, "The Colors of Desire."

What Mura has done is brave, partly because it is controversial, and inevitably will result in pain for, not just himself but also, his wife and friends. Indeed, the African American novelist Alexs Pate has told Mura that he thinks Mura is "reckless in (his) willingness to share secrets." As Mura describes in *WTBMM*, Pate questions, "Do you give people too much ammunition to condemn you?" Mura replies, "I tell him that I'm trying to explore what my life says about the issues of sexuality and race. The ways I hurt Susie (my Caucasian wife) and others in my early life are part of that exploration. I know people will criticize me not only for what I've done but also for writing about it. It goes with the territory. But what's the alternative? Pretending it didn't happen, that such issues don't exist?"

Mura's concerns extended to the landmark controversy for Asian Americans centered on the Broadway production of *Miss Saigon* and how his response to the incident caused him to lose some white friends. In his essay, "Secrets and Anger" (*Mother Jones*, Sept./Oct. 1992), he recalls:

Like many Asian Americans, ... I felt disturbed that . . . the British Jonathan Price, was playing a Eurasian, and that no Asian American actor had been given a chance to audition for that role. This repeated the casting discrimination which has been a mainstay of Hollywood since Warner Oland, the Swede, first played the sexual eunuch, Charlie Chan. Beyond that, I was upset by the Madame Butterfly plot of *Miss Saigon*, where an Asian woman pines for her white male lover (who, by implication, is always more desirable than the Asian men around her). I had thought that David Henry Hwang's *M. Butterfly* and its deconstruction of that stereotype would have rendered the use of such a plot absurd.

One day, I mentioned my anger to two white friends, Paula, a painter, and Mark, a writer. Both consider themselves liberals; Mark had been active in the anti-war movement during the sixties. He was part of my wedding and, at the time, perhaps my closest male friend. But neither of these people agreed with me about *Miss Saigon*. They argued that art represented the freedom of the imagination, was trying to get inside other people's skin. Isn't color blind casting what we're striving for? they asked. . . .

I don't recall exactly what happened after this. I think the argument trailed off into some safer topic as such arguments often do. . . But afterwards, as I thought of this conversation, I felt angrier and angrier and, at the same time, more despairing. I realized that for me the fact that Warner Oland played Charlie Chan and Keye Luke the bumbling number one son was a humiliating message. It did not show me that art was a democracy of the imagination. But though they were my good friends, neither Paula nor Mark could empathize with my sense of humiliation and shame before images of a white actor playing an Asian. It was secondary to their belief in "freedom" in the arts. . . .

But when I talked with a black friend, who's a writer, he replied, "Yeah, I was surprised too at the reaction of some of my white artists friends to *Miss Saigon*. It really told me where they were. It marked a dividing line. And I just backed away from certain people."

For a while, I avoided talking about my feelings when Paula and Mark. . . .

Finally, . . . I told Paula and Mark I not only felt that their views were wrong about *Miss Saigon* but that they were racially based. In these emotionally charged conversations, I don't think I used the word "racist" but I know they both objected to my lumping them together with other whites. Paula said I was stereotyping them, that she wasn't like other whites. She told me of her friendships with a few blacks when she lived back East, of the history of her mother's involvement in supporting civil rights. "It's not like I don't know what discrimination is," she said. "Women get discriminated against, so do artists." Her tone moved back and forth between self-righteousness and resentment to distress and tears about losing our friendship. . . .

Mark talked about his shame of being a WASP. "Do you know that I don't have a single male friend who is a WASP?" he said. I decided not to point out that within the context of color, the difference between a WASP male and say, an Irish Catholic, isn't much of a difference. . . .

A few months later, I had a few calmer talks with Mark, but they always ended with this distance between us. I felt I needed some acknowledgement from him that when we began talking about race, I knew more about it than he did, that our arguing about race was not the same as our arguing about say, free verse versus formal verse. . . .

It took me many months to figure out what had gone down with Paula and Mark. Almost invariably, when I talked about it with a friend of color, whether Asian American or African American or Hispanic American, I came away feeling better, with more understanding and self assurance. For instance, as my black friend Alexs and I talked about how whites desperately want to claim that they are victimized too, we came up with the term the "victim limbo."

When a white person is charged with racism or engages in a conversation about racism, the first thing they often do, as Paula did with me, is the victim limbo: "I'm a woman, I know what prejudice is, I've experienced it." "I'm Jewish/working class/Italian in a Wasp neighborhood/etc. I know what prejudice is, I've experienced it." If they are white, Wasp and male, like Mark, they are still able to do the victim limbo: "Yeah, I'm a white male. I know what that means—overly rational, uptight, oppressive, power hungry, racist"—a statement which implies, oh yes, they call all white males these things, but I'm not any of them, so I too am being unfairly labeled and judged.

The purpose of this limbo is to show the person of color that he or she doesn't really experience anything the white person hasn't experienced, that the person of color's social/ economic/political/cultural position is actually not very different from the white person's. Therefore, the white person doesn't have to feel guilty, doesn't have to acknowledge the system of racism in a direct way, since the white person is a victim too.

But Alexs and I both knew that the position of a person of color and a white person in American society is not the same. The victim limbo—which is offered by many as a token of solidarity: "I'm just the same as you"—is really a way of depoliticizing the racial question; it ignores the differences in power in this country which result from the system of race. . . .

None of this, though, assuages the pain and bitterness I feel over losing white friendships over race or the distance I have seen open up between me and white friends as I've become more and more conscious of race. Nor does it help me explain to my daughter why we no longer see Paula or Mark, when she asks about them or mentions their names.

The compensation for these changes I've been going through, for shedding my white identified consciousness, has been the numerous friendships that I've begun to have with people of color. My daughter will grow up in a household where the people who visit will be from a wider spectrum than those Japanese Americans and whites who visited my parents' house in the suburbs of Chicago.

It is no wonder that Mura unhesitatingly says he can't see himself writing "sunset poems or (poems about) the light on the lake — the kind that appear in magazines like *The New Yorker.*" Not only are many of these poems "crap, or at least bore (him) to tears," but, more importantly, Mura says, these "poems don't say anything vital to me or my life of the lives of a large majority of the world." Mura explains that he writes for "a Japanese-American audience, an Asian American audience, then an audience of people of color, then an audience beyond that."

Finally (and logically), Mura's approach also results in a bias towards long poems, such as "The Colors of Desire" which fuses his concerns about identity, race, sexuality and history.

"I obviously like to work on long poems. They allow me the opportunity to work for a long time and in great depth with the material; there's room to experiment and see how many different elements and approaches I can fit into the poem," Mura says. "In any poem obviously you want the language to work at a high level throughout, but I also want more at stake than simply the language; for me the material needs to contain many different thematic and psychological levels. Another way of putting it, to paraphrase Robert Bly, is I want a *knot* at the center of the poem, but it is even more interesting to me if there are several knots which reflect the range of my obsessions — race & identity, sexuality, history, politics, art."

—⁓—

The following presents some of Mura's drafting process for his poem, as divided into five sections. Within each section will be a discussion about his drafts and writing process. The five sections are:

- I.   First Draft With Title of "A Lynching: A Photo From In These Times" With Editing Marks Reflecting Drafting Changes Until The Poem Becomes Titled "PHOTOGRAPH OF A LYNCHING"
- II.  Writing Process On The Draft Titled "PHOTOGRAPH OF A LYNCHING"
- III. Writing Process For A Set of Drafts Titled "TRIPTYCH"
- IV.  Changes Between "TRIPTYCH" And Draft Titled "THE COLORS OF DESIRE":
- V.   Final Draft Titled "THE COLORS OF DESIRE"

*(Editing Marks: strikethroughs = deletions; underlined words = insertions/additions; [Del L] - deleted line breaks; [New L] = new line breaks; [Del P] = deleted stanza breaks; [New P] = new stanza breaks; bracketed)*

Section I.          First Draft With Title of "A Lynching: A Photo From In These Times"
                     With Subsequent Changes Reflecting the Poem's Development
                     Until The Poem Becomes Titled "PHOTOGRAPH OF A LYNCHING"

~~A LYNCHING: A PHOTO FROM IN THESE TIMES~~
**PHOTOGRAPH OF A LYNCHING**

*(Sections 4 and 5 are later deleted, though they naturally offer insight as to the thoughts running through Mura's mind. Section 6 ultimately becomes early draft of Section 4 of Final Draft's 4-section poem.)*

1

These men? Through the bagginess of their trousers, dented felt hats,
[New L] tilted to one side, [Del L] fingers tugging their suspenders or vests,
[New L] the way their faces are either a bit puffy or too lean,

[New P] and their eyes almost imperceptably too thin, too close together,

you can tell they are Southern, from the Thirties.
[New L] Of course they are white; [Del L] who else could create this

[New P] cardboard figure, face flat and grey like cardboard,
[Del P] eyes oversized and bulging, like some krazy kewpie doll
or some ancient totem the gang has dug up. At the far right,

[New P] with a small browed cap, [Del L] a boy of around twelve seems,
[New L] though it's hard to tell, to be smiling, [Del L] as if responding
[New L] to what's most familiar here: the taking of a picture.

[New P] It is the same with the rest. Though directly above them,
[New L] a branch [Del P] leashes the dead negro by a rope up in the air,
[New L] the men too remain [Del L] preternaturally intent on the camera,

[New P] the unseen eye. Which is, at this moment, us. [Del L] Or, more precisely,
[New L] me.  And for what purpose? We, I, have seen all of this before:
Horror, outrage, brutal depravity—the words by now

[New P] seem empty, abandoned, [Del L] devoid of sense.  Certainly,
[New L] nothing here surprises me. . . [Del P] So why am I writing this?
[New L] It goes deeper. Fifteen years ago. Behind the Green Door .

[New P] I am sitting in the dark of a theatre with a dozen other men.
(It's a scene I've visited before, and will, more and more often over the years.)
There's a woman laid out on a table, naked, the same one

[New P] on the Ivory Snow soap boxes, [Del L] holding a baby on her shoulder,
[New L] smiling her blond, more than pure white smile; [Del P] already
[New L] we've seen this woman , who a few hours earlier, was sitting on a patio above the valley,

[New P] being kidnapped, dragged in through the alley, black hooded figures
[New L] muscling her body [Del L] (perhaps the way, a few years earlier,
[New L] Patricia Hearst was "liberated" from her private world,

[New P] strapped to the wheel of history),  and now, after being prepared,
[New L] serviced, by a handful of women, each moving their hands
[New L] up and down the body, abstractly, half-smiling,

as one of them kneels and buries her face in her crotch,
[New L] now she is ready: [Del L] And now he walks in : — Lean, naked, black,
[New L] with streaks of white paint on his chest and face, [Del L] and a necklace of teeth,

[New P] it's almost comical, this fake garb of the jungle, Africa brought
before All-America, black and blond, almost comical
[New L] but for the sudden releasing surge of energy [Del L] when what has so long

been regarded

[New P] as the ultimate crime against nature [Del P] (so that even a glance,
[New L] a look by a black man, could bring this picture I now hold in my hands);
is suddenly there on the screen, the black man kneeling ~~, as did the woman,~~ to

[New P] ~~to~~ this kidnapped body; then sliding himself in, as the screen shows it all,
down to ~~the~~ her head shaking ~~back and forth of her head~~ like a seizure, ~~and~~ the final
    scream before
he lifts himself off her body, which is whimpering, quivering...

I walked out of that theatre as if bolted from a dream into a dream.
[New L] I stared at the cars whizzing by, watched the light change,
[New L] red, yellow, green, and the haze in my head from the hash,

[New P] and the haze in my head from the image, melded together, reverberating.
[New L] I don't know [Del L] what ~~happened next~~ I did afterwards. Only, night after night,
[New L] I will want to see it again and again—

[New P] like a miracle, a talisman, a rageful, unrelenting release.


2
So why am I writing this? How did I arrive here?
How speak without using the sentence, "Very early in my life,
it was already too late..." It is, of course, a question of desire:

How early did it start? The face I had at five, at twelve, at twenty five,
it is true, possessed the same lack of definition—soft, rounded,
overly fleshy—a woman's face really, and certain women I was with,

stroking my cheek, my chest, would remark on the smoothness,
the lack of hair (so that I wonder now if that  was what
attracted them—what I found so embarassing, so unmanly).

Certainly I see so much of this now through the face of that five-year-old,
his bluff of six guns pointed at the camera, holster of plastic bullets
strapped round his belly, already a bit too big, his cowboy hat black,

cocked at an angle. (How ridiculous: A cowboy? He's Japanese.)
He stands on the steps of the apartment on Broadway, a block from Lake Michigan,
in the windy city, city of gangsters, butchers, crooked politicians.

Next year, his hero will be Mickey Mantle, Roger Maris, Crazy Legs Hirsch;
but now, in the photo, his skin dark from the sun, he's Paladin,
squinting at the light, and he wears, like all boys in such photos,

an attempt at what—toughness? bravado? ease?—forgetting how,
each night, injuns, bad guys, robbers, the nightmares of childhood,
harmless hauntings, enter his room, shadows flittering about...

Yes, it all comes back now. Early summer, moths batter the screen.
Sounds of the Broadway traffic drift in; from the living room, the muffled t.v.
In the next bed, he hears his younger sister, taunting him, daring him

—he cannot hurt her, he cannot  hurt her —(Who knows
how long they have been talking like this, eyes open in the dark,
how long they have watched headlights flowing across the walls?)

And when his father slams open the door, and stands there,
the law decreed by his body, his shouts stalking the chaos
that's erupted in his house, who can recall—the sister? the brother?—

how, with his fist balled or his flat open palm, he descends
on the boy's body with the same swift motion that the boy,
like an animal, like a scared and angry little boy,

descended on his sister, beating her in the dark...


3
How little such incidents, such explanations, give us. Better to say
the soul entered this abyss, in the soul is this abyss, this voice, this demon;
to believe in the golden scales of incarnation, justice and retribution;

to believe the world is built on illusion, is nothing, to believe
it will all be redeemed, all be condemned, all will be well,
there's a plan, a meaning—Anything but the wheel of history

rolling on and on, past this glade where a crowd of men mill about,
pausing for a photo with their prize, strung from a rope;
past this bedroom where a boy crept over to his sister's bed,

where his father hauled him on his lap as he squirmed like a beetle;
past a studio where a naked blond woman lying on a platform, leans on her elbow,
and asks the grip man how long before the lights will be done...

I think of the time my father and mother came to therapy,
and my therapist got him talking of those years as a young man,
what he must have given up to make it, to feed his family, buy that home,

the prejudice, the pressures, hours and trips away. And I could see,
for a second, like heat lightning on the horizon of a summer night,

a faint, spidery redness etching the whites of his eyes, luring

this ripple from his muscles up his neck, past his chin,
through his cheeks, and just at the moment, I thought
the spasm would hit that redness just rising in his eyes,

an alarm went off, everything shut off, composure set in, no,
not composure, a look of what—bewilderment? confusion?—no
it seemed to me almost a gaze of stupidity, as if his knowledge

of himself, of the past, had reached its zenith, the blankness
in his eyes almost frightened, saying, ""No, no, it was what
I was supposed to do, what you did, there wasn't anything to it, anything at all..."

Somehow, uneasily, that incident connects with another awakening.
The fall I was twelve, home one day from school with a slight fever.
I enter my parents room, my mother's out shopping:

I slide back their closet door, start rummaging among the shoes,
all lined precisely, facing one way; then the garment bags, unzipping them—
what am I looking for? how did I know it was there?—

When I pull it out and open the pages, what spills before me
is only the image, the photo, millions of men, white, black, yellow, have seen,
though the body before me is white, eighteen, the breasts enormous,

almost frightening in their statement—the aureoles
seem large as my fist—and as the three unfolded pages
lay before me on the floor, I find myself touching myself,

and there is, in the back of my mind, some terror,
my mother will come home, I'll be found out,
some delight I have never felt before,

and I do not cry out, I make no sound...


(THIS ENTIRE SECTION 4 IS SUBSEQUENTLY DELETED)
4
Like travellers who cannot decide what possessions to let go,
we are, it seems, overburdened with history. Feminism, racism,
all the theories and castigations that leave us with the illusion

that justice is, justice was, possible (if only, if only, if only).
Addiction, pornography, the penal colony and its ghosts.
Trials and orders, crosses and posters, rifle towers, soldiers.

The legacy of families traveling on trains. The legacy
of arriving. Entering the gates. But the gates are different,
the stories not the same. Here flung into bright stars,

the intimate nights fold around us, cold gives in.
And we are huddled together, unfolding like blankets
our woolen deaths, little rooms in which to sleep.

Here all the earthly things of childhood: bread,
bottle, bib, rattle. A ship, a doll. Fear. Joy.
Here the mother's face, like a meadow at sunset,

a freshness and premonition, breathing like surf,
fragile as the dirt that drops from the edges of a grave.
And the transformations came like painters into a house.

And some walked out. And some did not—...No, no,
it was nothing like that. It was baseball, high school,
dances and big band. Bon-o-dori, mochi, mystery meat at the mess.

Poker, hana, dice in the back. Cigarettes stashed
beneath mattresses in the barracks. Rice in canvas sacks.
"Go for broke" and 442nd, No-no boys, Kibei, the loyalty oaths.

And if our realms of freedom were dimmed, so were the world's,
and really, when, in Jerome, we got on the buses,
we never thought, though the black faces too were beckoning,

saying "colored folks got to the stick together,"
we would ride anywhere but in the front.
Once, that is, the war was over. You see,

it was like my teacher once told me, "After the war,
this won't matter, it's all a mistake, but for your sakes,
you've got to be not one, but two hundred per cent American..."

For your sake...As a child, having been berated, spanked,
sent to bed with no supper, I would sometimes lie in my room,
pounding my stomach, thinking with the magic of my blows

each zag of pain sent its echo in my father, a bat quivering
back and forth between us in the summer scented dark.
How do we know when we are talking to ourselves?

And who are we blaming when we say they , twisting us around
like this, leaving us hanging? The crimes are not commensurate,

the justice more than uncertain. And we are forever taking our leave.

—A child's wish. Nothing I say can save this man...


5 4

Think of a man staring at a photograph of torture,
abmonination, rape, a land laid waste. Think of him
turning away, expunged, as if suddenly outside his door

he'd heard the sound of the river rushing past, as if
he'd waken out of a dream. Think of him turning back,
dripping with the unknown, holding before him the photo

amid that endless roar. Think of something streaming
inside him, the lashing foam, strafings of the current,
the jar of rocks and slap of stone. Think of him sinking.

It is like that moment when the priest raises the blade
above the quivering goat and then, with or without
the touch of lightning in the night summoned above him,

the blade and flesh enter each other, life force is released,
and the sacred screams back into silence. We are
hollow inside. Something fills us. Wandering in and out.

How could I know what was speaking inside me,
how many of the departed and dead, bodies I'd never seen,
aroused, waiting, what men, what women, hated me there,

and there, in a primal forest, spreading tendrils of leaf light
above the basin of root life, a little birth, a little ancient blood,
a small photo gutted with fathers was winking like an accomplice.

Atrocity smiled, and I smiled back. And I felt weightless,
dissolved, as if floating, as if in some arms of a mother,
thrown from her depths. And now, as if, from the drowsy lids,

some other weeping flows, I see in the face of the dead negro,
not just a  foretaste of sleep, undivided dreams, much less
the rage I want to call up and am hardly near, but the face,

delayed for a while, adapted to circumstance, expunged of his past,
of my father, of something he escaped and did not,
of what I run from and towards, as in the dream

where I stand by his bed, not knowing whether
he is asleep or not, whether, where, I should wake him,
why am I too late, why nothing can be done.

—That's all. The immovable eye can always watch.
Love, though this is not a word I might use,
what makes this so difficult has set in my hand this photo,

this constellation of images, and drawn them forth
like cards, one by one. How is it among them,
I found your face, fading before me on the table?

Or is it my hand that's covering it all?

6 5
A friend, reading all this, seemed bewildered, annoyed,
as if the self revealed here, were antithetical
not to some mild-mannered mask I wear,

like everyone else, on social occassions—
no, he's hardly that naive, has had his own demons,
breakdowns, incidents of ugliness he'd want to keep

sealed in a vault—No, it's precisely because he knows
what I've been through, that he wanted all that went between
then and now, how one day you wake with everything

collapsed about you, ruin, decay, shame; drugs, random bodies,
songs of self hatred; and suddenly you're tired,
and suddenly the sense you've always been broken

no longer makes sense. You ask for help, you resist,
you ask for help. It's so simple, though surely exhausting.
Redemption, a second chance, an old yet new song.

So why not provide that tune? Certainly, in these flickerings,
these faint wordings of the past, these recognitions
and recollections of the present, with all the confusions

the mind revives again, seeing where I stand
is so strange, even to me, seeing my asking
after history, after judgement, hints not just at desires

for knowledge or justice or even beauty, but that here,
in these turmoils, in the twistings of the boy, the man I was,

there's the exploration—how unlikely, how lucky—of pleasure.

And yet it is this pleasure I think now I have to let go.
For what matters now is not why, what explanations
can justify, ameliorate, forgive, but all I have incurred,

all I will incur. My tiny mortal sum.  Tonight it rains softly
on the roofs of my city, street lamps glow down the hill,
and my face is mirrored before me, dark on the glass.

In moments, the rain will glisten there as snow, snow
falling on the walks, on the porous earth, on the cobblestone street.
These nights in our bed, my head on your belly,

I can hear these thumps and later, when you fall asleep,
when I stand in our daughter's room, painted pink,
bare yet but for a simple wooden crib, something

plummets inside me, rises up, out of proportion
to the time I've been portioned on this earth.
And if what is granted erases nothing,

as the darkness rides into our hemisphere,
your belly still moves moonward, a small hill
on the horizon, swelling, floating with a child,

white, yellow, who knows, who can tell her,
oh what does it matter?

This early draft exemplifies what Mura calls "a stage where I try to allow anything to
come into the poem, where I cast my net as widely as possible.  I like the chaos of this stage, the
free wheeling and experimental mode.  I sometimes feel that students I've taught try to tidy up
their poems too quickly and therefore don't push themselves in new directions, don't make room
for unexpected discoveries.  Creativity comes in part from living with uncertainty, chaos, formless-
ness, from providing an arena for the unanticipated, for things coming from left field."

In this "free wheeling and experimental mode," Mura recalls his past when, in his twenties,
he would trawl bars and pornographic stores.  From *WTBMM*, Mura remembers:

There was something out there, some woman, some image, that would transform me, let
me enter that dream I was creating out of dope and booze and the magazines piled in my
closet, their glossy pages of copulation and flesh, their world where there is no other real-
ity but sex. *Playboy, Hustler, Swedish Erotica.*  Sometimes I went to the bars first, trying
my luck, often leaving at closing time for porno stores.

From that period, Mura recalls *Behind the Green Door*, a film released in the 1970s and star-
ring Marilyn Chambers.  One of the original "Ivory Soap" girls, Chambers was blonde, attractive in

a wholesome way and fittingly fulfilled the classic "girl next door" fantasy.  In the movie, Mura says, "She is kidnapped and taken to a club where she is stripped and first bathed with oil by four women who also stroke her body before is she laid upon a table on a stage.  A black man then emerges from behind a lighted green door at the back of the stage.  His face and chest are painted with streaks of white paint, a necklace of claws encirles his neck.  He is naked except for white stretch pants with a large circle cut out at the crotch.  They make love for a long time. . . ."

Mura describes the film's significance as:

> Amid (the movie's) welter of sexual acts, I know the movie has something to do with miscegenation, with what Susie (Mura's Caucasian wife) and I represent together.  I know this has something to do with the other I am not, the black man, representative of the primitive, of Africa, striding across the screen, larger than life.  Other myths, other taboos.  The images fuse with my own history.  I hear echoes of literary passages, of the glossy pages in my closet, of cheap paperbacks with their rumors of black prowess.  I know there is something missing, that I will never find my body, my Asian body, up there on the screen, and this rage erases all other considerations, consumes me.  In the twisted logic coagulating in my brain, I am determined to create my own damnation, to uncover the pornographic behind any facade of innocence, to prove that sexuality drives us, or should drive us all, if we were only bold and free enough.

Further into the poem, Mura includes a reference to himself as a "five-year-old./ his bluff of six guns pointed at the camer, holster of plastic bullets/ strapped round his belly, already a bit too big, his cowboy hat black,// cocked at an angle.  (How ridiculous: A cowboy?  He's Japanese.)" The reference relates to Mura's upbringing which he describes as growing up "cozily unconscious of race."  He says this "unconscious(ness)," is part of the Japanese American community's attempt to assimilate — explaining why the Nissei rarely speak Japanese and why Mura's father shortened the original family name of "Uyemura" to make it more pronounceable.  As Mura explains it in WTBMM, "Would my parents have spoken Japanese to us if they were fluent?  Probably not.  What purpose would it have served?  And those Japanese Americans who settled in the Midwest probably had less of a desire to return to the past or nurture their cultural roots than those who went back to the West Coast after the internment camps."

Such a state of affairs obviously is unsatisfactory to Mura.  As he says in sections of the poem (that, though later deleted in the final draft, reflect his thought process):

> From Part 3: "to believe the world is built on illusion, is nothing, to believe it will all be redeemed, all be condemned, all will be well,/ there's a plan, a meaning—Anything but the wheel of history/ rolling on and on, past this glade where a crowd of men mill about,/ pausing for a photo with their prize, strung from a rope"

> From Part 4: "Like travellers who cannot decide what possessions to let go,/ we are, it seems, overburdened with history.  Feminism, racism,/ all the theories and castigations that leave us with the illusion// that justice is, justice was, possible (if only, if only, if only)."

Another part of the "chaos" at this first draft stage is in Part 3, the moment when Mura says he "discovered (his) sexuality" as he looked at a June 1964 Playboy.  In Turning Japanese,

Mura describes this experience as similar to "many other American boys." But he also says that because the playmate was "white, her beauty seemingly self-evident. I sense somehow that she must be more beautiful than Asian women, more prestigious" even as the "forbidden quality of sex overpower(ed) any thought of race."

Because Mura is allowing himself "chaos" at this early drafting stage, it makes sense that much in this draft later would be deleted. For example, in looking at Part 4, all of which is later dropped, he says, "I can see several reasons for why I cut it: It lacks focus, some of it simply lists details from the camps, some of it echoes earlier imagery in a way that feels repetitive and prosaic; it doesn't have a clear sense of progression. Most likely I didn't try to reason my decision to cut; I simply felt intuitively the language wasn't working, it was second rate."

When asked whether this early draft reflected an approach of writing down themes for subsequent exploration and/or refinement, Mura responds, "That seems a bit too calculated a way of putting it. This may have happened; in other words, bits of the poem or the poem's theme that came in later started here. But I don't think of this as a conscious process of moving from abstract to the concrete or from a statement of a theme to its embodiment. It's more accurate to say I was experimenting with trying to use a more abstract language to embody what the poem was about. This reflects my belief that there are limits with the 'show don't tell' aesthetic; such an aesthetic would exclude a set of poetic influences that runs from Shakespeare to Donne to Browning to certain passages in Eliot to Milosz to various contemporaries."

It's also worth noting that in Part 6 of the poem, Mura introduces "A friend, reading all this, seemed befuddled, amazed." This reflects what Mura describes as his "general practice (wherein) I like to try arguing against the drift of any piece I am writing. I think we are contradictory creatures, that the truth is more complex than any one formulation. A poetic archetype for this for me might be something like Snodgrass's *After Experience* or some of Frank Bidart's poems about his father. In one of my performance videos I even argue with myself about whether race had anything to do with my adolescent sense of sexuality (when I do it on stage I argue with an video clip of myself; on the video for broadcast I'm split into two images)."

Mura's introduction of his "friend" also relates to real-life incidents of friends suggesting "that I sometimes present myself and the processes I've gone through in a harshly negative light. I think this is probably true. In *Turning Japanese*, for instance, I didn't spend any space describing the long hours my wife and I simply sat together in quiet peace reading or watching videos. I was more intrigued with our quarrels and in those quarrels I felt I needed to make sure I came off worse than she did. In part, this was because of a sense of fairness—I was telling the tale—and in part as a strategy towards winning the reader's trust—I wasn't going to try to use other people to make myself look better, I was going to tell the truth even when it made me look like a jerk."

Nonetheless, this method "where friends come in and challenge the drift of things," Mura says, "makes the writing more lively and complex and allows a more exploratory movement."

Finally, this early draft ends with the line, "Oh what does it matter." In the final draft, Mura changed the line to "Oh why must it matter." He says, "The 'what' seems more dismissive; the 'why,' while containing that sense, also opens things up to inquiry and speculation — it's more resonant, carries more meanings."

**PHOTOGRAPH OF A LYNCHING**

1

These men? ~~Through~~ In the bagginess of their trousers, their dented felt hats,
tilted to one side, fingers tugging their suspenders or vests,
in the way their faces are either a bit puffy or too lean,

and their eyes almost ~~imperceptably~~ imperceptibly too thin, too close together,
[New L] they seem, perhaps, too like the image you might have of the South,
~~you can tell they are Southern, from~~ the Thirties.  [Del L] Of course they are white;
        who else could create this

cardboard figure, face flat and grey like cardboard,
eyes oversized and bulging, like some krazy kewpie doll
or ancient totem the gang has dug up. At the far right,

with a small browed cap, a boy of around twelve seems,
though it's hard to tell, to be smiling, as if responding
to what's most familiar here: the taking of a picture.

It is the same with the rest. Though directly above them,
a branch leashes the dead negro by a rope up in the air,
the men too ~~remain preternaturally intent on the camera,~~ focus the blank beam of their
        gaze on

the unseen eye. Which is, at this moment, us. Or, more precisely, [Del L] me.
[New L] And for what purpose? We, I, have seen all of this before:
Horror, outrage, brutal depravity—the words by now

seem empty, abandoned, devoid of sense. Certainly,
nothing here surprises me...So why am I writing this?
It goes deeper. Fifteen years ago. Behind the Green Door .

I am sitting in the dark of a theatre with a dozen other men.
(It's a scene I've visited before, and will, more often through the years.)
There's a woman ~~laid out~~ splayed on a table, ~~naked~~ naked, the same one

on the Ivory Snow soap boxes, holding a baby on her shoulder,
smiling her blond, ~~virtually~~ practically pure white smile; already
we've seen this woman sitting on a patio above the valley,

being kidnapped, dragged in through the alley, black hooded figures
muscling her body (perhaps the way, a few years earlier,
Patricia Hearst was "liberated" from her private world,

strapped to ~~the~~ history's wheel ~~of history~~), and now, after being prepared,
serviced, by a handful of women, each moving their hands
up and down the body, abstractly, half-smiling,

as one of them kneels and buries her face in her crotch,
now she is ready: And now he walks in—Lean, naked, black,
streaks of white paint on his chest and face, a necklace of teeth,

it's almost comical, this fake garb of the jungle, Africa
before All-America, black and blond, almost ~~comical~~ a joke
but for the ~~sudden~~ surge ~~when what has long been regarded~~ that jolts across lines
          so long entrenched

as the ultimate crime against nature (so that even a glance,
a look by a black man, could bring this photo in my hands) ~~;~~ ,
is suddenly there on the screen, the black man kneeling to

this kidnapped body ~~; then sliding~~ , slipping himself in, ~~as~~ the screen ~~shows~~ showing it all,
down to her head shaking like a seizure, the final scream before
he lifts himself off her body, which is whimpering, quivering...

I walked out of that theatre ~~as if~~ , bolted from a dream into a dream.
I stared at the cars whizzing by, watched the light change,
red, yellow, green, and the haze in my head from the hash,

and the haze in my head from the image, melded together, reverberating.
I don't know what I did afterwards. Only, night after night,
I will want to see ~~it again and again~~ those bodies, black, white (who watches is the third) —

like a miracle, a talisman, a rageful, unrelenting release.

2
~~So why am I writing this? How did I arrive here?~~
~~How speak without using the sentence, "Very early in my life,~~
~~it was already too late..." It is, of course, a question of desire.~~

~~How early did it start? The face I had at five, at twelve, at twenty-five,~~
~~it is true, possessed the same lack of definition—soft, rounded,~~
~~overly fleshy—a woman's face really, and certain women I was with,~~

~~stroking my cheek, my chest, would remark on the smoothness,~~
~~the lack of hair (so that I wonder now if that—was what~~
~~attracted them—what I found so embarassing, so unmanly).~~

I know.  Perhaps, like the name of certain deities,
such things are better left unspoken.  Or like ancient relics,
buried in a tomb, in darkness, untouched.  And yet,

in a way, all I have, all I have become, begins
with the collusion of whatever inside me still responds
to degradation, destruction, intractable negation;

and what I want to bring forth now are not exactly causes—
as if the connection betwen these moments could ever
really be explained—but images, dreams, further allusions:

~~Certainly I see much of this now through the face of that~~ A second photo then, nothing
        like the first.  A five-year-old,
his ~~bluff of~~ six guns pointed at the camera, holster ~~of~~ , plastic bullets
~~strapped round~~ around his belly, already a bit too big ~~, his~~ ; cowboy hat black,

cocked at an angle. (How ridiculous: A cowboy? He's Japanese.)
~~He stands on the steps of the Broadway apartment, a block from Lake Michigan,~~
~~in the windy city, city of gangsters, butchers, crooked politicians.~~

~~Next year, his hero will be Mickey Mantle, Roger Maris, Crazy Legs Hirsch;~~
~~but now, in the photo, his skin dark from the sun, he's Paladin,~~
~~squinting~~ Squinting at the light, ~~and~~ he wears, like all boys in such photos,
[Del P] an attempt at what—toughness? bravado? ease?  ~~forgeting~~ forgetting how, [Del L] each
        night,

[New P] injuns, bad guys, robbers, ~~the nightmares of childhood,~~ [Del L] ~~harmless hauntings,~~
        enter his room, shadows flittering about...
[Del P] ~~Yes, it all comes back now.~~ Slowly it returns. Early summer, moths batter the screen.
        Whoosh
~~Sounds~~ of the Broadway traffic drift in; from the living room, the muffled t.v.

[New P] In the next bed, he hears his younger sister, taunting him, daring him
[Del P] —he cannot hurt her, he cannot  hurt her —(Who knows
how long they have been talking like this, eyes open in the dark ~~;~~ ?
~~how long they have watched headlights flow across the walls?)~~

~~And~~ Moments later, when his father slams open the door, ~~and stands there,~~
the law decreed by his body, his shouts stalking the chaos
that's erupted in his house, ~~who can recall  the sister?~~ does the brother or sister recall? —

how, with his fist balled or his flat open palm, he descends
on the boy's body with the same swift motion that the boy,
like an animal, like a scared and angry little boy,

descended on his sister, beating her in the dark...Wait.
Did that really happen? It's all seems so uncertain.
(And what family doesn't contain such scenes or squabbles?)

But of course, there are other photos, other dreams.
In the next one, home from school with a slight fever,
I wake to an empty house—my mother's out shopping—

and enter my parent's room. I slide back their closet door
start rummaging among the shoes, all lined precisely,
facing one way; then the garment bags, unzipping them—

When I pull it out and open the pages, what spills before me
is only the photo millions of men, white, black, yellow, have seen,
though the body before me is white, eighteen, the breasts enormous,

almost frightening in their statement—the aureoles
seem large as my fist—and as the three unfolded pages
lay before me on the floor, I find myself touching myself,

and there is, in the back of my mind, some terror,
my mother will come home, I'll be found out,
some delight I've never felt before,

and I do not cry out, I make no sound...

3

How little such incidents, such explanations, give us. Better to say
the soul entered this abyss, in the soul is this abyss, this voice, this demon,
to believe in the golden scales of incarnation, justice and retribution,

to believe the world is built on illusion, is nothing, to believe
it will all be redeemed, all be condemned, all will be well,
there's a plan, a meaning—Anything but the wheel of history

rolling on and on, past this glade where a crowd of men mill about,
pausing for a photo with their prize, strung from a rope;
past this bedroom where a boy crept over to his sister's bed,

where his father hauled him on his lap as he squirmed like a beetle,
past a studio where a naked blond woman lying on a platform, leans on her elbow,
and asks the grip man how long before the lights will be done...

I think of the time my father and mother came to therapy,
and my therapist got him talking of those years as a young man,
what he must have given up to make it, feed his family, buy that home,

~~the prejudice, the pressures, hours and trips away. And I could see,~~
~~for a second, like heat lightning on the horizon of a summer night,~~
~~a faint, spidery redness etching the whites of his eyes, luring~~

~~this ripple from his muscles up his neck, past his chin,~~
~~through his cheeks, and just at the moment, I thought~~
~~the spasm would hit that redness just rising in his eyes,~~

~~an alarm went off, everything shut off, composure set in, no,~~
~~not composure, a look of what—bewilderment? confusion?—no,~~
~~it seemed to me almost a gaze of stupidity, as if his knowledge~~

~~of himself, of the past, had reached its zenith, the blankness~~
~~in his eyes almost frightened, saying, ""No, no, it was what~~
~~I was supposed to do, there wasn't anything to it, anything at all..."~~

~~Somehow, uneasily, that incident connects with another awakening.~~
~~The fall I was twelve, home one day from school with a slight fever.~~
~~I enter my parents room, my mother's out shopping.~~

~~I slide back their closet door, start rummaging among the shoes,~~
~~all lined precisely, facing one way; then the garment bags, unzipping them—~~
~~what am I looking for? how did I know it was there?—~~

~~When I pull it out and open the pages, what spills before me~~
~~is only the image, the photo, millions of men, white, black, yellow, have seen,~~
~~though the body before me is white, eighteen, the breasts enormous,~~

~~almost frightening in their statement—the aureoles~~
~~seem large as my fist—and as the three unfolded pages~~
~~lay before me on the floor, I find myself touching myself,~~

~~and there is, in the back of my mind, some terror,~~
~~my mother will come home, I'll be found out,~~
~~some delight I have never felt before,~~

~~and I do not cry out, I make no sound...~~

4
~~Think of a man staring at a photograph of torture,~~
~~abmonination, rape, a land laid waste. Think of him~~
~~turning away, expunged, as if suddenly outside his door~~

~~he'd heard the sound of the river rushing past, as if~~
~~he'd waken out of a dream. Think of him turning back,~~
~~dripping with the unknown, holding before him the photo~~

amid that endless roar. Think of something streaming
inside him, the lashing foam, strafings of the current,
the jar of rocks and slap of stone. Think of him sinking.

It is like that moment when the priest raises the blade
above the quivering goat and then, with or without
the touch of lightning in the night summoned above him,

the blade and flesh enter each other, life force is released,
and the sacred screams back into silence. We are
hollow inside. Something fills us. Wandering in and out.

How could I know what was speaking inside me,
how many of the departed and dead, bodies I'd never seen,
aroused, waiting, what men, what women, hated me there,

and there, in a primal forest, spreading tendrils of leaf light
above the basin of root life, a little birth, a little ancient blood,
a small photo of fathers was winking like an accomplice.

Atrocity smiled, and I smiled back. And I felt weightless,
dissolved, as if floating, as if in the arms of a mother,
thrown from her depths. And now, as if, from the drowsy lids,

some other weeping flows, I see in the face of the dead negro,
not just a foretaste of sleep, undivided dreams, much less
the rage I want to call up and am hardly near, but the face,

delayed for a while, adapted to circumstance, expunged of his past,
of my father, of something he escaped and did not,
of what I run from and towards, as in the dream

where I stand by his bed, not knowing whether
he is asleep or not, whether, when, I should wake him,
why am I too late, why nothing can be done.

     — That's all. The immovable eye can always watch.
Love, though this is not a word I might use,
what makes this so difficult has set in my hand this photo,

this constellation of images, and drawn them forth
like cards, one by one. How is it among them,
I found your face, fading before me on the table?

Or is it my hand that's covering it all?

5

~~A friend, reading all this, seemed bewildered, annoyed,~~
~~as if the self revealed here, were antithetical~~
~~not to some mild mannered mask I wear,~~

~~like everyone else, on social occassions —~~
~~no, he's hardly that naive, has had his own demons,~~
~~breakdowns, incidents of ugliness he'd want to keep~~

~~sealed in a vault—No, it's precisely because he knows~~
~~what I've been through, that he wanted all that went between~~
~~then and now, how one day you wake with everything~~

~~collapsed about you, ruin, decay, shame, drugs, random bodies,~~
~~songs of self hatred; and suddenly you're tired,~~
~~and suddenly the sense you've always been broken~~

~~no longer makes sense. You ask for help, you resist,~~
~~you ask for help. It's so simple, though surely exhausting.~~
~~Redemption, a second chance, an old yet new song.~~

~~So why not provide that tune? Certainly, in these flickerings,~~
~~these faint wordings of the past, these recognitions~~
~~and recollections of the present, with all the confusions~~

~~the mind revives again, seeing where I stand~~
~~is so strange, even to me, seeing my asking~~
~~after history, after judgement, hints not just at desires~~

~~for knowledge or justice or even beauty, but that here,~~
~~in these turmoils, in the twistings of the boy, the man I was,~~
~~there's the exploration—how unlikely, how lucky—of pleasure.~~

~~And yet it is this pleasure I think now I have to let go.~~
~~For what matters now is not why, what explanations~~
~~can justify, ameliorate, forgive, but all I have incurred,~~
Once, at sixteen, a sharp, red, glistening sore
engulfed my penis—I was still a virgin;
how did the microbes know?—And while my father

applied the watery salve, I, in the mirror,
observed my face, trying not to look down.
For a moment his touch was gentle, sure.

"Don't move," he said;  and when I recall him there,
like an altar boy kneeling before the rail,

all I can see is his black, Brylcreamed hair....

Once there was a sweetness inside me like the story
someone tells each night till a boy grows old.
Why did that story take so long to find me?

Perhaps I should start again, embrace confusion,
contradiction, all the impossible puzzles of blame
the past brings forth, full of present illusions—

From father to son, from man to woman,
from niggers and japs, coolies and slaves,
from the years of Jim Crow and relocation...

—And yet perhaps there are simpler songs of grace.
[Del L] ~~all I will incur. My tiny mortal sum.~~ Tonight it rains softly [Del L] on ~~the roofs of~~ my
     city, street lamps
[New L] glow down the hill, [Del L] and before me my face

[New P] is ~~mirrored before me,~~ dark on the glass. [Del P] ~~In moments, the~~ Soon rain will
     be ~~glisten there~~ glistening
[New L] as snow, snow [Del L] falling on the walks, ~~on~~ the porous earth ~~, on the cobblestone
     street~~.
These nights in our bed, my head on your belly,

I can hear these thumps ; and later, when you fall asleep,
~~when~~ I stand in our daughter's room, ~~painted pink,~~ so [Del L] bare yet
[New L] but for a simple wooden crib, and something

plummets inside me, rises up, out of proportion
to the time I've been portioned on this earth.
And if what is granted erases nothing,

as the darkness ~~rides into~~ flows toward our hemisphere, your ~~belly~~ hollow
still moves moonward, ~~a~~ small hill on ~~on~~ the horizon,
swelling, floating with a child, white, yellow,

[New P] who [Del P] knows, who can tell her, oh what does it matter?


     In this drafting stage, Mura is cutting out "a lot of material that seems to be throat clear-
ing, that talks around the material or merely (serves) to introduce key images. Start as close as
possible to *in medias res*—in the middle of things." For example, Mura says about deleting the
lines that name Mickey Mantle, Roger Maris and Crazy Legs Hirsch, "One name will suffice; you
don't need to make the same point over and over." In the Final Draft, Mura referenced just one
boyhood hero: Paladin.

Yet Mura also deleted the reference in Part 3 to the therapy session. For about three years after graduate school, Mura worked with therapists to overcome depression until he got to a position where, as he describes it in *Turning Japanese*, he "was stuck. I kept calling my parents, shouting in anger, demanding that they acknowledge what they'd done — my father's physical abuse, my mother's put-downs ('David, you think too much of yourself')."

At the insistence of his therapists, he asked his parents to join him in a group session. After his parents reluctantly attended, they and Mura could not agree on the causes for his depression that manifested itself in years of sexual promiscuity and addiction to pornography. As Mura described this incident in *Turning Japanese*, he recalls one of the therapists whispering to him that he should tell his mother how much he needed her:

> "I can't," I hissed, "I can't."
>
> But he kept at me. Finally, I blurted out, "I need you, I love you I need you so much," and burst out in tears.
>
> My mother sat there, stunned. And then, to my surprise, she rose and hugged me. It was not a typical gesture. I was rippling with sobs.
>
> In Japan when I thought of that session, it seemed like a dream. Part of me wanted to pretend it had never happened that I couldn't have been so vulnerable.

In *WTBMM*, published five years after *Turning Japanese*, Mura recalls the incident again. This time, Mura characterized his mother's action as a "gift." Shortly after the poem describes this incident is the image of the father putting salve on the son's penis, which Mura describes in *WTBMM* as "a gesture of love." Consequently, Mura later would drop these two incidents from the poem because (in addition to the language being "too prosey") both "didn't fit with the thematic drift of the poem, (lacking) the sense of darkness that runs through the poem."

Mura also notes that many of his poems begin as "long lines" partly due to the influence of C.K. Williams and because "the long lines give me the freedom to say anything, no matter how prosey; they give my voice room to breathe and manuever, to fool with syntax and some rather prolix formulations. Much of this doesn't stay, but I don't think I'd get the bits that do stay without this room. In general I found early on that moving into longer lines helped relax my sense of language so that I could encompass a more colloquial mode."

"As I begin to shape the poem, the lines get shorter until in the final version they're in loose iambic pentameter, which is a very natural form for me (here the influence is perhaps the meditative poems of Wallace Stevens, such as *Esthetique du Mal*, which is also written in tercets, (as well as) Elizabeth Bishop. The iambic pentameter seems to lead me always into a more recognizably literary voice."

"As the drafts progress, I try to make the language more and more concise and this naturally begins to shrink down the lines," Mura continues. "The discipline of the iambic pentameter forces me to be more succinct, to experiment in word choice and syntax, and to push towards a more rhythmic expression. The tercets, which I later abandoned, also allowed me to discover shapes within the material and various ways of sculpting the material."

Mura adds that he deleted Section 3 as "too prosey" and Section 4 as "too unfocused and too much making clear what's already been presented."

III.   Set of Drafts Titled "TRIPTYCH"

## TRIPTYCH

1 ~~Photograph of a Lynching (circa 193__)~~   *Photograph of a Lynching (circa 193__)*

These men? In the bagginess of their trousers, their dented felt hats,
tilted to one side, fingers tugging their suspenders or vests,
in the way their faces are either a bit puffy or too lean,

and their eyes almost imperceptibly too thin, too close together,
they seem, perhaps, too like the image you might have of the South,
the Thirties. Of course they are white; who else could create this

cardboard figure, face flat and grey like cardboard,
eyes oversized and bulging, like some crazy kewpie doll
or ancient totem the gang has dug up. At the far right,

with a small browed cap, a boy of around twelve seems,
though it's hard to tell, to be smiling, as if responding
to what's most familiar here: the taking of a picture.

It is the same with the rest. Though directly above them,
a branch leashes the dead negro by a rope in the air,
the men too focus the blank beam of their gaze on

the unseen eye. Which is, at this moment, us. Or, more precisely, me.
And for what purpose? We, I, have seen all of this before:
Horror, outrage, brutal depravity—the words by now

seem empty, abandoned, devoid of sense. Certainly,
nothing here surprises me...So why am I writing this?
It goes deeper. Fifteen years ago. ~~Behind the Green Door.~~ *Behind the Green Door* .

I am sitting in the dark of a theater with a dozen other men.
On the screen a woman splayed on a table, stripped, the same one
on the Ivory Snow soap boxes, holding a baby on her shoulder,

smiling her blond, practically pure white smile; already
we've seen this woman sitting on a patio above the valley,
being kidnapped, dragged in through the alley, black

hooded figures muscling her body (perhaps the way,
a few years earlier, Patricia Hearst was "liberated"
from her private world, strapped to history's wheel),

and now, after being prepared, serviced, by a handful
of women, each moving their hands up and down
the body, abstractly, half-smiling, as one of them

kneels and buries her face in her crotch, now
she is ready: And now he walks in—Lean, naked, black,
streaks of white paint on his chest and face, a necklace of teeth,

it's almost comical, this fake garb of the jungle, Africa
before All-America, black and blond, almost a joke
but for the surge that floods the eye with the force

of the forbidden, what these lynchers regarded
as the ultimate crime against nature: the black man
kneeling to this kidnapped body, slipping himself in,

the screen showing it all, down to her head shaking
like a seizure, the final scream before he lifts himself
off her body, which is whimpering, quivering...

I walked out of that theater, bolted from a dream into a dream.
I stared at the cars whizzing by, watched the light change,
red, yellow, green, and the haze in my head from the hash,

and the haze in my head from the image, melded together, reverberating.
I don't know what I did afterwards. Only, night after night,
I will want to see those bodies, black, white (who watches is the third)—

like a miracle, a talisman, a rageful, unrelenting release.


2 ~~Photograph of the Author (circa 1957)~~ *Photograph of the Author (circa 1957)*

A second photo, nothing like the first. ~~A five-year-old,~~
I'm five, my six guns ~~pointed at the camera, holster of plastic~~ aimed at the lens;
~~bullets strapped round his belly, already a bit too big,~~
~~his~~ [Del P] cowboy hat ~~is~~ black, cocked at an angle.
~~(How ridiculous. A cowboy? He's Japanese)~~

[New P] Next year ~~his~~ my hero will be Mickey Mantle,
[Del P] but now, skin dark from the sun, ~~he's~~ I'm Paladin,
and squinting at the light, ~~he wears~~ I wear, like all boys

[New P] in such photos, an attempt at what—toughness?
[New L] bravado? ease? — (And yet, it seems so ridiculous.
How can I be a cowboy? I'm Japanese.)

forgetting how, each night, injuns, bad guys, robbers,
enter his room, shadows flittering about...
Slowly, the images return. Early summer,

moths batter the screen. Whoosh of the Broadway
traffic drifts in; from the living room, the muffled t.v.
In the next bed, he hears his younger brother

daring him he cannot hurt him, he cannot hurt him....
Moments later, when my father slams open the door,
Moments later, I'm riding with my father
in our Bel-Air, up Broadway, past the El,
my six guns pointed at cars whizzing past,

blast after blast, until, impatient, my father's
arm swings across the seat, and I sit
back, silent at last. I don't recall arriving

at Sears or what we bought, only that,
a half hour later, as I step out with my father,
a man in a green, grease stained suit,

steps forward, starts shouting, "Hey,
you a Jap? You from Tokyo? You a Chink?
Listen to me, boy. You a Jap? A Chink?"

Wobbling down the walk, he keeps it up,
the words with spittle jabbing like pebbles,
and as my father hustles us to the car, I keep

waiting for some explosion, some shot
like a balloon splattering shards, the way
his shouts slapped me just before his fist,

but no, nothing happens, just the key in the ignition,
just the man at the windshield, shouting, just
father's face, rigid as the wheel his fingers grasp...

Later that night in my bedroom, the whoosh
of traffic drifts in; moths, like fingertips, peck
the screen; from the living room, the muffled t.v.

In the next bed, my younger brother's taunting me—
you can't hurt me, you can't hurt me.... *you can't hurt me, you can't hurt me...*—
In the rhythmn of this night, the rhythmn of brothers,

who can explain where this chant began,
or why, when my father slams open the door,
the law decreed by his body, his shouts

stalking the chaos that's erupted in his house,
~~which brother can recall how, with fist-balled~~
~~or flat open palm, the father~~ he descends on ~~the boy's~~ [Del P] ~~body~~ his son with the same
        swift motion
[New L] that the ~~boy~~ son, [Del L] like an animal, like a scared and angry little boy,

[New P] descended on his brother, beating him in the dark?...


3 ~~Miss June 1984~~ *Miss June 1984*

~~Later, there are other photos, other dreams.~~
~~In the next one,~~ One last photo. I'm twelve, home from school
[New L] with a slight fever ~~;~~ . [Del L] I wake to an empty house—
[New L] my mother's out shopping— [Del P] and enter my parent's room.

[New P] I slide back ~~their~~ the closet door , [Del P] start rummaging
[New L] among ~~the~~ shoes, all lined precisely, [Del L] facing one way;
[New L] then the garment bags, unzipping them—

When I pull it out and open the pages,
[New L] what spills before me [Del L] is only the photo
[New L] millions of men, white, black, yellow, have seen,

[New P] though the body before me is white, eighteen,
[New L] the breasts enormous, [Del P] almost frightening
[New L] ~~in their statement~~ —the aureoles [Del L] seem large as my fist—

[New P] ~~and as~~ As the three unfolded pages [Del L] lay before me
[New L] on the floor, I find myself touching myself,
[Del P] and there is, in the back of my mind, some terror,

[New P] my mother will come home, I'll be found out,
some delight I've never felt before,
[Del P] and I do not cry out, I make no sound...


3 ~~Sonogram (1989)~~

~~Tonight, it rains softly on my city, street lamps~~
~~glow down the hill, and before me my face~~
~~is dark on the glass. Soon rain will be~~

~~glistening as snow, snow falling~~
~~on the walks, on the river with its barges,~~
~~and beyond, in the forest of the past,~~

~~on the dead negro, his chest bare,~~
~~lifeless as leather. Father,~~
~~I married a woman not of my color.~~

~~Tell me: what is it I want to escape?~~
So. Should I tell how long it took to see
that boy (or, really, any of these scenes),
without indulging a flood of shame?

Or how is it I've started to admit
whatever confusions my father must have felt?
Or by what other indirect and crooked paths

I arrived here? Tonight it snows softly
on my city, street lamps glow down the hill,
and before me my face is dark on the glass;

~~and later, when she falls asleep,~~
~~These~~ these nights in our bed, my head
on my wife's belly, I can hear these thumps,
[Del P] and later, when she falls asleep,

[New P] I stand in our daughter's room,
[New L] so bare yet [Del L] but for a simple wooden
[New L] crib [Del P] — ( on the bulletin board

[New P] I've pinned the sonogram [Del L] with
[New L] ~~its~~ black and white swirls like a galaxy
~~of stars~~ spinning about the fetal body — )

and something plummets inside me,
rises out of proportion to the time
I've been portioned on this earth.

And if what is granted erases nothing,
if history remains, implaccable as ~~this photo~~ these photos,
~~still~~ as darkness flows up ~~through~~ [Del P] our hemisphere,

[New P] her hollow still moves [Del L] moonward,
[New L] small hill on the horizon, [Del L] swelling,
[New L] floating with child, white, yellow, [Del P] who

[New P] knows, who can tell her, oh what does it matter?

The "TRIPTYCH" drafts may be seen as examples of a drafting attempt that failed to satisfy the poet. Mura says he might have just learned the word, "triptych," which encouraged him to experiment with its concept. Also, he recalls that, at the time, the material seemed like it could be divided into three parts. Ultimately, however, he says he couldn't get the material "to fit in a way that made poetic sense."

"I felt I was finally forcing the material into the form," he says. "Somehow Bishop's poems in *Geography* served as more appropriate formal models."

During the "TRIPTYCH" stage, Mura also introduces the scene at Sears (changed to IGA in the Final Draft) where a stranger yells at them, "Hey, you a Jap? You from Tokyo? You a Chink?" Whereas the boy in the poem expected his father to explode at the stranger, the father instead does nothing. The father only drives home in "rigid" silence. The poem, however, next moves into a scene that occurs later that night when the father ends up barging into his son's bedroom and beating the boy who had been engaged in noisy taunts with his brother; subsequently, the beaten boy also would beat up his brother. For Mura, the incidents have a wider significance.

"This is about the conditioning of the camps (where Japanese Americans were forcibly gathered in the mainland United States during World War II) and the conditioning brought to bear upon Asians in America and perhaps something of the Japanese cultural heritage and the relationship of the peasants to the samurai (the nail that sticks up gets hit on the head, shoo *ga nai* — it can't be helped). It is also about how racial violence or insults outside the family can be internalized within the family. This passage alludes to the unreleased rage of many of the Nisei men, their sense that they had to live within a narrow spectrum of behavior or expression, that they had to watch what they said and did."

It is an issue that makes Mura recall one of his epigraphs from *Turning Japanese* by Bruno Bettelheim that discusses the so-called "Stockholm syndrome" in the concentration camps in Europe: "Old prisoners who identified themselves with the SS did so not only in respect to aggressive behavior. They would try to acquire old pieces of SS uniforms . . . . When asked why they did it, the old prisoners admitted that they loved to look like the guards."

IV.  Changes Between "TRIPTYCH" And Draft Titled "THE COLORS OF DESIRE":

**TRIPTYCH**

1  *Photograph of a Lynching (circa ~~193——~~) 1930)*

These men? In ~~the bagginess of their trousers,~~ their dented felt hats,
~~tilted to one side,~~ in the way their fingers ~~tugging~~ tug their suspenders or vests,
~~in the way~~ with their faces ~~are either~~ a bit puffy or too lean, [Del P] ~~and their~~ eyes
~~almost imperceptibly too thin, too~~ narrow and close together,
they seem, ~~perhaps,~~ too like ~~the~~ our image ~~you might have~~ of the South,
the Thirties. Of course they are white;
[New L] who ~~else~~ then could create this [Del P]cardboard figure, face
[New L] flat and grey ~~like cardboard~~, [Del L] eyes oversized ~~and~~ , bulging ; like ~~some~~

~~crazy kewpie doll~~
~~or~~ <u>an</u> ancient totem ~~the~~ <u>this</u> gang has dug up. At the far right,
[Del P] ~~with~~ <u>in</u> a small browed cap, a boy of ~~around~~ twelve ~~seems~~ <u>smiles,</u>
~~though it's hard to tell, to be smiling,~~ as if responding [Del L] to what's most familiar here:
[New L] the ~~taking of a picture~~ <u>camera's click.</u> [Del P] ~~It is the same with the rest. Though~~
    <u>And though</u> directly above them,
a branch ~~leashes~~ <u>ropes</u> the dead negro ~~by a rope~~ in the air,
the men too focus ~~the~~ <u>their</u> blank beam
[New L] ~~of their gaze~~ on [Del P] the unseen eye. Which is, at this moment, us.

[New P] Or, more precisely, me. <u>Who cannot but recall</u>
~~And for what purpose? We, I, have seen all of this before:~~
~~Horror, outrage, brutal depravity—the words by now~~

~~seem empty, abandoned, devoid of sense. Certainly,~~
~~nothing here surprises me...So why am I writing this?~~
<u>how my father, as a teenager, clutched his weekend pass,</u>
<u>passed through the rifle towers and gates</u>
<u>of the Jerome, Arkansas camp, and, in 1942,</u>
<u>stepped on a bus to find whites riders</u>
<u>motioning, "Sit here, son," and, in the rows beyond,</u>
<u>a half dozen black faces, waving him back,</u>
<u>"Us colored folks got to stick together."</u>
<u>How did he know where to sit? And how is it,</u>

<u>thirty five years later, I found myself sitting</u>
~~It goes deeper. Fifteen years ago.~~ <u>in a dark theatre, watching</u> *Behind the Green Door* .
[Del P] ~~I am sitting in the dark of a theater~~ with a dozen ~~other~~ <u>anonymous</u> men. [Del L] On
    the screen
[New L] a woman ~~splayed~~ <u>sprawls</u> on a table, stripped, the same one
on the Ivory Snow soap ~~boxes~~ <u>box,</u> ~~holding~~ a baby on her shoulder,
[Del L] smiling her blond, practically pure white smile ~~; already~~ .
~~we've seen this woman sitting on a patio above the valley,~~
~~being kidnapped, dragged in through the alley, black~~

~~hooded figures muscling her body (perhaps the way,~~
~~a few years earlier, Patricia Hearst was "liberated"~~
~~from her private world, strapped to history's wheel),~~

~~and~~ [Del P] ~~now~~ <u>Now,</u> after being prepared ~~;~~ <u>and</u> serviced <u>slowly</u>
[New L] by a handful [Del L] of women, ~~each moving their hands up and down~~
~~the body, abstractly, half smiling,~~ [Del L] as one of them
[Del P] kneels ~~and~~ , buries her face in her crotch, ~~now~~
she is ready: And now he walks in—

[New P] Lean, naked, black, [Del P] streaks of white paint on his chest

[New L] and face, a necklace of teeth, [Del P] it's almost comical,

[New L] this fake garb of the jungle, Africa [Del L] ~~before~~ <u>and</u> All-America,

[New L] black and blond, almost a joke [Del L] but for the surge ~~that floods the eye with the force~~

[Del P] of ~~the forbidden,~~ what these lynchers regarded [Del L] as the ultimate crime

[New L] against nature: the black man [Del L] kneeling to this kidnapped

[New L] body, slipping himself in, [Del P] the screen showing it all, down

[New P] to her head shaking [Del L] ~~like~~ <u>in</u> a seizure, the final scream

before he lifts himself [Del L] off her <u>quivering</u> body, ~~which is whimpering, quivering~~...


I ~~walked out of~~ <u>left</u> that theater, bolted from a dream into a dream.

I stared at the cars whizzing by, watched the light change,

red, yellow, green, and the haze in my head from the hash,

[Del P] and the haze in my head from the image, melded together, reverberating.

I don't know what I did afterwards. Only, night after night,

I will ~~want to~~ see those bodies, black, white <u>(and where am I,</u>

[New L] ~~(who watches is~~ the <u>missing</u> third)— [Del P] like a ~~miracle, a~~ talisman, a rageful, unrelenting release.


2  ~~*Photograph of the Author (circa 1957)*~~ <u>1957</u>


~~A second photo, nothing like the first.~~
~~I'm five, my six guns aimed at the lens,~~
~~cowboy hat black, cocked at an angle.~~
<u>Cut to Chicago, June.  A boy of six.</u>
[Del P] Next year my hero will be Mickey Mantle,
but ~~now,~~ <u>this noon, as father eases the Bel-Air past Wilson</u>
<u>with cowboy hat black, cocked at an angle,</u>
<u>my</u> skin dark from the sun, I'm Paladin,
~~and squinting at the light, I wear, like all boys~~

~~in such photos, an attempt at what—toughness?~~
~~bravado? ease? (And yet, it seems so ridiculous.~~
~~How can I be a cowboy? I'm Japanese.)~~

~~Moments later, I'm riding with my father~~
~~in our Bel-Air, up Broadway, past the El,~~
<u>and</u> my six guns ~~pointed~~ <u>point</u> at cars whizzing past,
[Del P] blast after blast, <u>ricocheting the glass.</u>
<u>Like all boys in such moments, my face</u>
<u>attempts a look of what—toughness? bravado? ease?—</u>
[New L] until, impatient, my father's [Del L] arm <u>wails</u>
[New L] ~~swings~~ across the seat, and I sit [Del L] back, silent at last. ~~I don't recall arriving~~

~~at Sears or what we bought, only that,~~

~~a half hour later, as I step out with my father,~~
~~a man in a green, grease-stained suit,~~

~~steps forward, starts shouting, "Hey,~~

[New P]Later, as we step from IGA with our sacks,
a man in a serge suit—stained with ink?—
steps forward, shouts, "Hey, [Del L] you a Jap?
[New L] You from Tokyo? You a Jap?  You a Chink?
~~Listen to me, boy. You a Jap? A Chink?"~~
I stop, look up, I don't know him,
my arm yanks forward, and suddenly,
the sidewalk's rolling, buckling, like lava melting,
and I know father will explode,
shouts, fists, I know his temper.
And then,
I'm in that dream where nothing happens —
The ignition grinds, the man's face presses
the windshield, and father stares ahead,
fingers rigid on the wheel . . .

~~Wobbling down the walk, he keeps it up,~~
~~the words with spittle jabbing like pebbles,~~
~~and as my father hustles us to the car, I keep~~

~~waiting for some explosion, some shot~~
~~like a balloon splattering shards, the way~~
~~his shouts slapped me just before his fist,~~

~~but no, nothing happens, just the key in the ignition,~~
~~just the man at the windshield, shouting, just~~
~~father's face, rigid as the wheel his fingers grasp...~~

~~Later that~~ That night in my bedroom, ~~the whoosh~~ [Del L] ~~of traffic drifts in,~~ moths,
[New L] like fingertips, peck [Del L] the screen;
[New L] from the living room, the muffled t.v.
As I imagine Shane stepping into the dustry street,
[Del P] ~~In~~ in the next bed, my younger brother~~'s~~ starts
[New L] ~~taunting me~~ to taunt—[Del L] *you can't hurt me, you can't hurt me...—*
~~In the rhythmn of this night, the rhythmn of brothers,~~
[Del P] ~~w~~Who can explain where this chant began~~,~~ ?
~~o~~Or why, when ~~my~~ father ~~slams open~~ throws the door open,
~~the law decreed by his body, his~~ shouts [Del P] stalking ~~the~~ chaos ~~that's~~ erupted in his house,
he ~~descends~~ swoops on his son with the same swift motion
that the son, like an animal, like a scared and angry little boy,
[Del P] ~~descended~~ fell on his brother, beating him in the dark?

~~One last photo.~~ I'm twelve, home from school
with a slight fever. ~~I wake to an empty house—~~I slide back the door
~~my mother's out shopping—and enter my parent's room.~~
of my parents' closet—my mother's out shopping—
rummage among pumps, flats, lined in a rack,
unzip the garment bags, one by one.
It slides like a sigh from the folded sweaters.
I flip through ads for cologne, L.P.'s, a man
in a trench coat, lugging a panda-sized Fleischman's fifth.
Somewhere past the photo of Schweitzer
in his pith helmet, and the cartoon nude man
perched as a gargoyle, I spill the photo
~~I slide back the closet door, start rummaging~~
~~among shoes, all lined precisely, facing one way,~~
~~then the garment bags, unzipping them—~~
[Del P] ~~When I pull it out and open the pages,~~
~~what spills before me is only the photo~~
millions of men, white, black, yellow, have seen,
[Del P] though the body before me is white, eighteen~~,~~ :
~~the~~ Her breasts <u>are</u> enormous, almost frightening
—the ~~aureoles~~ <u>aerolas</u> seem large as my fist~~—~~ .
[Del P] As the three ~~unfolded~~ <u>glossy</u> pages ~~lay~~ <u>sprawl</u> before me ~~,~~
~~on the floor,~~ I ~~find myself touching~~ <u>start to touch</u> myself, [Del L] and there is~~,~~
[New L] ~~in the back of my mind,~~ some terror, [Del P] my mother will come home, ~~I'll be found~~
~~out,~~
some delight I've never felt before,
and I do not cry out, I make no sound...

~~So. Should I tell how long it took to see~~
~~that boy (or, really, any of these scenes),~~
~~without indulging a flood of shame?~~

~~Or how is it I've started to admit~~
~~whatever confusions my father must have felt?~~
~~Or by what other indirect and crooked paths—~~

~~I arrived here? Tonight it snows softly~~
~~on my city, street lamps glow down the hill,~~
~~and before me my face is dark on the glass,~~

~~these nights in our bed, my head~~
~~on my wife's belly, I can hear these thumps,~~
~~and later, when she falls asleep,~~

~~I stand in our daughter's room,~~
~~so bare yet but for a simple wooden~~
~~crib (on the bulletin board~~

~~I've pinned the sonogram with~~
~~black and white swirls like a galaxy~~
~~spinning about the fetal body),~~

~~and something plummets inside me,~~
~~rises out of proportion to the time~~
~~I've been portioned on this earth.~~

~~And if what is granted erases nothing,~~
~~if history remains, implaceable as these photos,~~
~~as darkness flows up our hemisphere,~~

How did I know that photo was there?
Or mother know I knew?
Two nights later, at her request,
father lectures me on burning out too early.
Beneath the cone of light at the kitchen table,
we're caught, like the shiest of lovers.
He points at the booklet from the AMA
—he writes their P.R.—"Read it," he says,
"and, if you have any questions..."

Thirty years later, these questions remain.
And his answers, too, are still the same:
*Really, David, it was just a magazine.*
*And the camps, my father's lost nursery,*
*the way he chased me round the yard in L.A.,*
*even the two by four he swung—why connect them*
*with years you wandered those theaters?*
*Is nothing in your life your own volition?*
*The past isn't just a box full of horrors.*
*What of those mornings in the surf*
*near Venice, all of us casting line after line,*
*arcing over breakers all the way from Japan,*
*or plopping down beside my mother,*
*a plateful of mochi, pulling it like taffy*
*with our teeth, shoyu dribbling*
*down our chins. Think of it, David.*
*There were days like that. We were happy....*

Who hears the rain churning the forest to mud,
or the unraveling rope snap, the negro
plummet to rest at last? And what flooded my father's eyes
in the Little Rock theatre, sitting beneath the balcony
in that third year of war? Where is 1944,
its snows sweeping down Heart Mountain,
to vanish on my mother's black bobbing head,
as she scrurries towards the cramped cracked barracks
where her mother's throat coughs through the night,
and her father sits beside her on the bed?
The dim bulb flickers as my mother enters.
Her face is flushed, her cheeks cold. She
bows, unwraps her scarf, pours the steaming
kettle in the tea pot; offers her mother a sip.
And none of them knows she will never
talk of this moment, that, years later,
I will have to imagine it, again and again,
just as I have tried to imagine the lives
of all those who have entered these lines...

Tonight snow drifts below my window,
and lamps puff ghostly aureoles
over walks and lawns. Father, mother,
I married a woman not of my color.
Tell me: What is it I want to escape?
These nights in our bed, my head
on her belly, I can hear these thumps,
and later, when she falls asleep,
I stand in our daughter's room,
so bare yet but for a simple wooden crib
(on the bulletin board I've pinned the sonogram
with black and white swirls like a galaxy
spinning about the fetal body),
and something plummets inside me,
out of proportion to the time
I've been portioned on this earth.
And if what is granted erases nothing,
if history remains, untouched, implacable,
as darkness flows up our hemisphere,

her hollow still moves moonward,
small hill on the horizon, swelling,
floating with child, white, yellow,
who knows, who can tell her,

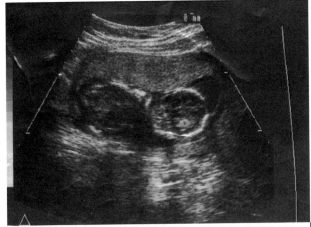

The sonogram for Samantha Sencer-Mura.

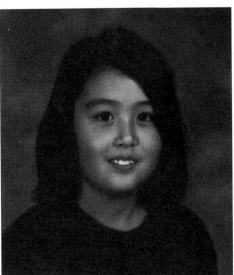

Samantha at age eight.

—ɷ—

[New P] oh ~~why must~~ <u>what does</u> it matter?

Mura says he chose what became the final title of the poem because "the new title incorporated the link between sexuality and the forces of racism that I was trying to explore, as well as rip off one of the titles to a Yuko Mishima novel."

As regards line breaks, Mura says, "I tend to break on syntactical pauses, but I want wherever possible for the break to add to the meaning." (He notes that an example of line breaks enhancing meaning may be seen in the end of the first stanza: "And though directly above them,/ a branch ropes the dead negro in the air,/ the men too focus their blank beam/ on the unseen eye. Which is, at this moment, us./ Or, more precisely, me."

It was also during this drafting stage wherein Mura expands on the section relating to his adolescent reading of *Playboy*, pushing further the poem's "sense of darkness" with the "father's lectures . . . on burning out too early." This line's background may be gleaned from the following — and wrenching — excerpt from *Turning Japanese* — an excerpt that details, too, the beginning of Mura's former sexual promiscuity and disease:

I don't know what she (mother) said to my father when she found I had gotten into his *Playboys*. I only know that later my father summoned me to the kitchen table and gave me a lecture that would serve as a model for the ones to come all through my adolescence, whenever she discovered pornography in my room. I see my father in his T-shirt and tortoiseshell glasses; his hair is shiny, brushed off his forehead. He is a little older than I am now. Some part of me must know he is uncomfortable, but I am only aware that some knot I can't untie is growing in my stomach, its strands tightening, engorging, twisting together.

He does not say much. He tells me, simply, "You will burn yourself out." I should stay away from girls; he can have the magazine because he is an adult, I must wait till I'm seventeen, eighteen—years away. And then he hands me a pamphlet from the AMA, where he works. "If you have any questions after you read this . . ."

I have no questions.

Later I do manage to observe technically my father's ban on dates. After all, I am going to a Jewish high school; most of the girls are not allowed to date "goyim." They can hardly pass me off to their parents as David Steinberg. And I am awkward, socially backward, more adept in the classroom or on the basketball court than at a dance. Once, in senior year, Laurie Brandt . . . does agree to go out with me, but at the end of the second date, at her doorstep, she bursts into tears. "I can't go out with you," she says. "My dad found out you weren't Jewish." I am dumbfounded. It feels like my fate. I do not go to homecoming or prom.

At nineteen — a late age for that period of "free love" — I lose my virginity to an upper-class woman at college. It is brief, joyless, done mainly because neither of us sees a reason not to. I feel relieved, the deed is done. But it does not wash away the feelings of inadequacy, the barriers I feel are there because of my looks. Is it my race or my own features? I cannot separate them; the matter is too hazy, too fraught with complications.

After this slow start, I break my father's ban with a vengeance. Steadily, surely, even after I meet Susie at the age of twenty, I come to woman after woman. My desires seem limitless, I take my father at his word. I begin to burn myself out.


V.    Final Draft Titled "THE COLORS OF DESIRE":

**THE COLORS OF DESIRE**

1  *Photograph of a Lynching (circa 1930)*

These men? In their dented felt hats,
in the way their fingers tug their suspenders or vests,
with faces a bit puffy or too lean, eyes narrow and close together,
they seem too like our image of the South,
the Thirties. Of course they are white;
who then could create this cardboard figure, face
flat and grey, eyes oversized, bulging like
an ancient totem this gang has dug up? At the far right,
in a small browed cap, a boy of twelve smiles,
as if responding to what's most familiar here:
the camera's click. And though directly above them,

a branch ropes the dead negro in the air,
the men too focus their blank beam
on the unseen eye. Which is, at this moment, us.

Or, more precisely, me. Who cannot but recall
how my father, as a teenager, clutched his weekend pass,
passed through the rifle towers and gates
of the Jerome, Arkansas camp, and, in 1942,
stepped on a bus to find whites riders
motioning, "Sit here, son," and, in the rows beyond,
a half dozen black faces, waving him back,
"Us colored folks got to stick together."
How did he know where to sit? And how is it,

thirty five years later, I found myself sitting
in a dark theatre, watching *Behind the Green Door*
with a dozen anonymous men?  On the screen
a woman sprawls on a table, stripped, the same one
on the Ivory Snow soap box, a baby on her shoulder,
smiling her blond, practically pure white smile.
Now, after being prepared and serviced slowly
by a handful of women, as one of them
kneels, buries her face in her crotch,
she is ready: And now he walks in—

Lean, naked, black, streaks of white paint on his chest
and face, a necklace of teeth, it's almost comical,
this fake garb of the jungle, Africa and All-America,
black and blond, almost a joke but for the surge
of what these lynchers regarded as the ultimate crime
against nature: the black man kneeling to this kidnapped
body, slipping himself in, the screen showing it all, down
to her head shaking in a seizure, the final scream
before he lifts himself off her quivering body...

I left that theater, bolted from a dream into a dream.
I stared at the cars whizzing by, watched the light change,
red, yellow, green, and the haze in my head from the hash,
and the haze in my head from the image, melded together, reverberating.
I don't know what I did afterwards. Only, night after night,
I will see those bodies, black and white (and where am I,
the missing third?), like a talisman, a rageful, unrelenting release.

## 2  1957

Cut to Chicago, June. A boy of six.
Next year my hero will be Mickey Mantle,
but this noon, as father eases the Bel-Air past Wilson,
with cowboy hat black, cocked at an angle,
my skin dark from the sun, I'm Paladin,
and my six guns point at cars whizzing past,
blast after blast ricocheting the glass.
Like all boys in such moments, my face
attempts a look of what—toughness? bravado? ease?—
until, impatient, my father's arm wails
across the seat, and I sit back, silent at last.

Later, as we step from IGA with our sacks,
a man in a serge suit—stained with ink?—
steps forward, shouts, "Hey, you a Jap?
You from Tokyo? You a Jap? A Chink?"
I stop, look up, I don't know him,
my arm yanks forward, and suddenly,
the sidewalk's rolling, buckling, like lava melting,
and I know father will explode,
shouts, fists, I know his temper.
And then,
I'm in that dream where nothing happens—
The ignition grinds, the man's face presses
the windshield, and father stares ahead,
fingers rigid on the wheel...

That night in my bedroom, moths,
like fingertips, peck the screen;
from the living room, the muffled t.v.
As I imagine Shane stepping into the dusty street,
in the next bed, my younger brother starts
to taunt—*you can't hurt me, you can't hurt me...*—
Who can explain where this chant began?
Or why, when father throws the door open,
shouts stalking chaos erupted in his house,
he swoops on his son with the same swift motion
that the son, like an animal, like a scared and angry little boy,
fell on his brother, beating him in the dark?

I'm twelve, home from school
with a slight fever. I slide back the door
of my parents' closet—my mother's out shopping—
rummage among pumps, flats, lined in a rack,
unzip the garment bags, one by one.
It slides like a sigh from the folded sweaters.
I flip through ads for cologne, L.P.'s, a man
in a trench coat, lugging a panda-sized Fleischman's fifth.
Somewhere past the photo of Schweitzer
in his pith helmet, and the cartoon nude man
perched as a gargoyle, I spill the photo
millions of men, white, black, yellow, have seen,
though the body before me is white, eighteen:
Her breasts are enormous, almost frightening
—the aureoles seem large as my fist.
As the three glossy pages sprawl before me,
I start to touch myself, and there is
some terror, my mother will come home,
some delight I've never felt before,
and I do not cry out, I make no sound...

How did I know that photo was there?
Or mother know I knew?
Two nights later, at her request,
father lectures me on burning out too early.
Beneath the cone of light at the kitchen table,
we're caught, like the shiest of lovers.
He points at the booklet from the AMA
—he writes their P.R.—"Read it," he says,
"and, if you have any questions..."

Thirty years later, these questions remain.
And his answers, too, are still the same:
*Really, David, it was just a magazine.*
*And the camps, my father's lost nursery,*
*the way he chased me round the yard in L.A.,*
*even the two by four he swung—why connect them*
*with years you wandered those theaters?*
*Is nothing in your life your own volition?*
*The past isn't just a box full of horrors.*
*What of those mornings in the surf*
*near Venice, all of us casting line after line,*
*arcing over breakers all the way from Japan,*
*or plopping down beside my mother,*

*a plateful of  mochi,  pulling it like taffy*
*with our teeth,*  shoyu *dribbling*
*down our chins. Think of it, David.*
*There were days like that. We were happy....*


4


Who hears the rain churning the forest to mud,
or the unraveling rope snap, the negro
plummet to rest at last? And what flooded my father's eyes
in the Little Rock theatre, sitting beneath the balcony
in that third year of war? Where is 1944,
its snows sweeping down Heart Mountain,
to vanish on my mother's black bobbing head,
as she scrurries towards the cramped cracked barracks
where her mother's throat coughs through the night,
and her father sits beside her on the bed?
The dim bulb flickers as my mother enters.
Her face is flushed, her cheeks cold. She
bows, unwraps her scarf, pours the steaming
kettle in the tea pot; offers her mother a sip.
And none of them knows she will never
talk of this moment, that, years later,
I will have to imagine it, again and again,
just as I have tried to imagine the lives
of all those who have entered these lines...

Tonight snow drifts below my window,
and lamps puff ghostly aureoles
over walks and lawns. Father, mother,
I married a woman not of my color.
Tell me: What is it I want to escape?
These nights in our bed, my head
on her belly, I can hear these thumps,
and later, when she falls asleep,
I stand in our daughter's room,
so bare yet but for a simple wooden crib
(on the bulletin board I've pinned the sonogram
with black and white swirls like a galaxy
spinning about the fetal body),
and something plummets inside me,
out of proportion to the time
I've been portioned on this earth.
And if what is granted erases nothing,
if history remains, untouched, implacable,

as darkness flows up our hemisphere,

her hollow still moves moonward,

small hill on the horizon, swelling,

floating with child, white, yellow,

who knows, who can tell her,


oh why must it matter?


—m—


At the conclusion of our interview, I asked Mura whether he was interested in making any last-minute changes to his poem before it was published in this book. He replied, "I've read this poem too many times out loud in public for me to think about changing it. It may not be perfect but it is now what it is. It's become, for me, historical. It is, I believe, a brave poem, one that took a lot out of me to write and one which forced me to cross various boundaries and deal with a certain amount of opposition—some actual in the process of the writing, some (correctly) anticipated and some internal. People are uncomfortable with putting race and sexuality together. It scared *me* to write the poem, made *me* uncomfortable. But I also recognize that that's part of my talent: I'm willing to go places and into rooms that other writers don't want to enter; some don't even want to acknowledge that they exist."

Mura notes, "One reviewer of the book *The Colors of Desire*, Gary Soto, charged that parts of the book were soft-core porn. In Dallas, at one reading of the poem, a couple of people walked out."

"Fear is not a bad thing or, at times, entirely unpleasurable. Giving in to fear, though, places limits on you. If I were going to do that, going to let others—critics, readers, my family, friends, whoever—limit what I write, I would have picked an easier calling. I would have worked in a corporation or wrote advertising and made more money and been less of a target."

Mura adds, "Robert Hass has criticized poems that come into the room and say all the right things, poems which won't ruffle a soul. Many of my best poems are not like that."

Finally, Mura concludes:

Perhaps this is a point for me to say that I think it is an abomination that the Asian American Studies Association did not give Lois Ann Yamanaka the award its own prize committee awarded her. Apparently people protested against the portrayal of Filipinos in her book of poetry, and yet it's obvious that the racial slurs in the book are coming from the mouth of a character, they are not the author's own views. That members of the AASA could not read a persona poem properly is quite troubling, even aside from the issues of fairness and literary openness. This spirit of policing authors ought to be criticized vigorously and by writers of all genres and persuasions. And the AASA ought to be ashamed of itself.

Though the AASA and Yamanaka controversy obviously are not part of the poem, "The Colors of Desire," it seems fitting to conclude with Mura's concerns on these issue. For this controversy, nevertheless, is part of his poetic concerns — what would "say anything vital to me or my life of the lives of a large majority of the world." Or, as he told Bill Moyers in *The Language of Life* (Doubleday, 1995):

The process of history is often permeated by a darkness that people don't want to look at, but I want my poetry to be a combination of those two things. I think that if poetry moves too far towards the realm of the aesthetic, the formal, and the beautiful and doesn't acknowledge the other side of existence — the history that we live in, the changes and the darkness of history — then the life goes out of poetry, and it becomes an escape.

# JOHN YAU

John Yau is a poet, fiction writer, curator, and critic who has written extensively on contemporary art for the past two decades. He has taught at various schools including Brown University, Pratt Institute, University of California at Berkeley, University of Texas at Austin, Hofstra University, Bard College, Emerson College, and is currently teaching, as well as directing the poetry reading series, at the Maryland Institute, College of Art. He has received fellowships and grants from the National Endowment for the Arts, the Ingram-Merrill Foundation, and the New York Foundation for the Arts, and has been awarded a General Electric Foundation Award, a Lavan Award (Academy of American Poets), the Brendan Gill Award, the Jerome Shestack Award (*American Poetry Review*), and The Richard Hugo Memorial Award (*Cut Bank*). As Ahmanson Curatorial Fellow (1993-1996), he organized a retrospective of paintings and drawings by Ed Moses, which opened at the Museum of Contemporary Art, Los Angeles in 1996. Other shows he has organized include *Joe Zucker: A Decade of Paintings 1983-1994* (1995), *Murder* (1995), and *Sex/Industry* (1997).

He has collaborated with American and European artists, such as Enrico Baj, Norman Bluhm, Max Gimblett, Edward Henderson, Bill Jensen, Suzanne McClelland, Ed Paschke, Jurgen Partenheimer, Archie Rand, Peter Saul, Patrick Surgalski, and Robert Therrien on books, prints, paintings, and drawings; and his collaborations have been exhibited in the Museum of Modern Art (New York), Phyllis Kind Gallery (New York), Bobbie Greenfield Gallery (Santa Monica), University of Northern Iowa Art Gallery, Feigenson-Preston Gallery, Huntington Woods (MI), Victoria and Albert Museum (London), and the National Library of Ottawa (Canada).

His poetry books include *Forbidden Entries* (Black Sparrow Press, 1996); *Berlin Diptychon* (Timken Books and Weidle Verlag, 1995); *Edificio Sayonara* (Black Sparrow Press, 1992); *Big City Primer* (Timken Books, 1991); *Radiant Silhouette: New & Selected Work 1974-1988* (Black Sparrow Press, 1989); *Corpse and Mirror* (The National Poetry Series Selected by John Ashberry) (Holt, Rinehart and Winston, 1983); *Broken Off by the Music* (Burning Deck, 1981); and *Sometimes* (Sheep Meadow Press, 1979). His books of fiction include *The Sleepless Night of Eugene Delacroix* (Release Press, 1980); *Hawaiian Cowboys* (Black Sparrow, 1995); and the forthcoming *My Symptoms* (Black Sparrow, 1998). His monographs and books of criticism include *The United States of Jasper Johns* (Zoland, 1996); *Ed Moses: Paintings and Drawings, 1951-1996* (Museum of Contemporary Art, Los Angeles and University of California Press, 1996); *In The Realm of Appearances: The Art of Andy Warhol* (Ecco Press, 1993); and *A.R. Penck* (Abrams, 1993). His reviews and articles have appeared in *Vogue, Interview, American Poetry Review, Art in America,* and *Artforum,* and he has contributed essays to catalogs on such artists as Brice Marden, Helmut Federle, Theresa Serrano, Joan Mitchell, Jackie Winsor, Dorothea Rockburne, Theresa Chong, Luis Cruz Azaceta, and Mary Heilmann. Current projects include editing an anthology of fetish fiction, which will be published by Four Walls, Eight Windows in 1998 as well as co-organizing a retrospective of Robert Creeley's collaborations with artists, which will begin its national tour in the fall/winter 1998.

In response to the question, "What advice would you give to a young poet?" John Yau responds:

> Unica Zurn, Anna Kavan, Alexandra David-Neel, Isabelle Gardner. Read lots of letters, journals.
> Don't be afraid to read anything, listen to all kinds of music, or look at art. Letters written to lovers,

editors, enemies, those outside of prison.  Rilke's *Letters To A Young Poet*.  The letters of Artaud, Keats, Crane, Hartley, Kees, and Kafka.  Journals.  Writers little known, hardly read.  The ignored and forgotten.  Don't be afraid to fall in love with a writer's work.  Don't be afraid to fall out of love with a writer's work.  Don't be afraid to sleep with the work beside you.  Don't be afraid to put the book away.  As Frank O'Hara so succinctly and elegantly stated: "Grace to be born and live as variously as possible."

# Approximating Midnight: Her Conversation With John Yau And

Constraints On Writing Up Interview With John Yau

1)      Split Up Eileen Tabios, the interviewer, into two selves: the self outwardly conducting the interview and the self observing the interview

2)      Between each paragraph of the interview, interject excerpts from poems in John Yau's latest poetry collection, *Forbidden Entries* (Black Sparrow Press, 1996).  The order of the excerpted poems — shown in italics below — will reflect the Table of Contents in *Forbidden Entries*.  However, the poem, "Conversation At Midnight," will not be excerpted because the poem will be printed in its entirety following the interview. (A)

Why These Constraints?

1)      To reflect John Yau's interest in the fragmented self

2)      Because Eileen Tabios has never written up an interview in this manner before

3)      Just to see what happens(B) — just as John Yau begins poems by writing them under "constraints" or arbitrary rules to generate a poem whose manifestation is unpredictable

—⁓—

*"I would say that the poetry of painting has to do with feeling.  It should be a kind of revelation"*
*— Robert Ryman*

July 24, 1997 (Flood warnings throughout the New York area):

She was hoping as she left you that you wouldn't think her boorish for not having looked at the many paintings on your walls.  You can tell something about me based on whether and how I look at the art in a place I visit, but not that day as I was too distracted over meeting you (too bad as she can tell something, too, about a person based on the art within a person's home).  She felt the rain beginning to harden outside.  She called out, "Oh, I left my umbrella in the hallway."  You said something she didn't quite catch, but undoubtedly innocuous, like "Good" or something like that.  But as she entered the elevator, she began castigating herself, "What a dimwit you are, so slow on the uptake.  Like, why didn't you ask whether he had a painting by John Way among those hanging on his walls?"  I tried to console her that you caught her unprepared when you expected to be interviewed and she had to wing those questions.  But she snapped back, "Come on, you were trained by crusty old crime reporters who never believed a female could do what they did."  All this while the rain hardened.  Once more, I tried, "But he was smiling at you as you shook his hand."  She sighed, "Yeah, there's that."

*All of us telling wait to be told something. There is the telling to be told. The something told, the something us, the something telling. Something telling is there. There telling us to be told something for which we wait. There is for the telling something of which we wait to be told. Something about us for the wait. Something about the telling to be told.*(1)

You told her you have a natural affinity for abstract art, primarily because you "believed in its importance when you were very young." You were about seven years old when you (and, later, your parents) met and started spending time with John Way, a father of a childhood friend and an abstract expressionist painter. "He was telling me about abstract expressionists while they were still alive and I grew up looking at reproductions of Robert Motherwell, Franz Kline, Willem de Kooning, Zao Wou Ki, a Chinese painter who worked in an abstract mode and lived in Paris, among others," you said. "I also grew up seeing an artist working in his house, and committed to abstraction." Consequently, when you began to write poetry at about age thirteen, you did so with the notion of also wishing to explore what was possible in and through poetry. Initially, you were inspired by Allen Ginsberg, Jack Kerouac and others connected to the Beat movement such as Gregory Corso and Ray Bremser. (I was delighted when you shared that you believe your "first poem was about chess and had a corny rhyme between 'fate' and 'checkmate'.")

*Now, if you're starting to think this is a message, you're wrong. I'm not a messenger, but a receiver, a crystal radio. I lift into the light the things that someone left behind, someone who wanted to point to where he had been and how he got there. With the kind of precision which does not derive its forms from a book, but from dancing alone, knowing the music will melt only once. It is not a where you can find on a map.*(2)

Subsequently, you came to be both an art critic and poet. You told her that over the years you figured out that at various points you have written about 300 to 400 pages a year about art to make a living. "A lot of art," you emphasized and she nodded her head. During the times you didn't have to write on art, you would write a poem. This is one reason why you begin to write poems by setting up a set of "constraints" or rules for writing a poem. You said, "I didn't want to wait for the poem to happen so this was a way of getting started." For example, you told her that you wrote the poem, "Conversation At Midnight" after reading *The New York Times* and the *Daily News* one day and, from your perusals, generating a list of about 30 words that you'd never used before in a poem. You said you decided to write a poem where each word would have its own line. And you also wished to write the poem as a conversation between a man and a woman, but you didn't want the poem's reader to know who's speaking, which person is male or female and when one person would stop or begin speaking. You thought you would discover something about the language of intimacy and boundaries through this method. Rudely, I am digging my elbows into her as she tries to shake me off and give you her full attention. But I am too excited. So, finally, she conceded, "I love this poem, 'Conversation At Midnight.' I remember first reading it in *American Poetry Review*. It made me look up your other works."

*Shouldn't stars start*
*igniting the sky*

*now that the world is rigid*
*earthen, yesterday*

*Aren't gasps of breath*
*invading our throats (3)*

I nudged her again. She agreed that you seemed pleased by the comment on "Conversation At Midnight." But she wouldn't let me tell you that that's the first poem I've ever read that inspired me to respond by also writing a poem. You took a drag on your cigarette and said that another reason you write under constraints is that you were inspired by OULIPO. Uh oh, I thought. She was relieved when you kindly volunteered before she could show her ignorance that OULIPO was a group of writers including Harry Matthews, Georges Perec, and Italo Calvino who wrote based on constraints — "wherein," you said, "the writer is the rat who constructs the maze from which he must escape." (I whispered to her, "I think he only mentioned Calvino because he suspected you might find that name more recognizeable than the others.") You said that you met Matthews in the mid-1970s and that OULIPO offered a way for you to get beyond the "I" in poetry and "against the mode of self-expression." It was Matthews who first told you about OULIPO and showed you various techniques to generate a poem. Later that evening, she and I would slosh our way through the wet, grey walls of an unseasonal storm as we hurried down Broadway to the Barnes and Noble library. There, a reference text revealed that Matthews is an American novelist who has lived mainly in France since the 1950s. A former editor of *Locus Solus*, the magazine of the New York School of Poets, he was a member of the OULIPO (Workshop of Potential Literature) experimental group whose interests extended back to Apollinaire, Roussel and Dada. The reference text describes Roussel's particular influence on Matthews as he "drew absurd logic, a highly artificial manner, texts-within-texts, incorporat(ed) maps, musical scores, indices, footnotes and road games." She observed (or did I?), "Ah, ha: constraints!"

*I was an adopted fan who yearned to grunt.*
*I was a bridge over which drunken hornets gathered.*
*I was a speckled cloud lolling in moustache filth.*
*These things I told myself*
*as if I was the one who was listening,*
*my cauliflower flap pressed to the door of medals. (4)*

"The use of constraints proposes that you can surprise yourself, as with a poem you've never written before," you explained. "Constraints help prevent you from repeating yourself, becomes a way to break yourself of your habits, like writing habits. I want to write poems beyond what I might have wished to write because whatever sense I have would have limited the poem. So I use words I wouldn't ordinarily use, say, from science and biology books, as well as from the newspaper or the dictionary. Poetry should be able to absorb all words. It's one of poetry's impossible tasks, but it's fun." Later, I reminded her that she had wanted to ask you why you thought the task "impossible" but sloppily dropped her train of thought when you continued, "Constraints allow me to see how to change whatever language I might use and break apart the notion of bounded ego or 'I'."

*I could have told you another white lie.*
*I could have heaped it on the mountain*

*gathering before you. Perhaps it would have*
*even been the truth, the whole truth,*

*but I wouldn't have known it, not then and not now. (5)*

She asked, "Why do you want to get away from the 'I'?" You replied, "Because when you think of poetry, the two divisions in my generation are that (i) language is the pure material of poetry or (ii) poetry is rooted in the fixed 'I' or ego. But I believe that there's subjectivity. That the 'I' is not whole but at best fragmented. But I didn't want my subjectivity to be solipsistic, (thus, I thought of) the concept of a conversation — except that the possibility that it's a conversation between two people doesn't preclude the conversation being with one's 'I', that one is filled with the traces of other voices." You noted that the poem's title was inspired by Samuel Taylor Coleridge who wrote a number of conversation-based poems. You added that you had learned to relate your concerns in your poems partly by reading certain poets who were "gay but used an 'I' that's not necessarily gay" (e.g. Frank O'Hara, John Ashberry and John Wieners).

*I don't know what else to attribute it to,*
*but I think we each have two different sets of personalities.*
*Yesterday you submitted an appended roster of vital statistics*
*to the uptown breeding contest, and tomorrow one of us*
*will enter our names in the registry*
*for future celebration and imminent disposal.*
*We like the hoopla, but not the late night apologies*
*draped in syndicated provender.*
*Perhaps the foil could be tinted a different color*
*and not reek of caloric melancholy and asteroid indifference.*
*Is this the inaugural gown you promised me?*
*or another informative sculpture*
*I am supposed to install beside our basalt hearth?*
*its tower of penetrated electric logs.*
*What is this surface over which giants fight and fall? (6)*

I asked her, "Isn't he great? And isn't this a great conversation?" Impatiently, she glared at me, "Knock it off. Just 'cause you like his poetry and what he's saying in the interview doesn't mean he's okay. Besides, have you forgotten he missed our earlier appointment?" Then she turned back to you. "Aw, come on," I insisted. "Look around: those papers and books strewn all over the floor, the ashtray heaped with butts and ash, the ringing phone (and isn't he gracious to ignore them for you?) — he's busy. He's kind to give you time." She muttered, "You're becoming histrionic. Now be quiet as I have to follow what he's saying so you don't sound stupid." You were saying, "It's like the way Robert Ryman paints. He works within constraints in an attempt to find out what is specific in a painting, what is real. I work within constraints to discover what will emerge." (Later, I would show her some of Ryman's writings, including the passages, "The use of white in my paintings came about when I realized that it doesn't interfere. It is a neutral color that allows for clarification of nuances in painting. It makes other aspects of painting visible that would not be so clear with the use of other colors."(c)) She asked, "Can one ever lose the 'I'?" You said, "No. But you can shift it to a different plane and that 'I' then has its own or different meaning from the one associated with 'You.' I think of abstract expressionism where the 'I' is the subject versus minimalism where the 'I' is the object. Is there an 'I' that is both object and subject, an 'I' seen in different profiles."

*You can't pretend your mind didn't wander off*
*and never returned, leaving me with a pail of bronze bulk.* (7)

You said that your exploration of the "I" as both object and subject is what has led you to create characters like Genghis Khan and Peter Lorre, who are under a section titled "Hollywood Asians" in your poetry collection, *Forbidden Entries*. "Peter Lorre," you noted, "was an Austrian actor who plays a Japanese detective in the Mr. Moto series. He was famous in Germany for his role of being a child molester and murderer in *M*, whereas in America he's a Grade B actor. And in at least one role, he was feminized. So, what if you take all those roles and say they are all true, then who is he? I played with this notion in the poem, 'Peter Lorre Dreams He Is the Third Reincarnation of a Geisha.' And wouldn't there be this anger he would have because he's trapped in his roles? I'm thinking of the nature of identity because I am interested in identity but, as a shifting, changing field, I'm not interested in the fixity of identity."

*One of them must always be the donkey when the other*
*is on the balcony, waiting for the film to start.*
*What is this? a voice on the golf course cries out,*
*the latest pebble added to the mound of sob glory?*
*Or just another bald-hearted attempt to pry open my sighs?* (8)

Later, when she read me "Peter Lorre Dreams He Is the Third Reincarnation of a Geisha," she insisted your "I" is clearly in the poem. If so, I still hoped much was "fictive"; I was saddened by the third stanza: "First I was delicate, a white peony, then I was a shiny delicatessen, something to snuffle over and return. Our leader said I was climbing the ladder of cultural evolution. I took mincing steps, I bowed and shuffled quietly across the rosewood floor, a prized worm. But I didn't mince words, they weren't mine to abuse. My teeth are straight and black in the proper manner. My thighs are long jade mirrors catching the moon's passage from one myth to another, a striped tiger unfurling its blurred banner. Why do you shun me? One of us inhabits a sad drama, the other entertains noisy guests. Don't squawk to me about nobility or honor. I took my raincoat to the cleaners, I learned to twirl spaghetti with a knife and spoon. I have something up my sleeve, something other than the arm you would amputate or lick with your leathery tongue. I want that tongue, and someday I shall have it. I am a reflection, a wall you have smeared with feces and blood. When you pluck your eyebrows, are you a chicken strutting through mud? A turtle crossing the road? Basho wrote, the journey itself is the home. And then highways and the theory of eminent domain ousted him from his solitude. My place in history is a mark left on a shirt. I was a waddling pug, and then I was plugged with rubber ballots. I made stone ducks gasp. I was a mulberry leaf the wind tugged loose from a branch, a ginko in a gazebo. My skin glistened on cue in the calculated light. I quivered until the audience mopped their brows with thick fingers. I live in a porous wall of moist projections. I am a dog oozing sweet oil in a butcher shop, a hatless traitor strung up by his heels. Bear claws are a necessary ingredient. Grind the rhinoceros horn to powder, lick the candle wax from your sleeve. Why spawn progeny? Why not choose extinction?"

*I want to doze while time continues flowing through this planetary circuit I've been sad-*
*dled with, its butter dish of blinking dreams. (9)*

She asked what you were like as a poet 20 years ago. You said that you were always "fictive but that you were more interested (then) in constructing that 'I'." Then you paused and thought for a bit before noting, "But almost from the beginning I wanted to get away from that 'I'. It was something I associated with Robert Lowell and Sylvia Plath: the 'I' as victim. There seemed to be something wrong with it, something privileged." I thought that was interesting and told her so. Her glance slashed as she said, "Thanks, Sherlock" before encouraging you to continue. You mentioned a poem you wrote in 1977, "Scenes From The Life of Boullee," where you pointed out that you used the word "I" only twice in a 16-section poem. You said, "At the time I was reading Jack Spicer, John Ashberry, Barbara Guest and O'Hara. O'Hara believed his life was immensely interesting and this is something that influenced poets in my generation. But I didn't see my life as that immensely interesting." At the time, you said that you were working at Books & Company, mostly consigned to the basement to unpack boxes and organize shelves.

*What path did you take to get here? What path will you take to leave? What is this here*
*you are in? What is a path? What makes this what it is? What name will you give it?*
*What names will circle the name you have given it? What will those other names bring you*
*to? What will be the name you don't give it? What is the name of the place you keep your*
*secrets in? (10)*

The concept of you not living an interesting life surprised me and she laughed at my fan-like presumptions that I concede can be quite tedious. While she was cackling, you answered before I could press her to ask why you felt that way, "Maybe it's part of being Asian American, that is, that my family spent hours talking about the importance of family versus the individual." She nodded encouragingly. You continued, "My family was dysfunctional, traumatized by the Second World War and by having to emigrate to American in 1949, penniless and largely without friends. They had to start over, but they could not let go of the past, about which they were unrealistic. So I didn't believe in the family, but I also didn't believe in the 'I' — particularly the 'I' as victim." She wanted to ask more, but I told her not to. "You're getting soft," she said. "Maybe," I said. "But let it go — this is poetry, not journalism." She quirked her eyebrow at me, as if to ask, "Sure? This could be interesting territory." I repeated, "Let it go."

*Did you see the bubbles trapped in the green dish*
*they keep locked in the cupboard*

*They claim it's a family heirloom*
*shipped from the piers of Baltimore and beyond*

*Why do some people point to their inheritance*
*as if an honored voice*

*is constantly being broadcast through*
*ant encrusted notes of an amber afternoon (11)*

Together, we cleared our throats and she asked, "And how does all this show up in your poetry?" You lit another cigarette while I squashed the maternal urge to pat your hand. You replied, "It shows up in my poetry as me being slightly disenfranchised, isolated, trying to communicate, and thinking communication is largely impossible." She couldn't help herself and baldly asked, "So, would you consider yourself a pessimistic person?" You laughed. You nodded and said, "Pessimistic? Well, maybe skeptical is more accurate. If you are a person of color in this country, you would be naive if you weren't skeptical."

> *Dairy wolves howl at empty spoons*
> *while I sleep in back mall*
>
> *lily padded trailer park*
> *answer the second*
>
> *second*
> *I'm stalled in a parallel stupor*
>
> *squeezed between red hurt of a fall potato*
> *and blue stones of a part-time seed shifter*
>
> *I'm one of the jilted*
> *eager to bite the crust (12)*

She asked if your attitude has changed over the years. You conceded that you're not as pessimistic as before. "Whereas before I was deeply pessimistic, I now am only skeptical so that I've moved from feeling it is completely impossible to communicate to feeling that, now, it's possible to communicate but the communication occurs with many layers and is always on the brink of not arriving, not being welcomed." I was glad she quickly followed up with how this affected your poetry. You replied, "The result in my poetry is an incremental rise of optimism in that there is more humor. It may be sarcastic, but the humor is there. And humor is based on the assumption that someone will laugh." Then, together, you and she laughed over a recent review of *Forbidden Entries* while I jealously watched. You shook your head as you said, "(The reviewer) didn't even notice that I told some jokes." Among other things, the reviewer had called you "too eager to probe his own pain, his own version of the *abject*" and cited Yeats to call your world one of " 'great hatred, little room'." She looked at me questioningly but I insisted, "This, too, you will let go."

> *I scoffed as if all this pointing*
>
> *reached me in the mirror*
> *where my resemblance once stood*
>
> *crouched in oil*
> *shot through*
>
> *with flakes of spit and gold. (13)*

Instead, you and she shared more laughs about the humor in your recent works. She said she had been "flat out on the floor, howling at the ceiling" when I read your story, "What She Told Him While They Pretended To Watch TV" in *Lingo 6 (A Journal of The Arts)*. Later, we looked up your story again and, once more, she bared her teeth and honked at excerpts like these: "He fixed me up with a woman once. He thought it would be good for me to fuck a woman. Everything had been arranged. We met this couple at a bar. The guy, some pretty boy in a muscle shirt, starts running his hand up his leg, squeezing his droopy ass whenever he got up to go to the bar, order another round of drinks. He tries to act sheepish, but he's not pushing him away, not making it clear where he stands on the matter. He's being a tease, as if he can still get away with it, still be the adored child. Remember, he's hit forty and he's way too old to be acting like some prince. Me, I'm looking at the woman and she's looking at me. No electricity, I might as well have been looking at a house or a car. She's dressed in a charcoal gray suit, you know a business nun who's taken the vow."

> *An ink storm swept across this emblazoned map*
> *where pompous couples prided themselves on their choice*
> *of emerging crowd pleasers and corncob furniture.*
> *A train full of inscribed pavement stones rattled through*
> *the tunnels, its polished bronze instruments*
> *swaying gently in the lower layers of the united dark.*
> *Each of us ends up a piece of luggage carried by others.* (14)

You said that, as with "What She Told Him While They Pretended To Watch TV," many of your stories come out of poems and in the form of a monologue. "Many of the stories are written from a woman's perspective," you said. "Like ranting — I was interested in how much of a ranting can one listen to." She said, "So, you're obsessive." You smiled, nodded, and added, "Somebody once said we're living in a society full of complaints. So I was interested in how much of a complaint can a complaint be and still be readable." She asked why you linked the female perspective to complaints. You said, "Because women often complain about men." You continued, "And men often complain about women. I have written stories exploring both perspectives. I was interested in the complaint, in what generated it."

*I was like you once*
*a moody slinker full of rain*

*Then I threw my dog badge into the bushes*
*and began counting backwards*

*until I learned to climb*
*the terraces of corporate lava*

*and paste the ashes to your lips*
*with my tongue (15)*

At a loss, she tossed you a meatball and asked whether, in your drafting process, the poem transcends the initial set of constraints you might have set up. "Of course," you said. Of course, I thought, feeling foolish. "At some point the poem does take over," you said. "And I just trace its trajectory. I don't impose any will on it. I see what happens. It's as when you look at certain paintings like by (Jackson) Pollock or Jasper Johns or Pat Steir — you can see that the painting takes over." She looked at me and, this time, she was the one who marveled, "Isn't this a great conversation?" I smiled back as we recalled how we long admired how Pollock was able to maintain a consistent harmonious balance across the surface of even the biggest of his drip paintings and yet the harmony is made up, ruptures and shifts. Just as Pollock's works, I felt, involved his encounters with the material of paint, you said that whatever happens "all has to come out of language — whatever happens is based on language." She asked when, in "Conversation at Midnight," the poem began to take over from the initial constraints. You opened your copy of *Forbidden Entries* to look at the poem and replied, "By the second line. (In the first line,) there's an 'I' and a 'You' but I then set up the reference to another couple. I wanted to get to the confusion right away. After all, my racial identity — if one wants to be exact — includes the fact that my father's mother was English, but claimed to be French."

*Virgin sushi*
*peel strangers*

*while Minnie*
*volcano rave (16)*

Later, battling the rain, she would conclude that, of course, your poem would have taken over right away. Otherwise, you probably wouldn't have considered it finished, would have worked over those initial lines. "Another dumb question," I joked but she didn't laugh. As with about 80% of your poems, you said that you typed in your computer the first draft of the poem. Then you worked on it for a few hours each day for about a week, generating about 15-20 different drafts. Because you work on the computer, you often do not keep traces of your process which goes between the sporadic and the concentrated in terms of time. "The poem has no attachment to me so that, at some point, when the poem becomes like it was written by someone else, then to me it's finished," you said.

*Xylophone duress initiates yank (17)*

Reflecting your view that what happens in your poems "is based on language," you expressed your appreciation of surrealism, which you defined as "language as material and the imagination as spirit in terms of what extends beyond physical being. If anything, that's one of the things that informs my work," you noted. This, too, reflects your appreciation of surrealism as being "politically and socially radical. Among modernist movements, surrealism is the only one who openly accepted people of color." And this, too, is linked with your overall interests in exploring identity. "I'm interested in identity but not the fixity of identity," you specified, noting that "multicultural issues sometimes want to fix identity but that's against multiculturality."

> *I am on the shrapnel inlaid verandah*
> *stalking the flower of your inimitable style*
>
> *when they begin speaking*
> *They say they are angels*
>
> *but I know they are just chemical transmissions (18)*

In turn, your concerns on identity — along with your general interest in popular culture — explain why you are working on a biography of the screen actress Anna May Wong as well as the fact that you own and watch many movies depicting the varied and insidious ways in which Asians are depicted. You said you considered the negative ways of presenting Asians as "pervasive" — from the movie "Fargo" which portrayed an Asian actor playing the role of a pathetic, lying sycophant to the David Letterman's wisecracks about Korean shopowners. You noted, "America proposes that it is black and white; everyone else is largely inconsequential."

> *Another corpse is dandled between swills of art*
> *Another fig sticks in the vertical (19)*

She asked what conclusions you've since made about identity, in terms of poetry. You replied, "That the identity issue is a major issue not being addressed by modernist and post-modernist poets. It's not been addressed by later modernist poets because many often want to assimilate and be part of the mainstream and, thus, do not question the mainstream's use of identity, how it fixes them with a narrow possibility. It's not being addressed by post-modernists because they say that the author is dead. But why is the author dead at a point when demographics have changed such that all these people who were once marginalized and silenced can now talk — but during a period when the author is supposedly dead? In that regard we are still silenced, because others are defining the limits of what can and cannot be written. Both approaches are exclusionary."

> *I never met a human being who didn't suffer*
> *the comedian announced*
>
> *as everyone leaned over their tables*
> *and waited patiently for his dirty red toupee*
>
> *to slip or fall (20)*

She asked you to focus once more on "Conversation At Midnight" and how it relates to your overall poetic concerns. Then she couldn't help herself from blurting out how the poem so impressed her and that long after she lost the copy of *American Poetry Review* in which she first read it, she held the poem's experience in her memory as one of the "greatest love poems" she had ever read, and in particular how the ending line so transported her: "If you want to lease me, go ahead and cry. You little parking lot." You nodded and said you had conceived it partly because you had wanted to explore whether it would be possible to write a love poem with humor, sympathy and anger — "a poem with sentiment but not sentimental, not idealized or idealizing."

*Why do I remember these words: You cannot become someone else's mirror no matter how hard you try. I am not a corpse, he thought, I am its shadow. (21)*

But equally significant, you said you had wished "Conversation At Midnight" to explore the nature of the "silly, weird" conversations — their unique vocabularies — lovers have with each other. Always, you explored language, just as your story "What She Told Him While They Pretended To Watch TV" explored the rant; or how in another poem, "The Executioner Meets Mister Ball and Chain," you explored aggressiveness in language. As regards the latter, you said, "In New York City, we live in a matrix of aggressive language, like rap music. There's a certain nastiness there. Where does this aggressiveness go? Who receives it? In poetry, so much ignores aggressiveness but it's a basic texture of language. I don't want to harangue the audience, but I am interested in the aggressive aspects of language — like in namecalling." For an example, you picked up your book and, from "The Executioner Meets Mister Ball and Chain," you read the line, "you tumescent vat of grimy scales warmed over pickled hyena spit." You paused, then added, "But I was also interested in the music of that line. Musically, the poem takes over. Albert Ayle and Charles Gayle are aggressive soloists."

*Let the violin show you its long black tongue*
*the one that flows across the wires wrapped around your neck (22)*

I began to rant myself as I raved to her, "Yes, yes! Music definitely takes over his poems — and it's rarely a single rising crescendo. His music has a back and forth, back and forth rhythm." She's trying to quiet me down but I'm too excited and I go on and on for a while about how your diction causes each syllable to participate in creating the ebb and flow of the emotion underlying the dialogues or monologues within your poems. Finally, I paused to catch my breath. "Are you done?" she asked, drumming her fingers. I ignored her question to continue, "It reminds me a bit of what Adorno once said about lyric poetry — that the lyric poem is also "in itself social in nature. It implies a protest against a social condition which every individual experiences as hostile, distant, cold and oppressive; and this social condition impresses itself on the poetic form in a negative way: the more heavily social conditions weigh, the more unrelentingly the poem resists, refusing to give in . . . and constituting itself purely according to its own particular laws.'(D)" She tossed me an impatient look and snapped, "Before you turn him into a Communist, can I get back to the interview?" She turned back to you and said that "Conversation At Midnight" perfectly mirrored the emotional path of similar conversations she's experienced with former lovers late into the evenings. In fact, she noted, that "Conversation At Midnight" epitomizes, for her, what an abstract painting would be in a poetic form — how the narrative was incidental to the emotions the artist sought to evoke. You nodded, saying, "It's what intrigues me about certain artists, de Kooning for example. In a de Kooning painting from the early 1980s, say, you get a mood out of his work that's both ecstatic and disappointed. It seems to me that many poems set their emotional register at the beginning and then the rest of the poem just fulfills it. But couldn't you get a more interesting poem if you lose control, like in de Kooning where you get both ecstasy and disappointment?" And, this desire to lose control also explained, you said, why you "wanted to choose words I'd never used before — to make myself do something I'd never done before. And if you choose words you've never used before, you give yourself a chance to write a poem that you've never written before."

*In the magical papyrus in Berlin: Make this child, or his mother, eat a cooked mouse. Put the bones around his neck, bound with a string in which seven knots have been tied.*

*Dioscorides says: It is well known that mice which run about the house can be very useful when cut up and applied to scorpion stings. If children eat them roasted, it helps them stop dribbling from the mouth. (23)*

She was monitoring the time because the poet Tan Lin(E) had called just after she entered your apartment and you had said you'd chat with him in an hour or so after the interview ended. So when she thought an hour passed, she asked, "Anything else you wish to share?" You said, "No."

*I hear your voices clamoring in the layers rubbing against the geological night, mercury tears drifting down tattooed skies. Glottal tubes twisting into gardens. Vibrato of clenched paws pounding red linoleum, demanding the silos be full and straight as the arrows entering General Custer's eyes. I'm one of those arrows. I fly again and again, spin through the wind. My yellow scarf hanging like spit from my shin. You can't disown me because you've never worn out my cashmere coat. I'm an engine of rebuilt fur. I'm what slips through your purified crave. (24)*

She walked out into the growing storm that soaked through my jeans and shoes. But that was okay, I told her, after she ducked into the subway, because you actually had given her more than an hour. Okay, she agreed easily. Then we thought about how well-mannered you were. Though the interview ended and an hour passed, you showed no eagerness for her to leave, even asking about me and the progress of *BLACK LIGHTNING*. In discussing *BLACK LIGHTNING*, she noted how she had been criticized in the past for her choice of 14 poets because it wasn't sufficiently representative. You sympathized when she explained that she had made her choices based simply on poets whose works she liked. But, she added, she was able to allay her critics when she explained that, given the nature of playing the reader of the subject poems, she wanted to rely on the criteria of finding poets whose works she appreciated. At the time, you nodded in seeming agreement. But as we waited for a train, I told her that your interview made me wonder whether I should have tried to do a poetry-in-progress piece with a poet whose works, at least initially, didn't move me. Just to see what would have happened. That certain *kind of revelation*. "Get a life," she replied.

Opium is the religion of the feeble, the game, and the assaulted. *This is a test, soon your*

*fortune teller will be returned to you. Do not switch the dial, you will only activate the*
*storm brewing on the horizon. Black mist drifts in loose bundles across the garden. I have*
*opened the shutters and let in the rain. (25)*

Later, she wondered whether your pessimism precluded idealism since you admired and
wrote a poem inspired by the French architect Etienne-Louise Boullee who concocted such impos-
sible-to-build designs as "Tomb of the Martyred Spartans." I said your search for *purity*, if that's
the right word, in language — perhaps similar to Boullee's search for architectural perfection —
did not translate necessarily to idealism. Then we agreed that we didn't know enough to continue
discussing this topic and contented ourself with learning more about Boullee. I found a book, *The
Built, the Unbuilt and the Unbuildable* (The MIT Press, 1994) by architecture critic Robert
Harbison. She was fascinated by this excerpt: "The other place (besides the page) where the flux
of invention often seems to continue into the spectator's present is in landscape gardens, also the
only other scene where one can expect to find small architectural impossibilities. Buildings scat-
tered or concealed like jewels in a perfected landscape may be episodes in a drama or variations
on a single idea. . . . Gardens are different because having it both ways is expected of them.
There one can build a dozen competing versions of one's ideal residence, carapace, or goal; dis-
satisfied with the finality of buildings, architects and their clients find an impossible freedom to
choose and not to choose in gardens. They are places for the indecisive who prefer their facts vir-
tual not actual, a vision which though permeating a whole landscape is broken into indistinguish-
able bits. Contrarily one reaches infinity in a single leap, with one engulfing image. Yet a surpris-
ing number of grandiose visions are dependent on concealed step by step narratives like journeys
through a garden. Boullee, one of the most relentless fabricators of infinitudes, often gains his
effect by specifying the separate grains of sand which make up his beach. Some would hold that
an idea expressed only in perspectives isn't truly architectural, and perhaps Boullee inhabits some
hinterland where the literary meets the visual."

*I pen these modest invasions, these veiled valentines, at night, when the moon is a tall cold*
*candle, a steady flame in the dark hills of Hollywood's dust bowls. I wanted to shed my*
*whine and become words vibrating in the folds of your brain. I need to know in which*
*bungalow I will finally take shape. To what island of lost trials am I condemned? Or was I*
*nothing more than a porcine spoon stirring planks of mud, a porcelain pork chop draped*
*over a fleur-de-lis scarf? Is that it? Was I just another tuxedo cruising the shallows of*
*clubbed waters? Another sack of flounders dropped onto an embossed plate? (26)*

She turned her attention to your poem, "Scenes from the Life of Boullee." A number of
sentence fragments resonated in view of your interview: "Only half the story is true. The next is
necessary, like clouds on a cloudy day . . . . Pieces of a piece. The face in the window larger
than the window facing in . . . . The light of topless dancing. Only half of you is there . . . . A
full garbage bag waiting for someone by not waiting for anything. Smoke on a horizon that exists
as a footnote . . . . When a place becomes a person, whose place is it . . . . The milky water
caused by adding a lemon . . . . Not what he had in mind but what he had . . . . The kind of pre-
cociousness found only in octogenarians . . . . Like a rope dangling from a tree, a site where there
is more conjecture than hard knowledge . . . . Counting the times as if they added up. . . .
Another autobiography sinking beneath its glittering reflections."

*All I could yield was this face. It was my spigot, my sword, and my shadow. Tarnish fol-*
*lowed me everywhere. A bleached doll's head twisted off at the neck, a klaxon brain's*
*bristling aquarium amplified through a window's rheumy membrance. Beady black eyes.*
*The kind you see in stuffed squirrels, a dusty acorn clutched in cobwebbed paws. Forever*
*was the rage that year. O to be mounted on the toothy pedestal of sweet taxidermy. O to*
*be embalmed in the camera's glowing formaldehyde. I was pluck lucky. I was ignited in*
*the prism halls. (27)*

We also found a book by Harry Matthews, *20 Lines A Day* (Dalkey Archive, 1988). He
had written it under the "constraint" of what he said in his Preface was "an injunction Stendhal
gave himself early in life: *Vingt lignes par jour, genie ou pas* (Twenty lines a day, genius or not).
Stendhal was thinking about getting a book done. I deliberately mistook his words as a method
for overcoming the anxiety of the blank page. Even for a dubious, wary writer, twenty lines
seemed a reassuringly obtainable objective, especially if they had no connection with a 'serious'
project like a novel or an essay."

> *There isn't time to measure the plunge of winter's corpse or trace the height of stacked*
> *shadows beckoning me to enter their tunnels of calcium ascending a blue ladder. (28)*

Matthews' first 20 lines included this recollection: "When I was fifteen, I felt the southern
sun and sea like a warm, soothing grace in which to let every kind of worry go." She turned to
me and said, "I bet Harry Matthews is not as pessimistic as John Yau." That's when we decided to
end our write-up on her interview with you. Though we were conversing with each other, the
conversation was becoming, in your words, "solipsistic."

> *I am a bat softener*
> *in the trade confession (29)*

—ɯ—

But then I reminded her of how some of your best poems reflect your obsessiveness —
how you keep going on and on, pushing the poem. I raised the example of your 28-couplet
poem, "Double Agent I" which contains such heart-breaking lines as "Now that all the tears have
been gathered and counted./ I will be the one who cuts them down from the sky." I told her that
I felt replete with emotion at some point in the middle of the poem and yet you were still exca-
vating, still pushing the poem. "So why don't we just keep going further with writing up this
interview since we've reached that first conscious decision to end?" I suggested. "Just to see what
happens?"

"Fine," she said, giving me that half-smile that betrayed her: it was not the first time she
was wondering whether my growing senility had reached an unmanageable state. We decided to
read one more book by you. We chose *IN THE REALM OF APPEARANCES* ("*REALM*") (The Ecco
Press, 1993) in which you critiqued both the art and what other critics have said about the art of
Andy Warhol. I had bought this book months ago but had not had time previously to read it.
And — in her words, "Wow!" — we discovered in this book a mirror to the concerns you
expressed in her interview of you. Note the following:

| Excerpt From *REALM* | As Reflected In The Interview |
|---|---|
| Critics define Warhol in either/or terms.  He is either an uncompromising genius or an accommodating charlatan, a brilliant artist or a dangerous fake, a numbing voyeurist or an accurate mirror, a producer of ground-breaking art or a purveyor of boring images, a creative presence or a destructive force. . . . Critics consider themselves the privileged citizens of one of two fictional worlds: Eden or Mammon. . . . For the critics who believe in Eden, art exists before experience and meaning, while the sages of Mammon have concluded that all experiences and meanings are known, and that nothing new, original, or even insightful and authentic, can be found in either art or life. . . . In both cases, critics are more interested in power than in art. . . .Rather than falling into the either/or argument and continuing, a discourse that has more to do with theory than with Warhol's art, . . . we ought first to remember that ideals are a combination of half-truths and notions of conformity that a society or group declares is necessary to cling to at a given moment. | Relates to the fixity of these critics' approaches versus how you feel Identity is not necessarily fixed. Touches on how you feel that both modernist and post-modernist poets don't deal adequately with the issue of Identity. Touches on how the two poetic approaches in your generation of choosing between (i) language as material and (ii) that the poem is rooted in the ego are both exclusionary, whereas you said that you feel there is *Subjectivity.* |
| The problem with either/or thinking is that it is concerned with . . . genealogy. . . . Most . . . critics find it is easier to develop and maintain the history of family trees than to explain the meaning of an artist's work.  For them, lineage takes precedence over purpose. . . . The result: Warhol's work is a blur, something we think we know but have failed to examine. | The review of *Forbidden Entries* had incorporated references to your middle-class upbringing and a car accident you were in while in college.  Yet, you observed, "(The reviewer) didn't even notice I told jokes," referring to what you actually wrote in your book.  The reviewer also presuppossed that because you are Chinese and went to an expensive college that you grew up middle class. |
| If art conforms to an external definition of what it should be like, doesn't this agreement between a specific work and theories about art (one could substitute "poetry" for"art") imply that the artist is an assimilationist, and that he or she wants to make work that has its place in someone else's narrative?  Might not Warhol (and he is certainly not alone in this) have consciously set out to make work which conformed to some accepted definition of radical and new?  And in | Touches on your observation of poets not challenging mainstream, flawed views on Identity because they want to assimilate. |

| Excerpt From *REALM* | As Reflected In The Interview |
|---|---|

doing so, didn't Warhol perpetuate the legitimacy of certain aesthetic theories and views. . . ?

Instead of leading to "hermeticism" and "legibility," . . . (Marcel) Duchamp's work embodies an unpredictable intersection of experience and aesthetics. Lodged inside a bird cage, a pile of sugar cubes carved out of marble, for example, raises questions about the relationship between appearance and identity. What we see is not what we get. In order to discover the nature of the sugar cubes, the viewer must investigate . . . .Looking at it is not enough. Viewers must overcome their aestheticizing eye and experience in a way that combines their physical, visual and mental capacities.

Touches on your how you use constraints to begin poems as a way of breaking yourself of your habits, including writing habits. You said, "I want to write poems beyond what I might have wished to write because whatever sense I have would have limited the poem."

(Jasper) Johns's sculpture (*Painted Bronze*) seamlessly integrates physical and visual properties. The viewer looks at the sculpture's painted surface and at the same time becomes aware of its tactile presence. . . . Johns's *Flag* and *Painted Bronze* are simultaneously physical and visual. They are things that underscore the bond between appearance and identity, between surface and substance.

Touches on your interest in the question: "Is there an 'I' that is both object and subject?" In the above interview, the excerpt immediately following the paragraph discussing this topic is "You can't pretend your indifference didn't wander off/ and never returned, leaving me with a pail of bronze bulk" — an interesting coincidence:    that *Bronze*.

The cliche "Don't judge a book by its cover" seems to have gained little credibility in the art world. Yet if one believes appearance can be separated from identity and experience, then one is in effect tacitly agreeing that racism and sexism are legitimate forms of recognizing someone who does not correspond with one's ideals. Whether modernist originality or postmodernist copy, the myths of beauty that culture continually revives are forms of denying, as well as speaking for, the other. This is an issue mainstream critics and aestheticians from John Ruskin on have managed conveniently to ignore.

Touches on your dissatisfaction with how Identity is addressed by both modern and postmodern poets.

Might not the end of history and the abolition of painting simply be a sign of the critics' frustration that the old rules of assimilation no longer hold and the next set of ideals has yet to be formulated? Might

Touches on your observation that in this multicultural society, people who used not to be able to talk are now allowed to talk — but this is occuring

| Excerpt From _REALM_ | As Reflected In The Interview |
|---|---|

not these solemn proclamations be a final, desperate defense thrown up against the growing awareness that certain narratives of history whether concerned with defining modernism or postmodernism, have been losing their validity from the moment they were first told? Might not all these new proposals be the latest set of arrogant attempts to assert America's dominance of the wider cultural landscape. Might not they be forms of censorship disguised as criticism? For those who construct the art world's standards, this must be an immensely frsutrating moment. . . .No doubt some individuals and institutions will appear to be reexamining the old standards and offering new ones. They will try to convince the public they are righting old wrongs. However, the issue will not be whether the new standards are new or not, but whether they, like the old standards, make denial an official and efficient program for looking at art.

during a period of time when it is being declared that "the author is dead."

(In _The New Yorker_ (May 18, 1992), Adam) Gopnik's ideal of the artist . . . as innocent or out-of-it child sounds like another version of the "Twinkie" defense. Gopnik takes this stance—How can we talk about the meaning of Koons's work when he himself isn't sure what he means—in order to get himself off the hook. . . . He goes on to say: "The old Warhol-soup-can question—did the person who did this intend it ironically or not—has been replaced by a new question: Does the person who did this even know what irony is?" . . . In Koons's case, the innocent child is a "nut," while in Jasper Johns's case, he is someone with no ideas at all. One has the feeling that Gopnik, like many other critics before him, cannot accept the possibility that the artist is a being capable of both thinking and doing, and may in fact know something that he doesn't. This would grant the artist the same rights as a thinking and doing critic.

Touches on your affinity for paintings and your statement — which I omitted from the write-up of the above interview — that "If painting is dead, then isn't painting a radical act?" I told her that when you play both critic and poet/artist, you are continuing what you learned as far back as when you were a seven-year-old hanging out with John Way: to push art and poetry as far as possible. She is a bit slow and asked haltingly, "So when John Yau is both critic and poet, he's playing a radical role?" I said, "I don't think he's playing" and left it at that.

About Art, (Warhol) said, . . . You should always have a product that has nothing to do with who you are or what people think about you. An actress should count up her plays, a model should count up her photographs, and a writer should count up his words, and an artist should count up his pictures so that you never start

"Counting the times as if they added up"—a line from your poem, "Scenes from the Life of Boullee."

thinking the product is you, or your fame, or your aura.

Finished the year before his death, _Camouflage Self-Portrait, 1986_, consists of a green, black, and gray camouflage pattern superimposed over the artist's face. The combination is telling: Warhol wanted to fit in, to be like everyone else, and he wanted to be noticed and singled out from the crowd. He wanted to hide, but he had to be seen. This is a paradox he could never resolve, the force that drove him from party to party and made him transfer the shadowy interior world of the voyeur to the viewer's experience of film. It is neither the American dream nor the Horatio Alger myth Barbara Rose had in mind when writing about Warhol. But it is the excruciating reality he lived. This was the role he couldn't drop and which he saw as necessary to his daily life. . . . And, like those who try to be loved by everyone, it is not surprising that he was willing to pretend whenever necessary.

What happens to Peter Lorre if all his roles came true? And if Peter Lorre, unlike Warhol, didn't want to pretend, doesn't he become angry? But if Peter Lorre, like Warhol, was willing to pretend, doesn't he still become angry?

—⁓—

You said that your pessimism has lightened up somewhat, that you now think it is possible to communicate although communication is multi-layered. Multi-layered, because you believe in Subjectivity, the non-fixity of Identity, the fragmentation of Self, the reductive perspectives of those who wish to retain positions of power, the existence of confusion (the validity of confusion?), the uncertainties and risk that come with your wish to push boundaries or go beyond boundaries to do something new, "the imagination as spirit in terms of what extends beyond physical being," and undoubtedly much more than could mentioned in an hour or two. So, she looked at me and suggested, "Let's read one poetic manifestation of his sensibility." I said, "Great," and reminded her, "Be sure to thank John Yau for the great ride."

Reader, here then is "Conversation At Midnight."

### _Conversation At Midnight_

Did I tell you about the couple who slipped into the well?
They got tired of proofreading the town daily,
    its expanding parcels of bungalow ooze and unregistered adults
that they had to freeze into orderly stems and vintage sequins.
The window was always glued down. You knew that.
I am sorry about the lump I left in your throat.
It was the latest joke someone sent me from another state.
Why did you say I was a camel when you meant something else?

There is supposed to be a fiber that will either

make it grow or make them flow. What do you mean

you have already been stapled to a post?

I would gladly accept your garnished buckets

if you had some twitching sauce as well.

It was the pluck of the claw if you ask me, which you weren't.

I will kiss your glue, but I will not miss your shoe.

One slipped through a slot, the other formed a neighborhood cult.

There is a rumor they preferred it gloved in steel.

Perhaps you would like to shift your flippers a bit,

make yourself more pungent than a fist clinging

to the grains of its last silver collar.

How would I know what kind of rust coats the inside of my dome?

You were always the expert on the proper insect retrieval systems,

the necessary buzz tones to a pendulum through the hair.

It depends on where you place the nylon and what you plan to do

with the extra row of teeth you keep beneath the other pillow.

Let us dust our nubs beneath the guardhouse beams, but this time

you be the crust and I will play the tropical raincoat.

You are not. I have lots of botched sobs in my cart too.

There is no need to pull the wings off what is certain.

It depends on when the one that marks the day begins to descend.

Don't talk to me like I am some style of perishable food

and you are the only minimum page burner around here.

I have all rinds of dirt. You want to tree some up or what.

Sonar finally brought them through the last truculent gates.

Why do they bang like that if they are not yours to keep.

If you want to lease me, go ahead and cry. You little parking lot.

—⧙⧘—

In response to a request for Yau to identify the thirty original words used to generate "Conversation At Midnight," Yau wrote the following essay:

### Excavating "Conversation At Midnight"

There was nothing due in the foreseeable future, no catalog essay, review, or article. It was morning and I had no appointments that I now remember. I had the whole day to myself. I was reading the newspapers, *The New York Times* and the *Daily News*, which I used to do every day, and becoming aware that I was procrastinating, that I was avoiding working on a poem. There was no poem at hand that I wanted to work on. Still, I thought that I should be writing instead of reading the paper, but, as I was reluctant to stop reading the paper, I began writing down words I came across that I was pretty sure that I had never used in a poem before.

I didn't have a sense of what I would do with the words until I had about fifteen or twenty of them. Around then I thought I would make a list of about thirty words and that I would use one word per line, which would compel me to shift attention from line to line. In each case, the word wasn't supposed to call attention to itself, to be more important than the other words in the line. I also decided that I didn't want to tell a story, but rather I wanted to see if I could make each line stand on its own. I got this idea from Jasper Johns, who, as I remember it, said of Paul Cezanne — "each thing mirroring the other." I thought that Johns meant that the brushstroke mirrored the thing (sky, tree) rather than mimicked it, and that in this sense everything stood on its own.

Reading the poem now, I am not always sure I know what words were the ones I picked from the newspaper. In the first line, it could have been "couple" or "well." In the second line, I'm sure it's "proofreading," though in the third line again I'm not sure. It could have been "parcels," "bungalow," or "unregistered." I think it's "unregistered." For some reason I'm sure that "orderly" was the word I chose and not "sequins," because I remember that "sequins" came from "sequence." I wanted to suggest "sequence" without using it. I wanted the trace of its sound to echo in the reader. "Glued," "lump," "joke," "camel," "fiber." I wanted the words to have no obvious connection to each other, to be more arbitrary than narrative. I tried at points to pick words that could have been both a noun and a verb: "post."

As for the poem itself. I didn't want to have one person (or character) speaking, but more than one. I didn't know who they were, nor did I want to know who they were, but I did want to find out what they could say. I didn't want a dialogue, but something less apparent, more a series of shifts and turns. Interruptions, segues, non-sequiturs. Often the familiarity that occurs within a relationship leads to using cliches, which may have some significance for both speaker and listener, but not for anyone else. I wanted to invent cliches, rather than use familiar ones. I wanted to discover if it was possible to invent cliches based on ones that already existed. I wanted to discover what kinds of feelings would emerge from using phrases that bordered on cliche. I didn't want the language to stay on the same plane, but to propose a space in which it might exist. I was interested in images that didn't become pictures of the relationship, picturesque reifications, harmonious designs. What does it mean, for example to be a "little parking lot"?

My resistance to a poem issuing from an authorial "I" and my interest in a poem whose plane has been ruptured stems from my engagement with postwar art, as well as from engagement with the art of this century. All of these aspects of my life — writing about contemporary art and art practices, organizing exhibitions, interviewing artists — play (I would like to think) a role in the way I write and what I write.

Footnotes:

A)       The constraint of excerpting from John Yau's poems fell away with the introduction of *IN THE REALM OF APPEARANCES*.

B)       One effect that occured almost immediately was the fragmentation of time in the narrative.

C)       from Robert Ryman's "Untitled Statements (1983)" published in *Theories and Documents of Contemporary Art* (ed. Kristine Stiles and Peter Selz, University of California Press, 1996)

D)       from Theodor Adorno's essay, "Lyric Poetry and Society" in *Telos 20* (Summer 1974). An expanded excerpt wherein Adorno counters the notion that lyric poetry is "the untouched virgin word . . . free of the impositions of the everyday world, of usefulness, of the dumb drive for self-preservation" is that the lyric poem "is in itself social in nature. It implies a protest against a social condition which every individual experiences as hostile, distant, cold and oppressive; and this social condition impresses itself on the poetic form in a negative way: the more heavily social conditions weigh, the more unrelentingly the poem resists, refusing to give in to any heteronomy, and constituting itself purely according to its own particular laws. Its detachment from naked existence becomes the measure of the world's falsity and meanness. Protesting against these conditions, the poem proclaims the dream of a world in which things would be different. The idiosyncrasy of poetic thought opposing the overpowering force of material things, is a form of reaction against the reification of the world, against the rule of the wares of commerce over people which has been spreading since the beginning of the modern era."

E)        By coincidence, Eileen Tabios had conducted a few months earlier an interview with L-A-N-G-U-A-G-E poet Tan Lin for *TEN*, the magazine of the Asian American Writers Workshop. Insights from this interview helped her with extemporaneous questions for her interview with John Yau. The interview with Lin is reprinted as follows:

## TAN LIN GIVES GOOD LOTION

*Suppose that there be a machine of which produces thinking, feeling, and perceiving; imagine this machine enlarged but preserving the same proportions, so that you could enter it as if it were a mill. This being supposed, you might visit its inside; but what would you observe there? Nothing but parts which push and move each other, and never anything that could explain perception.*

------ Gottfried Wilhelm Leibniz, *Monadology*

Tan Lin's first book, *Lotion Bullwhip Giraffe* ("LBG") (Sun & Moon Press, 1996), contains poems that both explode and implode language. A collection of innovative and unique poems, *LBG* reflects Lin's approach to poetry which he describes partly as "the putting together of words in a way like abstract expressionism in painting." As someone who began writing poetry in high school, he's come a long way from his earlier poetry which he recalls was influenced by Mark Strand, James Wright and Theodore Roethke. In 1979, he also won a *Mademoiselle* Poetry Prize judged by Marilyn Hacker and Robert Penn Warren.

Currently, Lin says he is interested in crafting poems that are written as if by machines. Referencing Leibniz's quote with which he begins "Ing Mage In," a poem in *LBG*, Lin says, "There's a question from Artificial Intelligence: can you create a machine that feels pleasure and pain? Can you generate a machine language that contains emotion?" To write in this manner, Lin follows arbitrary rules of composition. For example, he may write a poem by only using the keyboard's middle row of letters; concocting "prison escape" scenarios; ordering himself to use the same word seven times in seven lines; or choosing 12 words at random and then using those words in that same order, one word to a line (a technique he learned from John Yau). Most of the poems in LBG were written under such artificial constraints.

A professor of creative writing at the University of Virginia, Lin received a B.A. in English from Carleton College, followed by a PH.d in English from Columbia University. Lin says his students either hate or love his poems. "The danger is that you might end up creating nonsense. It comes close to nonsense, uncomfortably so for some people, but it's not nonsense," he says.

Though many people do not understand the poetry that Lin releases to the public, there are other efforts which he considers "failed poems." Yet the failures, he says, are as interesting as successful poems. It is worth noting that when Lin received the galleys for LBG, he changed almost everything in the manuscript. Although Lin typically finishes a poem's first draft quickly, most of his poems undergo 30 to 40 drafts. Ultimately, Lin concedes, "I'm trying to write in a way that I can't write. And it's very difficult because you can never get away from yourself."

Lin includes Gertrude Stein, John Ashberry, Jack Spicer, Frank O'Hara, Philip Lamantia, Andre Breton, Paul Eluard and Robert Desnos among his inspirations as he writes poems that reflect "the exploration of language. 'Pretty blue sea' is not as interesting as 'pretty glue watch.' Even more interesting is 'pretty glue godzilla'," he notes. Lin adds that Stein once said that she tried to put two words together that won't have a meaning, but found it impossible to do so. Similarly, he says he sometimes tries "to put two words together that have equal value and equal weight and that won't mean anything together. But the mind finds some meaning in the combination — like 'rooster rotisserie.' Part of the experiment lies in breaking down the line between words as things with physical densities and words that mean something else."

"My poetry is about violating boundaries," he continues. "In general, I try to avoid the word, 'I' and the whole range of confessional and personal poetry that the word calls up. Yet I'm not trying to get away from emotion. I'm only trying to get at it in a different way. It's an approach consistent with Stein, Williams, Pound and Eliot's wish for an 'impersonal poetry' — one that got at lyricism and subjectivity, but in very different ways from their predecessors."

As he developed as a poet, Lin says he did not consider creative writing courses necessary and learned mostly by questioning other writers about their works. An exception was a course taught by Yau at the 62nd Street YMCA in 1991. From Yau, Lin says he learned to incorporate "ugliness" in his poetry. "John is interested in the point where language becomes ugly and destroys the possibility for a common narrative or for personal expression. Neither of those two conditions causes the other but they're somehow related. I'm more interested in the purity of language. So he taught me about the dirt and ugliness inherent in language," he says. Lin defines "ugly" as combining words that do not belong together, such as "Lotion," "Bullwhip" and "Giraffe." When it was noted that beauty was found in the combination precisely due to its dissonance or perversity, Lin said, "Exactly. It's a different way."

When asked how Lin reads his poetry in public, given the nature of his poetry, he replies, "Usually, one reads poetry to make connections with the audience. I try to get away from that and that often results in a flat kind of reading."

Yet, notwithstanding Lin's consciously unemotional approach, his poems resonate with such passages as the following from his poem, "Tender Closings:"  *"A couple dimmed. A druggist wept.  It was like a consolation."*

Incidentally, Lin said "Lotion" symbolizes pleasure, "Bullwhip" pain and "Giraffe" what's "unquantifiable."  Perhaps this makes more accessible some lines from his poem "Patio Master Manual:"  *"Pristine mechanics sip from the organs of ranch hands and bullwhip the Vaseline peachfuzz"* and *"Pincushion lotion.  Vertical pageant.  Open giraffe."*  If not, bear in mind what Lin says in another poem, "Section Spicer," *"Poetry translates like pity."*

*The italicized excerpts are taken from the following poems:*

1)      Variations on a Sentence by Laura (Riding) Jackson
2)      The Sculptor Whispers in the Sleeping Poet's Ear
3)      Self-Portrait with Bruno Taut
4)      Hospital parking Lot Rendezvous
5)      Hoboken Palace Gardens
6)      Two Aztecs from New Jersey
7)      The Executioner Meets Mister Ball and Chain
8)      Castor and Pollux
9)      The Newly Renovated Opera House on Gilligan's Island
10)     Fifty for Richard Nonas
11)     One More Excuse
12)     Buffalo and Marshmallows
13)     Self-Portrait with Unidentified Painting
14)     Picadilly or Paradise
15)     The Star-Crossed Duet of Miss Burakumin and Mister Hollywood
16)     Bar Orient
17)     Nasty Orders Pacify Queen
18)     So Much Has Already Happened
19)     Epic Bone Hinge
20)     Blue Lizard Lounge
21)     After A Painting By Jasper Johns
22)     Whispers Inside The Garage
23)     M Is for Mouse and Medicine
24)     Peter Lorre Improvises Mr. Moto's Monologue
25)     Peter Lorre Dreams He Is the Third Reincarnation of a Geish
26)     Peter Lorre Confesses His Desire To Be A Poet
27)     Peter Lorre Wonders Which Artist Should Paint His Portrait
28)     Peter Lorre Prepares for His Final Soliloquy
29)     Genghis Chan:  Private Eye XXI

# ABOUT THE COVER
## ... AND MORE

## JOHN YAU REVIEWS THERESA CHONG'S PAINTINGS

*"My resistance to a poem issuing from an authorial 'I' and my interest in a poem whose plane has been rup-*
*tured stems from my engagement with postwar art, as well as from engagement with the art of this century.*
*All of these aspects of my life — writing about contemporary art and art practices, organizing exhibitions,*
*interviewing artists — play (I would like to think) a role in the way I write and what I write."*
*— John Yau, Poet and Art Critic*

One of the familiar patterns in art, one which might have finally become too familiar to us, is when an artist isolates a minor aspect of the preceding generation's accomplishments and builds upon that and that alone. These artists achieve a recognizeable signature capable of transmitting a frisson of aesthetic recognition, which carries with it a nostalgia for a previous idealized age and not much else. For these artists and for many viewers, the use of an aesthetically satisfying (and satisfied) style, and the flood of nostalgia it releases, become a surrogate for any meaningful and thus useful perception.

Theresa Chong, who isn't interested in satisfying our social desire for nostalgia-laden styles, has purposefully redefined various methodologies to arrive at perceptions which possess the potentiality for a wide range of meanings. She achieves this possibility by rigorously integrating two seemingly opposed perceptual possibilities within a single body of work. Done in either black on white or white on black, and painted wet on wet, Chong's square, intimately scaled, abstract paintings engage both our perceptions and intelligence. Thus, rather than taking one of two rather well-traveled paths in recent abstract art, Chong refuses to either indulge our physical body by constructing a purely sensual composition or appeal solely to our educated intelligence by illustrating the most recent (and recently fashionable) theory.

Beyond their engagement with the viewer's body and mind, what makes these paintings speak to us is that their methodology is not only attuned to basic human perceptions, particularly as they revolve around the poles of chaos and order, randomness and structure, surface and depth, but that it also incorporated nature. When (Jackson) Pollock declared, "I am nature," he wasn't making a grandiose statement; he was calling attention to the essential role gravity played in his methoddology. Chong's use of nature particularly as it involves the changing relationship of gravity, friction, resistance, and liquidity is what separates her from both the Minimalists and from the abstract artist who first gained attention in the 1980's.

For while we have seen art in which process determines the composition, as in Frank Stella's "Black" paintings of the late 1950's, as well as the use of repetition as parody, as in Ross Bleckner's optical "stripe" paintings of the early 1980's, Chong uses process in a less deterministic, more meaningful manner. Consequently, in contrast to Stella's impeccable sense of design, and his use of titles to contextualize his patterned compositions, as well as contrast to Bleckner's dandyish, op-art spinoffs, Chong focuses on the perceptual possibilities inherent in her methodology. Her art isn't painting about the death of painting, as it has been in Bleckner's case, but about our inextricable involvement with nature and time passing.

Chong's process involves an immense amount of control and planning seamlessly coupled with a willingness to succumb to accident, to remain open to the material willfulness of paint's liquidity, particularly in relationship to the forces of gravity. The paintings are done on incredibly smooth, gessoed wood panels. In Chong's case, the surfaces cannot be too smooth and in this regard they are like Formica or any other highly precise industrial material. And yet, the smoothness of the boards is something Chong achieves by repeatedly sanding the gessoed boards, by bringing both hand and machine to bear.

One could say that Chong doesn't make a painting in either the classical or modernist manner, for she neither repaints nor improvises. Rather, she initiates a highly defined sequence which requires her to be completely attentive to the linearity of time. In this regard, her methodology has much in common with those invented by composers or musicians. Like them, she both succumbs to time and redefines its passing. Chong's approach isn't surprising when one realizes that she spent many years studying classical music before switching to painting. For in her paintings it is clear that she not only brings a musician's highly acute sense of timing and sequence to bear in both her process and her compositions, her paintings and drawings, but that she has, in these paintings at the very least, and this is what is both surprising and engaging, invented a methodology which departs from those which previous generations of painters have commonly used. By doing so, she has enlarged the possibilities of what can be done in painting, recovered once again paintings' openness to the world.

Chong's process of applying the paint involves two distinct, though linked steps, which must be coordinated to occur within a sequence strictly determined by time. Onto a wet, smooth surface (either white or black), she releases paint, which eventually becomes a series of equally-sized vertical stripes (either black or white). The stripes are formed by the paint running down the surface from the top edge to the bottom one. In the case of both the wet surface and the subsequent layer of parallel stripes, the paint must possess a precisely defined liquidity; this enables the paint to run down the sticky surface, to spread at the edges but not run together. While the poured paint forms a row of highly uniform vertical stripes, the edges vary from stripe to stripe. Chong must know exactly what consistency of paint to use, so that the stripes never run together, prevented in each instance by the degree to which the underpainting sticks to, as well as holds, the subsequent application.

It is apparent to any discerning viewer that while Chong is sensitive to the material nature of paint and wood, she doesn't fetishize them, make their materiality become evocative of either transcendence or aesthetic sanctuary. Her paintings don't pull us away from the world, but toward it. And yet it is equally true that while their smooth surfaces are austere, even reticent, the optical interplay among the stripes and between the underpainting and the stripes pulls us closer to the paintings, causes us to become curious enough to scrutinize them from various distances. Because of the smoothness of the paint, it isn't immediately apparent which is in front, the underpainting or the stripes.

Chong's paintings are simultaneously bold and intimate, highly ordered yet full of randomness and natural occurences. Their compositions embody the essential instability contained within every stability, as well as acknowledge our desire to impose some kind of order upon chaos, make it meaningful. They define the poles or order and chaos between which we live and from which we cannot escape. If this weren't enough, Chong's paintings evoke gravity and time, thus underscoring our mortality. In contrast to Minimalism's insistence on a self-contained presence within a timeless aesthetic environment, or Postmodernist's pronouncement about the death of art, Chong's paintings are attuned to passage and transformation and thus the world both they and we inhabit. At the same time, in their use of gravity they do not reprise the gestural disclosure of Abstract-Expressionism.

Chong has done something that is of primary importance to this generation of abstract artists. She has found a way to use the past, rather than dream about it.

*The cover of* BLACK LIGHTNING *features the work of Theresa Chong. John Yau's review of Chong was first printed in the Catalogue for the show, "THREE GENERATIONS Towards An Asian American Art History: Tseng Ta-Yu, Phillip P. Chan and Theresa Chong" curated by Robert Lee and held at the Asian American Arts Centre (New York City) from April 3-May 17, 1997. As Yau's review also relates to his poetics, it seems fitting to reprint it in a book about poetry.*

**— *Eileen Tabios***

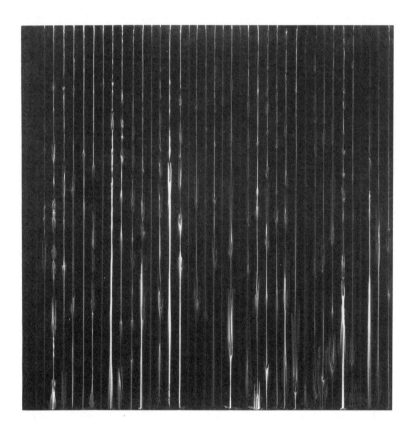

Cover Photo:
**"TWL"**
by Theresa Chong
1997 Oil on Wood, 20" x 20"
(Photo by Tom Powel;
Courtesy of Danese)

# AFTERWORD

## BLACK LIGHTNING As Performance Poetry

*"How do we know the other? By being madly in love."*
— *Charles Simic*


BLACK LIGHTNING is many things: a miracle, an exercise in trust, a conversation, an experiment, a matter of idealism, and, ultimately, a love affair.

In addition to discussing their art with each poet, I incorporated my own input as the poems' reader. Notwithstanding the limitations of my sensibilities, I didn't wish the subject poems to be bereft without a reader. The poet, after all, reaches out through a poem and I wished some-one there to respond. And after the Witter Bynner Foundation of Poetry, Inc. awarded a 1997 poetry grant to BLACK LIGHTNING, I came to treasure a poem by the foundation's namesake, "This Wave." I think that Witter Bynner's poem captures what I considered to be my role of con-tinuing the "progress" of the poem, by playing its *Other:*

### This Wave

Troughing at night,
Cresting at noon,
Down with the sun
And up with the moon,
Down with the moon
And up with the sun:
What was ended
Has begun.


Coincidentally, I had just begun to read and attempt to write poetry a few months before I wrote my first poetry-in-progress piece with Arthur Sze. I offer myself, therefore, as one more proof that poetry can be enjoyed by anybody — even the most ignorant about it as I was when I began this project. It seems to me that to read and enjoy poetry requires only an open heart and an open mind.

Two years from when I began BLACK LIGHTNING, I review the interview-essays, includ-ing my role as reader — as the "Other" to the subject poems. I can't fathom how I responded to some of them, and I undoubtedly would react differently today. I probably would respond almost 100% differently to Mei-mei Berssenbrugge's poem, "THE FOUR YEAR OLD GIRL." And I am sur-prised that, in reading Sesshu Foster's poem about "some dude deflowering a virgin, what mostly lingers is that brief slide of warm beer: 'a little sip in the stunning light.' " These, however, only prove to me how the poem can elicit different responses, reflecting the variety of personalities in its audience. Indeed, the poem can elicit different responses from the same individual as that per-son changes over time.

Nevertheless, what seems consistent to me is how interacting with a poem (as with any work of Art) draws forth that best part of ourselves. As Li Young Lee said, "Poetry enacts true identity." I am grateful to all of *BLACK LIGHTNING*'s poets for writing poems that enabled me to *enact* that best part of me — that self that responds to Art.

Consequently, I invite you, dear Reader, to savor the joys, the passion, the idealism, the desire of becoming the "Other" to poems. For these love affairs, simply open your mind and heart. For me, this project was a glorious ride that I would wish for you, too — stunning, as in Arthur Sze's poem:

> *And, stunned, I feel*
> *the nerves of my hand flashing*
> *in the dark, feel*
> *the world as black*
> *lightning.*

**— Eileen Tabios**

# POEMS' ACKNOWLEDGMENTS

Grateful acknowledgment is made to the publications which first published some of the works in this book. Unless noted otherwise, copyrights to the poems are held by the poets.

## From POETRY-IN-PROGRESS ESSAYS

Meena Alexander: "Muse" and "Passion" were published in *River & Bridge* (New Delhi: Rupa, 1995/ Toronto: TSAR Press, 1996). "Translated Lives" was published in *The World #53* (1997). "Gold Horizon" was published in *Weber Studies: Special Issue on Indian-American Writing* (1998).

Indran Amirthanayagam: "Letter from England" and "The City, with Elephants" were published in *The Elephants of Reckoning* (Hanging Loose Press, 1993).

Mei-mei Berssenbrugge: "The Four Year Old Girl" was published in *Conjunctions* (Annandale-on-the-Hudson, NY: Bard College, 1995).

Luis Cabalquinto: "Prelude" was published in *The Ibalon Collection* (Kalikasan Press, 1991). "The Dog-eater" was published in *The American Poetry Review*, Vol. 13, No. 6 (Nov./Dec. 1984). "Alignment" was published in *Trafika Quarterly*, No. 1 (Autumn 1993). "Depths of Fields" was published in *International Quarterly*, Vol. 2, No. 4 (1996).

Marilyn Chin: "The Phoenix Gone, The Terrace Empty" was published in *The Phoenix Gone, The Terrace Empty* (Milkweed Eds., 1994).

Sesshu Foster: All of his cited poems were published in *CITY TERRACE Field Manual* (Kaya Production, 1996)

Jessica Hagedorn: "Picture This (after the series of paintings entitled Gift Wrapped Dolls by James Rosenquist)" and "Lullaby (for Paloma)" were published in *Visions of a Daughter, Foretold* (Woodland Pattern Book Center and Light and Dust Books, 1994). Reprinted by permission of the author and her agents, Harold Schmidt Literary Agency. Copyright 1994 by Jessica Hagedorn.

Paloma Hagedorn Woo: "Wednesday Night" and "Pearl's Problem" were published in *Visions of a Daughter, Foretold* (Woodland Pattern Book Center and Light and Dust Books, 1994). Reprinted by permission of the author and her agents, Harold Schmidt Literary Agency. Copyright 1994 by Paloma Hagedorn Woo.

Li Young Lee: "The Father's House" was published in *Transforming Vision, The Art Institute of Chicago* (Ed. Edward Hirsch, A Bulfinch Press Book, Little Brown and Company, 1994).

Timothy Liu: "Vox Angelica" and "Canker" were published in *Vox Angelica* (Alice James Books, 1992). "The Road to Seder" was published in *Burnt Offerings* (Copper Canyon Press, 1995).

David Mura: "The Colors of Desire" was published in *The Colors of Desire* (Anchor, 1995) and *The Colorado Review*, Vol. XVIII, No. 2 (Fall/Winter 1991).

Arthur Sze: "Archipelago" and "Black Lightning" were published in *The Redshifting Web: Poems 1970-1998* (Copper Canyon Press, 1998).

John Yau: "Conversation At Midnight" was published in *Forbidden Entries* (Black Sparrow Press, 1996).

**From AFTERWORD**

"This Wave" by Witter Bynner is reprinted with the permission of The Witter Bynner Foundation.

Eileen Tabios and the Philippines' most
important English-language poet in the 20th century,
Jose Garcia Villa (1908-1997).
**Photo by Luis Cabalquinto**

*I unfell completely from*
*As I fell completely into:*
*The Act most pure.*
*— from "Divine Poems" by Jose Garcia Villa*

Eileen Tabios has a B.A. in Political Science from Barnard College and an M.B.A. in Economics and International Business from the New York University Graduate School of Business. To prepare herself for poetry, she has worked as a print and broadcast journalist; an economist; a secretary; a stock market analyst; a bystander in the 1980s contemporary art scene; a country risk analyst; an editor; a "temp typist"; and a project finance banker. In 1995, she began to write poetry, shortly before beginning *BLACK LIGHTNING: POETRY-IN-PROGRESS*. She recently released her own poetry collection, *BEYOND LIFE SENTENCES* (Anvil, 1997). Her next book will be *DOVEGLION* (Kaya Production, 1998), a recovery project on the Philippines' most important English-language poet, Jose Garcia Villa. Editor of *The Asian Pacific American Journal*, she has received a 1997 poetry grant from the Witter Bynner Poetry Foundation, Inc. as well as fellowships from the Virginia Center for the Creative Arts, Fundacion Valparaiso of Spain and the Helene Wurlitzer Foundation of New Mexico. Her poetry, fiction and essays have been featured in publications in the United States, Philippines, Guam, Canada and cyberspace.